PETER SINCLAIR

Unemployment
Economic Theory and Evidence

Basil Blackwell

For WRS and MNS

Copyright © Peter Sinclair 1987

First published 1987

Basil Blackwell Ltd
108 Cowley Road, Oxford, OX4 1JF, UK

Basil Blackwell Inc.
432 Park Avenue South, Suite 1503
New York, NY 10016, USA

British Library Cataloguing in Publication Data

Sinclair, Peter
    Unemployment: economic theory and
    evidence.
    1. Unemployment
    I. Title
    331.13′7′01   HD5707.5

    ISBN 0-631-14093-X
    ISBN 0-631-14094-8 Pbk

Library of Congress Cataloging in Publication Data

Sinclair, P. J. N.
    Unemployment: economic theory and evidence.

    Includes index.
    1. Unemployment.   2. Unemployment – Econometric
models.   I.   Title.
HD5707.5.S56   1987   331.13′7   86-17639
ISBN 0-631-14093-X
ISBN 0-631-14094-8 (pbk.)

Typeset in Monophoto on 10/11½ pt Times
by Advanced Filmsetters (Glasgow) Ltd
Printed in Great Britain by Page Bros (Norwich), Ltd

Contents

Preface

Unemployment is the central economic challenge of our times. It entails a massive loss of output, and a tragic waste of people's lives. This book has three aims: to chronicle and describe it; to explain it; and to evaluate alternative methods for reducing it.

The first chapter is designed to do the first of these. This is a substantial chapter, which draws upon and summarizes unemployment statistics for numerous countries. Attention is focused most closely upon the UK and the US, but data for Australia, Canada and much of the rest of Western Europe are also explored. The story starts in 1851, when the first hard evidence becomes available. An attempt is made to provide a long look at the phenomenon of unemployment since then, as well as a close scrutiny of the present position.

The middle part of the book deals with explanations for unemployment. It consists of chapters 2 to 15. The focus is largely (but not exclusively) theoretical. Analysis commences with the demand for labour (chapter 2), proceeds to explore general macroeconomic models where unemployment stems in part from wage-and-price stickiness (chapters 3 and 4) and then turns to a 'demand and supply' analysis of unemployment that brings out the significance of redistributive fiscal policies (chapters 5 and 6). Chapters 7 and 8 examine various short-term shocks that can generate unemployment, while chapter 9 investigates the microeconomic analysis of job-search by the unemployed. Chapter 10 expounds and assesses implicit contract models. This chapter, and its successor – chapter 11, which is devoted to the study of trade union behaviour – are designed to explain labour market phenomena that can predispose the economy to the risk of unemployment in adverse conditions. Chapter 12 returns to macroeconomic issues, to examine the links between unemployment and inflation; chapters 13, 14 and 15 concentrate upon particular issues of interest that bear upon this.

Chapter 16 surveys, contrasts and evaluates various policies that may be put to work to combat unemployment. It also contains a set of policy proposals with this end in view. For the first three decades or so after the Second World War, as the spectre of mass unemployment receded, academic debate on labour market problems was dominated by macroeconomic controversies about broad aggregates. Many of the lessons taught in the great inter-war works on labour markets, such as Hicks's *Theory of Wages* (1928) and Pigou's *Economics of Unemployment* (1937), slipped from memory. One camp followed Keynes in pressing for expansionary financial policies. Only these, it was claimed, would keep the demand for labour high enough to prevent a return to heavy unemployment. Their opponents, the 'monetarists', came to paint a picture where unemployment adjusted, with swift inevitability, to an equilibrium or 'natural rate'; reflation simply spelt inflation. This debate was often conducted at a great distance from the crucial microeconomic details. It was all too often silent on the incentives facing workers, unions and employers, and the contracts they enter into. The last 10 years or so have witnessed a welcome return to the central micro issues that can serve to explain the macro phenomenon of mass unemployment. Much of this work is reflected in the middle part of this book. Moreover, the policies recommended in chapter 16 are also primarily microeconomic in nature. Policies that offer the greatest chance of achieving a lasting reduction in unemployment should recognize – and then modify – the behaviour of individual employers, unions and workers.

My debts of gratitude in writing this book are numerous. Sue Corbett and her colleagues at Blackwells have been unfailingly kind and forgiving. I have learnt a great deal from the writings of many economists, and no less from discussions. To Willem Buiter, Max Corden, James Mirrlees, Derek Morris, Peter Neary, Steve Nickell, Andrew Oswald and Joe Stiglitz I am especially grateful; I hope that the many others to whom I also owe much will forgive me for not singling them out by name. I have been helped greatly by colleagues at Oxford and the University of British Columbia, by seminar audiences in Canada, the UK and the US, and by fellow participants at conferences; my editorial responsibilities with *Oxford Economic Papers* have taught me much, and I have learnt from graduate and undergraduate students. I should also like to thank Stephen Doe for his assistance with reading proofs. My greatest debt, by far, is to Shelagh Heffernan. Without her unstinting advice and support this book could not have been produced.

Brasenose College, *Oxford*

1 Unemployment: The Evidence

1.1 Introduction

This chapter is concerned with the evidence about unemployment. Section 1.2 discusses definitions of unemployment, and section 1.3 presents some contemporary international comparisons. Section 1.4 explores the historical record of aggregate unemployment data, with special reference to the UK, the US, Canada and Australia, from the point at which reliable data first become available. Sections 1.5 and 1.6 are concerned with the microeconomic features of unemployment; they attempt to answer the question: who are the unemployed? Finally, section 1.7 examines some consequences of unemployment.

1.2 The Definition of Unemployment

Unemployment is like an elephant: easier to recognize than to define. Definitions abound. Practices differ between countries. They are apt to change within countries, too; politicians beset by a sharp rise in unemployment on a given definition sometimes yield to the temptation to redefine their problem away.

Sometimes it is helpful to define unemployment negatively, by stipulating what it is not. Unemployment is clearly not employment. So the unemployed are a subset of those who are not employed. But even this is a hard proposition to stick to. What about those working part-time? Are they not partly unemployed, particularly if they normally work full-time or say that that is what they would prefer? What about the person who has lost his job, and occupies himself with sporadic tasks for which he may obtain some remuneration? These questions are generally answered by counting part-time workers as a separate group. The unemployed are out of work 'full-time', apart perhaps from a small amount of casual paid labour that they are allowed to undertake without endangering entitlement to unemployment benefits.

But the unemployed are only a subset of the non-employed. People under school-leaving age, and the retired, are typically excluded. So, too, are those deemed to be unavailable for work or not seeking work. But the terms 'availability for work' and 'seeking work' are hard to define. You may be available for work next week, or tomorrow, but not today. Your job-search may take different forms. There are inquiries to friends and relatives, 'situations vacant' columns in newspapers, or

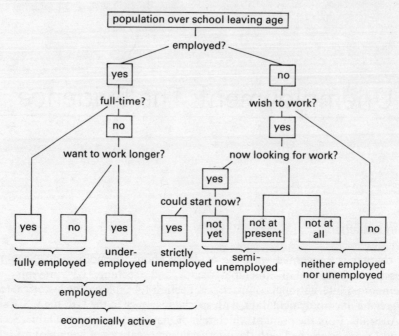

Figure 1.1   *A taxonomy of possible employment, unemployment and non-employment states*

submissions to public and private employment agencies. How frequently you scan the newspapers or visit agencies will vary.

One way of differentiating unemployment from employment and other types of non-employment is illustrated in figure 1.1. The taxonomy depicted in figure 1.1 takes the form of a tree, in which each branch begins with an answer to a particular question. The fully employed include those who work full-time, and part-time workers who do not wish to work full-time. These are on the left of the spectrum. At the opposite end lie those who do not wish to work, and those who are definitely not looking for it; they are neither employed nor unemployed, but perhaps best described as voluntarily non-employed. The remainder, in the middle, are unemployed. The strictly unemployed wish to work, are seeking work and would be available to take up work at once. The 'semi-unemployed' cover people who would not take up an immediate offer of a job, or who are temporarily not searching for employment.

Figure 1.1 shows many of the criteria laid down for the appropriate measurement of unemployment in a resolution of a recent conference[1] devoted to this subject: those above a specified age who were seeking work, out of work, and currently available for work. Those unemployed by the definitions of figure 1.1 are not infrequently identified by labour force surveys since 1973. An annual or biennial Labour Force Survey has been conducted in the UK, for example. The 1983 and 1984 surveys attempted to quantify the number of people without work who were actively seeking it. Such a definition corresponds with the 'strictly unemployed' of figure 1.1, and some, but not all, of the semi-unemployed. The 1984 survey was restricted to a sample of 1 in about 350 households in Great Britain, but the 57,000 observations thus provided were sufficient to pass all conventional requirements for statistical significance, at least as far as its broader aspects were concerned.

One of the most interesting findings of the British 1984 survey is the close similarity of its aggregate unemployment data with those of the monthly Official Unemployment Count (OUC). Since October 1982, Britain's OUC has been based upon the total numbers claiming unemployment benefit on a given week in each month. The OUC is not a sample; it is an aggregate figure. Before 1982, the OUC had enumerated everyone who registered as unemployed with an Employment Office (or Unemployment Exchange); the 1982 redefinition, from registered unemployment to claimant, and other accompanying changes, such as the removal of many men aged 60–4 from the figures, are thought to have reduced measured unemployment by some 110,000. Be that as it may, the comparisons between the post-1982 OUC and Labour Force Survey (LFS) figures are presented in table 1.1.

Table 1.1 shows that those revealed to be unemployed in the LFS added up to over 97 per cent of the number claiming unemployment benefit. This was true for both 1983 and 1984. All four numbers were just under 3 million.

But there are important differences lurking beneath the surface of these aggregate data. Female unemployment is decidedly higher by the LFS criterion, and male lower, by roughly offsetting amounts. Further, over one-quarter of the men and women revealed as unemployed on the LFS definition were not claiming benefit. Against that, a slightly higher proportion of claimants, the sample evidence suggests, were not really seeking work. This number appears to have risen somewhat between the two years. Given all this, one should conclude that the close similarity of the aggregate unemployment figures implied by the two approaches can only be a fortunate accident.

More generally, OUC data can come from either of two sources. They can be based upon registrations with public employment exchanges. This was the source of the British figures until the changes in October 1982. Registrations may include or exclude those in one job who apply for another. The second source is unemployment insurance data. The ratio of unemployment benefit recipients to the total insured population becomes the basis of the figure for the proportion out of work.

These two sources have different weaknesses. Not everyone registers as unemployed. Some people may rely upon other methods of searching for a job (private enquiries, answering advertisements and the like). Others may feel a sense of disgrace or harassment if they appear at such offices. The unemployment insurance statistics, on the other hand, may be incomplete. Self-employment is sometimes excluded. First-time job-seekers may not be insured. Some people may be too proud or too ill-informed to claim benefits due to them, while others may claim more than their due. For all these reasons, then, LFS data are widely regarded as being superior to OUC statistics of either type.

All three definitions are employed in practice; governments vary in this respect. The time has now come to investigate and compare the unemployment statistics of different countries. This is the subject of section 1.3, to which we turn next.

1.3 International Comparisons of Unemployment: A First Look at the Data

Unemployment has risen almost everywhere in the last two decades. In most countries, it is now more than double its post-war average. But countries differ

Table 1.1 Comparison of claimant count and LFS estimates of unemployment in Great Britain (in millions)

	Spring 1983			Spring 1984			Change Spring 1983 to Spring 1984		
	Males	Females	All	Males	Females	All	Males	Females	All
Survey unemployed (labour force definition)	1.85	1.06	2.91	1.77	1.13	2.90	−0.07	+0.07	−0.01
of which									
not claiming benefits[a]	0.22	0.54	0.76	0.25	0.62	0.87	+0.03	+0.09	+0.11
claiming benefits[a]	1.63	0.53	2.15	1.53	0.51	2.04	−0.10	−0.02	−0.12
Claimants[a] not unemployed (labour force definition)	0.54	0.30	0.84	0.56	0.36	0.94	+0.02	+0.06	+0.10
of which									
inactive (not seeking work)	0.44	0.24	0.67	0.44	0.30	0.74	−	+0.06	+0.07
employed	0.10	0.06	0.17	0.12	0.06	0.20	+0.02	+0.02	+0.03
Claimant count[b]	2.16	0.83	2.99	2.06	0.89	2.96	−0.08 (+0.01)[b]	+0.06	−0.02 (+0.07)[b]

Note: Figures are individually rounded to the nearest 10,000 and may therefore appear not to add.
  The 1983 figures have been revised since the previous article. The unemployed survey estimates for 1983 compared with the monthly counts' in the August 1984 issue of Employment Gazette. Revisions to LFS results included a change in definition of the survey unemployed to bring it into line with the current practice for deriving estimates of the labour force. As explained in the article 'Labour Force Survey preliminary results for 1984' in the May 1985 issue of Employment Gazette, from 1984, full-time students who are not available to start work within two weeks because they must complete their education are not now included in the labour force definition of unemployment. The figures given here for 1983 have been compiled on the same basis so that they are consistent with the figures for 1984. The 1983 claimant count figures given here have have also been revised from those given in the August 1984 article. The monthly figures have been more accurately weighted to reflect the pattern of interviews in the survey periods.
  [a]These figures are derived with reference to both the claimant count and the LFS results.
  [b]The changes in brackets allow for the effects of the 1983 Budget measures on the claimant count among older men between the respective survey periods. Certain men, mainly aged over 60, no longer need to sign on at Unemployment Benefit Offices in order to get supplementary benefit or national insurance credits. A total of about 180,000 men were consequently excluded from the claimant count, with the effect accumulating between March and August 1983. It is estimated that about 90,000 of these were excluded between the respective 1983 and 1984 LFS survey periods.
  Source: Reprinted from 'Unemployment: Estimates from the Labour Force Survey compared with the Monthly Claimant Count', Department of Employment Gazette, October 1985, pp. 393–6.

astonishingly widely in their levels of measured unemployment. It is this aspect to which the present section is devoted.

Table 1.2 presents unemployment data for all countries that report such figures in ratio form for inclusion in the *Bulletin of Labour Studies*, published by the International Labour Office (ILO).

The United States shares with South Korea the honour of being alone among these countries in experiencing lower unemployment in 1984 (or the last reported year) than 1981. In Hong Kong, unemployment was equal in these two years. Everywhere else, it advanced. The average unemployment increase was 2 per cent. In Chile and Switzerland it more than doubled, although from very different absolute positions.

Table 1.2 *Unemployment proportions for all countries reporting them to the ILO (men and women)*

		1981	1982	1983	1984	LFS information source
The Americas	Argentina	4.5	4.8	4.2	n/a	LFS
	Barbados	10.8	13.8	15.0	15.4	LFS
	Canada	7.5	11.0	11.9	11.3	LFS
	Chile (Gran Santiago)	9.0	20.0	19.0	18.4	LFS
	Colombia	8.1	9.3	11.4	n/a	LFS
	Jamaica	25.9	27.4	n/a	n/a	LFS
	Puerto Rico	18.9	22.8	23.4	20.7	LFS
	Trinidad & Tobago	10.2	10.0	11.0	n/a	LFS
	United States	7.6	9.7	9.6	7.4	LFS
	Venezuela	6.2	7.1	9.8	n/a	LFS
Asia	Cyprus	2.6	2.8	3.3	3.3	OUC(EE)
	Hong Kong	3.9	3.7	4.3	3.9	LFS
	Israel	5.0	5.0	4.5	5.9	LFS
	Japan	2.2	2.4	2.7	2.7	LFS
	S. Korea	4.5	4.4	4.1	3.9	LFS
Europe	Austria	2.4	3.7	4.5	4.5	OUC(EE)
	Belgium	11.1	13.8|	14.4	14.5	OUC(EE)
	Denmark	9.2	10.0	10.8	10.5	OUC(EE)
	Finland	5.1	5.9|	6.1	6.2	LFS
	France	7.3	8.0	8.0	9.1e	
	West Germany	5.5	7.5	9.1	9.1	OUC(EE)
	Ireland	10.5	12.8	15.3	16.8	OUC(EE)
	Italy	8.4	9.1	9.9	10.4	LFS
	Netherlands	9.1	12.6|	17.1	17.6	OUC(EE)
	Norway	2.0	2.6	3.3	3.0	LFS
	Portugal	8.2	n/a	n/a	n/a	LFS
	Spain	12.1|	16.3	17.8	20.5	OUC(EE)
	Switzerland	0.2	0.4	0.9|	1.2	OUC(EE)
	Sweden	2.5	3.2	3.5	3.1	LFS
	UK	11.1	13.1	13.1	13.1	OUC(EE)
	Yugoslavia	11.9	12.4	12.8	n/a	OUC(EE)
Oceania	Australia	5.8|	8.5	10.4	9.5	LFS
	New Zealand	3.6|	4.1	5.8	5.1e	OUC(EE)

LFS = Labour Force Survey
OUC(EE) = Official Unemployment Count, based on employment exchange data
e = estimate by author on incomplete data
| = series break
n/a = not applicable

The variation between countries is little short of extraordinary. Unemployment averaged below 1 per cent in Switzerland; in Jamaica, the data available give an average of nearly $26\frac{1}{2}$ per cent. Puerto Rico is little more fortunate than Jamaica, Barbados rather more so. Only Trinidad and Tobago, among the Caribbean countries, is able to maintain an average of less than 11 per cent.

The broad similarity of unemployment across the Caribbean is indicative of a more general tendency. One country is apt to resemble its neighbours. In Scandinavia, for example, Norway and Sweden are able to maintain an average of barely 3 per cent, and Finland of $5\frac{1}{2}$ per cent. Within the European Economic Community (EEC), three of the smaller countries (Belgium, Ireland and the Netherlands) and the UK have similar unemployment averages of about 13 per cent. France, Italy and West Germany average somewhat under 10 per cent. The two Alpine republics, Austria and Switzerland, both record unemployment far below this. Unemployment rates are similarly low in Japan, Hong Kong and South Korea, and again in Cyprus and Israel. Canadian unemployment averages not much more than in the US. There are exceptions to the rule: unemployment varies very widely in Latin America, for example, and Spain suffers far worse unemployment (it appears) than Portugal.

The bewildering variety of unemployment rates offers one important crumb of comfort. High unemployment is not inevitable. Some countries manage to avoid it. There is a panoply of possible reasons for this. First of all, the inter-country differences in unemployment rates may be partly due to different ways of quantifying it. Although there appears to be no systematic difference between countries employing the LFS and OUC (EE) data sources, differences in sampling techniques, registration habits and definitions within each method may be very large. There is unfortunately no means to hand of verifying this possibility. But there are other reasons, too.

Switzerland resorts to not renewing the work permits of aliens when its labour markets loosen; on one occasion, she even expelled them. Sweden offers guaranteed employment to those who would otherwise be the long-term unemployed. Norway devotes much of its enormous oil revenues to subsidizing production and employment in the private sector. Substantial private and public sector employment schemes are operated in New Zealand, and will undoubtedly have succeeded in moderating increases in unemployment there.[2] Hong Kong, Japan and South Korea have all benefited from economic growth rates far in excess of those prevailing in North America and Western Europe; and large Japanese private companies effectively offer a guaranteed lifetime contract to the majority of their employees, with a scheme of flexible bonus payments that ensures that it is wages, rather than employment, that will fall in temporary recessions.

Special factors are at work among the countries at the other end of the scale, as well. In Jamaica, the economic turmoil that attended the later stages of the Manley Government took unemployment to over 31 per cent in 1980. The new administration has had to contend with continuing apprehension on the part of foreign business, and adverse trends in world markets for her major primary product export, bauxite. There, and elsewhere in the Caribbean, tourist export revenues have faltered; furthermore, the traditional remedy for unemployment which worked well in previous decades–emigration–was often much harder. Falling export revenues have hit Chile (copper) and Venezuela (oil). These two countries, in common with everywhere else in Latin America, have suffered an explosion of overseas debt charges. Domestic investment projects and living standards had been supported by foreign borrowing in the 1970s. This suddenly dried up, as credit lines broke and overseas lenders baulked. In Spain, real labour costs continued to rise rapidly in the mid- and late-1970s, long after the economic growth rate fell; they were propelled upwards by the heady sense of political decompression that followed Franco's death in 1975. As in many other countries, unemployment also rose in Spain in the wake of tough disinflationary government policies undertaken in the early 1980s. (Chile offers a more dramatic example of this.) Unemployment may have been exacerbated in the three countries to join the EEC in 1973; Denmark, Ireland and the UK will have experienced some structural changes following the phased removal of tariff barriers with their Community partners. The sharp jump in Irish unemployment is also partly explained by the fact that jobs on the British mainland became suddenly much harder to obtain. A combination of sluggish economic growth and relatively generous unemployment benefit schemes may help to explain the very high levels of unemployment prevailing in Belgium and the Netherlands.[3]

So much, then, for our initial international comparisons of unemployment rates in the 1980s. We return below (in section 1.5) to examine this evidence more closely, in the context of other macroeconomic variables. At this stage, however, we turn our attention from contemporary data to the historical record. This is the subject of section 1.4.

1.4 The Historical Record: Aggregate Unemployment Rates

1.4.1 *Unemployment Before the First World War*

The first unemployment statistics were gathered from trade unions. An early function that the union performed was to insure its members against unemployment. Figures were kept on the numbers of both unemployment insurance beneficiaries, and contributors. The ratio of the former to the latter constitutes an unemployment rate. Unemployment statistics gathered in this way were sometimes reported to the government department responsible for the labour markets. In Britain's case, the Ministry of Labour received trade union unemployment returns going back to 1851.

The earliest figures must be treated with considerable caution. The labour force coverage is really minute. The first problem is that unemployment rates among different groups of workers do not necessarily move in parallel. There is often a strong positive correlation, but it is far from perfect, since industry is subject to sector-specific, microeconomic shocks as well as aggregate, macro movements. Then there are two important sources of bias. The early data are typically restricted to skilled labour; unskilled labour is likely to suffer higher unemployment, and greater swings in unemployment, if more recent figures are anything to go by. On the other hand, unemployment insurance usually starts in industries which are more vulnerable to unemployment. It is this that creates the demand for insurance in the first place. The construction sector, which is notorious for its high mean and variance of unemployment, usually figures prominently. These two biases run counter to each other. That does not mean that they cancel. But taken together with other observations (the absence of any time trend in unemployment as statistical

Table 1.3 *Unemployment rates in certain British trade unions,
1851–89*

		1860	1.9	1870	3.9	1880	5.5
1851	3.9	1861	5.2	1871	1.6	1881	3.5
1852	6.0	1862	8.4	1872	0.9	1882	2.3
1853	1.7	1863	6.0	1873	1.2	1883	2.6
1854	2.9	1864	2.7	1874	1.7	1884	8.1
1855	5.4	1865	2.1	1875	2.4	1885	9.3
1856	4.7	1866	3.3	1876	3.7	1886	10.2
1857	6.0	1867	7.4	1877	4.7	1887	7.6
1858	11.9	1868	7.9	1878	6.8	1888	4.9
1859	3.8	1869	6.7	1879	11.4	1889	2.1

Source: Mitchell and Deane (1962, p. 64). Until 1887, the figures are
based partly upon unemployment rates and partly upon unemployment
benefit outlays reported by unions. From 1888, they are computed from
the former alone

coverage widens, and the relative stability of the wage-change/unemployment
equations studied by Phillips (1958)), it suggests that the early British figures may
not be quite as untrustworthy as they might seem at first sight.

Table 1.3 presents these British unemployment data for the years 1851 (when
continuous figures begin) until 1889.

The information provided by table 1.3 is also presented in figure 1.2, and
summarized in table 1.4. Table 1.4 explores the swings and mean levels of

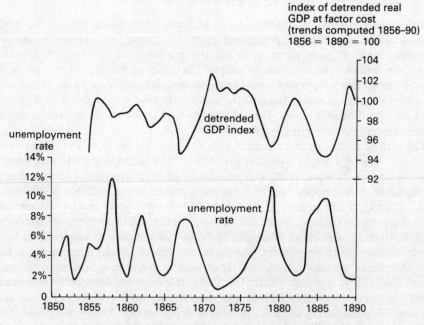

Figure 1.2 *UK unemployed, and detrended real GDP, 1851–90*
Sources: Feinstein (1972) for GDP; Mitchell and Deane (1962) for unemployment

Table 1.4 *Unemployment rates in certain British trade unions, 1853–89: summarized data*

	Mean	Maximum	Minimum
1853–9 inc.	5.2	11.9	1.7
1860–4 inc.	4.8	8.4	1.9
1865–71 inc.	4.7	7.9	2.1
1872–81 inc.	4.2	11.4	0.9
1882–9 inc.	5.9	10.2	2.1
1853–89	4.9	11.9	0.9

unemployment in each identifiable cycle. From the data presented in table 1.3, it is readily seen that some kind of cycle is indeed present. Troughs in unemployment occur on average once every 7.4 years. The periodicity is not particularly steady. It varies between a minimum of 5 and a maximum of 10 years. The years identified as troughs are 1853, 1860, 1865, 1872, 1882 and 1889. Unemployment peaks occur in 1858, 1862, 1868, 1879 and 1886.

The mean level of unemployment in the 37 years is just under 5 per cent. There is no discernible trend. Across the period as a whole, unemployment ranges from a minimum of 0.9 to a maximum of 11.9 per cent. The timing of the peaks and troughs of unemployment conforms nicely to that of troughs and peaks in real Gross Domestic Product (GDP).[4] The latter series reveals income peaks, relative to trend, in 1861, 1865, 1871, 1882 and 1889. Detrended income troughs can be placed in 1863, 1867/8, 1879 and 1886. Figure 1.2 illustrates the close association between the unemployment and GDP series. Indeed, one is almost the mirror of the other, when the GDP trend is removed.

Another macroeconomic variable with which the unemployment data are clearly well correlated is the pace of money wage changes. Money wages stagnate when unemployment is high, and income is close to its cyclical trough. But unemployment troughs witness annual money wage increases of 10 per cent or so. This relationship has been noticed for decades (see Fisher (1926), for example), but was first tested in detail by Phillips (1958) after whom it is now known.

British nineteenth-century evidence testifies, then, to close links between unemployment and (detrended) real output, and between unemployment and money wage rises. The question this finding provokes is which causes which. Economists are united in arguing[5] that money wage rises respond to unemployment (since this can be taken as some indication of whether the labour market was in excess demand or excess supply) and not the other way round. According to the Keynesian tradition, the output–unemployment link is explained by swings in aggregate demand, which generate broadly parallel movements in output and in the demand for labour. Many economists might today qualify this by arguing that output and (un)employment were best seen as simultaneously determined endogenous variables, both of them susceptible to direct and indirect shocks operating through demand and supply channels. But they might still accord pride of place to aggregate demand movements as the major explanation of year-by-year swings in unemployment. Perhaps the most satisfactory approach is to regard unemployment changes at, say, a quarterly or annual frequency, as the joint result of *two* sets of phenomena. They testify to swings in the demand for labour,

Table 1.5 *Unemployment rates in the UK and the US, 1890–1914*

	UK	US		UK	US		UK	US
1890	2.1	4.0	1900	2.5	5.0	1910	4.7	5.9
1891	3.5	5.4	1901	3.3	4.0	1911	3.0	6.7
1892	6.3	3.0	1902	4.0	3.7	1912	3.2	4.6
1893	7.5	11.7	1903	4.7	3.9	1913	2.1	4.3
1894	6.9	18.4	1904	6.0	5.4	1914	3.3	7.9
1895	5.8	13.7	1905	5.0	4.3			
1896	3.3	14.4	1906	3.6	1.7			
1897	3.3	14.5	1907	3.7	2.8			
1898	2.8	12.4	1908	7.8	8.0			
1899	2.9	6.5	1909	7.7	5.1			

Sources: UK: Mitchell and Deane (1962); US: Historical Statistics of the
United States: *Colonial Times to 1970*, US Department of Commerce, 1975

which can usually be traced back to aggregate demand movements. These
constitute the precipitating factor. But a second phenomenon matters, too: one has
to explain why it is employment levels, rather than wage rates or some other
variable, that absorbs the pressure of demand-for-labour swings. That is a question
of supply, not demand. The more elastic the short-run supply of labour, for
whatever reason, the more an economy is predisposed to swings in unemployment.

So much for unemployment up to 1889. What of the quarter-century between
then and the outbreak of the First World War? Fortunately, evidence for other
countries becomes available in this period. This is also based upon trade union
returns, at least in its first stages. Table 1.5 presents unemployment rates for both
the UK and the US, for the years 1890–1914. Table 1.6 depicts cyclical statistics
abstracted from table 1.5. The British figures continue to conform to a fairly steady
cycle, of between 7 and 10 years. Again, there is no unemployment trend. The range
within which unemployment fluctuates is similar to the earlier period.

In the US, on the other hand, cycles are harder to discern. Unemployment starts
off much higher, on average, than in the UK, and it displays a marked downwards
trend, at least until 1906–7 or so. This could indicate the workings of a longer cycle.
The cycles identified in the US data show a close timing association with the UK
cycle, with the latter leading by 2 years or so until the early years of the twentieth
century, then coincident. There is also evidence to suggest that unemployment
swings are rather more pronounced in the US. Close fits are observed between
unemployment and both detrended real national income and money wage
increases, as figures 1.3 and 1.4 testify.

Table 1.6 *Summary statistics for UK and US unemployment rates, 1890–1913*

United Kingdom				United States			
Cycle	Mean	Maximum	Minimum	Cycle	Mean	Maximum	Minimum
1890–9 inc.	4.4	7.5	2.1	1892–1902	9.8	18.4	3.0
1900–6 inc.	4.2	6.0	2.5	1903–6	3.8	5.4	1.7
1907–13 inc.	4.6	7.8	3.6	1907–13	3.7	8.0	2.8

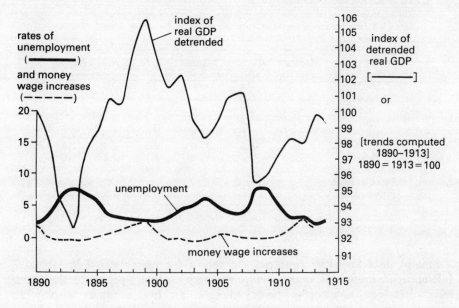

Figure 1.3 *Unemployment and money wage increases; detrended real GDP*
Sources: Mitchell and Deane (1962) for unemployment; Phillips (1958) for money wage increases; Feinstein (1972) for GDP

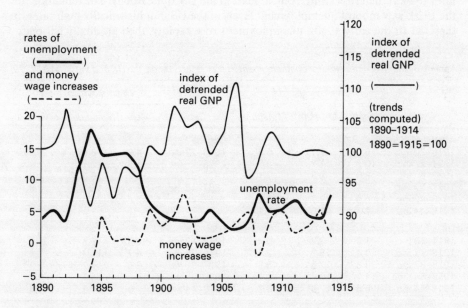

Figure 1.4 *Unemployment and money wage increases; detrended GNP, United States*
Sources: US Department of Commerce (1975) for unemployment and money wages; Kendrick (1962) for GNP

Table 1.7 *Unemployment rates in Australia, Belgium, Denmark, France, Germany and Norway, 1903–9*

	Australia	Belgium	Denmark	France	Germany	Norway
1903	9.2	3.4	n/a	10.1	2.7	n/a
1904	7.3	3.0	n/a	10.8	2.1	4.0
1905	5.3	2.1	13.3	9.9	1.6	4.4
1906	4.7	1.8	6.1	8.4	1.1	3.2
1907	3.6	2.0	6.8	7.5	1.6	2.5
1908	3.5	5.9	11.0	9.5	2.9	3.6
1909	2.9	3.4	13.3	8.1	2.8	5.0
No. of workers covered in 1909 (thousands)	–	48	91	216	429	18

Source: Abstract of Foreign Labour Statistics, HMSO (1911). For Australia, figure 13.1 in Jenson and Stevens (1985)

Finally, data for other countries are shown for years 1903–9 in table 1.7. Inferences are hazardous, since coverage averages less than 3 per cent of the labour force. But one noteworthy point emerges: all five countries display an unemployment trough in 1906 or 1907 which coincides with the peak of the boom in both the UK and the US. The twentieth century began, at least, with a truly international cycle in unemployment.

1.4.2 *Unemployment: 1914–44*

The First World War witnessed a sharp fall in unemployment, which remained low until 1920. It then rose swiftly, but, at least in the US, quite briefly. The remainder of the 1920s saw modest unemployment levels in the US, but historically high rates in the UK. In the early 1930s, unemployment rose rapidly, then gradually fell back.

Table 1.8 *Summary statistics for unemployment in Australia, Canada, the UK and the US: 1914–39*

	Unemployment rates				Unemployment rates		
Cycle	Mean	Maximum	Minimum	Cycle	Mean	Maximum	Minimum
Australia				Canada			
1916–20 inc.	6.4	7.1	5.8	1916–22 inc.	4.2	8.9	1.3
1921–2 inc.	10.3	11.2	9.3	1923–7 inc.	5.3	7.1	2.9
1923–6 inc.	8.0	8.9	7.1	1928–36 inc.	16.2	26.6	2.6
1927–37 inc.	17.1	29.0	7.0	1937–43 inc.	8.4	15.1	0.8
1938–42 inc.	6.3	9.7	1.1	1917–44 inc.	6.6	26.5	0.5
1918–44 inc.	7.9	29.0	1.1				
UK				US			
1914–18 inc.	1.3	3.3	0.4	1914–18 inc.	5.5	8.5	1.4
1919–27 inc.	9.4	15.2	2.4	1919–26 inc.	4.7	11.7	1.4
1928–37 inc.	12.6	17.6	8.2	1927–9 inc.	3.6	4.2	3.2
1938–44 inc.	4.1	10.2	0.2	1930–7 inc.	18.3	24.9	8.7
1918–44 inc.	6.6	17.6	0.2	1918–44 inc.	7.9	24.9	1.4

Sources: Australia and Canada: NBER. UK: until 1926, Mitchell and Deane (1962). From 1927, League of Nations *Monthly Bulletin of Statistics,* supplemented by author's estimates; data relate to wholly unemployed. US: as in previous tables

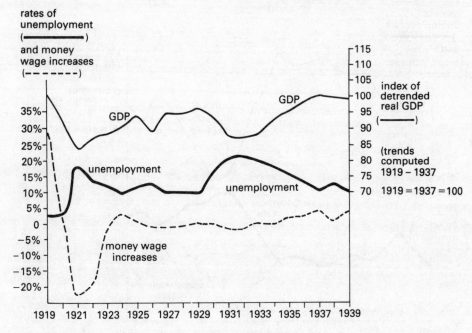

Figure 1.5 *Rates of unemployment and money wage increases, and detrended real GDP, United Kingdom, 1919–39*

Sources: Phillips (1958) for unemployment and money wage increases; Feinstein (1972) for GDP

But now it was America's turn to suffer a much higher average level of unemployment. The cyclical information for these two countries (together with Australia and Canada) is summarized in table 1.8. Figures 1.5 and 1.6 present rates of unemployment, and money wage increases, and detrended real national income, for the UK and US.

The pattern of the cycle is harder to discern in this period than in the years before 1914. The dominant phenomena are the sudden recessions that began in 1920–1 and after 1929. They both generate an immediate and very pronounced rise in unemployment. In the 1920s, Canada and the US recover quickly but Australia and the UK languish with an unemployment plateau close to 10 per cent; in the 1930s, the upswing is much faster in the UK. The 1927–9 minicycle in the US is barely a cycle at all, more a minor ripple, and the flatness of unemployment in the UK in the late 1920s makes the choice of trough arbitrary. Furthermore, 1937–8 really marks little more than a brief interruption in the long fall of unemployment down to the mid 1940s. But the similarity in timing between turning points in the UK and the US continues to appear, as do the close fits between unemployment, output and wage increases revealed before the First World War, at least in years of peace. This is revealed in figures 1.5 and 1.6. This brings us to the two most telling points to emerge from these figures. First, nothing reduces unemployment as swiftly or as far as the exigencies of a protracted war. This is especially true for Australia, Britain and Canada, for whom hostilities lasted longer, but is still striking for the United States as well. Second, the depths of the inter-war recessions take unemployment considerably above the maxima recorded in earlier statistics.

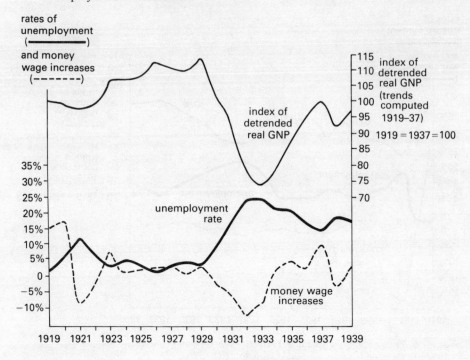

Figure 1.6 *Rates of unemployment and money wage increases, and detrended real GNP, United States 1919–39*
Sources: Department of Commerce (1975) for unemployment and money wage increases; Kendrick (1962) for GNP

Inter-war unemployment experience in other countries varies. Unemployment jumped almost everywhere in 1921, with the breaking of the post-war commodity boom. Germany was a rare exception to this: unemployment here fell from 2.4 per cent in 1921 to 1.3 per cent there in 1922, under the impact of the giddy hyperinflation that was by then in full swing. In 1923, as inflation accelerated, unemployment shot up to 12 per cent, and stayed high, if volatile, after the Schacht Currency Stabilization in November that year. Denmark, Norway and Sweden, like Britain, suffered from almost as much unemployment in the 1920s as the 1930s. In contrast Belgium, which was experiencing much faster inflation than its northern neighbours, saw unemployment fall to 2.7 per cent in 1922 and then stay below 2 per cent until 1930. Matters seem to have taken a similar course in France, as well, but the lack of credible official statistics on unemployment for this period means that one cannot be sure. In Australia, Canada and the Netherlands, data are rather closer to the US than the UK figures.

Australia and New Zealand were the first countries to witness a sharp rise in unemployment in the late 1920s, in 1926 in New Zealand, and in the fourth quarter of 1927 in Australia. The likely reason was that primary product prices were drifting downwards in this period, leading to lay-offs on the farms and in the mines. The available data suggest that Australia suffered worse unemployment in 1932 (29 per cent) than in the UK and the US, but it fell rapidly after that. In Canada, the depths were plumbed in 1933 (22.3 per cent). Recovery proceeded a little faster than in her southern neighbour; unemployment was down to 13.2 per cent 3 years later (as against nearly 17 per cent in the US). Among countries reporting official unemployment rate statistics, the Netherlands posted the highest level of joblessness: 36.3 per cent. This dreadful figure was attained as late as 1935, when every other country was benefiting from falling unemployment.

The 1920s and 1930s were by and large disastrous decades as far as unemployment is concerned. Even Japan saw unemployment climb to 6.8 per cent (in 1932). Of the other countries publishing official data on unemployment rates, the lowest maximum was recorded in the UK (17.6 per cent in 1932). But it was not equally disastrous for every country at any one time. One reason for this was that they adopted differing financial policies. The Australians, the British, the Dutch and the Scandinavians opted for tight money and a restoration of pre-war exchange rate parities in the 1920s at what proved to be somewhat overvalued levels. Unemployment stayed at historically high levels in all these countries (in 1927, for example, it ranged from 7 per cent in Australia to 25.4 per cent in Norway). The Germans debauched their currency and bought exceptionally low unemployment for a year or two (at a terrible price). The Belgians and the French kept inflation high, but not very high, until 1926, and then stabilized their currency at a set of low exchange rates, which gave their exporting and import-competing industries a large cost advantage. This kept their unemployment low throughout the 1920s. Australia and Britain went off gold in 1931, and the ensuing depreciation and period of low interest rates must have helped to cushion unemployment in 1932, if not reduce it later. The Dutch were among the last to devalue, in 1936; the fact that unemployment peaks so high and so late in the Netherlands must surely have something to do with this. Currency devaluations did little if anything to reduce world unemployment. They really only redistributed unemployment from the country that did it to those that did not. Import tariffs and quotas, which were widely employed in the mayhem of the 1930s, were another type of 'beggar my neighbour' policy, with the added feature that they may well have redistributed unemployment within national boundaries, as well.[6]

Inter-war evidence lends some support, then, to the Keynesian notion that macro financial policy can help to contain unemployment. It also testifies to the importance of external competitiveness as a major influence on the demand for labour and hence of exchange rate policies to affect this. Yet a further point, which emerges very clearly from the German experience, is that the unemployment cut you can buy by allowing inflation to soar may prove very short-lived.

There is lively contemporary debate among economic historians about the causes of inter-war unemployment. One school, led by Benjamin and Kochin (1979), maintains – at least in the British case – that unemployment was primarily benefit-induced. This is certainly a theoretical possibility. Chapters 5 and 6 are largely devoted to exploring why it can happen. Minford et al. (1983) provide a version of this story to explain contemporary unemployment in Britain, and elsewhere. We explore their theory in chapter 9. It is worth noting that most debate does not centre on the claim that unemployment benefits raise or raised unemployment. This is conceded. The point at issue is the size of the effect.[7] Its relative significance compared with that of others is also disputed.[8] Another group claims the existence of a powerful, negative link between employment and the real wage in inter-war Britain. This is at least consistent with, possibly confirmatory of, the 'classical unemployment' theories explored in chapter 3. Beenstock et al. (1984)

provide an elegant and rather persuasive paper on this. Animated discussion has followed.[9] A further group, of whom Hatton (1983) and Broadberry (1983) serve as examples, has tried to use inter-war data as a testbed for Keynesian versions of the quantity-rationing models of unemployment. (These models also form part of the subject matter of chapter 3.) This group claims qualified success for the hypothesis that aggregate demand movements were the real culprit behind the sharp changes in unemployment observed in the years between the wars.

1.4.3 *From 1945 to the Present: General Observations*

The first three decades after the Second World War offer a marked contrast with the two decades that preceded it. Unemployment was steadier, and very much lower. Everyone feared that it would climb after war ended, in the wake of recession: short-lived boom had been succeeded by slump after the First World War, and the Napoleonic War a century earlier. But no recession came. The 1950s and 1960s were characterized by the optimistic thought that mass unemployment had at last been conquered. The Keynesian macroeconomic doctrines, orthodox at this time, taught that unemployment could always be prevented by a sufficiently expansionary financial policy: indeed, the mere belief that the authorities would spend their way out of a slump might be enough to stop it.

The 20 years before 1940 had seen unemployment average nearly 12 per cent in the UK and $12\frac{1}{2}$ per cent in the US. The 30 years after 1945 witnessed averages of only 2.2 per cent and 4.3 per cent in these countries. Wherever statistical comparisons can be made, the same thing happened: Australia, Canada and New Zealand; Western Europe; Japan; Latin America. Not only unemployment averages fell. Rates of joblessness were steadier too. Unemployment cycles within countries increased in frequency, often to as little as 4 years or less, in contrast to the 7- to 10-year cycles that typified inter-war and earlier experience.[10]

Perhaps it was too good to last. Last it did not. Several countries witnessed a rising trend in unemployment rates as early as the 1960s. In the 1970s and early 1980s, this depressing development became almost universal. In 1985, five West European countries (Belgium, Ireland, the Netherlands, Spain and the UK) are

Table 1.9 *Average unemployment rates, 1948–84, OECD area*

Cycle	Mean	Maximum	Minimum
1948–50	3.5	4.1	2.7
1951–5	3.2	4.3	2.4
1956–60	3.3	4.5	2.5
1961–6	2.8	3.2	2.3
1967–73	3.0	3.6	2.4
1974–9	4.9	5.3	3.5
1980–4	7.4	8.6	5.7

Sources: for the US, as in previous tables up to 1970; for other countries: UN *Monthly Bulletin of Statistics* and ILO, supplemented by author's estimates, until 1958. From 1958 (1970, US) OECD standardized unemployment rates, from various issues of *Labour Force Statistics* and other publications displaying rates of unemployment that touch, or even surpass averages recorded for the inter-war period. The weighted average for the five of them, when taken together, is nearly 16 per cent. In the US, France, Italy and West Germany it has been undulating close to 10 per cent. Even in Scandinavia, Japan and the Alpine Republics, where it averages barely 3 per cent, unemployment has increased markedly over the past two decades. In 1969, unemployment in the Organization for Economic Co-operation and Development (OECD) area averaged 2.6 per cent. By 1984, this figure had more than trebled to 8.2 per cent.

Average unemployment rates throughout the OECD area (Canada, the US, Australia, Japan and most of Western Europe) displayed an upwards trend that appears to have begun in the mid-1960s. Table 1.9 reveals a cycle of approximately 5 to 6 years, at least after 1950. Experience within the constituent countries does not always support this, however, since there is far from perfect correlation between them. We turn now to investigate the behaviour of aggregate unemployment rates in some major countries.

1.4.4 *From 1945 to the Present: Aggregate Unemployment Rates in Selected Countries*

Both the United States and Canada have experienced eight post-war unemployment cycles, with an average (but irregular) periodicity of about $4\frac{1}{2}$ years (see table 1.10). Both countries exhibit a rising trend in unemployment throughout the period, briefly reversed between the mid-1960s and the early 1970s. Apart from Canada's first post-war cycle, unemployment consistently exceeds the OECD average. Canada's relative position, when compared with its southern neighbour, deteriorates throughout the period. She began with unemployment rates well below US levels, but ends up with a jobless rate more than $1\frac{1}{2}$ per cent higher. The brief dent in the unemployment statistics for both countries in the years between 1965 and 1972 probably owes much to the effects of the Viet-Nam War and its associated government expenditures. It is noteworthy that the US–OECD average comparison in the most recent cycle reveals a sharp relative improvement for the United States. This testifies to the fact that the US economy has grown much more strongly than that of Western Europe since 1982, under the combined impact of tax

Table 1.10 *Post-war unemployment cycles in the US and Canada*

	US unemployment rates					Canada unemployment rates			
Period	Mean	Maximum	Minimum	Relative to OECD average	Period	Mean	Maximum	Minimum	Relative to OECD average
1948–52	4.3	5.9	3.0	+1.2	1947–50	2.5	3.2	2.0	−0.8
1953–5	4.3	5.5	2.9	+0.8	1951–5	3.5	4.6	2.4	+0.3
1956–9	5.2	6.8	4.1	+4.7	1956–8	5.0	7.0	3.4	+1.3
1960–1	6.1	6.7	5.5	+3.5	1959–65	5.6	7.0	3.9	+2.8
1962–8	4.1	5.7	3.6	+1.4	1966–8	4.1	4.8	3.5	+1.6
1969–72	4.9	5.8	3.4	+1.7	1969–73	5.6	6.2	4.4	+2.4
1973–8	6.5	8.3	4.8	+1.9	1974–8	7.1	8.3	5.3	+2.3
1979–84	7.8	9.5	5.8	+0.8	1979–84	9.4	11.3	7.4	+2.4

Sources: as table 1.9

Table 1.11 *Post-war unemployment cycles in the UK*

	Unemployment rates			
Period	Mean	Maximum	Minimum	Relative to OECD average
1947–50	1.5	1.6	1.3	−1.8
1951–4	1.7	2.1	1.3	−1.4
1955–60	1.5	2.0	1.1	−1.8
1961–5	1.4	1.9	1.1	−1.5
1966–73	2.7	4.0	1.1	−0.2
1974–8	5.0	6.1	2.9	+0.2
1979–84	9.8	13.0	5.1	+2.8

Sources: as table 1.9

cuts and increased federal spending. US unemployment fell from 9.7 per cent in 1982 to 7.4 per cent in 1984, while the OECD average registered an increase from 8 per cent to 8.2 per cent. 1984 was the first year since the war when US unemployment fell below the OECD average. Canada has not shared this good fortune, although she did record a mild decline in the jobless rate from 1983 (11.8 per cent) to 1984 (11.2 per cent).

The United Kingdom experienced seven (or possibly eight) unemployment cycles in the years 1947–84. The ambiguity attaches to the period 1966–73, which would count as two cycles on other criteria (such as the swings in detrended GDP), and could perhaps be interpreted as two cycles on the unemployment evidence, too. Unemployment began the post-war era far below the OECD average, but has now climbed far above it. This change is first noticeable in the mid-1970s, but really only becomes marked after 1979. Table 1.11 furnishes the figures. There is a reasonable match in the unemployment turning point dates between the UK, and the US and Canada.

Britain's current unemployment rate is uncomfortably high, then, in relation to the OECD average. The phenomenon is recent, at least in the context of post-war evidence. One must return to the 1920s to find another period when the UK suffered relatively high unemployment, compared with the international average deducible from available statistics. Many observers attribute Britain's misfortune in the years after 1979 to an overvalued exchange rate, and the adverse effects this has upon the competitiveness of, and demand for labour in, British industries exposed to international trade. The years 1926–9, which also saw unemployment some 1–2 per cent above an international average,[11] witnessed the consequences of the 1925 sterling exchange-rate revaluation. The strong real exchange rates for the pound in the early 1980s can be blamed largely on the combined effects of North Sea Oil, high oil prices and perceptions and expectations of tight monetary policy.[12] Yet it is worth noting that Norway, where oil accounts form a much higher share of GDP than in the UK, has managed to contain unemployment in the 3–4 per cent range during this period, and has avoided any sharp appreciation in its nominal or real exchange rates; and unemployment shot up even faster than in the UK, in some countries, such as Belgium and Spain, where oil production is trivial.

The tightening stance of monetary policy in the UK since the late 1970s has undoubtedly succeeded in helping to lower inflation. This ran at 18 per cent in 1979;

by 1983 it had dropped to 4 per cent. But not dissimilar success has been recorded in several other countries. In the US, in particular, the unemployment cost of disinflation appears to have been quite trivial in comparison. One factor that distinguishes the UK sharply from the US is the pronounced differences in budgetary policy. In the UK, retrenchment in government spending and tax increases have brought the public sector financial deficit to barely $2\frac{1}{2}$ per cent of GDP; in the US, the reverse has happened. The US federal deficit has climbed steadily to reach nearly 7 per cent of GDP by 1985–6. The deficit, and the buoyancy of interest rates that has resulted, have led to massive inflows of foreign capital; this in turn led to a sharp appreciation of the US dollar, at least until the end of 1985. Appreciation leads to lower inflation, by limiting price increases for exportable and importable products, while its adverse effects on these domestic sectors' demand for labour have been more than offset by the fiscal stimulus. In Britain, the opposite happened, as sterling unwound from its excessive levels in 1980–1. To date, the net result has enabled the United States to obtain the best of both worlds: less inflation and less unemployment. There are grounds for thinking that America's success in this regard will prove transient, however. The scale of the deficit makes future tax increases and tighter constraints on government spending inevitable, while the downwards drift of the US dollar that began in 1985 will start to strengthen the inflationary momentum.

The US policy of attacking recession by fiscal stimuli has recently been followed in Australia, where unemployment has fallen (at the time of writing) to less than 8 per cent from its 1983 peak of 10 per cent. But before this recent success, the jobless rate had climbed sharply from its internationally low levels recorded until the mid-1970s.

Australian unemployment cycles occurred at just under 4-year intervals, according to the data presented in table 1.12. The periodicity is far from regular, and sometimes hard to define with precision. Turning point dates often fail to match those for other countries. But the upwards trend in unemployment, at least until its current reversal, closely mirrors that in the UK. The post-war era began with Australian unemployment far below that recorded in Canada or the US, but this gap has recently been all but closed. Australia's comparative success in holding

Table 1.12 *Post-war unemployment cycles in Australia*

Period	Unemployment rates			
	Mean	Maximum	Minimum	Relative to OECD average
1950–4	1.9	3.0	1.3	−1.6
1955–7	2.3	2.9	1.6	−1.0
1958–9	2.5	2.7	2.3	−1.2
1960–5	2.1	3.2	1.5	−0.7
1966–9	1.5	1.6	1.5	−1.0
1970–2	1.8	2.3	1.4	−1.6
1973–5	3.0	4.9	1.9	−0.9
1976–80	5.8	6.3	4.8	+0.6
1981–4	8.5	10.0	5.8	+0.6

Source: data calculated from statistics in ILO Yearbooks, and Jonson and Stevens (1985) for figures before 1965

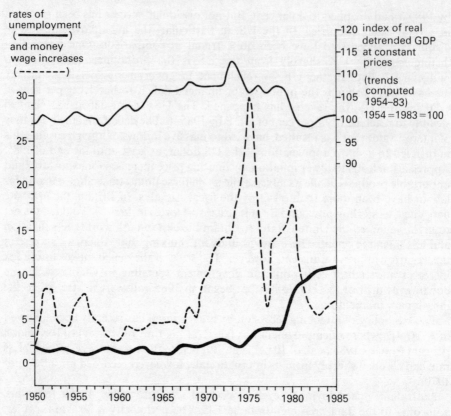

Figure 1.7 *Unemployment and money wage increases, and detrended real GDP, United Kingdom*
Sources: OECD Labour Force Statistics for unemployment; Economic Trends (basic weekly rates, manual workers) for money wage increases; IMF International Financial Statistics for GDP

unemployment down in the mid-1970s may owe something to the mineral boom, although its greatest effect may have been to draw employment away from other sectors that were squeezed in the ensuing real exchange rate appreciation. This mechanism appears to have operated in reverse in the first half of the 1980s.

Finally, figures 1.7 and 1.8 show the pattern of detrended national income, increases in money wages and unemployment over the period 1950–85 for the UK and the US. There continues to be a clear link between GDP and unemployment; the latter responds to the former with an average delay of nearly a year in Britain, less in America. The inflation–unemployment comparisons are more complex. It remains true that unemployment fluctuations usually coincide with inflation fluctuations within each cycle; inflation peaks at approximately the point unemployment reaches its cyclical minimum, or shortly thereafter. But the post-war period era as a whole points to something of a positive long-run association between these variables. For much of the 1960s and 1970s, at least, both inflation and unemployment rates were trending upwards together. In the early 1980s, this has ceased to be true; inflation has fallen quite sharply and the positive unemployment trend has continued, quickening in the UK and slackening in the US.

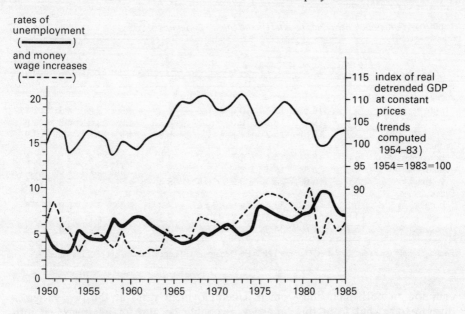

Figure 1.8 *Unemployment and money wage increases, and detrended real GDP, United States, 1950–85*

Sources: OECD Labour Force Statistics for unemployment; US Department of Commerce (1975) for money wage increases, to 1970, and thereafter Employment and Earnings, US Department of Labor (gross average weekly earnings); IMF International Financial Statistics for GDP

This, then, is the historical record for aggregate unemployment data. We turn now to examine some structural and micro aspects of joblessness. Who are the unemployed? How old are they? Are they men or women? What occupations did they have? How long are they out of work? What industries and regions suffer most? Which ethnic groups? It is to these questions that section 1.5 is devoted.

1.5 Who are the Unemployed? I: Certain Characteristics

1.5.1 *Which Age Groups are Most Prone to Unemployment?*

In the UK, a U-shaped curve can be plotted to show the relation between unemployment rates and age cohorts. The incidence of unemployment declines as age increases up to 40 or so. Then it rises, peaking rather before the age of retirement. This pattern is evident in UK statistics, as table 1.13 illustrates. It is

Table 1.13 *Unemployment rates by age, United Kingdom, October 1985*

Age group	All ages	Below 18	18–19	20–4	25–34	35–44	45–54	55–9	60 and over
Men and women	13.4	21.0	25.1	19.1	13.9	9.0	9.5	14.9	5.8
Men	15.7	23.5	27.3	21.5	15.5	12.0	12.3	18.6	8.4
Women	10.1	18.4	22.6	16.0	11.8	5.1	6.0	9.3	0.3

Source: Department of Employment Gazette, December 1985 (HMSO)

Table 1.14   *Unemployment rates by age: United States, September 1985*

Age group	All ages (16 and over)	16–17	18–19	20–4	25–34	35–44	45–54	55–9	60–4	65 and over
All races:										
both sexes	6.9	19.5	17.4	10.6	6.8	5.0	4.5	3.8	4.3	2.7
men	6.2	19.1	18.5	10.0	5.9	4.3	4.2	3.5	4.5	7.5
women	7.7	19.9	16.2	11.2	7.9	5.9	4.8	4.3	3.9	2.9
White:										
both sexes	5.8	16.2	14.1	8.7	5.7	4.5	3.9	3.3	3.9	2.2
men	5.3	15.9	14.4	8.5	5.0	3.9	3.4	3.1	4.0	2.0
women	6.6	16.6	13.8	8.9	6.6	5.4	4.5	3.7	3.8	2.5
Black:										
both sexes	15.1	47.5	39.4	24.5	14.4	9.3	9.3	8.2	6.8	7.6
men	14.6	44.0	43.6	21.2	12.9	8.3	11.1	7.1	8.6	9.3
women	15.7	51.8	34.3	27.9	16.0	10.2	7.5	9.4	4.9	5.9

Source: Employment and Earnings, October 1985 (US Department of Labor, Bureau of Labor Statistics)

common to both men and women. Unemployment rates at the two extremes diverge somewhat from this tendency, probably because many frustrated job-seekers under 18 or over 60 stay at school or opt for retirement. A somewhat different picture emerges from US statistics. Unemployment rates decline quite systematically with age, for both sexes and both black and white (table 1.14). There is a slight jump for some groups aged 60 and over, but that is all. As a reflection of the fact that UK unemployment was almost twice as high as in the US, virtually every group is more prone to unemployment. The sole exceptions are women in the 35–44 cohort, or aged 60 and over, who are statistically more likely to be jobless in the US.

One feature which the British and American data share is the high incidence of unemployment among the young. This is a ubiquitous phenomenon. In Canada, for example, joblessness in the 15–24 age group has been consistently 5–6 per cent higher than in the population as a whole since 1970. In West Germany, the 20–4 cohort experienced an incidence of unemployment $2\frac{1}{2}$ per cent above the national average in September 1984. Interestingly, West Germany displays a U-shaped unemployment–age relation similar to, if flatter than, the UK's: the risk of unemployment reached a minimum of 6.8 per cent for the 35–40 age group at that time.[13] Unemployment is also heavily skewed towards the young in Australia, as table 1.15 shows.

Table 1.15   *Unemployment rates by age: Australia, June 1984*

Age group	All ages (20 and over)	20–4	25–34	35–44	45–54	55 and over
Both sexes	7.7	13.3	8.0	5.7	5.5	5.2
Men	7.3	14.4	7.5	5.2	5.5	5.5
Women	8.6	11.8	7.4	9.3	5.5	n/a

Source: *Commonwealth of Australia Yearbook*, 1985

1.5.2 *Do Women Experience Higher Unemployment than Men?*

The data in tables 1.13, 1.14 and 1.15 do not tell a straightforward story. In the UK, men are more than 50 per cent likelier to claim unemployment benefit than women. In the over 35 cohorts, female unemployment runs at under half the equivalent rates for men. But as we have already seen, the LFS data suggest that true unemployment is more evenly spread between the sexes than table 1.13 suggests. In the US and Australia, female unemployment averages more than 1 per cent higher than for men.

Elsewhere, experience varies widely. Table 1.16 presents male and female unemployment rates for the most recent year available in the 1984 *ILO Yearbook of Labour Statistics*. In only 12 of the 45 countries given in table 1.16 do women face lower unemployment rates than men.

To Singapore goes the prize for achieving sexual equality in this grim statistic. Elsewhere, women are more prone to unemployment. This is especially true in the Caribbean (except for Puerto Rico), and Latin Europe. Portugal has the worst climate for female unemployment if one takes the ratio of the two statistics, Jamaica if one takes the difference. There is some indication that the bias against women is worst where the overall unemployment rate is highest: Puerto Rico and the UK provide rare counterexamples.

1.5.3 *What Occupations Did They Have (if any)?*

Unemployment rates are distinctly higher for those with working-class occupations than for managers, professionals and sales and technical personnel. This, at least, is

Table 1.16 *Unemployment rates by sex, all reporting countries*

	Female	Male		Female	Male
Australia	10.4	9.7	S. Korea	2.2	5.2
Austria	4.1	4.7	Malta	1.6	4.7
Bahamas	21.1	8.4	Netherlands	18.4	16.6
Barbados	19.8	11.0	New Zealand	6.2	5.5
Belgium	19.7	10.9	Norway	3.8	3.0
Canada	11.6	12.1	Panama	14.2	7.6
Chile	17.6	21.3	Philippines	5.3	3.4
Colombia	11.5	7.5	Portugal	12.3	3.7
Costa Rica	9.6	8.8	Puerto Rico	17.0	26.7
Cyprus	4.0	3.0	Singapore	3.2	3.2
Denmark	12.1	9.7	Spain	21.4	17.1
Finland	6.0	6.2	Sweden	3.6	3.4
France	11.0	5.9	Switzerland	0.9	0.8
French Guyana	13.7	5.0	Syria	10.6	4.3
Ghana	0.7	0.9	Thailand	0.7	1.0
Guam	9.9	9.4	Trinidad & Tobago	13.5	8.1
Hong Kong	3.5	5.0	United Kingdom	8.8	15.9
Ireland	13.4	16.1	United States	9.2	9.7
Israel	5.3	4.0	Uruguay	20.5	11.9
Italy	16.2	6.6	Venezuela	7.6	10.6
Jamaica	38.7	14.2	West Germany	10.1	8.4
Japan	2.6	2.7	Yugoslavia	18.4	9.1
Kiribati	10.8	6.0			

Source: ILO Yearbook, 1984

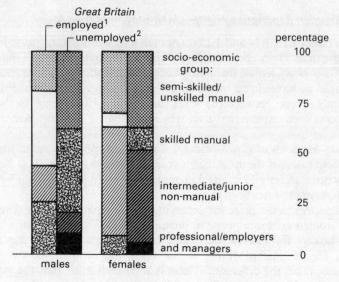

Figure 1.9 *The employed and unemployed by socioeconomic group and sex, 1984*
Source: Social Trends, 1986

the clear message of UK and US data. Figure 1.9 and table 1.17 give unemployment rates for various occupations in the UK and the US respectively.

1.5.4 *How Long Are They Out of Work?*

The older you are, the longer you take to be re-employed once you become unemployed. The data examined in section 1.5.1 suggested that unemployment rates generally decline with age, at least until prime age is reached. Consequently, the risk of experiencing unemployment declines very sharply with age, since the statistics in section 1.5.1 were essentially a product of two numbers: the proportion suffering unemployment, and the average duration of joblessness. Table 1.18 presents the author's estimates of median unemployment duration for different age cohorts in the UK.

These UK data point to a very sharp increase in median unemployment duration

Table 1.17 *Unemployment rates in different occupations: US, September 1985*

	Both sexes	Men	Women
Managerial and professional	2.7	2.2	3.3
Technical, sales and administrative	4.9	3.3	5.7
Service occupations	8.8	8.3	9.1
Precision production, craft and repair	6.7	6.1	12.3
Operators, fabricators and labourers	10.4	9.6	12.8
Farming, forestry, fishing	6.7	5.9	10.8
Total (16 years and over)	6.9	6.2	7.7

Source: as table 1.14

Table 1.18 *Median unemployment duration, by age: UK, October 1985*

	Age under 17	17	18	19	20–4	25–9	30–4
Weeks of unemployment							
Men	5	13	16	26	28	54	58
Women	5	14	14	25	22	25	25

	Age 35–9	40–4	45–9	50–4	55–9	60 and over
Weeks of unemployment						
Men	60	65	71	81	85	27
Women	26	40	42	55	86	145

Source: author's estimates, from data in *Department of Labour Gazette*, December 1985

as age rises. Duration increases steadily with age, with very few exceptions. Over half of the men who enter the unemployment register aged 25 and above take over a year to be re-employed. Half the teenagers in this position are employed after 3 months or so. The situation is apparently less gloomy for women, but this may be due to the fact that many may give up the struggle and stop registering as unemployed.

US figures also reveal a positive link between duration of unemployment and age. But the association is weaker, and the median duration very much lower than in the UK. Table 1.19 shows the comparable US figures, supplemented with some further information. As in Britain, women seem to be re-employed more quickly than men. This is also true of whites as opposed to blacks, and (doubtless because they are typically younger) of single as opposed to married people. Britain is not alone in displaying markedly more sluggish re-employment than the US. In West Germany, for example, the September 1984 data point to median (uncompleted) unemployment duration was over 30 weeks. In Canada, the proportion of the unemployed who have been out of work for at least 4 months has fluctuated between 24 per cent and 60 per cent in the past two decades. The median duration

Table 1.19 *Median unemployment duration, by age and other characteristics: the US, September 1985*

	Age 16–19	20–4	25–34	35–44	45–54	55–64
Weeks of unemployment						
Men	4.2	6.5	8.6	9.4	12.2	10.9
Women	3.9	4.3	5.5	5.6	6.7	9.2

Other characteristics	White	Black	Single	Married (spouse present)	Widowed, divorced or separated
Men	7.0	8.7	5.7	9.2	10.5
Women	4.6	6.2	4.5	4.9	6.7

Source: as table 1.14

Table 1.20 *Median unemployment data, by age: Australia, June 1984*

Age	15–19	20–4	25–34	35–54
Weeks of unemployment	21.0	21.0	24.3	31.1

Source: Commonwealth of Australia Yearbook, 1985

of unemployment in Australia in June 1984 is presented for various age cohorts in table 1.20. This shows a much higher interval of unemployment than in the US, but only a weak positive association between age and duration.

Median unemployment rates do not tell the whole picture. By definition, half gain employment more quickly, while half take longer. The latter group cannot be more numerous than the former. But the time they take to obtain re-employment – if indeed they ever secure it – is disproportionately longer. Mean unemployment duration data show this clearly: the mean typically exceeds the median by a large margin. In the United States, for instance, the median unemployment duration for the population as a whole was only 6 weeks in September 1985; the mean was nearly 15 weeks. Furthermore, this is a major difference between completed and uncompleted median unemployment spells. The latter have averaged nearly three times as long as the former in recent years in the UK.[14] The reason for this is the fact that the outflow from the unemployment register is a biased sample of those who remain there. The ex-unemployed are disproportionately young. Darby et al. (1985) argue that mild recessions and deep recessions differ: unemployment increases in the first case are largely confined to those who are likely to leave and re-enter the labour force frequently and quickly, but in the second case spread to 'permanent' employees who may find re-employment difficult.

1.5.5 *Which Industries Suffer Most Unemployment?*

In recent years, it has been the construction sector that has been most prone to unemployment. There is evidence of this in earlier periods too: 173 out of the 1149

Table 1.21 *Unemployment rates in various sectors: Australia, Canada, US, UK*

	Australia	av. 78–83	Canada	av. 75–83	UK	av. 74–82	US	av. 74–83
	1983		1983		1982		1983	
Agriculture, etc.	4.5	4.0	10.4	7.2	6.9	4.0	8.8	5.9
Mining & quarrying	6.6	n/a	13.7	7.8	10.1	6.4	16.5	7.1
Manufacturing	9.6	5.8	13.0	8.9	11.8	5.8	11.0	7.5
Electricity, gas, water	n/a	n/a	7.0	4.0	3.9	2.3	4.4	3.0
Construction	14.1	7.3	23.9	15.5	20.2	12.1	15.2	10.7
Trade, restaurants, hotels	7.9	5.2	12.5	9.0	9.1	5.2	9.3	7.5
Transport, storage, communication	3.2	2.5	8.5	6.2	7.4	4.3	7.1	5.2
Finance, insurance, etc.	3.7	2.5	8.3	5.6	4.9	2.7	6.1	5.0
Community, social, personal services	3.8	3.1	4.6	6.0	5.3	3.1	6.1	4.7

Source: ILO Yearbook of Labour Statistics and author's calculations

unemployed persons surveyed in Rowntree and Lasker's (1911) celebrated study of York in 1910 had been engaged in building and allied trades. Douglas and Director's (1931) study of unemployment estimates that there was only 1 year between 1897 and 1926 when the unemployment rate for building trades workers fell below 12 per cent in New York and Massachusetts.

Table 1.21 presents unemployment rates in nine major sectors for Australia, Canada, the UK and the US. The construction sector tops the list in almost every case. Manufacturing and mining and quarrying, are also high-risk sectors from the unemployment standpoint. Trade, restaurants and hotels occupy a position in the middle, and agricultural occupations are somewhat below average. Unemployment is lowest in the utility, transport and last two service sectors. Community, social and personal services display the smallest rates of unemployment.

1.5.6 *Which Regions Suffer Most?*

Unemployment rates differ between regions within countries just as much as between countries. Some generalizations can be made. At least in recent decades, unemployment is relatively low in agricultural regions, and high in coastal districts. It often tends to increase with distance from the country's economic centre. In urban agglomerations, it is typically much lower in the more prosperous suburban and commuting areas than in the inner city.

The UK exhibits all these tendencies. In November 1985, there were seven English counties and three Scottish regions where unemployment fell below 10 per cent. The former were all in the south of England, quite close (but not too close)[15] to London: Berkshire (7.2 per cent), Buckinghamshire (8.2 per cent), Cambridgeshire (9.6 per cent), Hertfordshire (7.1 per cent), Oxfordshire (7.7 per cent), Suffolk (9.5 per cent) and Wiltshire (9.19 per cent). One of the Scottish regions was an agricultural area (Borders, 9.0 per cent) and two were regions strongly affected by the oil industry (Grampian, 7.9 per cent, and Shetland, 5.7 per cent). There were eight English counties where unemployment exceeded 16 per cent. One was a remote, coastal county, Cornwall (19.2 per cent), which contained the district with England's highest jobless tally (Newquay, 29.2 per cent). The other seven were urbanized, industrial areas in the northern half of England (Cleveland, 22.2 per cent; Durham, 18.7 per cent; Humberside, 16.9 per cent; Merseyside, 21.0 per cent; South Yorkshire, 18.0 per cent; Tyne and Wear, 19.19 per cent; West Midlands, 16.5 per cent). All were suffering from declining traditional industries, such as coal mining, the docks, motor assembly, shipbuilding and textiles. Six Welsh counties also fell in this category: three of these could be described as remote or relatively remote coastal districts (Clwyd 18.5 per cent; Dyfed, 18.3 per cent; Gwynedd, 19.3 per cent), and three were urbanized (West and Mid-Glamorgan (16.1 and 18.7 per cent), and Gwent (16.7 per cent)). Of the four Scottish regions with unemployment over 16 per cent, two were predominantly urban (Central, 16.1 per cent and Strathclyde, 18.6 per cent), and two were remote coastal areas (Highland, 16.8 per cent and Western Isles, 18.3 per cent).

Canada shows a not dissimilar picture. As the data in table 1.22 show, unemployment is at present highest in British Columbia in the far west, and the Maritime Provinces of the Atlantic Seaboard. It has traditionally been lowest in Ontario, Canada's economic centre, in Alberta (favoured by oil), and the largely agricultural prairie provinces of Manitoba and Saskatchewan.

Table 1.22 *Unemployment rates in different Canadian regions: selected years*

	All Canada	Atlantic Provinces	Quebec	Ontario	Prairie Provinces	British Columbia
1964	4.7	7.8	6.4	3.2	3.1	5.3
1969	4.7	7.5	6.9	3.1	2.9	5.0
1974	5.3	8.3	6.6	4.4	3.4	6.2
1979	7.4	11.6	9.6	6.5	4.3	7.6
1983	11.9	15.0	13.9	10.4	9.7	13.8
1984	11.3	15.2	12.8	9.1	9.8	14.7

Source: *Bank of Canada Monthly Statistical Review*

Within the EEC, as constituted until the accession of Portugal and Spain, the highest unemployment rates have recently been recorded in Northern Ireland, Sardinia and the Belgian provinces of Hainault and Limburg. All registered unemployment rates of 16 per cent or so in 1983, nearly double the EEC average in that year (8.8 per cent). Other high unemployment regions included the northern and western areas of Britain, Corsica and the French Mediterranean coast, much of Italy south of Rome, and the less densely populated provinces of the Netherlands. All these areas are in varying degrees peripheral to the main centres of economic activity in their respective countries. The lowest jobless rates in the EEC (under half the EEC average) are to be found in areas close to the Swiss Border (in Val d'Aosta in the Italian Alps and some southern districts in Baden-Württemberg and Bavaria) and in Thrace in Northern Greece. There is some indication of relatively high unemployment in city districts: in Germany, the three city *Länder*, West Berlin, Bremen and Hamburg all display unemployment rates somewhat above the German average: Attica, which contains Athens, suffers an unemployment rate nearly 3 per cent higher than in Greece as a whole, and unemployment in Brussels exceeds the Belgian average. The Paris region is an exception to this, as it registers easily the lowest unemployment rate in France. EEC regions with unemployment above 12 per cent or below 6 per cent are highlighted in figure 1.9.

Table 1.23 *Unemployment rates, by state, in the US, August 1985*

Below 5%	5–6.4%	6.5–8.0%	Above 8%
Kansas 4.6	Colorado 5.4	Arizona 6.8	Alabama 8.3
Maine 4.0	Connecticut 5.1	California 7.3	Alaska 8.6
Maryland 4.3	Florida 5.8	Delaware 6.7	Arkansas 8.4
Massachusetts 3.7	Hawaii 5.6	Georgia 6.9	Dist. of Columbia 7.1
Nebraska 4.9	Minnesota 5.1	Idaho 6.8	Illinois 8.8
New Hampshire 3.4	Missouri 6.2	Indiana 6.9	Kentucky 8.6
New Jersey 4.4	N. Carolina 5.8	Iowa 6.9	Louisiana 11.1
N. Dakota 4.9	New York 6.1	Montana 6.5	Michigan 9.7
Rhode Island 4.2	Oklahoma 6.4	Nevada 7.7	Mississippi 10.5
S. Dakota 4.3	Utah 5.1	Oregon 7.7	New Mexico 9.0
Vermont 4.5	Virginia 5.3	Pennsylvania 7.3	Ohio 8.8
	Wisconsin 6.3	S. Carolina 6.6	W. Virginia 12.4
	Wyoming 6.0	Texas 7.0	
		Washington 7.2	

Source: *Employment and Earnings*, October 1985 (US Department of Labor, Bureau of Labor Statistics)

The United States also displays wide regional variation in unemployment rates. Table 1.23 presents these statistics for all US states in August 1985. Of the 11 states with jobless rates below 5 per cent in this month, five are in New England and four lie in the primarily agricultural mid-west. The remaining two, Maryland and New Jersey, provide residence for many of the better-paid commuters working in Washington DC, and in New York. Among the 12 states where unemployment exceeded 8 per cent, four are in the deep south; five (Illinois, Kentucky, Michigan, Ohio and West Virginia) suffer from undue concentration of older, declining industries (particularly coal mining, steel and vehicle-building); two (Alaska and New Mexico) are examples of peripherality; and one provides a clear instance of an inner-city (the District of Columbia). One broad generalization that could be made on the basis of table 1.23 is that unemployment rates are lowest on the Atlantic Seaboard and the outer mid-west, and highest in the large swathe of territory lying between these two groups of states. By contrast with the east coast, unemployment is somewhat above average on the Pacific Littoral. It should be borne in mind, however, that table 1.23 takes a still photograph of the regional variation of unemployment at one recent date; the fortunes of particular states sometimes change. There are some fixed points, however: West Virginia has consistently exhibited the highest unemployment rates in the United States since well before the last war. Marston (1985) finds that unemployment tends to be persistently higher in those US regions with high wages, high unemployment insurance and attractive amenities; labour is sufficiently mobile for changes in the fortunes of particular industries to have enduring effects on the spatial dispersion of unemployment.

1.5.7 *Are Ethnic Minorities Particularly Prone to Unemployment?*

US and UK evidence confirms that members of ethnic minorities are much more likely to be out of work than the rest of the population. The American data in table 1.14 tell a sorry tale. Blacks are as a whole more than twice as likely to be unemployed than whites in the United States in September 1985. The differences are most marked in the younger age cohorts; they are also somewhat more pronounced for men than women. More than two in five black teenagers in the labour force were unemployed. The proportion for whites was one in seven. As table 1.19 reveals, blacks also tend to suffer longer unemployment spells than whites, although the gap is much smaller than for unemployment rates.

The Hispanic minorities also suffer higher unemployment than whites, but their position is noticeably better than for the blacks. Table 1.24 gives unemployment rates for the various racial groups in the third quarter of 1985. Hispanics of Puerto

Table 1.24 *Unemployment rates for different ethnic groups: US, third quarter 1985*

	White	Black	All	Hispanic		
				Mexican origin	Puerto Rican origin	Cuban origin
Both sexes	6.0	15.2	10.4	10.6	13.6	7.9
Men, 16 & over	5.5	14.6	9.6	9.3	12.3	8.6
Women, 16 & over	6.6	15.7	11.7	13.0	15.4	6.8
Both sexes, 16–19	14.2	38.2	23.7	24.7	33.4	14.0

Source: as table 1.23

Table 1.25 *Unemployment rates by ethnic origin, all persons aged 16 and over, Spring 1984*

Ethnic origin	Male	Female
All origins	11.5	10.5
White	11.0	10.1
Minority	21.3	19.1
West Indian	29.0	17.0
Indian	13.0	18.0
of which from East Africa	9.0	20.0
Pakistani, Bangladeshi	34.0	40.0
Other	17.0	20.0

Source: *Department of Labour Gazette*, December 1985, p. 475

Rican origin fare much worse than the average for Hispanics, while those of Cuban origin are markedly more successful in gaining employment.

The British statistics for minority unemployment are equally depressing. Those of West Indian, Pakistani and Bangladeshi origin are particularly prone to unemployment. By contrast, joblessness for those of Indian origin is rather closer to the figures for whites. Table 1.25 presents data for the spring of 1984.

1.6 Who Are the Unemployed? II: Other Characteristics

1.6.1 *Attributes Identified in Previous Sections: Summary*

The unemployed, as we have seen, come disproportionately from fringe groups. They are much likelier, relatively speaking, to be in their teens or 20s than in older cohorts. In the UK (but not the US), unemployment is also more concentrated among those close to retirement. In most countries, but not the UK, women are over-represented among the unemployed. So too are ethnic minorities, especially blacks. They come disproportionately from the less skilled. White, well-educated prime-age males are relatively immune. The older you are, the longer you will take to find a new job if you lose or quit your old one.

1.6.2 *The Unemployed in York in 1910: Personal Characteristics*

The earliest and in some ways most interesting study of the unemployed is that of Rowntree and Lasker (1911). It is worth exploring the results of this important inquiry in some depth. The authors examined unemployment in the English city of York in June 1910. They investigated the personal characteristics of 1149 men and women unemployed at that time. This total was broken down as follows:

A   men previously in full-time work, now unemployed or at best casually employed   291

B   casual male workers, out of work on 7 June 1910, permanently underemployed but appearing to seek work actively   441

C construction workers (male) out of work	173
D women and girls unemployed	139
E workshy	105
	1149

Of those in category A, unemployment was attributed to the following characteristics:

age (dismissed as 'too old')	23.3%
physical handicap	7.2%
character faults (drink, gambling, theft, inefficiency, unpunctuality, laziness, etc.)	15.5%
both physical and character defects	3.1%

The remaining 50.9 per cent were found to be satisfactory on the last four criteria. Their joblessness was put down to 'economic' factors, such as depressed trading conditions, the bankruptcy of their employer or the like. The median (uncompleted) spell of unemployment was nearly 6 months.

Of those in category B, 83 had never been in regular work. Twenty had once served in the armed forces; alcohol appeared to be a factor for 14. Of the 358 who had once had a regular job, reasons for unemployment could be ascertained for 285. The median lapse of time since regular employment was $5\frac{1}{2}$ years. For these, and for the unemployed workers in building and allied trades, the reasons for unemployment were as shown in table 1.26.

The high incidence of unemployment among construction workers as a whole (10.5 per cent) owed much to the fact that the great turn-of-the-century building boom had come to an end in 1904–5.

Among the female unemployed, Rowntree and Lasker established reasons in some cases. Fourteen were deemed to be capable of work, but unable to find sufficiently remunerative employment. Twelve were 'not in distress', but clearly sought more work. Seven were 'needed at home', often to bring up children. Six were considered 'almost unemployable' for a variety of reasons. Of the 105 men identified as workshy, 55 had once worked regularly; drink was the most-cited reason for their joblessness. Thirty-two had never worked. In each case, infirmity of character was described as the root cause of unemployment. The workshy formed a recognizable group, but it is worth stressing that they were a small minority, accounting for less than 10 per cent of the unemployed men surveyed.

Table 1.26 *Reasons for unemployment, in York in 1910*

	Physical handicap (%)	Character fault (%)	Physical and character defects (%)	Satisfactory (economic causes) (%)
B	$12\frac{1}{2}$	27	$11\frac{1}{2}$	49
C skilled	17	2	2	77
C unskilled	2	8	14	52

Table 1.27   *Attitudes to work of 469 unemployed women*

	% under 25	% 25–44	% over 45	Total	%
Want factory work only	3	3	3	12	3
Want 'own job only'	8	10	13	51	11
Would take any available work	5	5	3	17	4
Not unwilling for residential domestic work	25	15	11	73	16
Not unwilling for non-residential domestic work	25	35	30	137	29
Expect to get work soon	14	10	8	51	11
Get seasonal work	5	5	5	25	5
Get casual work	2	3	1	10	2
No chance of getting work again	4	8	21	56	12

Want no work
  Availability
  doubtful
	11	6	5	37	8

Source: Pilgrim Trust (1937)

1.6.3 *Personal Reasons for Unemployment: Some Later Evidence*

The Pilgrim Trust (1937) conducted a statistical survey of the unemployed in various parts of Britain a generation after Rowntree and Lasker. By this time, unemployment insurance had come into force for the overwhelming majority of workers. The Pilgrim Trust study points to the existence of workshyness and even fraud among the unemployed. But this continues to be confined to a small minority.

One of the most interesting results of the Pilgrim Trust inquiry concerns the attitudes to work of 469 unemployed women sampled (table 1.27). Twelve per cent had become resigned to the fact that they could not, or would probably not, obtain work again. Their fatalistic attitude was far more pronounced among older women. The proportion identified as not wanting to work, on the other hand, fell sharply with age. The workshy, by this criterion, accounted for an even lower proportion of their respective demographic group (8 per cent as a whole) than in the Rowntree–Lasker study. The authors of the Pilgrim Trust report also found that pessimistic or workshy attitudes were more pronounced among young men than old men, and seemed to be sustained by an unemployment culture fostered by 'cellar clubs' in Liverpool and elsewhere. This might be one of several possible reasons for suspecting that natural rates of unemployment may be non-unique: the phenomenon is explored in a simple theoretical model in chapter 13.

Are the unemployed out of work because they left their job, or because they lost it? US evidence on this question merits scrutiny. Table 1.28 enables us to answer it, at least for present conditions. The statistics reveal that nearly four times as many people are unemployed because they lost their jobs than because they left them. Job-leavers are more frequently encountered among women than men, whites than blacks, teenagers than their elders. The numbers of new entrants, and re-entrants into the labour force roughly balance the job-losers. Job-leavers bear about the same proportion to the unemployed as the workshy in the Rowntree–Lasker and Pilgrim Trust studies.

Are the unemployed disproportionately likely to have unemployed spouses?

Table 1.28 Unemployed persons by reason for unemployment, sex, and race: United States (household data, not seasonally adjusted)

Reason for unemployment	Total unemployed		Men 20 years and over		Women 20 years and over		Both sexes 16 to 19 years		White		Black	
	Sept 1984	Sept 1985	Sept 1984	Sept 1985	Sept 1984	Sept 1985	Sept 1984	Sept 1985	Sept 1984	Sept 1985	Sept 1984	Sept 1985
Number of unemployed												
Total unemployed	8051	7984	3449	3302	3135	3328	1467	1354	5956	5840	1816	1880
Job-losers	3744	3695	2282	2182	1208	1247	254	265	2818	2710	802	886
On layoff	913	955	525	570	330	323	58	62	743	759	146	171
Other job-losers	2831	2740	1757	1612	878	924	196	203	2075	1951	657	715
Job-leavers	933	936	322	340	461	479	150	117	766	788	124	111
Re-entrants	2323	2450	692	679	1238	1375	393	397	1742	1757	508	597
New entrants	1051	903	152	101	228	226	671	576	631	585	382	286
Per cent distribution												
Total unemployed	100.0	100.0	100.0	100.0	100.0	100.0	100.0	100.0	100.0	100.0	100.0	100.0
Job-losers	46.5	46.3	66.2	66.1	38.5	37.5	17.3	19.6	47.3	46.4	44.2	47.1
On layoff	11.3	12.0	15.2	17.3	10.5	9.7	4.0	4.6	12.5	13.0	8.0	9.1
Other job-losers	35.2	34.3	51.0	48.8	28.0	27.8	13.3	15.0	34.8	33.4	36.2	38.0
Job-leavers	11.6	11.7	9.4	10.3	14.7	14.4	10.2	8.7	12.9	13.5	6.8	5.9
Re-entrants	28.9	30.7	20.1	20.6	39.8	41.3	26.8	29.3	29.2	30.1	28.0	31.8
New entrants	13.1	11.3	4.4	3.1	7.3	6.8	45.7	42.5	10.6	10.0	21.0	15.2
Unemployed as a per cent of the civilian labour force												
Job-losers	3.3	3.2					3.4	3.5	2.9	2.7	6.6	7.1
Job-leavers	0.8	0.8					2.0	1.6	0.8	0.8	1.0	0.9
Re-entrants	2.0	2.1					5.2	5.3	1.8	1.8	4.2	4.8
New entrants	0.9	0.8					8.8	7.7	0.6	0.6	3.1	2.3

Source: as table 1.23

Again, US evidence can be brought to bear. The picture is clear: the answer is yes. For unemployed husbands in September 1985, the incidence of spouse's unemployment was three times higher than for husbands as a whole (11 per cent against 3.7 per cent). Unemployed wives were also much likelier to have unemployed husbands than for wives as a whole (17.2 per cent against 5.7 per cent). Single household heads maintaining families were twice as likely to be unemployed (11.4 per cent for women, against 5.7 per cent for wives and 7.4 per cent for men, against 3.7 per cent for husbands). Dependent relatives in families maintained by single household heads were also disproportionately likely to suffer unemployment.

1.7 Some Effects of Unemployment

1.7.1 *Unemployment and Suicide*

Unemployment and suicide are tragically associated. An early statistical pointer to this was the large increase in Warsaw suicides attributed to unemployment after the onset of the Great Depression in 1930–1: 18.3 per cent in 1931, as against 5.2 per cent in the more prosperous conditions of 1928.[16] A recent British study by Overstone also suggests a positive link between unemployment and suicide. Forty-three per cent of attempted suicides, and 64 per cent of suicides in Edinburgh occurred among the unemployed or the retired (Overstone (1973)). A more recent study by Platt (1983), again on Edinburgh data, found a strong positive correlation between unemployment and attempted suicide, especially for those who had been out of work for a year or more. These and other papers are reviewed by Platt (1984). This does not rule out the possibility that unemployment and suicide were often joint symptoms of other causes, such as family break-up, illness, alcoholism or narcotic addiction, but the statistics are highly disturbing.

1.7.2 *Unemployment and Physical Health*

Micro data do not confirm that unemployment impairs physical health. The Department of Health and Social Security (DHSS) study by Moylan et al. (1984) of 2300 British unemployed men finds that only 8 per cent spent time out of work due to sickness in the year after first registering as unemployed, as against 12 per cent in the previous year. Worse health certainly meant a lower chance of gaining or retaining employment, but there was no direct evidence that health deteriorated due to unemployment.[17] Another British study by Narendranathan et al. (1982) found that, once the effects of skill levels were removed, no association between physical sickness and unemployment could be identified.

Aggregate time series data, on the other hand, do seem to suggest some link between unemployment, and other economic factors, and the general incidence of ischaemic heart disease. This is at least the claim of Brenner (1979, 1980). Gravelle et al. (1981) offer some trenchant criticisms of Brenner's evidence, however. On the other hand British inter-war evidence points to a clear link between unemployment and maternal childbirth mortality (Singer, 1937). In the EEC today, infant mortality is still far higher in some regions of high unemployment (such as Clydeside in Scotland, and the Italian Mezzogiorno) then elsewhere but there may be other reasons for this.

1.7.3 *Unemployment and Mental Health*

While the effect of unemployment on physical health remains controversial, or at least hard to establish, there can be no doubt about its adverse consequences for mental health. An early indication of this was provided by Halliday (1935). Psychoneurotic illnesses became progressively more common in proportion to sickness of all kinds, as the duration of unemployment increased. More recently, an Australian study by Findlay-Jones and Eckhardt (1981) of young unemployed workers suffering diagnosed disorders found that onset followed loss of job in 43 per cent of cases, in the apparent absence of other factors provoking it. British studies by Banks and Jackson (1982) and Jackson and Warr (1984) established that distress rises significantly after unemployment and falls with re-employment, and that the duration of unemployment gradually aggravates mental illness for a period of up to 6 months, for all but the youngest and oldest workers.

1.7.4 *Unemployment and Subsequent Earnings*

One would expect that a spell of unemployment would diminish a worker's subsequent earnings opportunities, if and when he regains employment. Clear evidence that this is indeed so is provided by Chowdhury and Nickell (1985). Studying US micro data, they find that earnings fall sharply after a spell of unemployment, but that the effect decays quite quickly, leaving a relatively small permanent effect. Yet the Chowdhury–Nickell results relate to the group – undeniably the great majority – that did regain employment. For those who do not, it is worth quoting Rowntree and Lasker's (1911) remarks about those in category B in section 1.6.2: 'It is obvious, even if we underestimate rather than exaggerate the value of the figures, that strong adverse influences have been at work, and almost all the men in this class are undergoing a more or less rapid process of deterioration.'

1.7.5 *Unemployment and Crime*

Unemployment furnishes both the opportunity and the motive for crime. There is a strong upwards trend in both unemployment rates and certain reported crimes in the UK over the past two decades. Robbery, assault, burglary, theft, murder and rape appear to have risen threefold, or worse; so has unemployment. Crimes appear to be much more common in inner-city areas, which also suffer well-above-average unemployment rates. In the United States, the trends in unemployment and reported crime are both less pronounced but there is still some positive correlation in both aggregate time series, and cross-sectional regional data. Possibly, the closest fit between unemployment and prison admissions pertains to Canada: figure 1.10, reproduced by kind permission from the 1982 House of Lords Select Committee Report, illustrates this.

1.7.6 *The Financial Consequences of Unemployment*

Unemployment entails a severe drain on the public finances. A man or woman out of work earns no wages, which would otherwise be subject to income tax. No contributions for social security are received from the worker or the employer. He or she spends less, so less is collected in indirect taxes. Finally, unemployment

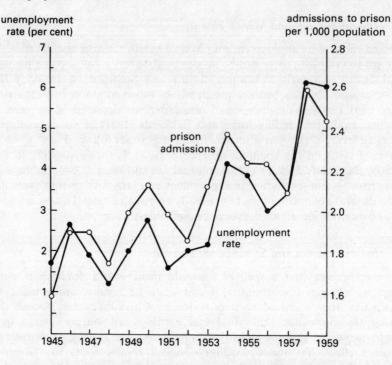

Figure 1.10 *Prison admissions and unemployment rate in Canada, 1945–59*
Source: House of Lords Select Committee on Unemployment Reports, 1982

benefit generally becomes payable, often supplemented by additional welfare payments in cash or kind.

The revenue losses borne by governments have been estimated by various authors. Reyher et al. (1979) put the average annual loss per unemployed German worker as DM 18,056 in 1978 (some £4100 at rates of exchange then prevailing): the total cost they estimated at over DM 23 billion. In the UK, Lord Cockfield announced, in answer to a Parliamentary Question, that the average Exchequer cost of unemployment was £436.81 per month for a single man with no dependants in 1980. This will have no doubt risen to some £6400 per year by 1986. Rates of unemployment benefit, employment taxes and marginal income tax rates are somewhat more modest in the United States, but even there $8000 per annum should be regarded as a conservative estimate in 1986 for federal and state authorities taken together.

1.8 Concluding Remarks

Unemployment varies widely over time, between economies, and between different groups of workers within economies. One of the few fixed points in the macro evidence is that high unemployment accompanies low output. When real national income is below trend, unemployment is typically above it. The macroeconomic links between output and employment that might explain this are explored in chapters 3 and 4, and the shocks that can generate changes in these variables are examined in chapters 7 and 8. These analyses all depend upon some relationship between unemployment and the demand for labour. It is therefore to this that we now turn in chapter 2.

2 Unemployment and the Demand for Labour

2.1 Introduction

Unemployment is often thought of as the excess supply of labour. That is, unemployment is the amount by which the available labour supply outstrips the demand for labour, at the going constellation of wage rates and prices. All else equal, a rise in the demand for labour should occasion a reduction in unemployment. Consequently no study of unemployment could be complete without a thorough examination of the forces that underlie the demand for labour. It is the purpose of this chapter to provide just that. Section 2.4 is devoted to exploring some reasons why the demand for labour might prove insufficient to eliminate unemployment, and why wages and prices might be less than fully sensitive to it.

2.2 The Demand for Labour by a Competitive Firm: The Simple Case

The natural starting place is the firm operating under perfectly competitive conditions. What makes the perfectly competitive firm an appropriate place to begin is not its realism, but its simplicity. Imperfect competition, in the form of monopoly or oligopoly, can then be explored straightforwardly as a relaxation of the assumption of price-taking behaviour in perfect competition.

We commence by laying down a list of assumptions that can form the basis of the simplest model of a competitive firm's demand for labour. Assume that the firm produces a single product, with a price of p which it cannot influence. Its output level, q, depends upon a single homogeneous variable factor of production, labour (n). Labour is applied to production instantaneously, and the forthcoming output is sold without delay. There are no taxes. The firm is fully apprised of its technology and prices confronting it, and aims to maximize its profit. Labour costs are summed up in a single number, w, which represents the money wage rate per unit of n.

The firm's profit, π will be the excess of its total receipts ($pq = pq(n)$) over its total wage bill (wn):

$$\pi = pq(n) - wn. \tag{2.1}$$

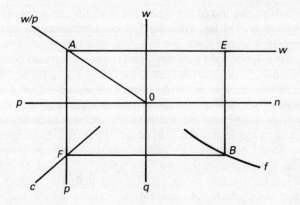

Figure 2.1 *Employment and output equilibrium for the competitive firm*

Profit will be maximized where the wage rate just balances the value of labour's marginal product (pq'):

$$pq' - w = 0. \tag{2.2}$$

If w were less than pq', it would pay the firm to expand employment: additional units of labour would add more to its receipts than to its costs. If w exceeded pq', profit would be increased by reducing employment. Only when (2.2) is true can profits be at a maximum. This situation, where the firm is in equilibrium, is depicted by point E in the upper right quadrant of figure 2.1. The supply of labour for the firm is given by the horizontal line w. This reflects the fact that the money wage rate, w, cannot be affected by the firm's actions. Its demand for labour is the value of labour's marginal product (pq'); that is shown by the downwards-sloping curve. The lower right quadrant presents the firm's production function, which gives the connection between the output of the product, q, and the level of employment. The function $q(n)$ is labelled f. In the lower left quadrant, the firm's output decision is illustrated. The vertical line, p, gives its average and marginal revenue (again reflecting the character of perfect competition, which requires the firm to be a price-taker in its product market). The curve labelled c shows the marginal cost of output, which increases with q since the production function, f, displays decreasing returns to labour (the increase in output occasioned by a negligible increase in employment drops as the level of employment increases). The upper left quadrant shows the real wage, w/p, which is the gradient of the ray OA.

Figure 2.1 shows a production function where returns to labour diminish. It might seem that this is a strong assumption. But in fact f *must* have this shape in the neighbourhood of equilibrium for the firm: if the equality of the wage rate with the value of labour's marginal product equation (2.2) is to be consistent with a maximum, rather than a minimum for profit, it is necessary that the latter (pq') *decline* as n increases. If w equalled pq' at a point where the latter was increasing, such a point would minimize profits, not maximize them. Profit would increase if employment were raised (since $pq' > w$ at higher employment levels) or reduced (since $pq' < w$ to the left).

Output and employment would both respond positively to a rise in the price level, p, or to a fall in the money wage rate, w. A higher price level would displace the price line leftwards in the lower left quadrant, and lift the pq curve in the upper right. The real wage would fall, rotating OA counterclockwise in the upper left quadrant. A drop in w would have just the same effect on the real wage ray; the w line would fall in the upper right quadrant, and the marginal cost curve, c, would be displaced downwards, to intersect the price line below F at a higher level of output. The magnitude of the increase in employment that would follow a fall in the real wage would depend on how pronounced was the curvature of the production function, f. If f were sharply curved, returns to labour would diminish rapidly, and only a modest gain in employment would occur. If f were almost linear, a large rise in employment would be needed to restore equality between labour's marginal product and the new lower real wage. The shape of f will be reflected in the elasticity of the labour demand curve, pq'. This elasticity (for a given p) will in fact equal the ratio of the elasticity of substitution between labour and the bundle of fixed factors of production, to the share of output not accruing to labour. The elasticity of the marginal cost (or supply) curve, c, will be the elasticity of pq', multiplied by labour's share in output.[1]

The final point to consider in the context of this single model is the consequence of a shift in the production function, f. Such a phenomenon could occur as a result of a change in technology, or an alteration in the quantity of the fixed factor(s) with which the firm operates. Technical progress, or a rise in the fixed factor(s), will push the f and c curves downwards in figure 2.1. At an unchanged real wage, output will necessarily rise. Employment will also go up, assuming that labour's marginal product (q') increases with the fixed factor(s), except in the extreme case of technical progress which is exclusively labour-augmenting[2] when the elasticity of substitution between labour and the fixed factor(s) is less than the share of output not paid out in wages (Sinclair (1981)).

The time has now come to investigate generalization of this simple framework. This is the subject of the following section.

2.3 Generalizing the Simple Competitive Model of the Demand for Labour

2.3.1 *The Firm and the Industry Under Perfect Competition*

Until now we have taken the price of the product, p, as an exogenous variable. As far as the competitive firm is concerned, this is quite appropriate; but for a competitive industry, the price is endogenous. The simplest thing to assume is that the price is determined by conditions of equilibrium and market clearing. Figure 2.2 illustrates this.

The demand for the industry's product is represented by a downwards-sloping curve, DD, in the lower left quadrant. The supply curve of labour for the industry is shown as an upwards-sloping curve, Ns, in the upper right. If the industry is to be in equilibrium, employment will be given by point E, where the wage rate equals the value of labour's marginal product in every firm. The industry's demand for labour curve, PQ', slopes down for two reasons: not merely will the marginal physical product of labour decline as employment increases as a result of the profit maximization condition (2.2), but now a rise in industry employment will occasion a fall in the price of the product, as the industry's output expands. The industry's

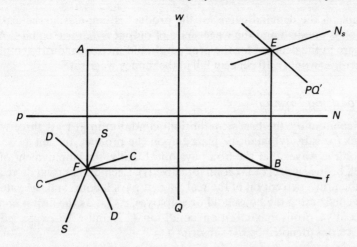

Figure 2.2 *Output, employment, wage and price in a perfectly competitive industry*

supply curve is rather complicated. If the existing number of firms in the industry is frozen, as is typically assumed in the 'short run', it will be given by the curve CC which is based on the summation of each firm's marginal cost curve. If, as in the 'long run', the number of firms is allowed to adjust to the point where (supernormal) profits vanish for the representative firm, industry supply is given by the curve SS. This latter curve will not be perfectly elastic in figure 2.2, since the industry's supply of labour is not depicted as horizontal. The curve f linking industry output (Q) to employment (N) is obtained by aggregating each firm's production function, subject to the condition that each has a common marginal product of labour.

The responsiveness of the industry's employment level, N, to the money wage rate and the level of demand for the product can be found by linking three relationships in rate-of-change from:

the demand for the product: $\qquad\qquad \tilde{Q} = \tilde{a} - \varepsilon\tilde{P}.$ (2.3)

the production function: $\qquad\qquad\quad \tilde{Q} = \theta\tilde{N}.$ (2.4)

the marginal productivity condition: $\sigma(\tilde{w} - \tilde{p}) = \tilde{Q} - \tilde{N}.$ (2.5)

A tilde (˜) above a variable represents a proportionate rate of change. In (2.3), $\tilde{a}$ is the change in the level of demand for the product, and ε is the elasticity of demand for the product, DD. In (2.4) θ denotes the share of output accruing to labour, the ratio of wN to PQ. θ will be the elasticity of the production function, f. In (2.5), σ stands for the elasticity of substitution between labour and the fixed factor(s) of production. All parameters, ε, θ and σ are positive (and θ lies between 0 and 1). Considering (2.3), (2.4) and (2.5), we can solve for the change in N in terms of changes in w and a:

$$\tilde{N} = \tilde{a}\frac{b}{\varepsilon} - b\tilde{w}$$ (2.6)

where

$$b = + \left[\frac{\theta}{\varepsilon} + \frac{1-\theta}{\sigma} \right]^{-1}.$$

For example, if the demand curve for the product is unit-elastic, the elasticity of substitution is one-half and the wage share of output is $\frac{3}{4}$, b will equal $\frac{4}{5}$. A 10 per cent increase in the demand for the product should increase industry employment by 8 per cent, as would a 10 per cent fall in the money wage rate.

2.3.2 *Introducing Taxation*

Taxation could affect the firm's equilibrium condition in at least three ways. An indirect tax (or subsidy) might be placed upon the product. Income tax might be levied upon the wages that the firm pays out. Finally, the employment of labour might itself be the subject of taxation (or subsidy). Each of these will drive a wedge between the firm's perception of the real wage it pays labour, and the value of the real wage confronting the household or employee. As far as the firm is concerned, the competitive profit-maximization condition (2.2) must be expressed in the employer's terms (denoted by the subscript f):

$$p_f q' = w_f. \tag{2.7}$$

Suppose that the government levies a sales tax on the good at the rate t_s an income tax on wage income at the rate t_i and an employment tax at the rate t_e. In that case, defining p_h and w_h as the price and wage rate facing the employee-household, (2.7) may be rewritten

$$p_h q' = \frac{(1+t_s)(1+t_e)}{1-t_i} w_h. \tag{2.8}$$

If at least some of the incidence of these three types of tax falls upon the firm, employment and output will be lowered as a result. Employment subsidies ($t_e < 0$) will have the opposite effect. We return to consider these issues in more detail later, in chapter 16.

2.3.3 *A Time-lag Between the Payment of Wages and the Sale of the Product*

Until now, the firm has been assumed to sell the product of the labour it hires at the same moment as it pays its wages. More often the payment of wages precedes the sale of the product. In that case, the firm will seek to equate the wage rate with the *discounted* value of labour's marginal product. If the product is sold at p in 1 year's time, and the rate of interest is r per year, the discounted price now is only $p/(1+r)$. Hence, if there is an interval of S years between the date at which labour is paid for its services, and the date at which the firm receives payment from the sale of its product, the competitive profit-maximization condition (2.2) becomes

$$pq' = w(1+r)^S. \tag{2.9}$$

For given p and w, the demand for labour decreases as either r or S increase. This establishes an important possible link between employment and monetary policy. The early 1980s witnessed a sharp jump in nominal and real interest rates. To the extent that money wage rates, and the expected prices received by firms, were given, employers experiencing a time interval between wage payments and product receipts will undoubtedly have faced a strong incentive to release labour. The sharp decline in employment that accompanied these interest rate increases – particularly in manufacturing, where the gestation period of production is important – may well have been exacerbated by them. Furthermore, to the extent that interest rate increases were taken to signal that the monetary authorities in the UK and the US planned to reduce forecast levels of inflation, expectations of the future selling prices of products will have fallen at the same time, reinforcing the cut in the demand for labour.

2.3.4 *Labour as a Less than Perfectly Variable Factor of Production*

The costs of hiring and firing are appreciable. Some workers remain with the same employer throughout their working lives. Seven out of every eight employees in the UK typically stay with the same company or public agency from one year to the next. In such conditions, an offer of employment will be seen partly as an investment decision by the firm making it. The assumption that labour is engaged only for the current period, then released, may once have been more realistic; today it applies only to a rather unimportant fringe of activities such as window-cleaning and temporary secretarial facilities.

Suppose, instead, that we consider the type of lifetime employment offers made by large Japanese concerns (or by central government to its administrative staff). Retain the competitive framework, and other assumptions, of the simple model discussed in section 2.2. In this case, the profit-maximization level of employment offers to the current generation of labour-force entrants that the firm will make should satisfy a greatly broadened version of (2.2). The new condition is that the stream of discounted values of labour's marginal product should equal the discounted stream of wage rates:

$$\int_0^T e^{-rt}p(t)q'(t)dt = \int_0^T e^{-rt}w(t)dt. \tag{2.10}$$

Equation (2.10) will be true, at least, for the case of a constant, time-invariant rate of interest, r, and a fixed career length, T. The discrete-time equivalent of (2.10) is

$$\sum_{i=0}^T p_i q_i'(1+r)^{-i} = \sum_{i=0}^T w_i(1+r)^{-i}. \tag{2.11}$$

Equations (2.10) and (2.11) will describe a state of affairs where the firm takes its current employment offers to the point where their net present value is maximized.

Several points emerge from (2.10) or (2.11). One is that the *current* value of the real wage pales into insignificance in comparison with what one might call the 'permanent', or average expected, relationship between wage rates and the price of the product. If the firm suddenly anticipates increased wage rates or depressed selling conditions in future periods, its demand for labour hired now will fall, even if current real wages are unchanged. Unemployment could be a *capital-theoretic* phenomenon, betokening pessimism on the part of employers about real wage rates in future periods, and only weakly sensitive, if at all, to their current values.

A second point concerns the rate of interest. Suppose that newly engaged labour is rather unproductive when it starts to work, but that productivity steadily rises with experience. Suppose that the skills which labour acquires are at least partly specific to the firm. Imagine that workers do not wish to earn a time profile of wages that mirrors the evolution of their productivity; rather, suppose that they are anxious to consume at a constant rate over their working lives, or at least keen that their consumption should start high in relation to their initial productivity level. Workers find it hard to borrow directly against the promise (or hope) of future

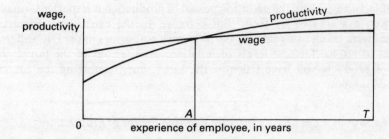

Figure 2.3 *Time profiles of wage rates and productivity with firm-specific skill acquisition and imperfect capital markets confronting workers*

wages. It will typically be easier for the company to do their borrowing for them. If this is so, the firm will make much more profit out of its workers later in their careers, and would experience outright losses, on a cash-flow basis, on the younger employees. The kind of wage and productivity time profiles to which this might give rise is illustrated in figure 2.3.

Now consider the effects of a once-and-for-all, unanticipated rise in the rate of interest. The discounted present value of the gains the employer anticipates in the longer future, when workers have been with it for more than the interval *A*, falls relative to that of the losses incurred in the nearer future. The net present value of the investment represented by engaging young workers now will go down. So the profit-maximizing volume of current employment offers must fall.

A further implication of this view of employment is that it will be the current generation of school-leavers and university-leavers that suffers the effects of swings in the overall demand for labour. Those already engaged have lifetime contracts. Dismissing them might even be illegal. It could certainly prove expensive, in a variety of ways. Older, more experienced workers will be much more valuable to the firm than new recruits, if the time profiles of wages and productivities resemble those illustrated in figure 2.3. The firm might have to buy them out of their explicit or implicit 'rights' to employment. It will tarnish its reputation as a good employer, and any young workers it may wish to hire in future years will not repose much confidence in its long-term employment offers. Morale among workers not dismissed as redundant could suffer; abler ones, who may command reasonable earnings opportunities elsewhere, may quit. The employer may also feel loyal to his current labour force for non-pecuniary reasons. He will hardly display less loyalty to the employees he knows than to job applicants unknown to him. An unexpected adverse movement in the overall demand for labour will induce firms to react by adopting a policy of hiring freezes, and 'natural wastage'. They will allow the labour force to fall as existing workers retire, resign or die. Depending upon the age structure of their labour force, and the extent of natural turnover due to quits, natural wastage may permit employment reductions of between 5 and 15 per cent per year. This may be enough to accommodate the fall in the overall demand for labour, if it is not exceptionally severe.

Natural wastage, supplemented if needs be by calls for voluntary (and compensated) redundancy, has been widely applied by West European and US concerns in recent recessions. Existing workers are by and large shielded. The onus of adjustment is thrust upon the hapless cohorts of young people leaving secondary and tertiary education, and on others, such as mothers with growing children wishing to re-enter the labour force. All this is distinctly unfair, and offends against canons of fairness between generations. One even wonders whether those unlucky enough to have been born in the 1960s will be prepared to subvent generous pensions for their seniors in the early decades of the next century, when the ratio of retired dependants to those of working age will be as much as twice its current level, given present demographic trends.

The final point to note in this connection is that the life-time employment-offer model is placed under considerable strain if the number of potential labour-force entrants varies sizeably from year to year. The 1950s and early 1960s witnessed a steady climb in births in most Western countries; a peak was reached of over 1 million in the UK in 1964, and over $4\frac{1}{2}$ million in the US in 1962. The fruit of the early 1960s birth bulge unfortunately coincided with the recessions of the early 1980s. It is easy to see in retrospect that special measures to subsidize youth employment would have been advisable to avoid the huge jump in the unemployment of young people at this time. Market forces would have called for a reduction in wage rates, paid at least for younger workers, if the baby-boomers were to be successfully accommodated within the labour force. In the event, labour markets proved far too rigid to allow this.

2.3.5 *Introducing a Second Variable Factor of Production*

Until now, labour has been treated as the only variable (or partly variable) factor of production. Suppose that we return to the case where labour is fully variable, but introduce a second variable factor. Call this factor 'energy', e, and label its price z. Profit maximization under perfect competition gives a condition analogous to (2.2): both labour and energy will be employed to the point where the value of their marginal products balances their prices:

$$
\left.
\begin{aligned}
w = p\frac{\partial q}{\partial n} &\equiv pf_n \\[2ex]
z = p\frac{\partial q}{\partial e} &\equiv pf_e.
\end{aligned}
\right\}
\tag{2.12}
$$

Equation (2.12) implies that the ratio of factor prices, w/z, will equal the ratio of their marginal products (f_n/f_e).

Will a rise in the price of 'energy', z, raise or reduce the demand for labour? If w and p are given, total differentiation of (2.12) reveals that the demand for labour will fall or rise accordingly as $f_{en} \gtrless 0$ (that is, depending on whether a rise in the supply of energy raises or cuts the marginal product of labour). It is highly likely, but not certain, that $f_{en} > 0$; only if labour and energy were close substitutes, and each were relatively complementary with a third (fixed) factor, capital, could f_{en} be negative.[3]

If we turn to the equilibrium of a competitive industry, the adverse effect of dearer energy on output, and also generally upon employment, is likely to be tempered by a rise in the price of its product. This will certainly be true if the industry in question sells its output to domestic consumers, rather than on international markets at an exogenously given price.[4] If so, a low enough elasticity of demand will allow employment to rise. For example, if there is a common elasticity of substitution between all three factors, capital, labour and energy, employment will rise following an energy price jump if the elasticity of demand is less than the elasticity of substitution. Dearer energy will also tend to raise employment in energy-producing industries, although this effect may be small since they are not likely to be particularly labour-intensive. Furthermore, if the country is a net exporter of energy (as Britain had become at the time of the second oil price shock in 1979) employment in other tradable industries is likely to be squeezed as a result of exchange rate appreciation.

2.3.6 *Imperfect Competition, I: Monopoly*

The framework of this chapter has so far been governed by the assumption of perfect competition. It is now time to investigate how the demand for labour is affected by the opposite premiss, of monopoly.

A firm enjoying a monopoly position will generally not set employment at the point where the wage rate equals the value of labour's marginal product (condition (2.2)). Monopoly means that an increase in employment, and hence in output, requires a cut in the price of the product if the additional units of output are to be sold. If the monopolist faces an exogenously given money wage for labour, and sets out to maximize profit, the level of employment will be chosen to ensure that the wage equals the *marginal revenue* resulting from labour's marginal product. In the absence of price discrimination (so that all units of output sell at a uniform price, p), this entails

$$w = pq'\left(1 - \frac{1}{\varepsilon}\right) \tag{2.13}$$

where ε, defined as a positive number, is the elasticity of demand for the product. (The right-hand side of (2.13) is known as labour's 'marginal revenue product'.) This is so because

$$\text{marginal revenue} \equiv p\left(1 - \frac{1}{\varepsilon}\right). \tag{2.14}$$

Given that q', the marginal product of labour, declines as employment increases (2.13) tells us that the level of employment in an industry will be lower under monopoly than under perfect competition (when $w = pq'$). A profit-maximizing monopolist must charge a higher price, produce less and employ less labour, than a set of perfectly competitive small firms.

Figure 2.4 illustrates this comparison. For simplicity's sake, the supply of labour is assumed horizontal in the upper right quadrant. The curve C in the lower left represents the marginal cost curve of the monopolist, and equally the summed supply curves of all firms when the industry is perfectly competitive. The vertical line S depicts the industry long-run supply curve in perfect competition, which will be perfectly elastic given the horizontal labour supply curve, and the absence of any interdependencies affecting the costs of individual firms. The perfectly competitive industry is in equilibrium with the rectangle $EBFA$, which will give employment at Np, and price at Pp. By contrast, the profit-maximizing monopolist sets employment at point C, where the marginal cost of labour (w) balances the marginal revenue product of labour. This is in accordance with (2.13). The dashed

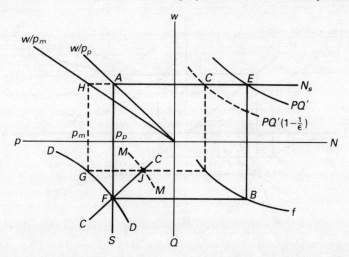

Figure 2.4 *Comparing employment and output under monopoly and perfect competition, for a horizontal labour supply curve*

curve, $PQ'(1-1/\varepsilon)$, lies below the solid curve, PQ', because the monopolist – unlike his perfectly competitive counterparts – recognizes that employing more labour entails a cut in the price of output, not just on the additional units but on all intramarginal units, too. It is this that restrains his demand for labour. Point C in the upper right quadrant corresponds with point J in the lower left, where marginal cost (CC) intersects marginal revenue (MM) in the product market. So the monopolist's equilibrium position is described by the rectangle $HCDG$.

The message of figure 2.4 is simple. Monopoly cuts the demand for labour. It squeezes real wage rates (expressed in terms of goods supplied by the monopolist), or employment levels, or both. These effects are reinforced if the firm enjoys monopsony as well as monopoly power. If it faces an upwards-sloping supply of labour, and cannot discriminate between its labourers by paying them different wage rates, it will be the *marginal cost* of labour, and not the wage rate, that is equated with its marginal revenue product. Once the labour supply curve slopes up, raising employment means increasing the wage rate and, in the absence of discrimination, this entails increasing rates of pay to all existing employees just as much as for the new hirer. The relation between the marginal cost of labour and the wage will be given by a condition analogous to (2.14):

$$\text{marginal cost of labour} \equiv w\left(1+\frac{1}{\alpha}\right) \qquad (2.15)$$

where α is the elasticity of the supply of labour to the wage rate. Accordingly, profit maximization implies

$$w\left(1+\frac{1}{\alpha}\right) = pq'\left(1-\frac{1}{\varepsilon}\right). \qquad (2.16)$$

Equation (2.16) is a generalization of both (2.13) (when $\alpha \to \infty$) and (2.2) (when both α and $\varepsilon \to \infty$). Monopsony inhibits employment and production still further. Just like monopoly, the effect of monopsony is to raise the value of labour's marginal

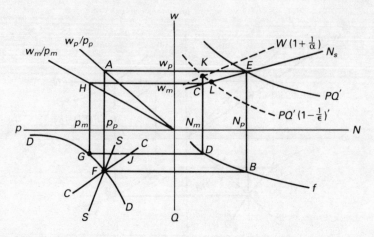

Figure 2.5 *Company employment and output under monopoly–monopsony and perfect competition, for an upwards-sloping labour supply curve*

product relative to the wage, and since employment increases must only lower pq', for profits to be at a maximum, that can only imply less employment. Figure 2.5 depicts this.

The perfect competition case is illustrated by the rectangle $AEBF$, as before. The product real wage is Wp/Pp, given by the slope of OA in the upper left quadrant. Employment will be at Np. Industry equilibrium occurs at F in the product market and E in the labour market. The price of the product equals its marginal cost, and the wage rate, Wp, just balances labour's marginal product. When the industry is represented only by a single firm, however, profit maximization entails employment at point K, where labour's marginal revenue product equals its marginal cost. Hiring more labour calls for an increased wage rate, since the labour supply curve slopes up, and because the firm does not discriminate between its employees, the higher wage must be paid to everyone. This is the reason why the marginal cost of labour, $w[1+1/\alpha]$ lies above the average cost, represented by the labour supply curve N_S. Under monopoly–monopsony, the real wage will be only Wm/Pm (the slope of the ray OH); employment is kept down to N_m, and full equilibrium is given by the rectangle $HCDG$.

It seems, therefore, that monopoly and monopsony are unambiguously adverse in their effects upon the demand for labour. This is certainly their general tendency. But there are a number of factors that could soften the blow. One of these arises from the fact that a monopolist, unlike the perfectly competitive firm, may not wish to maximize profits. If a competitive firm fails to do this, it must in the long run make losses, and is hardly likely to survive. So profit maximization is enforced by a Darwinian mechanism. Not so in monopoly; the monopolist may be able to earn positive profits indefinitely, due to the existence of barriers to entry. So the question arises as to whether it will actually seek to maximize profits. Suppose, instead, its objective is to maximize a weighted average of profits and total revenue. If its maximand were $\beta\pi+(1-\beta)pq$ where $1 \geqslant \beta \geqslant 0$ (so that β represented the profit weight, and $1 - \beta$ the sales weight) (2.16) would become

$$\beta w \left(1 + \frac{1}{\alpha} \right) = pq' \left(1 - \frac{1}{\varepsilon} \right).$$ (2.17)

The lower the value of β, the lower the marginal revenue product of labour in relation to its marginal cost, and the higher employment will be.

A second factor that may make monopsony less adverse in its impact upon employment than figure 2.5 suggests is is the possibility of discrimination between employees. If a different wage can be paid to each worker, it ceases to be true that attracting more workers entails paying higher wages to intramarginal employees. Profit maximization would then imply employment at point L in figure 2.5, where labour's marginal revenue product intersects the labour supply curve. Intramarginal workers would earn less, but at least employment and output would be higher.

A third point to consider concerns barriers to entry. Suppose that firms are free to enter the industry, and incur no delays or sunk costs in doing so. Suppose, too, that the monopolist is constrained to sticking to his published prices, while customers can migrate immediately to an alternative supplier should he present himself. These conditions will make the industry fully 'contestable'.[5] If, in addition, both the incumbent firm and all potential rivals enjoy common, horizontal average costs of production, the monopolist will be forced to behave as if the industry were perfectly competitive. Price will be driven down to the common value of average and marginal cost. Any excess of price above this level would at once attract new entrants, and entail a complete loss of custom. It is worth stressing that these conditions are rarely likely to be fulfilled in practice; but barriers to entry may not always be sufficiently formidable for incumbent monopolists to exploit their position as fully as figures 2.4 and 2.5 imply. Competition from the unseen hypothetical entrant may well be enough to keep prices lower, and employment and output levels higher, than what is suggested in these diagrams.

Finally, there can be special cases where monopoly can increase employment *above* its perfectly competitive level. If the labour supply curve is backwards-bending (so that employment and the real wage paid to labour are negatively associated), and monopoly profits are fully taxed, or paid abroad, or confined to a small group of individuals, monopoly will lead to higher employment than perfect competition. The cut in real wages that occurs when the price of the monopolist's product is increased, will induce an increase in the overall supply of labour. Similar results may ensue if the products of monopolists are relatively complementary with leisure, or less labour intensive than competitive industries, or act as intermediate inputs which are closer substitutes for labour than for other factors in other sectors.

2.3.7 *Imperfect Competition, II: Oligopoly*

Oligopoly is an industry composed of few firms. Oligopoly occupies much of the middle ground between the extremes of monopoly and perfect competition. It is possible that all existing firms co-operate to maximize their joint profits. In this case, there will be no real difference in total output and employment between oligopoly and monopoly. But if the oligopolists to some extent compete with each other, output and employment will be higher. Consider the case described by Cournot (1838) where each oligopolist sets his own output (and employment) independently, to maximize his own profit as he sees it, on the assumption that his rivals' output–employment choices are given independent of his own actions. In this case, each firm's conjectures of his rivals' responses to his own decision are all zero: the 'conjectural variation' parameter is nought. In such circumstances, each firm will take its employment to the point where

$$w = pq'\left[1 - \frac{1}{\varepsilon m}\right] \qquad (2.18)$$

assuming that there are *m* firms in the industry; that each takes the wage rate, *w*, as given; and that they sell undifferentiated products with a market share of $1/m$ for each. In the Cournot case, the number of firms is a variable of central importance. The larger is *m*, the greater the industry's employment and output will be. Equation (2.18) embraces both monopoly and perfect competition as special cases: (2.18) reduces to (2.2) when *m* is infinite, and to (2.13), the simple monopoly example, when *m* is only one. The disappearance of firms, by amalgamation for instance, will push the industry further from the competitive to the monopoly solution, and will entail an unambiguous cut in industry employment levels.

Equation (2.18) can be generalized to cover other situations. If each firm expects its rivals to react to its own employment decision, by raising its labour force by *v* for each one-unit rise in its own level of employment, (2.18) will become

$$w = pq'\left[1 - \frac{1 + (m-1)v}{\varepsilon m}\right]. \qquad (2.19)$$

When $v = 1$, the oligopolists act like a monopolist, since (2.19) simplifies to (2.13). Equation (2.19) collapses to (2.18) when $v = 0$. If *v* is negative, as in Stackelberg's (1934) example of disputed 'leadership',[6] employment will be higher than in the Cournot or collusive (monopoly) cases, since the contents of the square bracket will be larger than $(1 - 1/\varepsilon m)$. The variable *v* acts as a gauge of the degree of co-operation or conflict between the firms. Co-operation (a high positive value of *v*) is inimical to the interests of labour.

2.3.8 *Imperfect Competition, III: Increasing Returns in Oligopoly*

We saw in section 2.2 that, under perfect competition, the marginal product of labour had to decline as employment increased. No profit-maximizing firm would ever choose a range of employment levels where this were not so, because profits could only go up by increasing employment until its diminishing returns to labour were apparent. Our discussion of imperfect competition has continued to operate under the assumption that q', the marginal product of labour, diminishes with *n*. But it need not. This section is devoted to exploring some implications of relaxing the assumption.

The reason that q' need not decline as *n* increases is that profit maximization calls for a somewhat different condition under imperfect competition. What is needed is that the firm's perception of its marginal revenue product, what we labelled $pq'[1 - 1/\varepsilon]$ in the monopoly case, should cut the marginal cost of labour from above. It is not necessary that q' decline for this to be true.

If q' need not fall as *n* rises, it ceases to be true that employment increases call for a reduction in the real wage paid to labour. Indeed, it is even possible to construct cases where a rise in employment could go hand in hand with a rise in the real wage. Consider the following example of oligopoly in which this can occur.

Suppose that the demand for the product of an oligopolistic industry is inversely proportional to its price, but positively related to the money income of households, M, and to the level of expenditure on the good by an external agent, for example the government, G:

$$Q = (aM + G)/p. \tag{2.20}$$

Suppose that each firm's output, q, is related to its employment of labour, n, by the equation

$$q = -f + gn \qquad f, g > 0. \tag{2.21}$$

Equation (2.21) gives a constant, positive marginal product of labour, g; but there are fixed costs of production, in the sense that n must exceed the level f/g for output to be positive. An industry where firm's production functions are given by (2.21) cannot be perfectly competitive, because small firms are severely handicapped by the existence of fixed costs. If labour were paid the value of its marginal product, as perfect competition requires, the firms would all make losses.

Finally, assume that the money wage, w, is given, and that there is free entry and exit from the industry. The number of firms, m, will be such as to ensure that each firm just breaks even. From what has been said, it is clear that m must be finite. Since labour is the only factor of product, this break-even condition implies that its wage bill will just exhaust the value of its output.

$$wn = pq(= p(gn - f) \, (\text{from (2.21)}). \tag{2.22}$$

Profit maximization, with each firm behaving in the Cournot fashion and treating its rivals' output and employment levels as given, will entail

$$pg\left(1 - \frac{1}{m}\right) = w. \tag{2.23}$$

Equation (2.23) is a special case of our earlier Cournot oligopoly equilibrium condition for the firm, (2.18), since the marginal product of labour, q', is now equal to g, and the elasticity of the demand for the product, given (2.20), is unitary. Combining (2.22) and (2.23) establishes that the equilibrium number of firms is given by

$$m^2 = g(aM + G)/wf. \tag{2.24}$$

Since each firm's output will equal $f(m-1)$, the real wage paid to labour equals its average product (given (2.22)), and

$$\frac{w}{p} = \frac{q}{n} = g\frac{m-1}{m} = g\left[1 - \sqrt{\frac{wf}{g(aM+G)}}\right]. \tag{2.25}$$

Equation (2.25) shows that a rise in government spending will unambiguously *raise* the real wage. It will also increase industry employment, $N \, (= mn)$, since

$$N = (aM + G)/w. \tag{2.26}$$

This example of oligopoly under increasing returns to labour has some features in common with Weitzman's (1982) model of monopolistic competition. Here

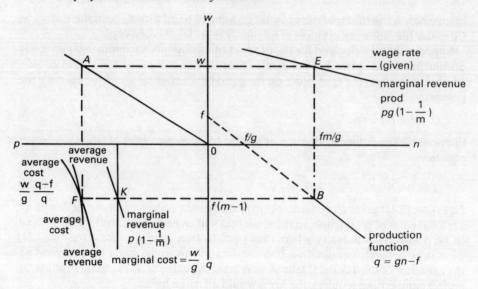

Figure 2.6 *Long-run equilibrium for the oligopolistic firm*

again, an exogenous increase in demand for the product raises both employment and the real wage, and increases the number of firms in the industry. The rise in the real wage follows from the fact that the number of firms needed for the industry to break even increases by a smaller proportion than industry output and employment – just as in (2.24) – so that the average 'overhead' cost per firm goes down. Consequently the price of the product drops somewhat, and the real wage is brought up.

The geometry of the oligopoly model just examined is presented in figures 2.6 and 2.7. Figure 2.6 depicts the equilibrium for the firm, and figure 2.7 that for the

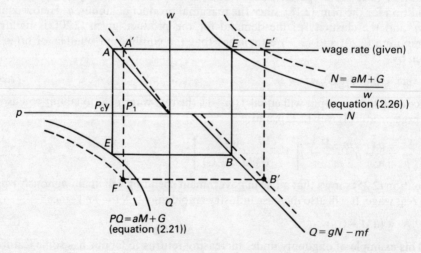

Figure 2.7 *Oligopolistic industry in long-run equilibrium*

industry as a whole. The lower right quadrant of figure 2.6 depicts the production function linking the firm's output, q, to its employment level, n. This illustrates equation (2.20). If n is zero, output will equal $-f$; but as employment increases, output rises with a constant marginal product, g. The upper right quadrant depicts the profit-maximizing employment level, E, and corresponds to (2.23). The firm's output decision is given by the intersection of marginal cost (w/g) with marginal revenue ($p(1-1/m)$) at K in the lower left quadrant. If the industry is to be in equilibrium, so that m adjusts to eliminate profits and set the real wage equal to labour's average product, as given by (2.22), point K will correspond to a point of tangency between the oligopolist's perception of his average revenue, p, with his average cost ($w(q-f)/gq$). The real wage will be given by the gradient of the ray OA. Hence the full equilibrium is shown by the rectangle $AEBF$.

For the industry as a whole, figure 2.7 depicts the full equilibrium. The industry production function will be the sum of each firm's production function, so that $Q = gN - mf$. The product demand curve (2.21) is illustrated in the lower left quadrant, and the labour demand curve (2.26) in the upper right. Both are rectangular hyperbole. If the government's spending upon the product increases, both curves move outwards. The equilibrium shifts from $AEBF$ to $A'E'B'F'$. The number of firms increases slightly, so the industry production function moves somewhat to the right (reflecting the higher fixed costs). But since m rises only in proportion to the *square root* of the demand $aM + G$, average fixed costs per unit of output go down. It is this that brings about a fall in the price of the product from P_0 to P_1, and a corresponding rise in the real wage.

2.3.9 *Imperfect Competition, IV: The Profit Mark-up Model*

Let us return to the simple model of monopoly examined in section 2.3.6. The monopolist's profit-maximizing level of employment was given by equation (2.13), repeated here for convenience.

$$w = pq'\left(1 - \frac{1}{\varepsilon}\right). \tag{2.13}$$

Another way of writing (2.13) is to express it as a pricing equation:

$$p = \left(\frac{w}{q'}\right)\left(\frac{1}{1 - 1/\varepsilon}\right). \tag{2.27}$$

In (2.27), the term w/q' represents the marginal costs of production. The second bracketed term on the right-hand side is the profit-maximizing mark-up of price above marginal cost. This depends negatively upon the elasticity of demand, ε. If ε is 3, price is 50 per cent above marginal cost; if ε were 2, price rises to double marginal cost.

It is very likely that the value of the elasticity of demand varies with the level of demand. Only when the product demand curve can be written in the log-linear form

$$Q = aP^{-\varepsilon} \tag{2.28}$$

will this not be so. With (2.28), the elasticity of demand remains equal to ε, no matter what the values of a (the parameter reflecting the strength of demand) or P. If, more generally, we represent the demand curve by

$$Q = ag(P) \tag{2.29}$$

it is not true that ε will be a constant, independent of the level of demand (as indicated by the value of *a*). In general, then, the strength of demand for the product can affect the relationship between the real wage and the marginal product of labour. The direction of this effect is ambiguous. A rise in *a* will raise or reduce the demand for labour at a given *real* wage, depending on whether demand becomes more or less elastic as a result.

There are other conditions in which the level of demand can alter the demand for labour at a given real wage. One particular case that has received considerable attention (Layard and Nickell (1985), Nickell (1985)) arises when firms employ a *full-cost-pricing* rule. The simplest form this takes will depict the firm as setting a fixed price, $\bar{p}$. This gives it a horizontal supply curve. The firm simply produces for the level of demand at $\bar{p}$, if we ignore inventories; if labour is the single freely variable factor of production, the elasticity of employment to the level of demand for the product is just the reciprocal of the elasticity of output to employment. Aggregate employment will be highly sensitive to movements in product demand, if the economy is typified by firms that behave in this fashion. By contrast, if perfect competition is the rule, or if production is undertaken by profit-maximizing monopolists subject to constant-elasticity demand curves of the form of (2.28), demand fluctuations will have no effect upon employment if real wage rates and technological factors governing the marginal product of labour are frozen.

2.3.10 *When Markets do not Clear*

Until now, it has been assumed that the employer has no difficulty in securing sales for his products, and the level of employment he wishes, at the going constellation of wages and prices. The firm is always able to achieve a point of equilibrium on its demand curve for labour. It is never rationed in its output by deficiency in demand or in available labour.

This optimistic assumption may sometimes fail to hold. The firm may face a given price for its product, but be limited in the amount it can sell at that price. An obvious example of this occurs when an exporting firm is subject to a quota in its foreign markets. Since 1983, dairy farmers within the EEC have been subject to ceilings on their milk production. British universities have recently been forced to restrict their admission of 'home' students, under the threat that their government funding will be reduced if quotas are infringed. A demand constraint on firm's ability to sell at given prices is an essential feature of models of Keynesian unemployment, which are examined in detail in chapters 3 and 4. These two chapters also investigate cases where the firm is rationed in the labour market. Such a state of affairs is known as 'repressed inflation'. The framework of these two chapters is, for the most part, governed by an assumption that wage rates and prices are sticky. It is the purpose of the next section to describe possible reasons for this.

2.4 Some Reasons why Wage Rates may be Sticky in the Face of Unemployment

2.4.1 *Wage Stickiness and Informational Asymmetry: The Plight of the Outsider*

Suppose an unemployed worker asks an employer to offer him a job. The latter replies that he already has all the labour he needs. So the unemployed man responds with a plea for work at a wage below what existing workers are being paid. 'The Union won't allow this' may be the reply. Even if the union were to permit it, the employer may be reluctant to engage him at a lower wage for fear that it would contravene some principle of equity, that it could endanger his reputation for being a good employer or that other workers might fear dilution, and even dismissal.

Yet there is an important further reason why the employer may not wish to take him on. When the unemployed job-seeker tries to gain employment by offering to work for less than the going wage, he emits a low-quality signal. 'Well, he must be lousy if that is all he offers his services for', the employer may think. 'What does he know about his ability – or lack of it – that I do not?' This is where informational asymmetry comes in. People vary in ability, or at least are widely thought to do so. Often the individual is a better judge of how well he will work than a prospective employer. Someone out of work may not be regarded as having average ability. The employer's estimate of his ability is likely to lie below the population mean, if only for the very reason that he is out of work. When the job applicant offers to work for less, the employer's estimate of his efficiency may fall still further.

In circumstances such as these, the job-seeker's chance of being offered employment may be negatively related to the wage at which he offers his services. He may have to offer himself for next to nothing before the employer is prepared to engage him, or at least at a wage which is even less attractive than living on the dole. Shaked and Sutton (1984) examine a related phenomenon: firms may treat the unemployed 'outsider' as an imperfect substitute for 'insiders'. Involuntary unemployment can result from this.

2.4.2 *Wage Stickiness and Informational Asymmetry: The Insiders*

An employer may know little about the efficiency of his existing workers, either. He can of course observe their aggregate output. But he may be far from well-informed about how well particular individuals perform their tasks. Even when he can monitor productivity at the level of the individual worker – which is typically rare in large, centralized businesses – chance factors may make inferences about the quality of his or her labour input very hazardous.

Members of the existing labour force are likely to vary, then, in their efficiency, in ways that are imperfectly observable to their employer. There will be good workers, and relatively less good workers. They are likely to be paid alike. The better workers will probably be better at performing other functions, too. Quite possibly they will have higher reservation wages – wages below which they will quit – if only because their self-employment prospects may be brighter.

What this suggests is that the firm may not wish to respond to conditions of slack in the rest of the economy's labour markets by reducing the wage. A wage cut carries the danger that the best workers will quit. The average quality of labour will fall. It could even fall enough to reduce the firm's receipts by more than the saving in wages. If this is so, the firm's profits will fall if the wage rate is cut below a critical level. This hypothesis is known as the 'efficiency wage model'. The model was originally developed in the context of poor countries, where a lower wage was thought to imply a reduction in nutrition and consequent fall in labour and productivity; it helped to explain why relatively high industrial wages coexisted with conditions of urban and rural unemployment. The efficiency wage model can be extended to advanced countries too. The argument would not rely on the idea that the worker's efficiency is boosted by his calorific intake, so much as on the notion of average quality or morale effects dependent on the wage. Morale effects could be important: people may become soured and unproductive if they think they are being underpaid. Then there is the related idea, urged by Solow (1980), that the entrepreneur may wish to secure a reputation for being a 'good employer' by keeping wages up in bad times.

The essential flavour of the efficiency wage model can be demonstrated simply. Consider a range of perfectly competitive firms. Each has a production function

$$q = f(en) \tag{2.30}$$

where n is the number of workers, and e the efficiency with which each works. The variable e increases with w, the wage paid. The firm's job is to choose w and n so as to maximize

$$pq(e(w)n) - wn \tag{2.31}$$

with respect to both w and n. The first-order conditions for this are

$$pq' = \frac{w}{e} = \frac{1}{e'}. \tag{2.32}$$

Equation (2.32) implies that the wage will be set where the marginal effect of the wage on efficiency equals the ratio of e to w, and that employment, n, will be governed by the condition that the value of labour's marginal product, pq', equals the wage per unit of e. If the resulting level of employment fails to match full employment in an economy where this is the only sector, there will be involuntary unemployment. Figure 2.8 illustrates this. The efficiency–wage function, $e(w)$, is depicted by the curve in the left quadrant. Point A represents the position where the elasticity of the $e(w)$ curve is unitary. This accords with the optimum wage. The demand for labour at this wage is given by point B in the right quadrant. So employment will be OC, given the wage OE and efficiency level OD. Point B is surrounded by isoprofit loci; profits fall away the further the firm moves from point B. If the diagram is magnified to represent the whole economy, and OF denotes the labour force, CF will be the level of involuntary unemployment. If the firms are prevented from paying OE, for example by government legislation, and have to

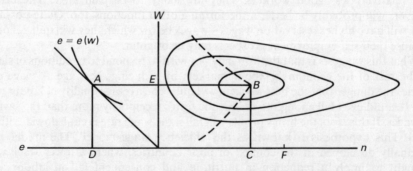

Figure 2.8 *Wage, employment and efficiency in the efficiency wage model*

take the wage rate as exogenously given, the relation between n and w will resemble the dashed curve. Employment will typically fall if the firms are forced to pay a lower wage.

2.4.3 *Wage Stickiness and Implicit Contracts*

A further line of argument that can be advanced to explain why wages vary little between boom and slump invokes the concept of implicit contracts. The worker is averse to risk. He lacks access to insurance and capital markets. He would rather work for a guaranteed wage, in good times and bad, than earn a fluctuating income that depended on the vagaries of the demand for his employer's product. He could even prefer the former to the latter when it involved the possibility of being laid off in bad times, provided that there was appropriate compensation for unemployment. If the firm is neutral to risk, it will be efficient for it to offer its workers a form of income insurance that achieves this. This is the implicit contract. Chapter 9 is devoted to exploring these ideas in detail.

2.4.4 *Unemployment as a Way of Disciplining Workers*

In a fully employed economy, where everyone is paid the same, the sack is not much of a punishment. You can go and work at once for someone else. But if the wage is lifted above the market-clearing level, dismissal is painful. It may be hard to get another job. Not every worker may enjoy his work. Some will be tempted to take it easy. 'On-the-job leisure' is costly to the employer, since it entails less output. The individual worker's effort is also costly. So employers deliberately pay 'over the odds' in order to create a reward for hard work. The reward takes the form of not being dismissed if you are found not to have been slacking. The equilibrium wage exceeds its full employment level. The unemployed cannot bid it down. No firm will employ them for less, for fear that they will take so much more on-the-job leisure that profits fall as a result.

One difficulty with this story, told skilfully by Shapiro and Stiglitz (1984), is that unemployment of this kind could be avoided if workers could be fined, rather than sacked, when observed to be slacking. On the other hand, the workers and the firm must both be able to observe the on-the-job leisure, and to have it (or its absence) certified by some third party in the case of disputes, to avoid the unpleasant dangers that the firm might otherwise declare that some of its workers had been slacking when they had not. Such behaviour would bring the firm a tidy income in fines, not to mention the sharpened incentive effect upon other workers (*pour décourager les autres*). In the absence of full observability, then, the unemployment–discipline mechanism will be a second-best which at least has the merit of keeping employers honest.

2.4.5 *Training Costs and Unemployment*

Stiglitz (1985b) offers a powerful model of training costs and wage distributions that opens up the possibility of unemployment equilibria. The essence of this Stiglitz model consists of two relationships: a positive link between the wage rate a firm pays its workers and the proportion of those workers who remain with it, and a positive relation between the costs of training and the proportion who quit. The firm minimizes its labour costs by setting the wage at the point where training costs just equal the reciprocal of the marginal effect of the wage upon the quit rate. It is there that the marginal cost of the wage balances its marginal benefit in terms of reduced costs of training. Those who quit consist of the irreducible minimum overtaken by *anno domini*, plus those who leave because they get a better offer elsewhere. The former are exactly balanced at any moment by new arrivals into the labour force, who are presumed to know nothing about alternative wage rates and simply accept the first job on offer. Stiglitz shows that it is not impossible that there is more than one value of the wage rate at which labour costs are minimized, and what is more, minimized at a common value of profits. What is needed for this boils down to a set of restrictions upon the distribution of wages offered by other firms (which are known in general to each firm, but only in very limited form to its employees). This can permit the construction of a set of equilibrium wage distributions (with their associated quit rates). It includes, as one possibility, the case where all firms pay the same. When the firms are subject to diminishing returns to labour, unemployment can easily emerge in this case, because no firm has an incentive to alter the wage rate which it sees being paid by all other firms. If it were to cut its wage, what it saved in wages would be swamped by the additional costs of training; if it raised the wage, savings in training costs would fail to compensate for the higher wage bill. So *any* wage could be an equilibrium distribution, and full employment would only be a freak. Similar results emerge for both single and multiple wage distributions when firms vary in their non-pecuniary job characteristics, and workers in evaluating them.

A curious feature of Stiglitz's model is the wide gulf of knowledge separating firms and workers. Firms are assumed to know the distribution of wages offered (to otherwise identical labour). But new job applicants, just entering the labour force, are completely in the dark. Gradually they build up their own personal inventory of information about this, but only as a result of their own searching. This slow accumulation of knowledge on the part of aging workers, who gravitate tardily towards higher paying or more attractive jobs, is balanced by the continual recreation of ignorance, as new young workers replace those who die. One suspects that in practice workers – even those entering the labour force for the first time – are typically better informed about wages paid by different employers than the model allows. Against this, inter-firm wage relativities can and do change over time, so that information about past wage offers may be untrustworthy. Furthermore, Stiglitz's central claim, that firms may be reluctant to lower wages for fear of incurring the higher costs that inevitably accompany increased turnover, is an attractive and cogent factor than can certainly help to explain wage stickiness, even in the face of substantial unemployment.

2.4.6 *Some Further Observations on Wage and Price Stickiness*

Labour is not hired on a spot-auction market. Wages are typically predetermined for a period of a year or more, throughout West European and US manufacturing industry. One explanation for this has already been given briefly, in section 2.4.3, and is the subject of detailed inquiry in chapter 9. There can be other reasons for the phenomenon, too. The costs of wage negotiations are substantial. Bargaining is a time-consuming activity. There is always the danger of a breakdown in discussions. Threats of strikes or lockouts are not infrequent. The frequency of contract renegotiation is an endogenous economic variable. It will surely decline with an increase in the fixed costs of negotiations, or a reduction in the 'noise' affecting the environment within which wages are bargained (the variance of inflation, and firm-specific demand or technology shocks). Furthermore, both worker and employers make some long-term investment commitments after engagement, in the form of firm-specific training costs and the like. Frequent *ad hominem* wage renegotiations could expose each party to the risk of being held to ransom by the other. Long-term contracts provide a way of avoiding such dangers.

It is costly to change product prices, too. First, there are the fixed costs of issuing new brochures, altering price tags, rewording and revising advertisements. Then there is the customer ill-will that producers sometimes fear will be incurred if they are seen to be exploiting opportunities for price variation. When prices vary frequently, the buyer who observes a price at one date will realize that his investment in information depreciates rapidly afterwards. In an industry characterized by imperfect information on the part of customers, the firm may reason that unilateral price cuts will only persuade its existing customers to buy more, while price increases will provoke many of them into search, and possible defection. Furthermore, a high degree of price variability, at the level of the individual firm, would hardly be conducive to the stability of tacit or overt agreements with fellow oligopolists. There is also a connection between the optimum frequency of price revision and the costs of inventories. If stocks of finished goods can be run down or built up with relative ease, it may prove cheaper to keep selling prices independent of modest shifts in demand than to incur the numerous costs associated with frequent price revision.

There are numerous reasons, therefore, for suspecting that wage rates and prices are sluggish, and respond little, and slowly, to high unemployment. It would be wrong to consider the various explanations as alternatives. Probably they all have some role to play.

2.5   Concluding Remarks

This chapter has examined what determines the demand for labour in both perfect and imperfect markets. The level of employment has often been seen to vary negatively with the real wage, but an assumption of increasing returns, studied in 2.3.8, allows for a positive association. Section 2.4 was devoted to explaining various types of wage rigidity, and why market forces cannot always be relied upon to eliminate unemployment. It is to the consequences of such rigidities for unemployment that we now turn in chapter 3.

3 The Quantity-rationing Model: A Geometrical Account

3.1 Introduction

This chapter is concerned with the consequences of market failure. The central questions are: How and why does unemployment arise if markets fail to clear? What does this imply for government policy? The chapter is devoted to exploring the effects of incomplete wage and price flexibility. Section 3.2 sets out the chapter's fundamental assumptions, and section 3.3 examines the Walrasian equilibrium, full-price-flexibility case which serves as a useful benchmark and comparator for what follows. Section 3.4 introduces the various non-clearing regimes which are then analysed separately in later sections (Keynesian unemployment in section 3.5, classical unemployment in section 3.6, repressed inflation in section 3.7). Finally, section 3.8 presents a brief account of extensions to an open economy and a multi-period framework.

Algebra is kept to the barest minimum in this chapter. Instead, the emphasis is placed on geometrical and verbal presentation of the issues. A more technical account of quantity-rationing models is provided in chapter 4. Many of the central ideas in both these chapters go back to the seminal work of Barro and Grossman (1971), and extensions (among others) by Benassy (1975), Malinvaud (1977) and Muellbauer and Portes (1978).

3.2 Fundamental Assumptions

The framework of this chapter is deliberately kept as simple as possible. We shall take a still photograph of an economy at just one date. The households that comprise it will be identical in their preferences, in their endowments of labour time and wealth and in what happens to them when they try to sell their labour time to buy goods. There will be only one product, and just one type of firm that makes it. The firms and the households will be numerous, and equal in number. In the diagrams that follow, we shall analyse the behaviour of 'representative' firms and households. Because they are identical and behave identically, it does not matter which we pick to illustrate their actions and interactions.

The households will be assumed to derive satisfaction from three things. These are the amount of the good they can consume, the amount of leisure time that is left to them after subtracting work hours from their endowment of time and the level of their money holdings, measured in real terms (that is, in units of the good). It is clear why households must benefit from consumption, at least at low levels; they will starve if they don't consume. Making them view leisure and real money holdings as 'goods' is less obvious and more controversial.

Lying behind the notion that leisure is a good, may be the fact that households can put their leisure time to use. Leisure should not be thought of as a spell of inactivity, on this view; it is time devoted to activities such as reading, cooking and travelling which are essential inputs into the creation of 'home-made' goods which people do enjoy. The pleasure of entertainment, meals and visiting friends would be examples. The justification for including real money holdings in households' preferences is twofold. They constitute one form in which spending power can be held over for future periods; this is the 'store of value' role of money. They also save their holder time, trouble and various types of cost in effecting transactions. These benefits from money holdings reflect the use of money as a medium of exchange.

The simplest assumptions one can make about the preferences of households have the following implications:

1. households aim for a given ratio of real money holdings to consumption;
2. labour supply does not vary with real wage rates, in full equilibrium;
3. labour supply is reduced by an increase in non-wage income, and, out of equilibrium, by an increase in the real financial resources available to the household.

These three results follow directly from the Cobb–Douglas utility function employed in chapter 4. The Cobb–Douglas function expresses the household's utility as a weighted geometric mean of the goods in which it is interested.

On the production side, we assume that there are positive but diminishing returns to labour. To be more specific we suppose that the production function for each of the firms is also Cobb–Douglas. This implies that, in full competitive equilibrium, the share of output accruing to labour as wages is a given number, such as three-quarters, which stays constant in the face of any changes in workers' preferences, technology or resources. The assumption of perfect competition, allied to that of diminishing returns, ensures that there is an inescapable negative link between the real wage rate paid to labour, and the volume of employment that firms, if in equilibrium, will offer at that wage.

The picture is completed by denying the existence, for the time being, of any economic role for the government (except controlling the money supply); budgetary variables, such as tax rates or spending, will be removed from the scene for the present. Our economy also excludes any economic links with other economies. There is no 'foreign sector'. Firms will not be allowed to accumulate assets in the form of investment, in order to keep matters as simple as possible. This means that the sole source of demand for production comes from households, in the form of consumption spending. Capital, on the other hand, can enter the picture as a given factor of production which co-operates with labour. The income earned on capital, profits, is assumed to go straight to households, without delay or deduction, as non-wage income. The production function displays constant returns to scale, since this guarantees that competitive payments to labour and capital will exactly exhaust the total product.

3.3 Walrasian Equilibrium

We can now put this apparatus to work. Walrasian equilibrium is the name given to a state of affairs where all markets clear. In this model, that amounts to saying that:

1   households' preferred consumption, c^*, matches the output firms wish to supply, q^*;
2   The nominal demand for money, m^*, matches the supply the authorities have determined, m; and
3   the labour time that households wish to offer for remunerated work, L^*, matches the volume of employment that firms are seeking, n^*.

Our diagrammatic approach will concentrate upon the first and third of these markets, namely those for goods and labour. The market for money will be implicit, behind the scenes. Take the goods market first. The demand for goods, c^*, will bear a constant proportionate relationship to the real level of money holdings, m/p. This is true by virtue of the money-market clearance condition (2 above) and the first implication, 1, of the households' preferences discussed in the previous section. This means that the demand for goods is inversely proportional to their price, p, and directly proportional to the nominal money supply, m. The result is illustrated in figure 3.1.

The demand for goods is a rectangular hyperbola, or unit elastic. Its position is governed by $\bar{M}$, and also by the preference parameters of households. If the demand for money went up, the curve DD would drop; a rise in the supply of money would have the opposite effect.

Now consider the supply of goods. We have already seen that there is a negative association between the real wage paid to labour and the volume of employment demanded by firms. This stems from the assumptions of diminishing returns to labour, which implies that the marginal product of labour is reduced if employment goes up, and of perfect competition, which entails that the real wage rate, and the marginal product of labour, will be equal for the firm to be in equilibrium. Now since employment and output are positively associated, and employment and the real wage rate are negatively associated, it follows that there must be a negative link between the real wage rate and the level of output firms will seek to produce. The reason for this is that firms must have a rise in their selling prices, or a fall in labour costs, before they will be willing to increase their labour force and produce more output.

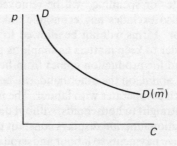

Figure 3.1 *The demand for goods*

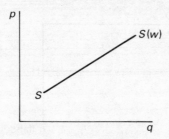

Figure 3.2 *The supply of goods*

The negative effect of a higher real wage rate upon the firm's chosen output level translates into a positive effect from an increase in the price level, p, if the money wage rate, w, is given. This is what is illustrated in figure 3.2. When the money wage is given, a rise in p is needed to provide the incentive for firms to raise their levels of output and employment. A jump in the money wage rate would displace the supply curve SS to the left: firms will need a compensating rise in the price level if they are not to cut their output. A rise in the stock of capital available to firms, or an improvement in technology, would have the opposite effect of moving SS to the right. The elasticity of SS will in fact equal the ratio of wages to profits, since the production function is assumed to be Cobb–Douglas. Full Walrasian equilibrium in the goods market is reached where the demand and supply curves for goods cross. But Walrasian equilibrium demands more than this. The labour and money markets must also clear. How are the goods and labour markets related?

The most direct link is that between output, q, and employment, n. This is the production function. We have assumed positive but diminishing returns to labour. So the shape of the function will be as illustrated in figure 3.3. When it is drawn upside-down (for a reason that will soon become apparent), it has a negative gradient, suggesting that a rise in n is needed to raise q; and it is concave, reflecting the assumption of diminishing returns. A rise in the stock of capital, or a technical improvement would move this curve to the right.

The labour market, like that for goods, will be subject to the forces of both supply and demand. We have assumed that the supply of labour, in equilibrium, does not vary with the real wage rate. So when other relevant variables, such as households' preferences and the level of profits, are given, the supply of labour can be drawn as a horizontal line in a diagram which displays the real wage rate as a horizontal-axis

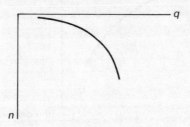

Figure 3.3 *The production function*

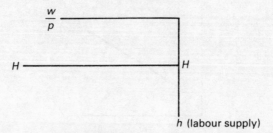

Figure 3.4 *The supply of labour*

variable, and labour supply (*h*) on the vertical axis. This is what is depicted in figure 3.4, as the horizontal line *HH*.

The demand for labour, on the other hand, will vary with the real wage rate: there must be a negative association between these variables as has already been discussed. Figure 3.5 illustrates this. As the production function is Cobb–Douglas, the elasticity of *n* to the real wage will in fact equal the reciprocal of the profit share of output. The curve will be displaced downwards by a rise in the stock of capital or by an improvement in technology, under these conditions. Labour market equilibrium will be attained where the curves *GG* and *HH* cut.

The groundwork has now been done to permit us to assemble these separate pieces together. The result is figure 3.6. The upper right quadrant displays the goods market, the bottom left the labour market, and the bottom right the production function which links them. The upper left quadrant contains a curve for the remaining loose end, the money wage rate. Since this must be the product of the price level *p* and the real wage *w*, the shape of this curve must be a rectangular hyperbola. It is important to stress that the value of the money wage rate is not a given, exogenous variable in Walrasian equilibrium. On the contrary, it is endogenous; it is determined by the rest of the system. One exogenous variable on which it depends is the nominal money supply, *m*. The curve in the upper left quadrant therefore depicts the *equilibrium* money wage rate, *w**.

The rectangle *ABCE* traces the links between the interdependent goods and labour markets, in Walrasian equilibrium. It is now a fairly simple matter to see what happens, in Walrasian equilibrium, if any of the exogenous variables (capital,

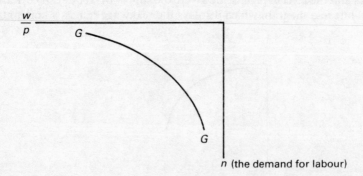

Figure 3.5 *The demand for labour*

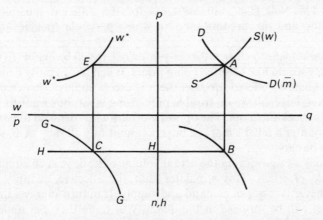

Figure 3.6 *Walrasian equilibrium*

technology, preferences, money supply) is to change. We shall run through these quickly and in reverse order. A higher nominal money supply pushes up the demand for goods. The fleeting tendency to excess demand in the goods market will be met swiftly by a rise in the price level, and excess demand for labour will cause the money wage rate to rise similarly. Full equilibrium will be restored at unchanged levels of output, employment and real wage rates (points B and C of the 'equilibrium box' remain fixed), by the equiproportionate increases in the money wage rate and the price level. A rise in the demand for money (keeping households' preferences between consumption and leisure unchanged) will have exactly the opposite effect, of depressing the price level and the money wage rate, but keeping real variables unchanged. A rise in the demand for leisure (keeping households' preferences between consumption and real money holdings unchanged) will reduce the labour supply (pushing HH upwards) and raise the real wage rate, the money wage rate and the price level, and cut production. A technological improvement, on the other hand, would raise output, lower prices and raise real wage rates, and similar effects would follow from a rise in the capital stock; in both cases, GG would be displaced leftwards, and the production function would move to the right.

3.4 What Can Happen when Markets Fail to Clear: A Taxonomy of Quantity-rationing Equilibria

The Walrasian equilibrium is attained when all markets clear. Continuous, complete market clearance requires complete flexibility of all prices. In the remainder of this chapter, we shall be concerned with the consequences of price and wage inflexibility. Instead of allowing the price of goods and the wage rate for labour to react at once to any incipient excess demand, or supply, suppose that both the price level and the money wage rate are locked at arbitrary values. This is of course exactly the opposite assumption to full price and wage flexibility. In practice, we observe elements of both flexibility and inflexibility in prices. But the fact that price and wage flexibility is patently incomplete, especially over the short run, is itself a good reason for exploring what happens when wage rates and prices are locked. This will give valuable clues for the different possible causes of unemployment, and the circumstances in which particular policies may help to reduce it.

When a market fails to clear, either buyers or sellers will be unable to trade in the quantities they would like to at the going prices. When the quantity demanded falls short of the quantity offered for sale, there is excess supply. This characterizes a buyer's market: buyers have no trouble purchasing what they want to buy. Sellers will be eager to seek them out. The opposite occurs when demand outstrips supply. Here we encounter a seller's market; buyers cannot buy all they wish, while sellers can afford to be choosey.

The essential idea governing the actual volume of trade in such circumstances is the *short-side principle*. This stipulates that the effective quantity transacted will be whichever is lower of demand and supply. It in turn suggests that one side of the market will be *rationed* in the quantity of trade they can undertake. The easiest form of rationing to work with, if not the most realistic, is one which has equal impact upon all economic agents. If the market for labour is in excess supply, for example, households are rationed in the employment they can obtain, and every household is constrained to accept a shorter period of employment as a result. The principle that if one buyer (or seller) of a good or factor is rationed, then so must all be, has the great advantage in allowing us to continue working with the concept of the 'representative' household or firm.

If agents are rationed in one market, their actions in other markets, where they still have the freedom to transact as they wish, are likely to change as a result. This gives rise to an important distinction between *notional* and *effective* demands or supplies. The notional demand for goods by households, for example, is the quantity they would like to buy, at the going set of prices and wages, *if they are able to achieve their desired trades in all other markets*. If they are not, as a result, let us say, of excess supply prevailing in the labour market, their effective demand for goods will be the amount they wish to buy, once they know that they will be unable to sell all the labour time they want.

In the simple one-good, one-factor, one-time-period set-up that we are considering, there are only three possible types of quantity-rationing equilibria that can occur. These are generally known as Keynesian unemployment, classical unemployment and repressed inflation. In Keynesian unemployment (KU), there is excess supply in both goods and labour markets. Firms are quantity rationed in the market for goods. Households are quantity rationed in the market for labour. Both markets are buyer's markets. Classical unemployment (CU) also displays excess supply in the labour market, but, in contrast with KU, there is excess demand for goods. So households are quantity rationed in both labour and goods markets, while producers are rationed in neither. The third regime is repressed inflation (RI). This is the exact opposite of KU: both goods and labour markets are in excess demand. Households cannot buy the goods they wish; firms cannot secure the employment they demand. These three possibilities are shown in figure 3.7.

The set of feasible quantity-rationing equilibria is reduced by a number of considerations. Sellers and buyers cannot both be rationed in the same market. Furthermore, if one market fails to clear, then so must at least one other. These two principles allows us to eliminate all the cells of figure 3.7 which are left empty. One anomaly needs to be explained. This is the cell labelled 'underconsumption'. The underconsumption regime is characterized by excess demand in the labour market

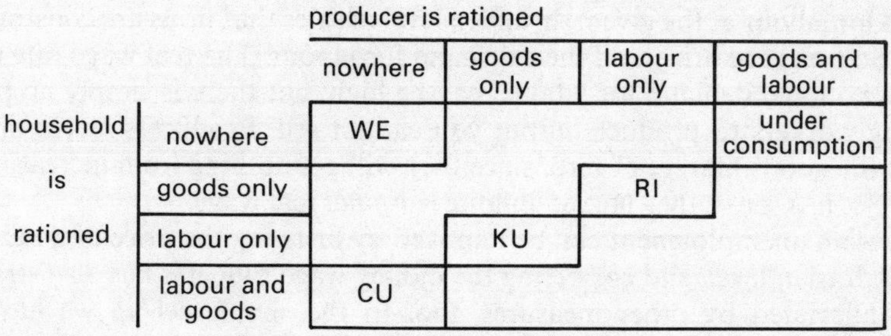

producer is rationed

household		nowhere	goods only	labour only	goods and labour
	nowhere	WE			under consumption
is	goods only			RI	
rationed	labour only		KU		
	labour and goods	CU			

Figure 3.7 *Quantity-rationing equilibria*

and excess supply in the market for goods. It cannot arise in the simple one-period framework we are considering because of the fact that the firm will react by revising its notional demand for labour and supply of output in the face of the constraints it faces. If it cannot sell all the output it wishes to produce, it must revise downwards its demand – its effective demand – for labour. Similarly, if it cannot obtain all the labour it would like to employ, its effective supply of output will be cut. These reactions ensure that the goods market cannot be in *effective* excess supply when there is excess demand for labour, and that the labour market cannot be in *effective* excess demand if there is excess supply of goods. The top left cell in figure 3.7, labelled WE, denotes Walrasian equilibrium, which can arise as a very remote possibility if *p* and *w* are arbitrarily imposed.

It is now time to take a closer look at the three other cases, Keynesian unemployment, classical unemployment and repressed inflation. We examine each in turn.

3.5 Keynesian Unemployment

Keynesian unemployment suffers from generalized excess supply. Demand is deficient for both labour and goods. Perhaps the simplest way of reaching it is to start at Walrasian equilibrium, and raise the price level, all else equal.

Firms will react to the cut in the real wage that a higher price level implies, when the money wage is given, by wanting to employ more people and sell more output. This will be the change in its *notional* demand and supply. But it will be frustrated. Why?

The problem centres on the demand for goods. A higher price level, when the nominal money supply is unchanged, means a fall in the households' real financial wealth. They will seek to cut back their spending. We have assumed that consumption bears a constant proportionate relation to their real money holdings. So down consumption will go.

Firms will perceive that they are forced to accept a reduced volume of sales, despite the incentive to increase production that the higher price level brought. They have no choice in the matter. They simply cannot sell everything which it is profitable to produce at the new price level. They are driven off their supply curve in figure 3.2. That is not the end of things. If they are to produce less, they do not need to employ so much labour. The production function can be inverted to give the demand for labour at the given, shrunken level of sales that firms are constrained to accept. So firms are driven off their demand for labour. The real wage rate may be low; the notional demand for labour may be high; but there is simply no point in engaging workers to produce output you cannot sell. Producers face a marginal price in the goods market of zero, since they will get nothing from increasing their output. So, in a sense, they face an infinite *marginal* real wage.

Keynesian unemployment can be removed by bringing the price of goods down to its Walrasian level, and correcting the money wage rate, if it has also strayed. It can be alleviated by other measures, too. In the simple set-up we have been examining, a rise in the money supply will raise the effective demand for goods. In extended models where fiscal policy instruments are brought into play, increases in government spending or transfer payments, or cuts in taxation will have similar effects. Once the demand for goods has gone up, firms will need to employ more labour; the effective demand for labour will rise, and unemployment should fall. But aggregate demand stimulation by itself will not necessarily restore Walrasian equilibrium, since the real wage rate needs to be brought to its Walrasian value too.

The geometry of Keynesian unemployment is illustrated in figure 3.8. The rectangle $ABCE$, drawn with a thin border, represents the Walrasian equilibrium. This is just as it was depicted in figure 3.6. It will hold when $w = w^*$, $p = p^*$ and $M = \bar{M}$ (with other parameters, such as household preferences and the production function, given as before).

The price level is now raised to p^{**}. Firms' notional demand for labour rises to point Q on GG in the lower left quadrant, which corresponds with point N on the production function. Their notional supply of output goes up from A to M in the upper right quadrant. But these notional equilibria for firms are unsustainable. There is excess supply of FM in the goods market. Household demand sinks from A to F, because real money balances have fallen from m/p^* to m/p^{**}. Firms need less

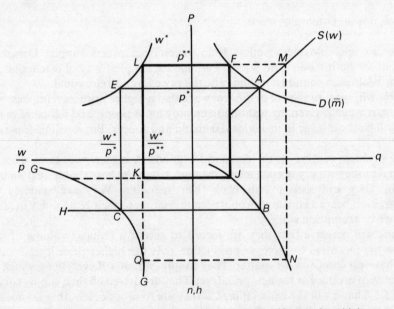

Figure 3.8 *Keynesian unemployment: the price level imposed too high*

labour, not more, in order to produce this shrunken output level. Their effective demand for labour will be at point K. Firms will behave *as if* they faced a real wage at R in the lower left quadrant, and a price level at S in the upper right. Q and S have been called the *virtual* real wage, and price level confronting firms. Virtual prices are the prices that would have led agents to choose the actual levels of demands and supplies they are forced to accept. This helpful concept was first introduced by Neary and Roberts (1980). The thick-bordered rectangle, $FJKL$, depicts the Keynesian unemployment equilibrium.

We have already seen what would happen if the money supply were increased above $\bar{M}$ – the demand curve for goods in the upper right quadrant would be displaced rightwards; effective demand would rise in the goods market and, through the production function, also in the labour market. A higher money supply would raise the virtual price of output confronting firms, and reduce the virtual real wage they face. It would also exert another effect. The supply of labour H would be reduced (shifted upwards in the lower left quadrant), since households could now rely upon increased real balances to finance more of their consumption, and would not need to offer as much labour time as before. But, provided that the money supply increase was not very large, there would still remain some unemployment in the labour market, and households would still be rationed there. If the money supply increase was large enough, the economy would shift regimes, from Keynesian unemployment to repressed inflation, which we shall examine below.

It is worth seeing how the Keynesian unemployment rectangle would respond to other changes. A higher preference for real money holdings would make matters worse, by shifting the demand for goods curve leftwards. An increased price level would also depress output and employment, as a result of a fall in demand. A rise in the stock of capital, or technical progress, would shift the production further upwards in the lower right quadrant. More output could be produced from a given employment level; the labour requirements for a given output rate would drop. It is the second of these interpretations that is relevant here, since the demand for goods may be regarded as given, and provides the key to everything else. So employment would go down. The base of the rectangle $FJKL$ would be displaced upwards.

If the assumptions of our model were changed to allow wage income to be spent, but profits to be saved, in part at least, matters would deteriorate even further. The increase in capital, or technical progress, would lead to a transfer of income from wages to profits. This would then cause the demand for goods to fall. The rectangle $FJKL$ would become narrower as well as shorter, to reflect a reduced level of output. Indeed, a multiplier process would ensue, since the output drop would cause a further fall in employment, and hence in wage income, which would imply yet another fall in the demand for goods.

Profits may be partly saved, perhaps because profits retained in companies are not perceived as income by households, or for other reasons (they might be treated as more volatile, or they could be concentrated among richer households, with a smaller marginal propensity to consume, for example). Figure 3.9 shows how the Keynesian unemployment equilibrium is altered by this assumption. The demand for goods now depends not just on the money supply $\bar{M}$, but also the amount of money income paid out as wages (defined as B). In Walrasian equilibrium, this is B^*. Now $B^* = (w)^*n^*$.

But when the price level is p^{**}, and employment falls as a result of the deficiency in the demand for goods that ensues, nominal wage income falls. So the demand

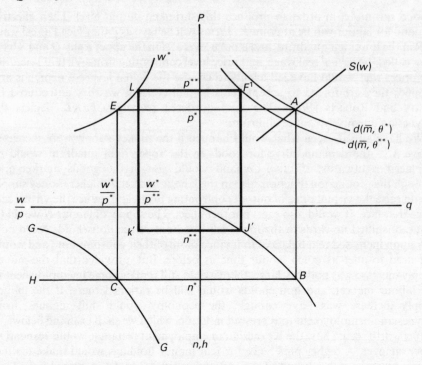

Figure 3.9 *Keynesian unemployment equilibrium, when profits are partly saved*

curve moves leftwards, setting in motion a secondary round of falls in employment and output. The process stops at F, where B^{**} equals w^*n^{**}, and n^{**} is given by J on the production function.

In this amended story, a rise in the money wage rate will exert important, beneficial effects. It will increase B, and therefore stimulate higher demand in the goods market, with subsequent gains to employment and output. This will not happen in the circumstances depicted in figure 3.8, because a higher money wage rate simply relabels some fraction of household income, hitherto profits, as wages, and there is no difference in the way people are assumed to spend them.

The Keynesian unemployment rectangle could also shrink, as in figure 3.9, as a result of a multiplier process, for other reasons. One would arise when leisure was more complementary with real money holdings, than with consumption, in household demand. As the worker was forced to consume more leisure, his choices between money and consumption would change, and the *effective* demand for goods would move leftwards.

The difference between the two cases is interesting, and has major implications for policy. The classical solution to unemployment is to lower wage rates. Sometimes this proposal is cast in nominal terms, so that it is a fall in money wage rates that is advocated; sometimes proponents of this view urge a fall in *real* wages. There certainly can be circumstances in which either, or both, will help to reduce unemployment. The classical unemployment case, to which we turn next, is a prominent example. Economists of a Keynesian persuasion have taken their cue from an intriguing if annoyingly incomplete chapter in Keynes' *General Theory*

(1936, chapter 19) and urged opposition to wage cuts. One element in Keynes' argument is the possible adverse effect of a money wage fall upon consumer demand; others centre on its considerable effects, of uncertain direction, upon investment and the trade balance. It is primarily the consumption argument that concerns us here. We have seen that everything turns on whether aggregate demand responds to a switch between wages and profits. The issue cannot easily be settled a priori. There are cogent reasons for suspecting that aggregate consumer spending responds more quickly, and perhaps more substantially, to wages than to profits. An increase in future expected wage costs provides an incentive to more capital-intensive production methods. But there is no denying a rich set of influences running from profits to investment. An increase in a company's profits provides it with an enlarged source of cheap funds (retained earnings); it may be taken to indicate higher profits on possible future projects than had been anticipated; and it makes it easier to borrow. Whether money wage increases would help to bring unemployment down in the circumstances of pure Keynesian unemployment must remain a moot point, with much to be said on both sides. Economic evidence on the effects of profits on consumption and investment is unfortunately inconclusive and disputed. The fairest conclusion is that wage increases might stimulate higher employment under conditions of deficient aggregate demand, but that there are far less risky ways of trying to achieve this; furthermore, since pockets of Keynesian and classical unemployment will typically co-exist in a complex economy, there is every chance that some unambiguously adverse effects on employment have to be set in the balance against rather questionable gains elsewhere.

3.6 Classical Unemployment

In classical unemployment, households are rationed in product and labour markets. They cannot buy as much as they would like, and they are forced to work less than they wish. By contrast, firms are not constrained at all. They can choose

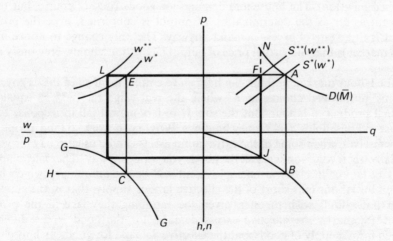

Figure 3.10 *Classical unemployment: the money wage rate is too high*

their levels of employment and production, without let or hindrance. Classical unemployment will certainly ensue if an economy departs from Walrasian equilibrium as a result of an increased money wage rate, all else equal.

Figure 3.10 illustrates the money wage is raised from its Walrasian value, w^* to w^{**}. A new rectangular hyperbola, further out from the origin, appears in the upper left quadrant. Firms respond to the higher real wage rate by lowering their demand for labour, from C to K on the curve GG in the lower left quadrant.

In the upper right quadrant, depicting the product market, the higher money wage displaces the supply (or marginal cost) curve to the left, from $S^*(w^*)$ to $S^{**}(w^{**})$. The classical unemployment equilibrium rectangle is $FJKL$, in contrast with Walrasian equilibrium ($ABCE$).

Consider now what will happen if other variables changed. A rise in the price level (so long as it was not too great, otherwise Keynesian unemployment could ensue) will trim the real wage rate. Firms would expand production along $S^{**}(w^{**})$, and raise employment along G. A higher stock of capital, or a technical advance, would increase output for a given employment level; the excess demand in the product market would certainly come down, as the supply curve would shift to the right. In the labour market, a capital stock increase would raise the demand for labour at a given real wage: in a two-factor model, with constant returns to scale and diminishing returns to each factor, a rise in one factor must raise the marginal product of the other (in more complicated cases, this result is open to qualification, as will be seen in the three-factor case explored in chapter 8). Technical progress must raise the demand for labour at a given real wage rate if it is capital-augmenting, and may do so if it is labour-augmenting (the condition for this is that the elasticity of substitution between capital and labour should exceed the profit share (Heffernan (1980, 1981) and Sinclair, 1981). The Luddites of nineteenth-century England, who destroyed machines in order to try to save their jobs, would have argued their case on the basis of Keynesian rather than classical unemployment.

In sharp contrast to its effects under Keynesian unemployment, a rise in the money supply will not do anything to increase output and employment. This is certain, at least, if it is not large enough to provoke a change of regime (into repressed inflation). The household demand for goods rises, of course, but this is irrelevant as far as the determination of output is concerned, since the product market is in a state of excess demand anyway. The only change to notice in the goods market is that the virtual price of output facing households, previously at N, will go up.

In the labour market, nothing can happen to employment since this is governed by firms' unrationed choices at K, where the real wage rate w^{**}/p^* equals the marginal product of labour. But the supply of labour will fall in response to the increase in households' real money holdings. Why try to work so long, people will ask themselves, when some of the extra liquid assets can be used to pay for goods, especially when you cannot get all the goods you want, anyway? The *effective* excess supply of labour in classical unemployment will be the amount by which firms' demand for labour falls short of the effective labour supply, that is, the supply of labour households wish to offer, given the rationing they face in the product market. (Similarly, the effective excess demand for the good is the difference between firms' supply of goods and the effective demand for goods by households, given the rationing on households in the market for labour.) A money supply increase should lower this effective excess supply in the labour market, even though it does nothing to raise employment.

The most direct and effective cure for classical unemployment, at least in the simple model considered here, is to act directly on the incentives facing firms. Either the demand for labour must be raised at a given real wage rate, by encouraging changes in technology or the supply or prices of other factors, or the real wage rate perceived by employers must be brought down. Employment subsidies would be a direct method of achieving this, provided that they were not absorbed completely by employees in the form of higher real after-tax earnings. So would cuts in employment taxes, such as employers' contributions to national insurance. Even income tax cuts would help, if some of the benefit was passed on to employers in the form of lower gross-of-tax real wage rates. This would certainly happen if unions are thought of as imposing a given after-tax real wage rate, since this would translate income tax into a pure employment tax.

Classical unemployment arises when excess supply in the labour market is combined with excess demand in the product market. The last of the three regimes, repressed inflation, exhibits a shortage of goods, too, but with a state of excess demand, not excess supply, in the labour market. It is the exact opposite of Keynesian unemployment: instead of generalized excess supply, there is general excess demand. It is to repressed inflation that we turn next.

3.7 Repressed Inflation

Repressed inflation can be induced by imposing a lower money wage rate, all else being equal, on an economy hitherto in Walrasian equilibrium. What this will do is to provide firms with an incentive to increase employment and output, just as a wage increase led them to cut them in classical unemployment. But these are the effects of firms' *notional* demand and supply. As in Keynesian unemployment, they will find themselves unable to achieve these higher, notional, levels of employment and production. Why?

In Keynesian unemployment, the problem for the firms is where to sell the extra output that it looked profitable, prima facie, to produce. Not so now; the product market poses no difficulty for them. The obstacle to higher output lies elsewhere: insufficiency of labour. Under the assumptions of this model, what really determines households' labour supply is the ratio of the money wage rate to the money supply. If this goes up, people will want to work more. The opportunity cost of leisure will have risen. The opposite occurs when, as in our case, the money wage rate falls in relation to the nominal money supply.

If the labour supply falls, despite firms' wishes to increase employment, so must production. Producers' *effective* supply of goods falls, even though their notional supply goes up. So the product market falls into a state of excess demand. Households are rationed there. The unavailability of goods, in the amounts desired, could easily cause households to reduce their effective supply of labour still further, setting a supply–supply multiplier process in action (less labour supply would imply a still lower level of production, hence a tightening of the product market rationing on consumers, in response to which labour supply would fall again); this would certainly happen if leisure were less complementary in demand with consumption than with real money holdings.

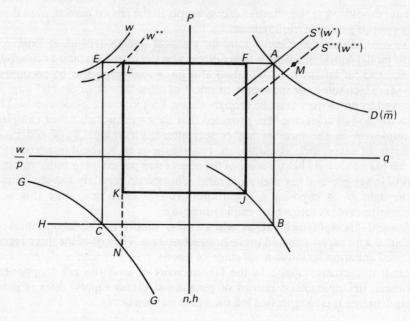

Figure 3.11 *Repressed inflation: too low a money wage rate*

The geometry of repressed inflation is presented in figure 3.11. The money wage rate, cut from w^* to w^{**}, displaces the notional product supply curve rightwards, from $S^*(w^*)$ to $S^{**}(w^{**})$ in the upper right quadrant. Producers' notional output supply is at point M, and their notional demand for labour at N in the lower left quadrant. But the money wage cut reduces labour supply to K, and hence, through the production function, keeps the effective supply of output down at point F. $FJKL$ depicts the repressed inflation equilibrium rectangle, in contrast to the Walrasian equilibrium rectangle, $ABCE$. Repressed inflation will be associated with low levels of output and employment, just like the other two regimes, but for quite different reasons. The shortfall in employment takes the form of voluntary underemployment: the problem lies with the incentives facing households.

Employment and output will therefore react strongly to a change in the environment facing households. A higher money wage rate would raise labour supply, and increase production. A higher money supply would exert the opposite effect, since incentives to work, depending as they will on the ratio $w/\bar{M}$, can only worsen further. A higher stock of capital, or technical advance, would increase output at a given labour supply, and hence relax the product market rationing constraint upon households. This might cause households to work longer, leading to a virtuous circle. From a policy standpoint, the most disastrous response to a state of repressed inflation could follow from misdiagnosis: if vigorous monetary expansion were accompanied by tight restrictions on money wage rates, repressed inflation would only get worse. This combination of policies looks rather appealing in Keynesian unemployment. It was tried from time to time in several Western countries in the post-war period, most recently, and most dramatically, in 1972–3 in both the UK and the US.

3.8 Some Extensions

3.8.1 *Fixed Money Wage, Endogenous Price Level*

In section 3.1, both the price level and the money wage rate were fixed at arbitrary values. Unless both happen to be imposed at the levels that would obtain in Walrasian equilibrium, we saw that some form of quantity rationing will ensue.

Sometimes the prices of goods remain unchanged for quite long periods. Manufacturers face costs of changing prices. New brochures have to be printed; new lists of prices have to be disseminated to wholesalers and traders who buy from them; advertisements may have to be changed. It is not uncommon for the prices of manufactured goods to be altered at no more than 6-month intervals, at least when there is little overall inflation. But primary commodity prices change day to day, even hour to hour, although substantial trading also occurs on fixed-price contracts. Money wage rates, on the other hand, are often renegotiated annually, or even less frequently. Two- and three-year wage contracts are common in the United States. Money wage rates are typically less flexible than the prices of goods.

This suggests that it is worth looking at what happens when money wage rates are given, and the prices of goods adjust to eliminate effective excess demands. Broadly speaking, the three quantity-rationing regimes we have considered collapse into two: there will either be effective excess demand in the labour market, or effective excess supply. The first situation arises when the price level goes up to place the economy on the borderline between repressed inflation and Keynesian unemployment. In the second, it adjusts to bring firms and households to the boundary between Keynesian and classical unemployment. There is excess demand for labour in the first case, and excess supply in the second.

Figure 3.12 depicts the RI/KU boundary. Because effective demand exceeds

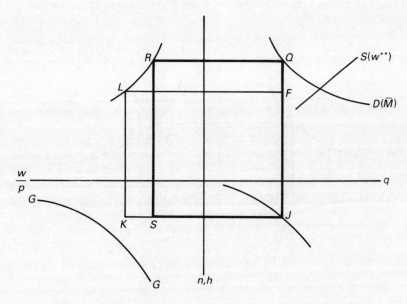

Figure 3.12 *The repressed inflation/Keynesian unemployment boundary*

effective supply in the product market, the price level must rise until it is eliminated. The price level rises to Q.

The real wage falls to R on w^{**}. The resulting equilibrium will be the rectangle $QJSR$, instead of $FJKL$ as in figure 3.11. Effective excess demand in the product market vanishes (although notional excess supply increases). Effective excess demand in the labour market is aggravated by the drop in the real wage. Employment remains at its old, sub-Walrasian value, because nothing has happened to the critical ratio, $w/\bar{M}$, upon which the labour supply depends. The implications of changes in exogenous variables remain much as in the pure repressed inflation case, although they are now altered by induced changes in the price level.

The second possible state of the economy is the Keynesian/classical unemployment boundary. This is the situation examined in Keynes' *General Theory* (1936): the price of final output is assumed to rise if unemployment is classical, or fall if it is Keynesian, until it is on the borderline between the two. Suppose unemployment is initially Keynesian, with an equilibrium rectangle indicated by $FJKL$. The price level drops, since effective supply exceeds effective demand in the goods market. The process continues until equilibrium is established at Q. The fall in the price level increases output and employment because it induces a rise in effective demand, stemming from the increase in consumers' real wealth or money holdings. The final equilibrium is illustrated by the rectangle $QTSR$, drawn in bold. Alternatively, if the unemployment is initially classical (as shown by rectangle $F'JK'L'$, corresponding to $FJKL$ in figure 3.10), the price level rises to choke off the effective excess demand for goods, until rectangle $QTSR$ is reached.

Classical unemployment will always turn into the Keynesian/classical 'compromise' unemployment illustrated by $QTSR$; prices can only go up. But Keynesian unemployment could develop into the KU/RI boundary phenomenon illustrated in figure 3.12. This would have happened in figure 3.13, had the supply of labour line lain above, rather than below, point S in the lower left quadrant.

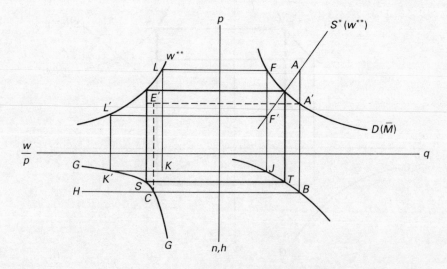

Figure 3.13 *The Keynesian/classical unemployment boundary*

In the circumstances of figure 3.13, it is interesting to see that *both* Keynesian *and* classical remedies for unemployment may be expected to help. Monetary expansion would displace the product demand curve rightwards. If point *B* on the production function defines the Walrasian equilibrium, an increase in the money supply required to eliminate unemployment (or, at least, to eliminate non-Walrasian unemployment) may be inferred from point *A*.[1] This gives the Walrasian equilibrium price level, for a money wage rate of w^{**}. In a suitably expanded model, reflationary fiscal policy would in principle serve just as well to achieve this objective. The increase in prices is needed in order to strengthen the incentive for producers to employ more labour. These incentives matter now, since producers are no longer rationed in the product market. An alternative, classical route to Walrasian equilibrium would take the form of money wage cuts. A fall in the money wage would displace the product market supply curve to the right. Walrasian equilibrium at *B* calls for product market equilibrium at *A'*, which is consistent with a money wage rate given by the product of the co-ordinates of point *E'*.

Figure 3.13 leaves one with two distinct impressions, both of them rather optimistic. One is that price flexibility on its own will help to rebuild employment: output and employment are both higher at *T* than at *J*, the initial equilibrium in the two cases of 'pure' Keynesian or classical unemployment with which we began. The second is the conclusion that reflating demand, and money wage cuts, are both impressive candidates for policy measures that could eliminate unemployment. This is an appropriate juncture at which to consider some serious objections.

Consider first the benefits that appear to occur from falling prices in Keynesian unemployment. They can be problematical for several reasons. First, they may be rather implausible. Negative price inflation has not been observed in the UK, other than for the odd freak month, for over half a century. Second, there are grounds for questioning whether the increase in the real money supply that might occur in a spell of negative price inflation really will increase spending. All but the narrowest definitions of the money supply include deposits placed with banks. If you have deposited £100 in a bank, and prices come down, the purchasing power of your deposit undeniably rises. But your £100 deposit typically has a counterpart of £80 or £90, perhaps even more, in the form of claims by your bank on someone else. To companies or individuals who have borrowed from the banks or other financial institutions, a fall in the price level implies a direct increase in the real value of their liabilities. They will not react by spending more; all the pressures will be on them to spend less. The decline in prices transfers wealth from borrowers to holders of financial claims. The net increase in society's real wealth may be very small. There could be asymmetries: borrowers may cut back their spending by more than deposit holders increase theirs. There are indeed two powerful reasons for expecting just this pattern of asymmetries. An increase in the real value of debt charges, which will follow a general decline in prices, must increase the chance of bankruptcies. Banruptcies act as a sudden, unanticipated destruction of wealth, and will entail a discontinuous fall in the spending of those unlucky enough to suffer in this way. Bankruptcies also have unpleasant and pervasive knock-on effects not least because of the highly intricate network of trade credit between producers in a modern economy. The second reason for expecting asymmetries is that large deposit holders are most unlikely to be constrained by credit-rationing limits on their spending; they can always decumulate deposits if they wish; and the additional spending that will follow a pure windfall, in the form of increased purchasing power of their deposits, is therefore likely to be slight. Borrowers, on the other hand, are rather likely to be credit-constrained; why else are they borrowers? Higher real debt charges may cut the amount available for spending one for one in such circumstances.

There are other problems with falling prices. Take the example of an industry composed of a small number of large firms, experiencing a recession. Each will recognize that a price war would lead to collective suicide. A cut in prices will reduce the profit margin on sale immediately, and demand may respond little, or slowly, to lower prices. Oligopolistic collusion, tacit or overt, may succeed in preventing price cuts. Many buyers have loyalty to their current suppliers, and may be unaware of prices offered by rivals. A firm on its own may reckon that a unilateral price cut may not win it an appreciable increase in business, especially if attempts to publicize the reduction to poach custom from other firms are thought likely to provoke retaliation.

Rising prices, in situations of classical unemployment, may not be as helpful as they seem, either. Price inflation is popularly regarded as a grave social ill, perhaps quite incorrectly; but it is at least perceived as a threat to living standards. A rise in prices when money wage rates are given will create pressure from compensating wage increases. If the burden of classical unemployment is borne by a minority of unemployed workers, while the majority are continuing to work for hours they regard as reasonable, the cut in real wages for the latter group which a general price rise induces will be greeted by howls of protest. Furthermore, even if money wage rates fail to respond, it is not clear how much additional output and employment a price increase will create. Production may be held back by shortages of equipment, by indivisibilities in plant, by firms' apprehension that the price rise may soon be reversed. There could also be asymmetries at work here, too. Trees are slow to grow, and quickly felled. It may be the same with jobs, especially in manufacturing industry.

One must be cautious, therefore, in welcoming price increases in conditions of classical unemployment, or price cuts in Keynesian unemployment. This will be particularly true if classical and Keynesian unemployment are hard to tell apart in practice, as they may be, or co-exist in a complex economy with many different kinds of goods and labour. This note of scepticism must extend both to the classical arguments in favour of money wage cuts (which rely upon the disappointingly slender need of the 'real balance effect' – the idea that consumer spending increases with M/p) and the Keynesian case for aggregate demand expansion (which turns critically, in the context of figure 3.13, on the highly uncertain elasticity of the supply curve, and the questionable assumption that money wages will stay down when prices rise).

3.8.2 *Two Further Extensions to the Simple Quantity-rationing Model*

Two of the most noteworthy extensions to the simple macroeconomic quantity-rationing model introduce an open economy, and explore intertemporal elements in the story. What follows is a thumbnail sketch of these two strands of thought.

One interesting issue that arises in an open economy is whether Keynesian unemployment in an open economy can really occur at all. The influential early studies of quantity rationing (Barro and Grossman (1971), Benassy (1975) and Malinvaud (1977)) had confined attention to a closed economy. If there is an excess supply of goods at home, why cannot firms sell their extra output overseas? Dixit (1978) produced a one-sector model of a small open economy, in which Keynesian unemployment was impossible for this reason. There are, however, two ways of restoring the possibility of Keynesian unemployment in an open economy. One is to introduce rationing at the world level. The home country's exporters may find themselves subjected to quota ceilings on their sales into foreign markets. In deep international recessions, such quotas are apt to become more widespread and more severe. This was especially true of the international slump of the 1930s. One country's quota against the exports of others is a perfect example of how rationing restraints on producers can operate. Keynesian unemployment, in short, can be a worldwide phenomenon.

The other approach is to split the economy into traded and non-traded sectors. Non-traded goods suffer from such high tariff barriers or transport costs that they cannot be traded across international boundaries. The possibility of Keynesian unemployment arises now because non-traded goods can be in excess supply. If home demand for these goods is insufficient to match the output levels that their producers wish to achieve, the option of switching into foreign markets is denied to them. It is Neary (1980) who develops a formal model to explore this. The domestic money wage rate and price of non-traded goods are locked. The prices of traded goods are also frozen by a commodity arbitrage condition: the home price of these goods is governed by the exchange rate and the foreign currency prices in international markets.

Neary examines the effects upon employment, output and the trade balance of various parameter changes in this framework. Devaluation raises the home currency price of traded goods. Production and employment rise in this sector because real wages in terms of these products will drop (unless there is excess demand for labour and that sector is rationed there). What happens in the non-traded sector depends greatly on the regime. In Keynesian unemployment, spending on non-traded goods rises because of the higher employment and income levels in the traded goods sector, and also because the relative price change encourages consumers to switch, but this effect may be weakened by the squeeze on real money balances that devaluation entails. Domestic spending on tradable goods is also likely to go up quite sharply. In classical unemployment, there is excess demand for non-traded goods anyway, so employment and output cannot budge. Turning to fiscal policy, an important difference emerges between the effects of increased government spending on traded and non-traded goods. The former spills over one-to-one on the trade balance, and can do nothing to soften unemployment, under either Keynesian or classical conditions. But the latter works powerfully to cut unemployment of the Keynesian (but not classical) variety. Money supply increases act like a combination of the two.

Intertemporal extensions of quantity-rationing models begin with Muellbauer and Portes (1978), but the fullest treatment is offered by Neary and Stiglitz (1983). The latter authors study a two-period world where the first period money wage and the second period price of goods are imposed arbitrarily (and at typically non-Walrasian levels). Labour will be in excess supply in the first period if the former is too high. Unemployment will be Keynesian if the latter is low enough, otherwise classical. A low future price of goods weakens the incentives for current consumption and investment. The Neary–Stiglitz analysis explores three different types of expectational assumptions: beliefs that markets will clear in the next period; exogenously given beliefs about what regime will prevail in the next period; and what are termed rational constraint expectations. In the second case, unemployment is more likely to be Keynesian now if Keynesian unemployment is anticipated in the following period (households and firms will spend less now); similarly, classical unemployment expectations for the future make classical unemployment more probable now. Rational constraint expectations impose the condition that what people expect must be consistent with what will actually happen. Interestingly, they imply that the output and employment consequences of government policy decisions are more powerful, not less powerful, than when rationing expectations are arbitrary. In a sense, virtuous or vicious circles can be triggered. This contrasts sharply with what rational expectations suggests in a world where prices clear, as we shall see in chapter 12.

One objection to quantity-rationing models is that they fail to explain why wages and prices are rigid. These critical variables are just imposed. Furthermore, as time passes, the assumption itself becomes less and less plausible. The reply to this must be that at least temporary rigidities in wages and prices are observed, and explicable in a variety of ways. We have already encountered these arguments in the last chapter (pp. 54–9). Yet it must be conceded that quantity rationing provides a much more appealing way of explaining short-term swings in unemployment, than long-term trends. For accounts of the latter, one may wish to look elsewhere: the demand and supply analysis of fiscally induced unemployment, contract theories, or trade unions for example. The first of these forms the subject matter of chapters 5 and 6, while the latter two are examined in chapters 9 and 11 respectively. And even if we confine attention to the short run, it will be necessary to explain the various types of shock that will generate changes in unemployment during the period when prices are sluggish. These shocks are the subject of chapters 7 and 8. Lastly, in defence of quantity-rationing models, it should be emphasized that they have formed the basis of a vast number of econometric studies, particularly in France and Belgium. Many of these are reviewed or referred to, in a recent survey by Laffont (1985). UK empirical studies include that by Andrews and Nickell (1986). So quantity-rationing models offer a theory that has been made to work, successfully, on data.

4 Fix Price Models: Some Detailed Analysis

This chapter should be seen as a kind of technical appendix, or extension, to chapter 3. The reader who prefers to avoid these details is advised to proceed directly to chapter 5.

4.1 Introduction

It is the purpose of this chapter to supply the technical details that underpin the analysis of chapter 3. Chapter 3 relied upon geometry and verbal explanations of how unemployment can result from wages and prices stuck at non-market-clearing levels. The present chapter backs this up with a more formal treatment.

Section 4.2 examines a simple static general model. Analysis starts with the Walrasian case where all markets clear (4.2.1). This acts as a convenient platform for examining the consequences of wage and price rigidity: classical unemployment is explored in 4.2.2, Keynesian unemployment in 4.2.3 and repressed inflation in 4.2.4. The effects of allowing prices to vary when wages are locked are studied in 4.2.5, while 4.3 proceeds to analyse the Cobb–Douglas special case that forms the basis of chapter 3. Section 4.4 deals with a multi-sector extension, and section 4.5 with the case when rationing in labour markets takes the form of unemployment for some and full employment for others. Finally, section 4.6 is concerned with the behaviour of investment, and extensions to a multi-period framework.

4.2 The Simple Static General Model (SSGM)

4.2.1 *The Walrasian Case: Perfect Price and Wage Flexibility*

The elements of this simple model, where all households and products are identical, one good is produced, and a single time period is allowed, depend upon four considerations: the behaviour of households, producers and government; and market-clearing conditions.

Assume that households receive financial resources equal to $\bar{M} + (1 - T)(\bar{\pi} + WH)$.

These represent nominal money endowments, plus taxed wage and profit income. The budget restraint requires that $M + PC$, end of period nominal money holdings plus the value of consumption, not exceed this. Utility is derived from three goods: real money (M/P); leisure ($1-H$); and consumption (C). Let utility be increasing, concave and additively separable in these three. The utility derived from good i is multiplied by a parameter B_i, which represents the strength of preference for that good. Denote by δ_i the reciprocity of the elasticity of the marginal utility of good i (defined as a positive number).

Household optimization thus implies

$$\frac{m-p}{\delta_1} - b_1 = \frac{c}{\delta_3} - b_3 \tag{4.1a}$$

$$= w - p - t - \frac{H}{1-H}\frac{h}{\delta_2} - b_2 \tag{4.1b}$$

given that the budget restraint binds. Lower-case letters refer to proportional changes in upper-case variables, except that t is defined as $dT/(1-T)$. Differentiating the budget restraint yields

$$\bar{M}\bar{m} - (\bar{\pi} + WH)dT + (1-T)(d\bar{\pi} + WH(w+h)) = Mm + PC(p+c). \tag{4.2}$$

Equation (4.2) states that the change in total financial resources for the household equals the change in its total disbursements.

All *producers* have an identical production function

$$Q = f(A_k K, A_n N) \tag{4.3}$$

which displays constant returns to scale, and diminishing returns to the two factors employed (capital, K and labour, N). There is perfect competition. Marginal productivity factor pricing entails

$$w - p = \frac{\sigma-1}{\sigma} a_n + \frac{q-n}{\sigma} \tag{4.4a}$$

$$r - p = \frac{\sigma-1}{\sigma} a_k + \frac{q-k}{\sigma} \tag{4.4b}$$

where σ is the elasticity of substitution between capital and labour, and w and r are proportional changes in the money wage rate and nominal rental on capital. A_k and A_n in (4.3) denote capital-augmenting and labour-augmenting technology parameters, so that a_k and a_n in (4.4a) and (4.4b) will represent corresponding rates of technical change for these two. Further, since (4.3) implies

$$q = \theta(a_k + k) + (1-\theta)(a_n + n) \tag{4.5}$$

(where θ denotes the competitive share of output accruing to capital as profits), (4.4a) can be re-expressed to give a demand curve for labour in rate-of-change form:

$$w - p = a_n\left(\frac{\sigma-\theta}{\sigma}\right) + \frac{\theta}{\sigma}(a_k + k) - \frac{\theta_n}{\sigma}. \tag{4.6}$$

A similar equation can be derived for capital from (4.4b) and (4.5). The change in profits will be

$$d\bar{\pi} = PQ(p - w(1-\theta) + \theta(a_k + k) + (1-\theta)a_n). \tag{4.7}$$

The Government is assumed to tax all income, profits and wages, at a single rate

T. It devotes its tax receipts, TQ in real terms, to direct spending on final output, G. Its budget is balanced, so that its fiscal activity has no impact upon the nominal money supply, $\bar{M}$.

There is full price and wage flexibility. Consequently the goods market clears to give $Q = C + G = C[1 - T]^{-1}$, and similarly with the labour market $(N = H)$. Units are chosen so that the numbers of households and producers are equal. The money market also clears, hence $\bar{M} = M$.

The real endogenous variables of the system include two relative prices (the real wage rate W/P and the real capital rental R/P), as well as four quantities: output, Q; consumption, C; employment, H (or N); and lastly real money holdings, M/P. We now proceed to solve for equilibrium changes in these six variables. The changes will represent responses to disturbances in exogenous variables. There are eight of these in all: three resource parameters $(A_k, A_n$ and $K)$; three preference parameters $(B_1, B_2$ and $B_3)$; and two government parameters, $\bar{M}$ and the spending share (or tax rate) T.

To obtain these solutions, begin by deleting the monetary terms $\bar{M}\bar{m}$ and Mm from (4.2): money market clearance must imply that they are equal. Use (4.7) to eliminate $d\bar{\pi}$, and divide through by PQ. Equate the right-hand side of (4.1a) and (4.1b) to derive a second equation linking c to h, and eliminate c. The result will be a labour-supply equation (in rate-of-change form):

$$h(1 + y - \theta) = t(1 - \delta_3) + \delta_3(b_3 - b_2 - p + w) - \theta(a_k + k) - a_n(1 - \theta) \tag{4.8}$$

where $y \equiv \delta_3 H/\delta_2(1 - H)$. Labour market equilibrium entails that $h = n$. Hence (4.6) and (4.8) can be linked to solve for the (change in the) real wage rate:

$$(w - p)z = (a_k + k)(1 + y) + a_n\left(y + \eta\left(\frac{\sigma}{\theta} - 1\right)\right) - t(1 - \delta_3) - \delta_3(b_3 - b_2). \tag{4.9}$$

In (4.9), $z \equiv \eta + y\sigma/\theta + \delta_3$ and $\eta = \sigma((1 - \theta)/\theta)$ (the elasticity of supply). Substitution of (4.9) into (4.6) or (4.8) furnishes a solution for employment:

$$nz = a_n\left[\delta_3\left(\frac{\sigma}{\theta} - \eta\right)\right] + (a_k + k)(\delta_3 - \sigma) + \frac{\sigma}{\theta}[t(1 - \delta_3) + \delta_3(b_3 - b_2)]. \tag{4.10}$$

Output changes can be obtained by substituting (4.10) into (4.5):

$$qz = a_n\eta\theta(y + \delta_3) + (a_k + k)(\sigma y + \delta_3) + \eta[t(1 - \delta_3) + \delta_3(b_3 - b_2)]. \tag{4.11}$$

Changes in consumption follow directly from (4.11), since $c = q - t$, and real money changes emerge from (4.1a). The last of our six real endogenous variables, the real capital rental, can be found by eliminating q in (4.4b) by the use of (4.11).

One notable feature is the irrelevance of the nominal money supply, $\bar{M}$, as far as these real variables are concerned. Our results are consistent with the neutrality of money. Furthermore, all but the real balance equation are unaffected by a change in the demand for money (b_1). Fiscal policy, on the other hand, is generally non-neutral. As (4.10) and (4.11) show, employment and output rise in response to an increase in the tax rate if $1 > \delta_3$, and fall if this inequality is reversed. The first case corresponds to a victory of the income effect of higher taxation over the substitution effect upon labour supply, the second to a defeat. When utility is Cobb–Douglas, $\delta_3 = 1$ and the two effects cancel. More complex effects of a change in t would have arisen, had some of the proceeds of tax been devoted to transfer

Table 4.1 Response elasticities to exogenous parameters

Endogenous variables	Exogenous parameters						Technology parameter
	Tax rate t	Nominal money supply $\hat{m}$	Demand for money b_1	Demand for leisure b_2	Consumption demand b_3	Capital stock k	labour-augmenting a_n
Employment $(h = n)$	$\dfrac{\sigma(1-\delta_3)}{\theta z}$	0	0	$\dfrac{\sigma\delta_3}{\theta z}$	$\dfrac{\sigma\delta_3}{\theta z}$	$\dfrac{\delta_3-\sigma}{z}$	$\dfrac{\delta_3\frac{\sigma-\theta}{\theta}-\eta}{z}$
Output (q)	$\dfrac{1-\delta_3}{\eta z}$	0	0	$\dfrac{\eta\delta_3}{z}$	$\dfrac{\eta\delta_3}{z}$	$\dfrac{\sigma y+\delta_3}{z}$	$\dfrac{\eta\theta(y+\delta_3)}{z}$
Consumption (c)	$\dfrac{1-\delta_3}{\eta z}-1$	0	0	$\dfrac{\eta\delta_3}{z}$	$\dfrac{\eta\delta_3}{z}$	$\dfrac{\sigma y+\delta_3}{z}$	$\dfrac{\eta\theta(y+\delta_3)}{z}$
Real wage $(w-p)$	$\dfrac{\delta_3-1}{z}$	0	0	$\dfrac{\delta_3}{z}$	$-\dfrac{\delta_3}{z}$	$\dfrac{1+y}{z}$	$\dfrac{y+\eta\frac{\sigma-\theta}{\theta}}{z}$
Real capital rental $(r-p)$	$\dfrac{\eta}{\sigma}\dfrac{(1-\delta_3)}{z}$	0	0	$\dfrac{\eta\delta_3}{\sigma z}$	$\dfrac{\eta\delta_3}{\sigma z}$	$\dfrac{-\eta}{\sigma}\dfrac{(1+y)}{z}$	$\dfrac{\eta\theta}{\sigma}\dfrac{(y+\delta_3)}{z}$
Real balances $(m-p)$	$\dfrac{\delta_1}{\delta_3}\left[\dfrac{1-\delta_3}{\eta z}-1\right]$	0	δ_1	$\dfrac{\eta\delta_1}{z}$	$-\dfrac{\delta_1}{z}\left(\dfrac{\sigma y}{\theta}+\delta_3\right)$	$\dfrac{\delta_1}{\delta_3}\dfrac{\sigma y+\delta_3}{z}$	$\dfrac{\delta_1}{\delta_3}\dfrac{\eta\theta(y+\delta_3)}{z}$
Nominal income $(p+q)$	$\eta(1+\delta_1-\delta_3)+\delta_1\left(1+\dfrac{\sigma y}{\delta_3\theta}\right)$	$+1$	$-\delta_1$	$(\delta_1-\delta_3)\dfrac{\eta}{z}$	$(\delta_3-\delta_1)\dfrac{\eta}{z}$	$(\delta_3-\delta_1)\dfrac{\sigma y+\delta_3}{\delta_3 z}$	$(\delta_3-\delta_1)\dfrac{\eta\theta(y+\delta_3)}{\delta_3 z}$
Money wage (w)	$\dfrac{\delta_1(1+\eta)+\delta_1(1+\eta)-1+\frac{\delta_1\sigma y}{\delta_3}}{z}$	$+1$	$-\delta_1$	$\dfrac{\delta_3+\delta_1\eta}{z}$	$\dfrac{\delta_3+\delta_1\eta}{z}$	$\dfrac{1+y-\frac{\delta_1}{\delta_3}\sigma y-\delta_1}{z}$	$\dfrac{y\delta_3-\delta_1\eta\theta+\eta\left(\frac{\sigma-\theta}{\theta}-\delta_1\theta\right)}{\delta_3}\dfrac{\eta\theta(y+\delta_3)}{\delta_3 z}$
Nominal rental (r)	$\dfrac{\frac{\delta_1\sigma y}{\delta_3\theta}+\delta_1(1+\eta)+\frac{\eta}{\sigma}(1-\delta_3)}{z}$	$+1$	$-\delta_1$	$\dfrac{\eta}{z}\left(\delta_1-\dfrac{\delta_3}{\sigma}\right)$	$\dfrac{\eta}{z}\left(\dfrac{\delta_3}{\sigma}-\delta_1\right)$	$\dfrac{-\left[\frac{\eta}{\sigma}(1+\eta)+\frac{\delta_1}{\delta_3}\sigma y+\delta_1\right]}{z}$	$\dfrac{\eta\theta}{z}\{y+\delta_3\}\left(\dfrac{1}{\sigma}-\dfrac{\delta_1}{\delta_3}\right)$
Price level (p)	$\dfrac{\delta_1}{\delta_3 z}\left[\dfrac{\sigma y}{\theta}+\delta_3(1+\eta)\right]$	$+1$	$-\delta_1$	$\dfrac{\delta_1\eta}{z}$	$-\dfrac{\delta_1\eta}{z}$	$-\dfrac{\delta_1}{\delta_3 z}(\sigma y+\delta_3)$	$-\dfrac{\delta_1}{\delta_3 z}(y+\delta_3)\eta\theta$

Note: Capital-augmenting technical progress $(a_k > 0)$ affects all endogenous variables except the nominal and real capital rentals exactly like a rise in the capital stock.

payments, or had government spending been allowed to affect consumers' marginal rates of substitution between leisure and consumption.

Turning to the other parameters, (4.11) shows that technical progress of either kind (capital-augmenting or labour-augmenting) must increase output. So will a rise in the stock of capital. How employment responds to such changes, evident from (4.10), is ambiguous: much depends upon whether the labour supply curve slopes up ($\delta_3 > 1$) or bends back ($\delta_3 < 1$). A higher stock of capital, or level of the capital-augmenting technology parameter, must imply a higher real wage rate. Labour-augmenting technical progress may well do so, but need not. Higher capital brings down the real rental on it; labour-augmenting technical progress will boost it, and capital-augmenting technical progress may do so. A higher demand for leisure ($b_2 > 0$) reduces employment and output, and raises the real wage; a higher demand for consumption ($b_3 > 0$) exerts the opposite effect.

Solutions for the nominal endogenous variables can be found from (4.1a) and the money market clearance condition $m = \bar{m}$. Substituting the solution for c (from (4.11) and the goods market clearance condition $q = c - t$) yields an equation for the change in the price level:

$$zp = \left[\bar{m} + \delta_1(b_3 - b_1) + \frac{\delta_1}{\delta_3}t \right] z - \frac{e_1}{e_3} \{ a_n \eta \theta(y + \delta_3) + (a_k + k)(\sigma_y + \delta_3)$$

$$+ \eta[t(1 - \delta_3) + \delta_3(b_3 - b_2)]. \} \qquad (4.12)$$

(4.12) shows that anything which induces a rise in output, with the exception of b_3 and possibly t, must cause the price level to drop. Rises in B_3 or T will necessarily increase the price level. Prices rise one-for-one with the nominal money supply. They fall, with elasticity $-\delta_1$, if the demand for money increases. Changes in the money wage rate, the nominal value of national income (PQ) and the nominal rental on capital can be obtained by substituting (4.12) for p in the corresponding solutions for these variables in real terms. PQ, W and R are all proportional to $\bar{M}$. The complete results are presented in table 4.1.

The full results presented in table 4.1 are a little daunting. They are given in qualitative form in table 4.2, where the cells display + or − to describe positive or negative effects. When the relevant exogenous variable has no effect on the

Table 4.2 *Qualitative responses to exogenous parameters*

Endogenous variables	Exogenous parameters							
	t	$\bar{m}$	b_1	b_2	b_3	k	a_k	a_n
n	?(0)	0	0	−	+	?(0)	?(0)	+
q	?(0)	0	0	−	+	+	+	+
c	−	0	0	+	+	+	+	+
$w-p$	?(0)	0	0	+	−	−	+	?(+)
$r-p$	?(0)	0	0	−	+	+	?(+)	+
$m-p$	−	0	+	−	−	−	+	+
$p+q$	?(+)	+	−	?(0)	?(0)	?(0)	?(0)	?(0)
w	?(+)	+	−	+	−	?(0)	?(0)	?(0)
r	?(+)	+	−	?(0)	?(0)	−	?(0)	?(0)
p	+	+	−	+	−	−	−	−

endogenous variable in question, there is a zero, and when the effect is ambiguous, a question mark. Finally, a bracketed sign or zero after a question mark gives the effect when the production and utility functions are specialized to a Cobb–Douglas form. Then all the δ_i collapse to unity, as does the elasticity of substitution, σ. (The Cobb–Douglas special case will be examined in detail in section 4.3, since it has the great attraction of giving explicit solutions to the levels of variables, and not just to their rate of change.)

Twenty-three of the 80 cells in table 4.2 display qualitative unambiguity. In the Cobb–Douglas special case, all the question marks disappear, usually to be replaced by noughts. The real usefulness of these tables, and the model on which they rest, is that they act as a platform, or basis for comparison, for seeing what happens when markets fail to clear. This is the subject of the remaining parts of section 4.3 of the present chapter.

4.2.2 *Rigid Wage Rate and Price Level, I: Classical Unemployment*

We now replace the assumption of perfect price and wage flexibility, which governed the Walrasian system just examined. Instead, suppose that W and P are locked at arbitrarily selected values. It is just conceivable that the economy could be in Walrasian equilibrium if this is done. But this would be a mere fluke.

It was seen in chapter 3 that if the money wage rate is raised above its Walrasian value, while the price level remains at this point, classical unemployment will ensue. This is a state of affairs typified by excess effective demand for the product, and excess effective supply of labour. Households are rationed in both these markets, firms in neither. Producers can attain their notional equilibria in both employment and output. As far as these variables are concerned, household behaviour is simply irrelevant.

The determination of output and employment rests with producers. We can confine attention to the production function (4.3) and its allied marginal productivity condition for labour, (4.4a). Together these give rise to the demand for labour equation (4.6). (4.6) can be inverted to give the change in employment:

$$n = a_k + k + a_n \frac{(\sigma - \theta)}{\theta} + (p - w)\frac{\sigma}{\theta}. \tag{4.13}$$

This states that employment responds one-to-one with capital-augmenting technical advances, or capital accumulation. How it reacts to labour-augmenting technical progress is unclear. When the substitution elasticity exceeds the profit share, the demand for labour rises; it falls when the opposite is true. A rise in the real wage rate (recall that this is now an exogenous variable) must reduce the demand for labour. The elasticity of this relationship, σ/θ, is the ratio of the substitution elasticity to the profit share.

Output changes can be obtained directly by substituting for n in (4.5):

$$q = a_k + k + \eta[a_n + p - w] \tag{4.14}$$

where η (defined in 4.1.1) is the supply elasticity, $\sigma((1 - \theta)/\theta)$. Capital accumulation or capital-augmenting technical progress raise output in proportion (just as they did to employment). Labour-augmenting technical improvements also increase output. In all three cases, they serve to reduce the marginal cost of production, and thereby ensure a higher level of production since the price level is given. In the first two, they also displace the demand curve for labour, so as to yield a higher level of employment at the given real wage; in the third case, it may well do this but need not. A higher money wage rate raises marginal costs; a price level increase ensures that price equals marginal cost at an enhanced volume of production.

The household preference parameters, and the money stock, are notable absentees from the two equations above. This simply reflects the fact that households are rationed in both labour and good markets. The tax rate (or government spending share of output), T, also fails to appear. This reflects an assumption that it is the firms' perception of the money wage rate, the gross-of-tax wage, that is fixed. If instead we suppose that the net-of-tax wage rate is locked, perhaps because of union behaviour, employment and output do respond to T. They will fall if t increases, because the incidence of the tax now falls fully on producers, raising their perception of labour costs. More generally, if ζ is defined as the elasticity of W to $1 - T$ (presumably ζ will lie somewhere between nought and unity), and $\bar{w}$ is defined as an autonomous change in the net-of-tax wage rate, the above equations become

$$n = a_k + k + a_n \frac{(\sigma - \theta)}{\theta} + \frac{\sigma}{\theta}(p - \zeta t - \bar{w}). \tag{4.15}$$

$$q = a_k + k + \eta[a_n + p - \zeta t - \bar{w}]. \tag{4.16}$$

A higher value of T will depress employment and production except in the limiting case where ζ vanishes. One question of particular interest from a policy standpoint is how T affects total tax receipts, TQ. Some observers have followed Laffer in claiming that an income tax cut could so stimulate production that TQ rose as a result. From the above, the elasticity of TQ to T will be

$$\frac{\frac{dT}{T} + q}{\frac{dT}{T}} = 1 - \eta\zeta\frac{T}{1 - T}. \tag{4.17}$$

The value of this is, indeed, ambiguous. If this model accurately depicts contemporary economy, where labour's share of output, $1 - \theta$, is approximately two-thirds, and substitution elasticities between capital and labour may be cautiously placed in the range from $\frac{1}{2}$ to 1, it looks unlikely that Laffer's optimistic view of the tax receipts effects of tax cuts will be warranted. Even if ζ and σ are at the upper ends of their range of possible values, at unity, the tax rate T must exceed one-third for this to follow. If ζ and σ are both one-half, T will have to exceed two-thirds.

A second way in which the government's fiscal authority may affect output and employment in classical unemployment arises if firms' production functions are altered by government spending. Infrastructural investment in the road network, or energy programmes, for example, can have a direct effect upon firms' cost conditions. Educational expenditure may raise the quality of the labour force, and therefore lead to $a_n > 0$. Subsidies for research and development, or capital formation, will also have an obvious direct impact.

Yet further means at government's disposal include employment subsidies and direct labour market intervention to affect w. Provided that employment subsidies succeed in lowering firms' perceptions of wage rates – so that they are not simply swallowed up in increased net-of-tax incomes for employees – employment and output should respond favourably. It is more than possible that they could be self-financing in such circumstances. Not merely would the government recoup higher income tax receipts on increased economic activity, there would also be a direct saving in reduced unemployment benefits. Other measures to influence w could take the form of limits on public sector pay, or more overt and thoroughgoing types of incomes policy. Indeed, it is in classical, not Keynesian unemployment, that the possible benefits of such policies really show through. We return to examine these issues in chapter 16.

A final point of note in this discussion of classical unemployment concerns the possible link of w to p. At one extreme, money wage rates may be indexed formally to the price level. Such has been the case in Italy, where money wage rates are tied to the price index by a so-called *scala mobile*. Indexation of money wages was employed in the UK from 1918 until 1923, when it was abandoned once sharp price declines led to money wage cuts which were strongly resisted by organized labour. Britain also saw a brief return to a form of wage indexation under the Threshold Scheme in 1973–4. It is also more than possible that some association between w and p emerges naturally as a result of pay-bargaining. To assume anything short of equiproportionality of w to p in the long run is to accuse labour market participants of money illusion. Accordingly, if k is defined as the elasticity of the gross money wage rate to the price level, equations (4.15) and (4.16) will be amended to give

$$n = a_k + k + a_n \left[\frac{\sigma - \theta}{\theta} \right] + \frac{\sigma}{\theta}(p(1-k) - \zeta t - \bar{w}) \tag{4.18}$$

$$q = a_k + k + \eta(a_n + p(1-k) - \zeta t - \bar{w}). \tag{4.19}$$

Full equiproportionality ($k = 1$) will destroy any output or employment effects emanating from the price level.

4.2.3 *Rigid Money Wage and Price Level, II: Keynesian Unemployment*

In Keynesian unemployment, excess effective supply in the labour market is combined with excess effective supply, not demand, in the product market. Households are rationed in the employment opportunities they receive, as before; but they can at least choose how to allocate their shrunken financial resources between consumption and money holdings. Firms, on the other hand, are more constrained, since they cannot succeed in selling their notional output level. They are demand-constrained in the goods market. As a result, they will limit their offers of employment to the minimum necessary labour input to produce for this reduced level of output. Their effective demand for labour will be considerably lower than the notional demand.

It is easier to assume that the rationing scheme works in such a way that if all agents are rationed on one side of a market, all are rational to an equal extent. This allows us to continue employing the device of a representative agent. (Below, in section 4.5, we shall investigate the possible consequences of relaxing this assumption.) Consequently, involuntary unemployment takes the form of every household being constrained to accept reduced time at work. No one is completely unemployed; everyone is partly unemployed. An analogous assumption for firms ensures that they all suffer equally from the excess effective supply in the product market.

As we saw in chapter 3, Keynesian unemployment will arise when the price level is raised above its Walrasian value (while the money wage rate, for simplicity's sake, is pegged at that value). Our assumptions about households' utility, to be specific the assumption of additive separability, have the helpful implication that the trade-off between two goods where choice is exercised is unaffected by rationing, or changes in the available quantity, of any third good where it is not. In Keynesian unemployment, households are denied the power to choose H. But they can still select M and C. Consequently (4.1a) continues to hold. (4.1b), on the other hand, does not.

Equation (4.1a) provides the key that unlocks the formal analysis of Keynesian unemployment equilibrium. Money market clearance enables us to replace m by $\bar{m}$. Consequently (4.1a) may be rewritten

$$c = \delta_3 \left[b_3 - b_1 + \frac{\bar{m} - p}{\delta_1} \right]. \tag{4.1a$'$}$$

Equation (4.1a)$'$ shows that consumption spending is unambiguously boosted by money supply increases (so long as they are not cancelled, in real terms, by inflation). Price increases serve to squeeze consumption. A higher demand for money ($b_1 > 0$) acts like the familiar effect of a higher propensity to save in traditional Keynesian models. An increase in B_3, on the other hand, raises consumption directly. These effects on consumption are exactly mirrored in their impact upon output, since $q = c + t$. This last condition also informs us that a rise in government's spending, as a share of national income, will necessarily increase output, in accordance with the balanced budget multiplier.

Changes in employment are found simply by inverting (4.5) to give

$$n = -a_n - \frac{\theta}{1-\theta}(a_k + k) + \frac{1}{1-\theta} \left\{ t + \delta_3 \left[b_3 - b_1 + \frac{\bar{m} - p}{\delta_1} \right] \right\}. \tag{4.20}$$

Supply-side influences (technical progress and capital accumulation) played no role in influencing output. But they do affect employment. Their impact is disastrous. Because firms must take output as given, they can only serve to cut the labour requirement for producing at that level. Anything that raises aggregate demand, on the other hand, whether it be rises in T, B_3 or $\bar{M}$, or falls in B_1 or P, will increase the need for labour.

Equation (4.20) says nothing about what will happen if the money wage rate changes. Indeed, C and N are independent of it. This is because households are assumed to receive the profits of firms, without delay or deduction (save for tax). The consequences of amending this assumption have already been discussed at length, in chapter 3. Section 4.6 of the present chapter enriches the models of Keynesian (and classical) unemployment by introducing firms' investment spending into the story. The determination of the unemployment rate is also examined below, in section 4.5.

4.2.4 *Rigid Wage Rate and Price Level, III: Repressed Inflation*

Repressed inflation is the exact opposite of Keynesian unemployment: both product and labour markets languish in a state of effective excess demand, not supply. Producers are rationed in the labour market, households in the market for goods. The additive separability assumption on utility allows us to carry (4.1b) over from the Walrasian model. The household trade-off between money balances and leisure governs this regime. Setting $m = \bar{m}$, (4.1b) can be re-expressed

$$h = \delta_2 \left(\frac{1-H}{H} \right) \left[w - p - t - b_2 + b_1 - \left(\frac{\bar{m}-p}{\delta_1} \right) \right]. \tag{4.1b}'$$

Labour supply is stimulated by a higher money wage rate or an increased demand for money, and lowered by rises in the money supply, the tax rate or the demand for leisure. The effect of a higher price level is ambiguous, since it cuts the real wage rate (discouraging labour supply) but also lowers real money holdings (making people keener to go out and earn more to rebuild them). In the Cobb–Douglas case, when $\delta_1 = 1$, these two effects cancel.

Events in the product market can be seen by setting $h = n$ and combining (4.1b)' with (4.5) to yield

$$q = \theta(a_k + k) + (1-\theta) \left[a_n + \delta_2 \left(\frac{1-H}{H} \right) \left(w - p - t - b_2 + b_1 - \left(\frac{\bar{m}-p}{\delta_1} \right) \right) \right]. \tag{4.21}$$

Output responds favourably to any development that increases the labour supply in (4.1b)'. It is also stimulated by technical advance or capital accumulation. Either of these forces must increase the output which can be forthcoming with a given supply of labour. From a policy standpoint, perhaps the most important results are that monetary expansion, and government spending increases financed by higher income taxation, will serve to lower output and employment. This occurs because they inhibit the supply of labour. Any policy to curb w will also damage these variables. Policy responses to low employment suggested under Keynesian unemployment are not just inappropriate in repressed inflation (as they were in classical unemployment); they are the precise opposite of what is needed to put matters right. As already observed in chapter 3, the dangers of repressed inflation are greatest in a Western economy when its government tries to combine vigorous monetary expansion with tight limits on money wages. We turn now to examine a case when that combination of policies, if successfully applied, looks rather appealing.

4.2.5 *Rigid Money Wage Rate and Perfectly Flexible Price: The Boundary Between Keynesian and Classical Unemployment*

Suppose now that the price level adjusts instantaneously to remove effective excess demand or supply in the product market. To that extent, at least, we step back towards the Walrasian world of 4.2.1. But the money wage rate is still exogenous, and the labour market is in a state of effective excess supply.

This is a mongrel model: both Keynesian unemployment and classical unemployment relationships hold. The one novelty is that the price level is no longer an exogenous parameter. It is now an endogenous variable. We therefore combine (4.13 and 4.14), the output and employment equations under classical unemployment, with their Keynesian unemployment counterparts (4.1a)' and the condition linking c to q, $q = c + t$. This results in

$$q \left[1 + \frac{\eta}{\delta_4} \right] = a_k + k + \eta(a_n - \bar{w}) + \eta t \left(\frac{1}{\delta_4} - \zeta \right) + \eta(1 - \ell)[\bar{m} + \delta_1(b_3 - b_1)] \tag{4.22}$$

$$n\left(1+\frac{\delta_4}{\eta}\right)(1-\theta) = \theta\left(\frac{\delta_4}{\sigma}-1\right)(a_k+k)+a_n\left[\frac{\sigma-\theta}{\sigma}\delta_4-(1-\theta)\right]$$

$$+t\left(\frac{\delta_4-\zeta}{\delta_4}\right)+\delta_3\left(b_3-b_1+\frac{m}{\delta_1}\right)-\bar{w}\delta_4 \qquad (4.23)$$

where $\delta_4 \equiv \delta_3/\delta_1(1-k)$. Equation (4.22) tells us that output reacts favourably to technical progress and capital accumulation, and also to monetary expansion and increased consumer demand. Higher demand for money, or autonomous money wage increases will restrain output. The government spending-cum-income tax parameter is ambiguous, because of its conflicting demand-side (positive) and supply-side (if anything, negative) effects. The only qualification to all this is that the demand-side influences are all completely neutralized if $k = 1$, when real wage rates will effectively be locked.

Employment changes, given by (4.23), are rather less straightforward. Capital accumulation and both types of technical progress can either raise or lower unemployment. In the pure Cobb–Douglas case, when $\delta_1 = \delta_2 = \delta_3 = \sigma = 1$, they will all be neutral if $k = 0$ and favourable if $k > 0$ (since any tendency to falling prices will then be matched by some cut in the money wage rate). The tax rate is ambiguous, as it was for output. Money wage pressure is adverse. Monetary expansion, higher consumption demand and reduced demand for money all raise employment, except in the limiting case where $k \to 1$.

The mixed classical–Keynesian unemployment regime is of direct interest for several reasons. It comes closest to the framework explored by Keynes' *General Theory* (1936), and therefore serves to encapsulate, or at least interpret, most central tenets of Keynesian and post-Keynesian thinking, while providing the explicit micro foundations for it which are so often, and so confusingly, ignored. No less important, it is probably a step towards greater realism than the 'pure' fix price models offer. There is much more evidence of price flexibility than wage flexibility in a brief period of, say, several months. In the longer run, the wage rate should respond to labour market disequilibrium. Equations (4.22) and (4.23) at least tell us what we can expect from this, even if they are silent on the form and speed of such responses. As the interval of time lengthens, the assumption of price and wage rigidities comes to look increasingly silly. But this is not to say that the Walrasian model comes back fully into its own, nor that quantity rationing is irrelevant in the long run because of its temporary nature. Short-run output changes can have enduring and powerful long-run effects, through a variety of mechanisms. Anything that influences today's investment alters the capital stock for tomorrow, and for years to come. Volatility in income, and other macroeconomic variables, can affect the forms in which wealth is accumulated, and even the demand and supply of labour.

If prices are flexible and the money wage rate is locked, the boundary between classical and Keynesian unemployment is not the only possible family of equilibrium. Price adjustments could take the economy towards the boundary between Keynesian unemployment and repressed inflation. Solutions for q and n can be found by connecting (4.1a)' with (4.14), and (4.15) with (4.1a)' to eliminate p.

4.3 The Cobb–Douglas Special Case

The advantage of restricting production and utility functions to the Cobb–Douglas form is that solutions can be found for the levels of the endogenous variables, and not just for their rates of change. It therefore provides useful illustrative guidance.

In the Walrasian case, where prices and wages are perfectly flexible and all markets clear, assume that households select M, H and C to

$$\operatorname*{Max}_{M,H,C} \left(\frac{M}{P}\right)^{\alpha} (1-H)^{\beta} C^{\gamma} + \lambda[\bar{M} + (\bar{\pi} + WH)(1-T) - M - PC] \tag{4.24}$$

$$\Rightarrow \frac{U}{\lambda} = \frac{M}{\alpha} = \frac{PC}{\beta} = \frac{W(1-H)(1-T)}{\beta}. \tag{4.25}$$

We can simplify further by imposing the condition that $M = \bar{M}$ when obtaining households' all-important consumption–leisure trade-off, and by noticing that a Cobb–Douglas production function

$$Q = AK^{\delta}N^{1-\delta} \qquad 1 > \delta > 0 \tag{4.26}$$

entails that $\bar{\pi} = \delta PQ = (\delta/1 - T)PC$. Substitution into the first-order conditions for household optimization gives solution for H (or N) and C:

$$H = [1 + \beta/\gamma(1-\delta)]^{-1}$$

$$C = \frac{W}{P} \frac{1-T}{1-\delta} [1 + \beta/\gamma(1-\delta)]^{-1}.$$

Producer optimization entails that $N = K[PA(1-\delta)/W]^{1/\delta}$, $Q = KA^{1/\delta} \times [P(1-\delta)/W]^{(1-\delta)/\delta}$. Real endogenous variables can now be solved, since $N = H$ and $(1-T)Q = C$. The nominals can all be found from the consumption–money trade-off $P = (\beta/\alpha)(\bar{M}/C)$.

The classical unemployment results for N and Q are provided directly from the producer optimization conditions, at least in the simple case where W is independent of P and T. In Keynesian unemployment, the consumption–money trade-off condition can be invested to give

$$Q = \frac{\beta}{\alpha} \frac{\bar{M}}{P(1-T)}. \tag{4.27}$$

This displays the favourable output effects of real balance or tax increases. Employment can be found by inverting the production function (4.26) so that

$$N = \left[\frac{\beta}{\alpha} \frac{\bar{M}}{P(1-T)}\right]^{1/(1-\delta)} [AK^{\delta}]^{-1/(1-\delta)} \tag{4.28}$$

The adverse consequences for jobs from technical progress (A rises) or capital accumulation are directly evident. The repressed inflation results follow at once from households' money–leisure trade-off, $\bar{M} = \alpha/\beta[W(1-H)(1-T)]$. Making H the subject:

$$H = 1 - \left[\frac{\beta}{\alpha(1-T)} \frac{\bar{M}}{W}\right] \tag{4.29}$$

so that

$$Q = \left[1 - \frac{\beta}{\alpha(1-T)} \frac{\bar{M}}{W}\right]^{1-\delta} AK^{\delta}.$$

Lastly, the classical unemployment Keynesian unemployment boundary, where P is an endogenous variable, gives rise to

$$N = \frac{1-\delta}{W}\frac{\beta}{\alpha}\bar{M}$$

$$Q = AK^\delta\left[\frac{1-\delta}{W}\frac{\beta}{\alpha}\bar{M}\right]^{1-\delta}.$$

(4.30)

4.4 Extension to Many Sectors

This section extends the Cobb–Douglas model of the previous section from one sector to many. Each good i (of which there are n in all) is produced subject to the Cobb–Douglas production function

$$q_i = T_i k_i^\delta n_i^{1-\delta} \qquad i = 1,\dots n$$

(4.31)

which all firms making that good share. Capital is allocated equally among such firms. Every household has a utility fraction

$$U = \prod_{i=1}^n \left(\frac{M}{P_i}\right)^{\alpha\gamma_i}(1-h)^\beta(c_i)^{\gamma_i} \qquad \begin{array}{l}\sum\gamma_i = 1 \\ \alpha, \beta, \gamma_i > 0.\end{array}$$

(4.32)

Each shares a common budget restraint

$$\bar{M} + \sum_i (\pi_i + whi_i) - M - \sum_i P_i C_i.$$

(4.33)

Households supply labour to, and derive wage and profit income from, each product sector. The household's notional equilibrium, achieved when it is rationed in no market, occurs when the following first-order conditions are fulfilled:

$$\frac{M}{\alpha} = \frac{w(1-h)}{\beta} = \frac{P_i C_i}{\gamma_i} \qquad \forall_i i = 1,\dots n.$$

(4.34)

The producers' notional equilibria are obtained by maximizing profits $P_i q_i - wn_i$ subject to (4.31). This gives rise to

$$n_i = k_i\left[\frac{P_i(1-\delta)T_i}{w}\right]^{1/\delta}$$

(4.35)

$$q_i = k_i T_i^{1/\delta}\left[\frac{P_i(1-\delta)}{w}\right]^{(1-\delta)/\delta}.$$

(4.36)

In what follows, we shall assume the presence of involuntary unemployment. Any good in effective excess demand will display output q_i given by

$$q_i = k_i T_i^{1/\delta}\left(\frac{P_i(1-\delta)}{w}\right)^{(1-\delta)/\delta} < \frac{\gamma_i\bar{M}}{\alpha}.$$

(4.37)

For good j in effective excess supply, on the other hand,

$$q_j = \frac{\gamma_i\bar{M}}{\alpha} < k_j T_j^{1/\delta}\left(\frac{P_j(1-\delta)}{w}\right)^{1-\delta/\delta}.$$

(4.38)

Producers of good i are unrationed in their product market, while firms producing j are rationed by insufficient demand. Suppose that w and all prices are frozen, and that the first m of the n goods markets are in a state of classical unemployment ((4.37) applies), while the remainder are in Keynesian unemployment (when (4.38) holds). The economy's total effective demand for labour, N, will be given by

$$N = \sum_{i=1}^{m} k_i \left(\frac{P_i(1-\delta)T_i}{w} \right)^{1/\delta} + \sum_{j=m+1}^{n} \left[\frac{\gamma_i \bar{M}}{\alpha P_i T_j k_j^{\delta}} \right]^{1/(1-\delta)}. \tag{4.39}$$

The nominal value of national income, meanwhile, will be

$$\sum P_i q_i + \sum P_j q_j = \left(\frac{1-\delta}{w} \right)^{(1-\delta)/\delta} \sum_{i=1}^{m} [K_i T_i^{1/\delta} P_i^{(1-\delta)/\delta}] + \left(\frac{\bar{M}}{\alpha} \right) \sum_{j=m+1}^{n} \gamma_j. \tag{4.40}$$

Total employment will be boosted by price increases, technical progress or capital accumulation in the classical sectors, and damaged by them in the Keynesian ones. A higher wage rate squeezes employment in the classical sectors, and leaves it unchanged in the Keynesian industries (since profits are distributed in full to households, and a higher wage rate simply relabels households' incomes). Monetary expansion stimulates output and employment in Keynesian sectors, and has no effect on these variables among the classical industries. If capital is free to move across industries, there may be a tendency for employment to grow, to the extent that profit rates may be higher in the classical industries than in their Keynesian counterparts.

If we now assume that the money wage rate is locked, but that goods prices adjust to remove effective excess supplies and demands in product markets, and that the economy remains in an unemployment state, P_i and P_j will move to transform (4.37) and (4.38) into strict equalities. In this case, total employment reduces to

$$N = \frac{\bar{M}}{w} \frac{1-\delta}{\alpha}. \tag{4.41}$$

Equation (4.41) is an arrestingly simple result. Employment is directly proportional to the ratio of the money supply to the money wage rate, and unaffected by technical progress, the level or allocation of the capital stock or the pattern of consumer demand.

4.5 Extension to Partial Rationing Among Households

Previous sections have assumed that, if any household is rationed, all are rationed. Unemployment takes the form of everyone having to accept less time at work than they would wish. In this section, we show how this can be relaxed. Instead, proportion θ of households will be totally unemployed, with no wage income at all. The remaining $1-\theta$ can work as long as they like. To simplify matters, we return to the single-sector framework of section 4.3.

Every household has the utility function

$$U = \left(\frac{M}{P} \right)^{\alpha} (1-h)^{\beta} c^{\gamma} \tag{4.42}$$

which the unconstrained households are fortunate enough to be able to maximize freely, with respect to their three choice parameters M, and c, subject to the restraint

$$\bar{M} + \bar{\pi} + w - M - w(1-h) - PC = 0. \tag{4.43}$$

The consumption level of these households, $C_{1-\theta}$, emerges directly:

$$C_{1-\theta} = \frac{\gamma}{P}(\bar{M} + \bar{\pi} + w). \tag{4.44}$$

The unemployed households maximize (4.42) with respect to their two choice variables, M and C, subject to simplified budget restraints

$$\bar{M} + \bar{\pi} - M - PC = 0. \tag{4.45}$$

Their level of h is constrained at zero. The consumption of the unemployed, C_θ, will be

$$C_\theta = \frac{\gamma}{\alpha + \gamma} \frac{\bar{M} + \bar{\pi}}{P}. \tag{4.46}$$

Aggregate consumption per head, $\tilde{C}$, will be a weighted average of (4.44) and (4.46). The weights will be given by $1 - \theta$ and θ. Hence, where $v \equiv \beta\theta(\alpha + \gamma)^{-1}$,

$$\tilde{C} = \gamma\left[\frac{\bar{M} + \bar{\pi}}{P}(1+v) + \frac{1-\theta}{P}w\right]. \tag{4.47}$$

(We have assumed that all households, employed and unemployed alike, receive the same endowments of money and profits.) The labour supply of those at work, $h_{1-\theta}$, also emerges from the first-order conditions for maximizing (4.42) subject to (4.43):

$$h_{1-\theta} = 1 - \beta\left[\frac{\bar{M} + \bar{\pi} + w}{w}\right]. \tag{4.48}$$

Since profits, $\bar{\pi}$, will equal $P\tilde{C} - w(1-\theta)h_{1-\theta}$, we can solve for $\bar{\pi}$:

$$\bar{\pi}\alpha^{-1} = \frac{\bar{M}[\gamma(1+v) + \beta(1-\theta)] - \alpha w(1-\theta)}{(1+v)}. \tag{4.49}$$

Substituting (4.49) into (4.47) gives us the simple result

$$\tilde{C} = \frac{\gamma}{\alpha}\frac{\bar{M}}{P}. \tag{4.50}$$

Now assume the presence of Keynesian unemployment. Producers are therefore rationed in the goods market. If they share the production function

$$q = Tk^\delta n^{1-\delta} \Rightarrow n = \left[\frac{\tilde{C}}{Tk^\delta}\right]^{1/1-\delta} \tag{4.51}$$

(we assume that households provide the only source of effective demand for final output, so that $q = \tilde{C}$). The model can be solved for the employment level, $1 - \theta$, by linking (4.48), (4.49) and (4.51) to the condition $n = (1-\theta)h_{1-\theta}$:

$$1 - \theta = \left[1 + \frac{\alpha + \gamma}{\beta}\frac{\alpha - \beta\dfrac{\bar{M}}{w}}{x}\right]^{-1}. \tag{4.52}$$

In (4.52),

$$x \equiv \left[\frac{\delta \bar{M}}{PT(\alpha k)^{\delta}} \right]^{1/(1-\delta)}.$$

Equation (4.52) reveals that the unemployment rate, θ, increases unambiguously in the following circumstances:

1   if the money supply falls,
2   if the wage rate rises,
3   if the price level rises,
4   if technical progress occurs ($dT > 0$),
5   if there is capital accumulation.

There are two reasons for (1). A reduction in the money supply squeezes the consumption of those in and out of work, as is evident from (4.44) and (4.46). Secondly, it increases the labour supply of those in work, as (4.48) testifies. This cuts the number of jobs available. The second of these effects also operates in the case of a money wage increase, case (2). The remaining possible adverse influences on unemployment, (3), (4) and (5) are familiar from the simpler quantity-rationing model studied in section 4.3.

These results arise in Keynesian unemployment. How does the model apply to classical unemployment? We must return to the production function, (4.51). Since firms will now be able to achieve their notional equilibria in the goods and labour markets, profit maximization establishes

$$n = k\left[\frac{(1-\delta)PT}{w} \right]^{1/\delta}, q = kT^{1/\delta}\left(\frac{(1-\delta)P}{w} \right)^{(1-\delta)/\delta}. \tag{4.53}$$

Furthermore, $\bar{\pi} = \delta PQ$ and $\bar{\pi}/w = \delta n(1-\delta)^{-1}$.

If we assume that employed households are able to satisfy their consumption demands, (4.48) will give their hours of work. $\bar{\pi}/w$ will be replaced by $\delta n(1-\delta)^{-1}$. Labour market equilibrium will occur where the demand for labour, given by (4.53), balances (4.48) multiplied by the proportion of those in work, $1-\theta$. Consequently we can solve for $1-\theta$:

$$1-\theta = \left[\frac{1 - \beta\left(1 + \dfrac{\bar{M}}{w} \right)}{k}\left(\frac{w}{PT(1-\delta)} \right)^{1/\delta} - \frac{\beta\delta}{1-\delta} \right]^{-1}. \tag{4.54}$$

Equation (4.54) shows the following effects. Unemployment (θ) increases unambiguously if:

1   the money supply falls,
2   the capital stock increases,
3   there is technical progress,
4   the money wage rate increases.

Results (2) and (3) are familiar from our inquiry into classical unemployment in section 4.3. Result (1) arises because a money supply increase reduces preferred work hours of those in work (see (4.48)). This increases the number of jobs available for the unemployed. The adverse effect of a higher money wage rate is twofold: firms cut back on employment and production (see (4.53)), and unrationed households seek to supply more labour time, squeezing the number of jobs free for everyone else.

If the price level adjusts to remove effective excess supply (or demand) in the product market, both (4.52) and (4.54) hold, with the price level moving to ensure that they are consistent. When $\delta = \frac{1}{2}$, for example, we find

$$\frac{1-\theta}{\theta} y - \frac{1}{1-\theta} = \beta \tag{4.55}$$

where

$$y \equiv \left(\frac{2\alpha}{\gamma}\right)^2 \left[\frac{w}{\bar{M}}(\alpha+\gamma) - \beta\right] \left[\frac{(\alpha+\gamma)\left(\alpha\dfrac{w}{\bar{M}} - \beta\right)}{\beta}\right].$$

In (4.55), θ will increase with y for given β, and since y increases with the ratio of w to $\bar{M}$, we obtain the result, familiar along the boundary between Keynesian and classical unemployment that unemployment is lowered by monetary expansion and increases with the money wage rate. It is interesting to note that increases in capital or technology have no effect on unemployment in this case, just as in the corresponding equation (4.41) in section 4.4.

4.6 Wages and Investment

Until now, the capital stock has been an exogenous parameter. The emphasis has been placed upon static models. Changes in variables have taken the form of hypothetical, instantaneous disturbances, or immediate reactions to them. The analysis has been comparatively static. Furthermore, no attention has been paid to firms' investment decisions: it has been the consumption decisions of households that has governed aggregate demand in the product market.

In this section, a simple model of investment will be set up. For the sake of convenience we shall abstract from such matters as taxation, differences between capital goods, forecasting mistakes and the costs of adjusting the stock of capital, in order to illuminate the central relationships as economically as possible.

Investment can have two major effects on unemployment. While it is occurring there are jobs to be had in the industries that produce the capital goods. A burst of investment will have a powerful if transient impact on aggregate demand. If the economy suffers from a Keynesian form of unemployment, the boost to jobs will be direct. Under classical unemployment, higher output in the capital goods industries has no immediate special impact on total employment, since there is already excess demand for goods. The second effect of investment on unemployment is indirect, and gradual. Investment today increases tomorrow's stock of capital. As we have seen, a higher stock of capital will imply increased producers' demand for labour in a world of classical unemployment, and reduced demand under Keynesian conditions. When the economy lies on the boundary of the two types of unemployment, the two effects can cancel directly (as they did in (4.41) and (4.55)).

We start with Keynesian unemployment. Imagine that firms know that they are rationed in the product market. They face a current demand constraint $\bar{q}_0$ (at date 0). Similar constraints are known for subsequent periods $(\bar{q}_1, \bar{q}_2, \ldots)$. They face a money wage rate of w_0 for labour hired now, and $w_1, w_2, \ldots$, for subsequent periods.

Employment can be switched on and off like a tap; there are no costs of hiring or firing, and employment is renewed afresh in each period. They share a common production function for date t:

$$q_t = Tk_t^\alpha n_t^\beta \qquad 1 > \alpha, \beta > 0. \tag{4.56}$$

For simplicity's sake, T, the technology level, is taken as constant.

Capital goods are bought, not rented. The price of a machine at date t is M_t. The sequence of $M_0, M_1, \ldots$ is known. The capital goods industry which produces these objects is assumed to employ labour as a sole factor of production, and there are constant returns to scale there. Assuming perfect competition, the price of capital goods will equal their unit production costs:

$$M_t = w_t/\theta. \tag{4.57}$$

θ denotes the productivity of labour; like T, it is constant. Capital always depreciates at the rate δ, so that a machine produced at date 1, for example, will command a price of $(1-\delta)^2 w_3/\theta$ two periods later. We shall assume that firms who want to sell old machines are never rationed in that market.

The amount of investment at t, I_t, is assumed to be added in full to the capital stock in the following period. Consequently,

$$k_{t+1} = (1-\delta)k_t + I_t = (1-\delta)^2 k_{t-1} + (1-\delta)I_{t-1} + I_t = \ldots. \tag{4.58}$$

Since firms are rationed in the product market, they will seek to minimize their total costs of production. Equation (4.56) can be inverted to give

$$n_t = \left(\frac{\bar{q}_t}{T}\right)^{1/\beta} k_t^{-(\alpha/\beta)} \tag{4.59}$$

so that wage costs at t will be $w_t k_t^{-(\alpha/\beta)}(\bar{q}_t/T)^{1/\beta}$. The advantage of additional capital is that it allows the firm to save on labour costs. The drawback is the price paid for acquiring it. Profit maximization entails a trade-off between capital and labour where the marginal cost of capital just balances the marginal reduction in wages it permits.

If r is the rate of interest (which we shall assume to be constant over time, and the same for borrowing and lending) and $v \equiv (1+r)^{-1}$, the discounted present value of profits, at date 0, will be

$$\pi_0 = P_0 \bar{q}_0 + P_1 \bar{q}_1 v + P_2 \bar{q}_2 v^2 + \ldots$$

$$- w_0 \left[\frac{\bar{q}_0}{T}\right]^{1/\beta} k_0^{-(\alpha/\beta)} - v w_1 \left[\frac{\bar{q}_1}{T}\right]^{1/\beta} (k_0(1-\delta) + I_0)^{-(\alpha/\beta)} - \ldots$$

$$- m_0 I_0 - m_1 I_1 v - \ldots$$

$$= \sum_{i=0}^{\infty} \left\{ P_i \bar{q}_i v^i - v^i w_i \left[\frac{\bar{q}_i}{T}\right]^{1/\beta} \{k_0(1-\delta)^i + I_0(1-\delta)^{i-1} + \ldots \right.$$

$$\left. + I_{i-1}\}^{-(\alpha/\beta)} - m_i I_i v^i \right\}. \tag{4.60}$$

The firm will seek an investment plan, I_0^*, I_1^*, I_2^*, that makes (4.60) as high as possible.

Differentiating π_0 with respect to I_0, and setting the result equal to zero, gives

$$0 = -m_0 + \frac{\alpha}{\beta} \sum_{i=1}^{\infty} v^i w_i \left[\frac{\bar{q}_i}{T} \right]^{1/\beta} \{k_0(1-\delta)^i$$

$$+ \sum_{j=1}^{i-1} (1-\delta)^{i-j} I_j\}^{-(\alpha/\beta)} (1-\delta)^{i-1} \quad (4.61)$$

and a similar condition for I, yields

$$0 = -m_1 v + \frac{\alpha}{\beta} \sum_{i=2}^{\infty} v^i w_i \left[\frac{\bar{q}_i}{T} \right]^{1/\beta} \{k_0(1-\delta)^i$$

$$+ \sum_{j=1}^{i-1} (1-\delta)^{i-j} I_j\}^{-(\alpha/\beta)} (1-\delta)^{i-1}. \quad (4.62)$$

Subtraction of (4.62) from (4.61) establishes the optimum investment level for the current period

$$I_i = -k_0(1-\delta) + \left[\frac{\frac{\alpha}{\beta} v w_1 \left(\frac{\bar{q}_1}{T} \right)^{1/\beta}}{m_0 - m_1 v(1-\delta)} \right]^{\alpha/\alpha + \beta}. \quad (4.63)$$

Using (4.57), and assuming that x represents the rate of increase in money wages, (4.63) can be re-expressed as

$$I_0 = -k_0(1-\delta) + \left[\frac{\alpha\theta}{\beta \left(\frac{1+r}{1+x} - 1 + \delta \right)} \right]^{\beta/\alpha + \beta} \left(\frac{\bar{q}_1}{T} \right)^{1/\alpha + \beta}. \quad (4.64)$$

Some quite predictable results emerge from (4.64). Gross investment is negatively related to the rate of interest, r. It varies positively with the level of demand expected in the next period, $\bar{q}_1$. Replacement investment is boosted, and net investment restrained, by the depreciation rate, δ. But there are also surprises. The level of technology (in the industry employing the capital good) exerts a negative effect upon investment. This testifies to the Keynesian unemployment: a technical improvement lowers the demand for inputs, capital or labour, to produce an exogenously given quantum of output. More surprising is the effect of x, the rate of wage inflation. Investment is boosted by x. The reason for this is that faster wage inflation means a faster rate of increase in the price of new capital goods. It will become more attractive to pre-empt them, and perhaps sell them later. The cost of renting capital decreases when the price of capital goods is expected to rise more quickly. On the other hand, if higher x is fully reflected in a higher value of the rate of interest, r, the level of investment is unaffected. Similar results can be found for the growth in investment, $I_1 - I_0$.

While investment is occurring at a substantial rate, employment in the capital goods industry will be high. But unless the sequence of qs rises fast enough, capital accumulation will serve to undermine employment in the other, consumption–goods sector. Define total employment at date t, n_t^T, as the sum of n_t^I and n_t^C (the employment levels in these two industries). From (4.59) and (4.64), and the capital–goods sector's production function $I_t = \theta n_t^I$, we have

$$n_0^T = \left[\frac{\bar{q}_0}{T k_0} \right]^{1/\beta} + \frac{1}{\theta} \left[\left[\frac{\alpha\theta}{\beta \left(\frac{1+r}{1+x} - 1 + \delta \right)} \right]^{\beta/(\alpha + \beta)} \left(\frac{\bar{q}_1}{T} \right)^{1/(\alpha + \beta)} - k_0(1-\delta) \right]. \quad (4.65)$$

Total employment in later periods can be found by similar means. Previous investment is damaging to current employment, all else equal, because it will have come to be incorporated in the present capital stock, k_0. The higher k_0 is, all else equal, the lower the demand for labour in both sectors, as (4.65) shows.

The simple model of investment under Keynesian unemployment sketched here points out an interesting issue. There is a time dimension to the demand for labour. Employment can be boosted in one period, but at a cost in reduced employment later. If monetary policy succeeds in pegging the rate of interest well below the rate at which money wage rates are advancing, investment will be high. This is illustrated clearly by (4.64). The current level of employment will also be high, because of the strong demand for labour in the capital-goods sector. But policy of this kind is not really curing unemployment. It is *retiming* it. Jobs are being borrowed from the future. In most of the post-war period, money wages increased rather faster than the level of the interest rate. In the late 1960s and 1970s, there were years when x exceeded r by as much as 5 per cent or 7 per cent on an annual basis, in the UK. Not dissimilar magnitudes could be observed in the United States. The 1950s and 1960s witnessed a high and growing level of capital formation in most Western economies. But by the late 1960s the expansion in investment started to taper off, perhaps chiefly as a response to falling rates of profit on capital on many definitions. It was becoming progressively harder to coax companies into substantial investment projects. By the 1970s, particularly after the first oil shock, private sector investment outlays fell heavily, and unemployment began to climb.

Employment losses were particularly acute in the UK, Germany, France and the US in the steel, automotive and construction sectors most directly affected by the faltering level of investment. These trends became increasingly painful in the late 1970s and early 1980s. They were no doubt accentuated by the behaviour of nominal and real interest rates. The 1970s was a decade of mainly negative real interest rates. This perhaps reflected governments' anxiety at the time to combat the rise in unemployment by trying to sustain capital spending with a low ratio of $1+r$ to $1+x$. But with the emergence of high real interest rates in the 1980s, $r-x$ swung positive. Nominal earnings have grown at between 3 per cent and 6 per cent below the annualized Treasury Bill rate of interest for most of periods since 1981, in both the UK and the US. It is natural to blame these developments for some of the current high levels of unemployment. Yet the massive increases in unemployment in the early 1930s may be seen as a consequence of high, perhaps excessive levels of investment in previous periods. This argument has particular appeal in the case of the United States. The capital stock grew there by over 30 per cent in the 1920s, when the average unemployment rate was under 4 per cent. Between 1930 and 1933, gross private investment fell by over 80 per cent in the United States, and unemployment climbed to over 30 per cent. It is more than possible that some of the weakness in the labour markets in the early 1980s can be traced to the long investment boom of the previous three decades. Many economists think that the UK is now faced, in a sense, with the opposite problem. Years of Keynesian recession may have led to such an erosion of the capital stock, at least in certain sectors, that employment may be held back by shortages of capital. Keynesian unemployment can become classical.

So much for investment under Keynesian unemployment; what of classical unemployment? In these circumstances, producers will be able to attain their notional equilibrium in labour and product markets. The output rates q_t become endogenous variables, chosen by firms. The present-value-of-profits function,

(4.60), now becomes

$$\pi_0 = \sum_{i=0}^{\infty} [P_i T k_i^{\alpha} n_i^{\beta} - w_i n_i - m_i I_i] v^i \qquad 1 > \alpha, \beta > 0. \tag{4.66}$$

The firm will seek an investment plan $(I_0^*, I_1^*, \dots)$ and an employment plan $(n_0^*, n_1^*, \dots)$ to maximize equation (4.66). Together these will imply an output plan $(q_0^*, q_1^*, \dots)$. We shall assume that α and β sum to less than unity. (If $\alpha + \beta = 1$, the scale of the ns and Is will be indeterminate.) For simplicity's sake, assume further that $\beta = \frac{1}{2}$. In other respects, previous assumptions made in the Keynesian unemployment case carry over to this one.

Marginal productivity pricing will give rise to relations between n_t^* and k_t^*:

$$n_t^* = \left(\frac{P_t T k_t^{*\alpha}}{2w_t} \right)^2. \tag{4.67}$$

The optimum investment levels will follow the sequence

$$I_0^* = -k_0(1-\delta) + \left[\frac{P_1 T}{w_1} \right]^{2/(1-2\alpha)} \left[\frac{\alpha\theta}{2\left[\frac{1+r}{1+x} - (1-\delta) \right]} \right]^{1/(1-2\alpha)}$$

$$I_1^* = \left[\frac{P_2 T}{w_2} \right]^{2/(1-2\alpha)} \left[1 - (1-\delta) \left[\frac{P_1 T}{w_1} \right]^{2/(1-2\alpha)} \right] \left[\frac{\alpha\theta}{2\left[\frac{1+r}{1+x} - (1-\delta) \right]} \right]^{1/(1-2\alpha)}$$

$$\vdots \qquad\qquad\qquad \vdots$$

$$I_t^* = \left(\frac{P_t T}{w_t} \right)^{2/(1-2\alpha)} \left\{ 1 - (1-\delta) \left(\frac{P_t - 1^T}{w_{t-1}} \right)^{2/(1-2\alpha)} \right\} \left[\frac{\alpha\theta}{2\left[\frac{1+r}{1+x} - (1-\delta) \right]} \right]^{1/(1-2\alpha)}$$

$$\tag{4.68}$$

Optimum employment levels can be solved from (4.67) and (4.68). The time path of investment depends primarily upon the course taken by the product price, P, and the wage rate, w. The lower the product real wage at date t, the more attractive it will be to offer substantial employment then, and to build up the capital stock to exploit profit opportunities to the full. But other variables, such as r and x, matter too. The faster the expected increase in machine prices (and that means the more quickly money wage rates are expected to climb) the greater the inducement to invest. This is evident from (4.68), and resembles our findings in the Keynesian unemployment case. A higher value of r, on the other hand, has the conventional disincentive effect upon investment.

5 Fiscally Induced Unemployment: A Geometrical Account of the Demand and Supply of Unemployment

5.1 Introduction

This chapter presents an introductory, geometrical account of how unemployment interacts with the government's fiscal policy instruments. It is concerned with how unemployment can emerge as an incidental and unwanted by-product of policy measures to reduce economic inequalities. Section 5.2 lays down and discusses assumptions, while section 5.3 explores the 'demand' for unemployment. The 'supply' of unemployment is the subject of sections 5.4 and 5.5, which offer a contrast between benefits conferred to those out of work and unconditional transfers paid to everyone. Section 5.6 integrates these demand and supply relations, and section 5.7 poses optimum policy choices under different assumptions about social objectives. Section 5.8 presents an important qualification.

Algebra is almost wholly avoided in this chapter. A more technical account of the subject matter covered by it is presented in chapter 6.

5.2 Assumptions

In this chapter, we shall retain three features of the basic quantity-rationing model examined in the last. We shall continue to operate with an economy which produces just one good; the analysis will again be confined to a single time period; and household preferences will again be captured by a Cobb–Douglas utility function.

But that is where the similarities end. Two important new elements now enter the story. First, the government taxes incomes in order to finance transfer payments which are designed to improve the welfare of the less fortunate members of society. Second, households are now allowed to differ in their ability to earn. Those who can command the highest wage rates are the most advantaged and the most unlucky are those who can earn least.

In order to simplify matters, some features of the last chapter now drop out. We get rid of money: households' preferences now relate only to consumption and leisure. Markets now always clear. Instead of diminishing returns, we adopt the more convenient assumption for our present purposes, which is that of constant returns to labour. Capital disappears as a factor of production, and so do profits earned on it.

Some special assumptions, which we shall now and then have occasion to relax, are: (a) the distribution of abilities in the population is uniform between a maximum of 1 and a minimum of 0; (b) original (wage) income is taxed at a single rate t; and (c) all tax proceeds are returned as transfer payments, either to everyone or only to the unemployed as a form of dole.

It is now time to see what these assumptions imply.

5.3 The Demand for Unemployment

Consider, first, the case where tax receipts finance unemployment benefit payments confined to those out of work. The assumptions of the last section will then imply that total unemployment benefits paid out must equal total income tax receipts. Total tax receipts are the product of national income, Q, and the tax rate, t. Total unemployment benefits paid will equal the rate of benefit, b, multiplied by the numbers out of work who receive it, U. If q and u represent the level of income per head, and the rate of unemployment, respectively, we have the equation

$$bu = tq.$$

It is worth stressing the conditions under which this holds: government financial outflows must be restricted to the payment of unemployment benefits, and exclude, for example, any direct expenditure by the state; the budget is balanced, so that disbursements are matched by tax receipts; and taxation takes the form of a single-rate tax on all original incomes (that is, wage earnings, in this model).

What does the equation $bu = tq$ tell us? The central implication is that for given levels of t and q, b and u must be negatively related. Indeed, when total tax receipts are given, b and u are inversely proportional to each other. A curve showing the relation between b and u for given t and q will be a rectangular hyperbola. This is depicted in figure 5.1.

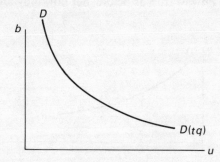

Figure 5.1 *The demand for unemployment, for a given total yield of taxation*

The curve in figure 5.1 is what can best be called the demand curve for unemployment. Hence its label *DD* in the diagram. There is a problem with the curve as drawn. This is the assumption that both *t* and *q* are given. The tax rate may rightly be treated as a parameter, chosen by the government, or at least set by them so as to balance their budget. But *q* varies with the unemployment rate, *u*. The higher the level of unemployment, the less work will be done, and the smaller the level of income per head. We can write $q = q(u)$ in recognition of this fact.

Our equation $bu = tq(u)$ can be re-expressed to give *b* in terms of *u* and *t*:

$$b = t\frac{q(u)}{u}.$$

This is a helpful rearrangement. It shows that an increase in unemployment will tend to reduce the scale of benefit payments, when the tax rate is given, for *two* reasons. First, there is the fact that the benefits have to be spread over more recipients: this is captured by the term *u* on the denominator. Second, a rise in *u* means a drop, perhaps not a large one but an inevitable drop nonetheless, in *q*: and this also implies a lower value of *b*. Allowing for the dependence of *q* upon *u* causes us to modify figure 5.1 somewhat. The demand curve for unemployment is a little more elastic than the rectangular hyperbola presented in figure 5.1: this is in recognition of the fact that there are really two influences running from *u* to *b* when *t* is given, both of them negative, and not just one as in figure 5.1. Hence the revised picture in figure 5.2. The demand curve will cross the horizontal axis at an unemployment level of 100 per cent. If no one is at work, nothing gets produced, and tax receipts vanish, too.

As we shall see later, it is the less able who are most prone to unemployment. Hence an increase in the level of unemployment is liable to cause a greater loss of output when unemployment is high, rather than low. This suggests that the demand curve should get progressively less elastic as unemployment increases. Were government spending to enter the picture, its effect would be to displace the demand curve leftwards. A higher rate of tax would push the demand curve to the right.

If transfer payments are made to everyone regardless of whether he or she is at work or not, our critical equation becomes

$$c = tq(u).$$

This states that the transfer payment, *c*, equals average tax receipts per head (the tax rate *t*, multiplied by original income per head). The demand curve for unemployment slopes downwards, as before, but now only for one reason: the fact

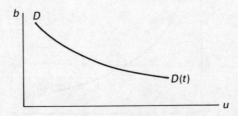

Figure 5.2 *The demand for unemployment, for a given tax rate*

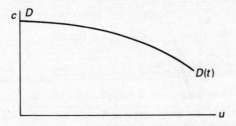

Figure 5.3 *The demand curve for unemployment: the unconditional transfer and the unemployment level, for a given tax rate*

that higher unemployment accompanies reduced output. Since the output loss implicit in a rise in unemployment increases as the unemployment level bites deeper into the distribution of abilities across the population, the shape of the demand curve is concave, rather than convex. Figure 5.3 illustrates this. The curve crosses the horizontal axis at an unemployment rate of 100 per cent, however, just as in figure 5.2.

5.4 The Supply of Unemployment, I: The Unemployment Benefit Case

In the model of this chapter, people choose whether or not to participate in the labour force. In marked contrast to the quantity-rationing model examined in the last two chapters, unemployment in this chapter is essentially voluntary. Those who do not work are unemployed because they are better off that way: their utility out of work is higher than the best that they could achieve in work.

This does not mean that those out of work are happier than those who are employed. In fact, the reverse will be true. The employed must be better off in work than out of it, because that is what they have chosen to do. If everyone has the same preferences, the utility received by being out of work will be the same for everyone who is unemployed. They all receive a common benefit payment, b, and they all enjoy the same, full ration of leisure time.

The higher your ability to earn, the greater your income if you work, and the more you can spend on consumption. Hence utility will increase with ability-to-earn when a cross-section of the population is compared. Figure 5.4 illustrates this idea, with the concave curve labelled FF. It must slope up, because income and

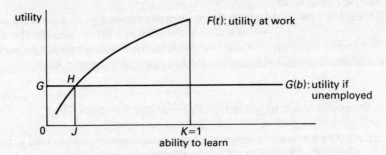

Figure 5.4 *Utility and ability-to-earn and the supply of unemployment*

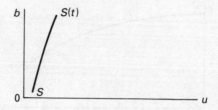

Figure 5.5 *The supply of unemployment, for a given rate*

consumption increase with ability-to-earn. It is concave if the marginal utility of consumption diminishes (the Cobb–Douglas utility function ensures that those at work will all opt to work for the same length of time, no matter how high the real wage rate per unit time that they can command). Those out of work, on the other hand, will all gain a utility level OG. The height of OG depends on b, and nothing else.

Those with lowest ability to earn will have greater utility from unemployment (OG) than what could be gained by working (FF). Everyone with ability-to-earn less than or equal to J will opt for unemployment. Point H, where GG (a horizontal line depicting the utility of unemployment) intersects FF, is the cut-off point which gives the ability-to-earn of the ablest unemployed individual (point J on the horizontal axis). Everyone with ability above this will prefer to be in work. Figure 5.4 depicts the paradox that the unemployed are better off not working, but are worse off than everyone at work.

We have stipulated that abilities to earn are distributed uniformly across the population between a ceiling of 1 and a floor of 0. Figure 5.5 therefore gives us the unemployment rate, u: the ratio OJ/OK will be the proportion of the population out of work. There are two variables that determine this 'supply of unemployment'. One is the rate of benefit. An increase in benefit will raise the utility of unemployment. The horizontal line GG will be pushed up, intersecting the FF curve further to the right, implying a higher level of unemployment. The other factor that governs the supply of unemployment is less obvious. It is the tax rate, t. A higher income tax rate will imply a reduction in the after-tax income, and hence consumption, enjoyed by those in work. So the utility to be had from employment will fall. The curve $FF(t)$ will drop a little. Again, the new point of intersection with the utility-of-unemployment line is to the right of the old one. The supply of unemployment therefore increases with b and with t, although it will probably be more sensitive to b than to t.

These ideas are now presented in a new diagram, figure 5.5. This gives the supply of unemployment as a function of b, for a given level of t. Given what has been said, the curve SS must slope up, and must be displaced rightwards by an increase in the tax rate, t. It will be concave (as drawn) if FF is concave in figure 5.4.

5.5 The Supply of Unemployment, II: The Transfer Payment Case

When tax receipts are used to finance a lump-sum transfer paid to everyone, and not just a benefit for those out of work, the supply of unemployment becomes rather more complicated. The clue is to explore what determines people's preferred

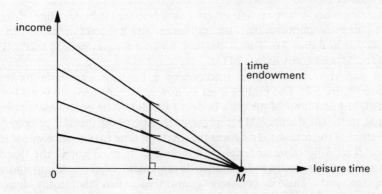

Figure 5.6 *Labour supply and income levels, when the transfer payment is zero*

hours of work. Suppose, to start with, that no transfer is paid. From our Cobb–Douglas utility assumption, we know that everyone will seek to work for the same length of time, no matter what wage they can command. Figure 5.6 depicts this.

The locus of points of tangency between successive budget lines rotated through point M, the time endowment point, and indifference curves, will be the vertical line drawn up from point L. The different budget lines show the differing opportunity sets of our individuals: those who can earn most have the steepest; the least

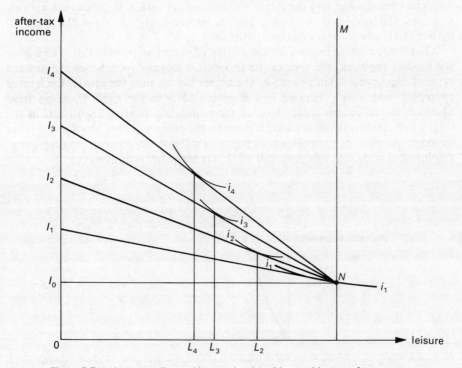

Figure 5.7 *Labour supplies and income levels, with a positive transfer payment*

fortunate member of society effectively has a horizontal budget line, if we are to stick to our assumption that the minimum ability level is zero. No one is unemployed in figure 5.6. This is because no transfer payment is made. They all work for *LM*, and enjoy leisure of *OL*.

Now consider the effects of introducing a positive wage-sum payment for everyone (figure 5.7). The budget lines all now move upwards. *M* is no longer the lowest right-hand limit of people's budget restraints. The endowment point shifts upwards, to *N*. The distance *MN* represents the size of the transfer payment made.

The effect of the transfer is to lower the length of time that anyone wants to spend at work. This follows immediately if leisure is a 'normal good', the demand for which rises with an outward, parallel displacement of the relevant individual's budget restraint. This is certainly guaranteed when the utility function is Cobb–Douglas. Those with high ability to earn do not lower their labour supply very much, since the transfer payment seems quite modest to them, given their large earned income. But those with low ability, whose budget restraints are very flat, will reduce preferred work time quite dramatically. Indeed, if their ability to earn is low enough and the transfer payment large enough, they will stop work completely, and 'consume' at point *N*. In the diagram, everyone with an ability to earn comparable to, or lower than, the budget restraint *I*, will opt for unemployment. Those with abilities above this will remain at work, although for shorter periods. The relevant factor determining what proportion of the population drops out of employment is the proportion with a budget restraint no steeper than the gradient of indifference curve *i*, passing through point *N*. This is determined by two things: the height of the transfer payment, *c* (indifference curves crossing the vertical line *MM* get steadily steeper as you go up); and the size of the income tax rate, *t*. If the income tax rate increases, the slopes of everyone's budget restraints (which show the trade-off between time and *after-tax* incomes) will fall.

What the foregoing implies for the supply of unemployment is this. The higher the transfer payment, the greater the proportion unemployed, hence the upward slope of the curve *SS(t)* in figure 5.8. The higher the tax rate, the greater the level of unemployment; so an increase in *t* displaces *SS(t)* to the right. If, as we have assumed, the minimum ability level in the population is zero, *SS(t)* starts at the origin. If the minimum ability level is positive, the curve will have a positive vertical intercept. A sufficiently small transfer payment will not cause anyone to drop out of employment (although everyone will still lower his or her time at work).

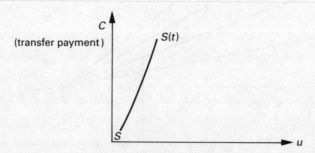

Figure 5.8 *The supply of unemployment: the unconditional transfer and the unemployment level, for a given tax rate*

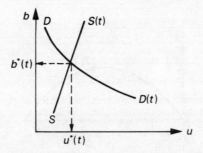

Figure 5.9 *Unemployment and benefit for a given tax rate: demand and supply in equilibrium*

5.6 Combining the Demand and Supply Curves for Unemployment

The scissors of demand and supply can now be joined. The supply curve depicted in figure 5.5 can be combined with the demand curve of figure 5.4 to show how the levels of unemployment, and unemployment benefit, are simultaneously determined for a given level of tax. This is portrayed in figure 5.9. Similarly, figure 5.10 superimposes the supply curve of figure 5.8 on the demand curve of figure 5.3 to illustrate the determination of the conditional transfer payment, c, and the unemployment rate, again for a given income tax rate. An increase in t, the income tax rate, displaces both $S(t)$ and $D(t)$ to the right in both diagrams. Unemployment must increase. What happens to b, the unemployment benefit in figure 5.9, or c, the transfer payment made to everyone in figure 5.10, is not clear. They go up when unemployment is low enough, but will drop when u is high. Figures 5.11 and 5.12 depict the relationships between u, the unemployment rate, and b and c respectively. There will exist maxima at X or Y. These give the unemployment rate at which unemployment benefits, or transfer payments, are as high as possible. In the diagrams, the curves show b (or c) at zero when unemployment is at either extreme, of zero or one. When everyone is unemployed, nothing will be produced, and taxation, no matter how high the rate, will yield nothing. So b, or c, must be zero. The curves will start at the origin if, as we have assumed, the minimum ability to earn in the population is zero. If the lowest ability level were positive, the levels of

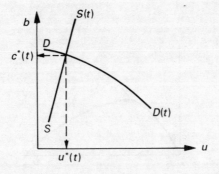

Figure 5.10 *Unemployment and the transfer payment for a given tax rate: demand and supply in equilibrium*

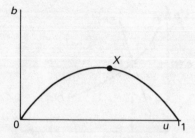

Figure 5.11 *The relation between benefit and unemployment in equilibrium*

b and c consistent with no unemployment could be positive, and, just as the supply curves of unemployment could exhibit a positive vertical-axis intercept, the curves in figure 5.11 and figure 5.12 would start above the origin, too.

It may be the authorities set the level of b, or c, and adjust the rate of income tax to achieve a balanced budget. This will lead to a different kind of demand-and-supply analysis under the two cases. Figures 5.13 and 5.14 illustrate this. The demand for unemployment at any level of b or c is an increasing function of the tax rate: higher tax rates imply that society can 'afford' more unemployment. But since the loss of output becomes progressively more serious as unemployment increases, the amount of extra unemployment a given rise in the tax rate 'buys' comes down. Hence the convex shape of the D curves in figures 5.13 and 5.14. The supply curves also slope up, because an increase in the marginal income tax rate on wages lowers the attractiveness of being employed (benefit case) or reduces chosen hours of work (transfer case). It is convex, to reflect the fact that unit increases in t exact accelerating downwards pressure, proportionately speaking, on the fraction $(1-t)$ of marginal earnings that households are allowed to keep, and it is this that governs their labour-force participation decisions. A rise in t from 0.1 to 0.2 lowers $(1-t)$ by only one-eighth; when t increases from 0.8 to 0.9, $(1-t)$ halves.

The effect of a higher value of b in figure 5.13 will be to push the demand curve up. A higher level of benefits means higher taxes or fewer recipients. But it displaces the supply curve to the right: more people will elect for unemployment. If b is pushed too high, the demand and supply curves will be pushed apart, and equilibrium will cease to exist. This is evident in figure 5.11, too: if the benefit level exceeds its value

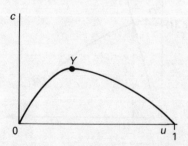

Figure 5.12 *The relation between transfer payment and unemployment in equilibrium*

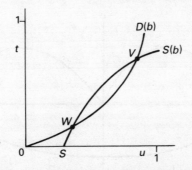

Figure 5.13 *The demand and supply of unemployment as functions of the benefit rate*

at point X, no equilibrium is possible. An increase in the unconditional transfer payment, c, has similar effects upon demand and supply in figure 5.14.

We are now in a position to integrate all the pieces of the analysis, and present the complete set of relationships between national income, unemployment, taxation and the two kinds of benefit, b and c. Figure 5.15 displays these when tax receipts are applied to paying unemployment benefits, while figure 5.16 illustrates the case of unconditional transfers paid to all. They extend the relationships portrayed in figures 5.11 and 5.12 respectively.

Both diagrams show a heart-shaped curve linking these four variables. Under the assumptions with which we have been working, society can choose its level of redistribution from the more to the less fortunate members of society. Greater redistribution brings greater equality, and quite possibly a perception of greater fairness. It also tends to lower the size of national income, and induce an increase in the level of unemployment. A completely *laissez-faire* government could achieve no unemployment and the highest level of national income, by scrapping income taxation and the welfare payments it finances. At the other extreme, a government that insisted on perfect equality could achieve it by imposing an income tax rate of 100 per cent; but this would imply no employment, and a disappearance of national income, under the assumptions of this chapter. In between these limits, the government has the opportunity to trade off gains from greater equality against the efficiency, output and employment losses to which redistribution will give rise.

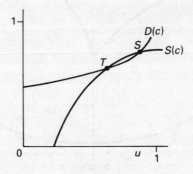

Figure 5.14 *The demand and supply of unemployment as functions of the unconditional transfer payment*

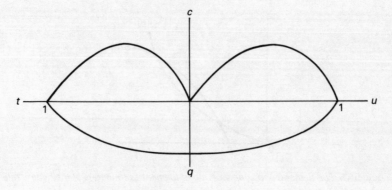

Figure 5.15 *National income, taxation, unemployment and benefits: the full system*

Exactly where this balance is struck is the subject of the next section. But before we proceed to explore this, one important point deserves mention at this stage. This is the sensitivity of the shape of the curves depicted in figures 5.15 and 5.16 upon the assumptions made. For example, had the lower limit to ability to earn been placed above zero, the two curves in the upper panels of the two diagrams would not cross the origin, but start with a positive intercept on the vertical axis. Had the utility functions for agents displayed less substitution between taxed income and leisure than the Cobb–Douglas function, the curves linking q to t would display a positive association between them at low tax rates (modest taxation could increase national income by raising the labour supply of those in work). Were government to coerce individuals to supply labour, or were output to depend on other factors as well as labour, even 100 per cent taxation at the margin could be compatible with a positive level of output and transfer payments.

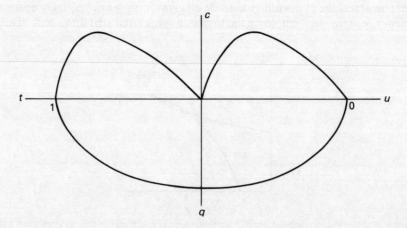

Figure 5.16 *National income, taxation, unemployment and transfers to all: the full system*

5.7 Optimum Levels of Unemployment

The notion of an 'optimum' level of unemployment strikes one as paradoxical, even perverse. How would a right-thinking person ever want to deprive someone else of a job? Surely unemployment is always bad?

This is quite a natural reaction to the concept of 'optimum' unemployment. The misery conspicuously suffered by millions of poor, jobless people in the world makes it more than understandable. But there is another side to not working that merits consideration. Words like 'vacation', 'free evening', 'week-end' and 'sabbatical' have a most agreeable, even magical ring to them. The Law of Natural Cussedness suggests that nothing could be more enticing than the prospect of leisure, provided you are denied it. Furthermore, there must be a very high rate of unemployment among heirs and heiresses to vast fortunes. They may be busy reprimanding their servants, losing at roulette, killing birds and foxes and enduring the ordeals of social competition, and they may be far from happy; but at least they serve to remind us that unemployment may not always be a miserable, involuntary state of privation. More importantly, they show how unemployment can emerge as an unwanted and perhaps unwelcome side-effect, of increasing people's financial wellbeing.

Government will hardly be indifferent to the wellbeing and utilities of members of society. It can be made tautological to say that government's task is to maximize social welfare, as it sees it, subject to the restraints which it perceives. Social welfare is related to the utilities of the individuals who together comprise society. Pareto laid down that a society must be counted as having gained if the welfare of everyone inside it rises. This is unexceptionable. The difficulties arise when individuals' interests clash. If a particular change brings gain to some and loss to others, as it is almost inevitably bound to, what can be said about the change in society's welfare?

One possible answer to this is provided by the Benthamite, or utilitarian,

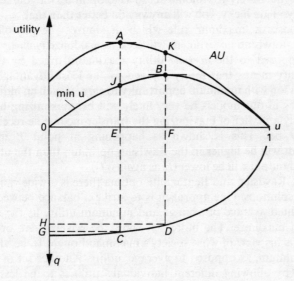

Figure 5.17 *The utilitarian and Rawlsian optima for unemployment and national income*

suggestion that society should be interested in maximizing the *sum* of everyone's utility. This is equivalent to maximizing average utility. When the size of the national income is given, and everyone has a diminishing marginal utility of income, this is achieved by transferring income between people until everyone's marginal utility of income is equal. If everyone shares the same utility function, it will also imply an equalization of incomes and utilities. But the essential feature of our model is that the size of national income is *not* given. In figures 5.15 and 5.16 it is drawn as declining when the marginal income tax rate is increased. The utilitarian will therefore restrict himself to something short of perfect equality. But that does not mean he will refrain from any income redistribution. Figure 5.17 illustrates this.

If everyone has a diminishing marginal utility of income (as they certainly will if they share a utility function that expresses utility as the geometric mean of income and leisure), transfers from richer to poorer should tend to increase average utility so long as the tax rate is sufficiently low. So average utility, shown by the curve *AU* in figure 5.17, is drawn initially increasing with unemployment. But a point will be reached where the sacrifice of output entailed by redistribution taxation imposes a marginal cost that balances the marginal gain from redistribution. This is shown as happening at *A*, where average utility is maximized. Beyond that point, further redistribution squeezes the utilities of the better-off members of society by more than it increases the gains for the worse off. For a Benthamite government, point *A* defines the optimum rates of tax and benefits; it also implicitly defines optimal values for unemployment and national income.

A very different social objective is proposed by Rawls (1971). Imagine that everyone is unaware of the ability-to-earn with which he will be endowed, and highly averse to risk. Rawls suggests that if, at this early stage, people were to assent to a contract which governed such matters as rights and economic redistribution, they would 'play safe' by agreeing upon a set of rules which made life as attractive as possible for the least advantaged member of society. No one knows who that will be. It could be you. Surely you should act so as to optimize for yourself in this worst eventuality; if you are lucky, you will anyway do better than that.

Rawls proposes a 'maximin' rule which maximizes the pay-off to the least fortunate. The Rawlsian government will seek to maximize *minimum* utility in our context, as opposed to the *average* utility maximand urged by the utilitarian. Minimum utility means that utility enjoyed by the least advantaged member of society, the person with minimum opportunity to earn. If such an individual is to be unemployed, as in our models he very likely will be, maximizing his utility then becomes simply a matter of maximizing the transfer income he receives (*b* or *c*, as the case may be). This is shown as happening at point *B* in figure 5.17. Unemployment will be higher in the Rawlsian optimum than the utilitarian (*F* as against *E*); and output will be lower (*H* as against *G*).

Between the Rawlsian and Benthamite optima there is a wide range of possible 'compromise' solutions. One approach is to strike a balance between the two by taking a weighted average of average and minimum utility as the objective that society should maximize. The more 'left-wing' the government, or the observer claiming this as his view of what society's maximand ought to be, the heavier the weight on minimum, as opposed to average, utility. Another set of compromises can be found by allowing different individuals' utilities to be less than perfect *substitutes* in social welfare (which is what they are in the utilitarian set-up, which

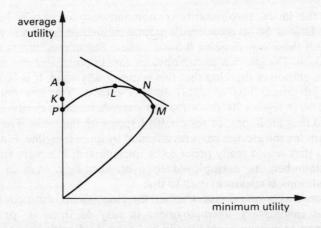

Figure 5.18 *The trade-off between average and minimum utility*

takes welfare to be the sum of everyone's utility), but equally less than perfect *complements* (which is how the Rawlsian objective function views them). The 'elasticity of substitution' between different individuals' utilities in social welfare can be introduced as a parameter that reflects society's aversion to inequality in utility; the greater this is, the closer to the utilitarian end of the range. If this is recast in terms of income, the elasticity of substitution gives society's aversion to income inequality. This can be identified (under utilitarian assumptions) with individuals' aversion to risk. The more risk-average everyone is, the more quickly the marginal utility of income declines as income rises, and the greater the sacrifice in aggregate output that it is worth undertaking to bring people's marginal utilities of income closer together. The precise implications of these two approaches to compromising between the Rawlsian and Benthamite objectives are studied with examples in the more technical account of these issues presented in chapter 6. A pictorial view is provided in figure 5.18.

Figure 5.18 illustrates the trade-off between average utility and minimum utility implicit in figure 5.17.

5.8 An Important Qualification

Throughout this chapter we have assumed that people derive positive satisfaction from leisure. This has meant that those unlucky enough to be out of work at least have the compensation of greater free time at their disposal. It must be admitted that whether people enjoy leisure is open to doubt. It is a cruel paradox that you probably enjoy time not spent at work most when it is scarcest. A change of scene and opportunities for recreation, entertainment, travel and rest are very pleasurable when you have been busy at work and know that you will soon return to it. But when you are out of work, unemployment should not be seen as an agreeable protracted holiday. Some of those out of work may opt for that. But it is very doubtful whether this is true of more than a modest minority of the unemployed.

A sharp distinction is traditionally drawn between those out of work by choice and the remainder of the unemployed. The former group are said to be voluntarily unemployed; the latter, involuntarily. Economic analysis usually has choice-theoretic foundations. So an economist's natural inclination is to treat joblessness as a state which those experiencing it have chosen. Sometimes, this is a perfectly realistic approach. The idle rich are an obvious case in point. But one must guard against the temptation of thinking that this is universally valid. It is certainly not. Losing your job means loss of status and self-esteem. You lose contact with colleagues. Surveys repeatedly show that an overwhelming majority of those in work state that they are happy, or reasonably happy with their jobs. The employed may often yearn for the greener pastures afforded by more free time. But that does not mean that they would really prefer to be unemployed. The mere fact that the employed outnumber the unemployed so overwhelmingly, even in the most depressed conditions, is testament itself to that.

Yet reflection makes one doubt whether the clear, sharp, distinction between voluntary and involuntary unemployment is easy to draw in practice. An unemployed man or woman could usually find some paid work, sooner or later, if really forced to. Regaining employment would entail certain costs, possibly prohibitive costs. Employment opportunities might be available only at greatly reduced wages. They might entail disagreeable, possibly degrading work. They might mean lengthy commuting, a costly move of house and severance of ties from family and friends. They could require costly searches, involving time, travel and other financial outlays. They could involve exclusion from the chance of better-paid work, or jobs closer to home, which might subsequently become available. The lower the rewards – both pecuniary and psychic – from such jobs as may be available, the greater the incentive to acquiesce in unemployment with the limited financial resources provided by benefits. The more one considers the complex balance of factors influencing search, the more blurred the distinction between voluntary and involuntary unemployment becomes.

There are other reasons for questioning this distinction, too. Contracts may be struck between workers and employers that leave open the possibility that the latter will lay off the former in sufficiently adverse conditions. The worker, or often the trade union representing him, will attempt to strike a point of balance between the attractiveness of higher wages in better states, against the chance of lay-offs. The laid-off worker has not chosen to be unemployed; rather, he, or his agent, has entered a contract that allows for the possibility of this. Perhaps he may have erred on the side of optimism, and failed to perceive that the probability of unemployment was as high as it was. Perhaps he or his union treated the employer's claim that higher wages *could* entail higher risks of lay-offs as an empty bluff designed to keep labour costs down. Quite possibly, an adverse swing in the employer's demand for labour may come as a complete surprise, testifying to an unanticipated deterioration in the probability distribution governing the employer's demand for labour. All these factors are examined in greater detail in chapter 10.

Then there is the problem that unions may negotiate wages, and possibly employment levels too, for a large group of workers. The union may balance the benefits of higher wages for those in work against the numbers that can enjoy it. This is the approach explored in a subsequent chapter (chapter 11). The luckless job-losers have not chosen to be unemployed. The union's bargain with the employer decided that, at least in probabilistic terms. Those who retain their jobs, probably a large majority, may be reluctant to sacrifice some of their own earnings to secure the employment or re-employment of others. In such a case, at least the chance of unemployment is in a sense dictated by the choices of those in work, not those out of it. And the greater their success in preserving their high wages, perhaps by the device of restricting entry into their labour market, the harder it will be for unemployed workers to find jobs. Workers and their unions may be caught in an ugly Prisoner's Dilemma. All might agree that almost everyone would be better off with a flexible labour market without entry barriers. But if other unions limit entry into other industries, it is in your interests to do the same. If you do not, you risk loss of jobs and livelihoods as the unemployed flock into your sector and bid down wages against you. And even if other sectors do not impose entry barriers, your wages may be higher and safer if you do.

Furthermore, one should not necessarily treat time spent outside the formal labour market as pleasurable (or disagreeable) inactivity. Tasks are performed within the household no less than in factories and offices and other places of formal employment. Within limits you often choose between supplying additional time to the formal labour sector, to gain higher earnings, and devoting it to household production. One might supply another hour to formal employment, for £5 or $10, let us say, and dine in a restaurant, or alternatively devote the time to shopping, cooking and dishwashing and eating more cheaply at home. This view of household behaviour was first developed by Becker (1965). Raising children, making repairs, redecoration and countless other domestic tasks are time-consuming alternatives or adjuncts to formal employment. It is not impossible to view the unemployed as often opting to undertake more of such activities albeit at the cost of reduced income. The greater the effective marginal tax on earnings, the level of unemployment benefit, the trouble and expense of job-search and the reduction in pay on regaining formal employment, the likelier this becomes. There is also the possibility of seeking out a precarious livelihood by performing such tasks, informally for neighbours and friends, possibly on a reciprocal basis. This has been variously described as the shadow, black or informal economy.

Finally, it is not unthinkable that the marginal utility of leisure time is negative when you are out of work, and positive for the employed. Indifference curves drawn between leisure (horizontal) and income (vertical) might be U-shaped. That would make unemployment a less enjoyable state than the downwards-sloping indifference curves which underlay earlier sections of this chapter. But the analysis of the unemployment benefit model, at least, could carry over quite straightforwardly to this new case. The supply curve of unemployment would be displaced leftwards and the resulting unemployment rate (for any income tax rate) would be reduced. The critical individual would be indifferent between unemployment and employment, as before. All that would happen is that there would be fewer people out of work.

6 The Optimum Distribution of Income and Unemployment: Further Analysis

Just as chapter 4 was a technical extension to chapter 3, this chapter performs the same function for chapter 5. The reader who wishes to avoid technical details is advised to go straight to chapter 7.

6.1 Introduction

This chapter supplies the technical details that underlie chapter 5. Section 6.2 explores the optimum distribution of income in general terms. The linear income tax system is the subject of section 6.3: general discussion in section 6.3.1 is followed by a scrutiny of particular examples that serve to emphasize the possible determinants of 'optimal' unemployment (section 6.3.2). Some of the key assumptions are relaxed in section 6.3.3 and the overall findings are summarized in section 6.3.4. Section 6.4 moves on to look at the determination of optimum unemployment in unemployment benefit models. Lastly, a different approach to optimum unemployment is sketched out in section 6.5. The ideas developed and discussed in this chapter owe a great deal to Mirrlees' pioneering study of optimum income taxation (Mirrlees (1971)).

6.2 The Optimum Distribution of Income

6.2.1 *The Two Ideal Requirements*

Let us begin by assuming that society is interested in maximizing the sum of every member's utility. This is the Benthamite, utilitarian objective. It is equivalent to maximizing average utility. Assume, further, that everyone's marginal utility of income declines as his income increases.

The optimum distribution of incomes across individuals will prescribe equality in the *marginal* utilities of their incomes. Violate this condition, and you can raise average utility by redistributing income from those with lower to those with higher marginal utilities of income. Call this the efficient distribution rule, or EDR for short.

If average, or total utility is to be maximized, it must not be possible to raise one person's utility without reducing someone else's. The allocation of resources is Pareto-efficient when utilities are maximized in this sense. Pareto efficiency calls for a large set of marginal equivalences, at least in an ideal society: every pair of consumers must have common marginal rates of substitution between every pair of goods they each consume; every pair of producers must have common marginal rates of substitution between every pair of factors they each employ; the common marginal rates of substitution between consumed goods must equal the marginal rate of transformation between them. One important extension, or application, of this third condition is that the worker's marginal rate of substitution between leisure and a good must equal the marginal real wage, expressed in terms of this good, that he receives for the sale of his labour time. The ratio of the marginal utility of leisure to that of consumption must equal the marginal real wage the individual commands. Call this the efficient allocation rule or EAR.

6.2.2 *One Difficulty with the EAR and EDR: Possible Incompatibility*

The utilitarian objective calls upon us to fulfil both the EAR and the EDR. But this may be impossible. One reason for this is that utility functions may be such as to make the two rules incompatible.

Consider an individual i, who commands a wage (or ability level) w_i. He or she has utility $U(c_i, 1-h_i)$ if we endow the person with one unit of time, define work time as h_i and restrict the analysis to the case of a single good, the consumption of which is c_i. The EDR requires us to set the marginal utilities of consumption equal across the population. So $\partial U/\partial C_i$ is a constant, for all i. The EAR prescribes equality between the marginal rate of substitution between leisure and consumption with the individual's (marginal) wage. Hence:

$$\frac{\partial U/\partial C_i}{\partial U/\partial [1-h_i]} = \frac{1}{w_i}.$$

The problem that concerns us here is that these two rules may conflict. Suppose, for example, that utility takes the form

$$U_i = c_i^\alpha (1-h_i)^{1-\alpha} \quad 1 > \alpha > 0. \tag{6.1}$$

The EDR implies that

$$\alpha \left(\frac{1-h_i}{c_i}\right)^{1-\alpha} = \text{constant (say } k). \tag{6.2}$$

But the EAR implies

$$\frac{\alpha}{1-\alpha} \frac{1-h_i}{c_i} = \frac{1}{w_i}. \tag{6.3}$$

It is clear that if these two individuals have different wage rates, (6.2) and (6.3) cannot be applied simultaneously.

This is not just a freak consequence of the utility function, (6.1). It will happen whenever utility displays 'constant returns to scale' in both leisure and consumption (or income). If doubling your income and your leisure time makes you twice as well off as before, that is, the EAR and EDR cannot be applied simultaneously.

6.2.3 *A Second Difficulty with the EAR and EDR: The Incentive Problem*

Of course, utility does not have to display constant returns to scale. This will only be a special case. Let us consider an example where it does not:

$$U = \alpha \ln c_i + (1-\alpha)\ln(1-h_i) \quad 1 > \alpha > 0. \tag{6.4}$$

Equation (6.4) gives the marginal utility of consumption as α/c_i. Equalizing this across the population, following EDR, implies equalizing consumption (given that α is common to everyone).

What will EAR imply? The marginal utility of leisure will be $(1-\alpha)/(1-h_i)$. Setting the ratio of the marginal utilities equal to person i's wage implies

$$\frac{\alpha}{1-\alpha}\frac{1-h_i}{c_i} = \frac{1}{w_i}. \tag{6.5}$$

Define k to be the common marginal utility of consumption (α/c_i). Equation (6.5) then can be rewritten

$$1 - h_i = \frac{1-\alpha}{kw_i}. \tag{6.6}$$

Equation (6.6) tells us that the individual's work time will be positively related to his wage.

Suppose everyone is in a position to choose his hours of work. Suppose we adopt a *laissez-faire* attitude and allow them to do this with no fiscal intervention by the authorities. Each person faces a budget restraint

$$w_i h_i - c_i = 0. \tag{6.7}$$

If (6.4) is maximized subject to (6.7), we find that h_i will equal α. Everyone will work for the same length of time. But if their wage rates differ, that will be no good: we get an immediate conflict with (6.6), which imposed the requirement that the more able should work for longer than the less able.

One straightforward way out of this conundrum is to impose a person-specific transfer payment, a_i, of as yet undetermined sign or magnitude. Amend (6.7) to read:

$$w_i h_i - c_i + a_i = 0. \tag{6.8}$$

Maximizing (6.4) subject to (6.8) yields

$$h_i = \alpha - \frac{a_i}{w_i}(1-\alpha). \tag{6.9}$$

We are now in a position to find the value of a_i, in terms of k and w_i, that makes individual choice (equation (6.9)) consistent with the requirements of EAR and EDR. Link (6.6) and (6.9):

$$a_i = \frac{1}{k} - w_i. \tag{6.10}$$

The lump-sum transfer payment that we make to an individual will go down one-for-one with his wage.

Suppose that society consists of an equal number of high-wage people (facing a wage of w_1) and low-wage people (with w_2). Assume that the transfer payments are chosen so as to break even in aggregate: $\sum a_i = 0$. Hence

$$a_1 = -a_2. \tag{6.11}$$

Equations (6.10) and (6.11) now enable us to solve for the common marginal utility of consumption:

$$k = \frac{2}{w_1 + w_2}. \tag{6.12}$$

The two groups' work time will be given by

$$h_i = 1 - \frac{1-\alpha}{2} \frac{w_1 + w_2}{w_i} \quad i = 1, 2. \tag{6.13}$$

We can then find the utility level of each group by substituting (6.13) and (6.12) into (6.4):

$$U_i = \alpha \ln \alpha + (1-\alpha) \ln (1-\alpha) + \ln (w_1 + w_2) - \ln 2 - (1-\alpha) \ln w_i. \tag{6.14}$$

Equation (6.14) tells us at once that the abler group will be *worse off*, in utility terms, than the less able. They will consume at a common rate, but the less able will enjoy more leisure than the others.

The average level of utility, AU, will be

$$AU = \alpha \ln \alpha + (1-\alpha) \ln (1-\alpha) - \ln 2 + \ln (w_1 + w_2) - (1-\alpha) \ln (\sqrt{w_1, w_2}). \tag{6.15}$$

We shall have succeeded in maximizing this unambiguously. But we immediately face an awkward problem. It pays the more able to pretend to be less able. Playing dumb gives you a higher utility; you work less and your consumption is subsidized, rather than taxed, by the receipt of the lump-sum transfer. Recall that a_1 will be negative, and a_2 positive.

So the difficulty to which the combination of EDR and EAR gives rise is that there are incentives to lie. The fiscal arrangements just described are said to be *incentive-incompatible*. Taxing abilities, for that is what this system amounts to, runs foul of the problem that it pays to be less able, or at least to pretend to be less able. Ability taxation would also create havoc with training and education, if these are ways of increasing your efficiency at work, or of signalling your efficiency to your employer. The reader is referred to Roberts (1984) for a most penetrating abstract analysis of the ways in which incentive-compatibility difficulties impede redistributive schemes.

6.2.4 *A Third Difficulty: Corner Solutions*

So far we have assumed that people can choose their hours of work. Equation (6.9), for example, gives preferred work time for each person in the model of the previous section; and (6.13) gives an exact solution. One question that needs to be addressed is whether these labour-supply equations are feasible.

It is not possible for someone to supply negative hours of work (short, perhaps, of employing domestic servants to carry out your personal household chores). So we should strictly rewrite (6.13), for instance, as

$$h_i = \text{Max}\left[0, 1 - \frac{1-\alpha}{2}\frac{w_1 + w_2}{w_i}\right]. \tag{6.16}$$

A closer look at (6.13) and (6.16) reveals that this time constraint ($h_i > 0$) could easily be infringed. There is no risk of this happening for the more able. But for the less able, commanding a wage of w_2, could easily run into their time constraint. This will happen if

$$w_2 < (1-\alpha)\frac{w_1 + w_2}{2} \quad \text{or} \quad w_2 < \frac{1-\alpha}{1+\alpha}w_1. \tag{6.17}$$

If inequalities (6.17) apply, each group will consume $\alpha w_1/(1+\alpha)$; the less able will not work at all; and the utilities will be given by

$$\left.\begin{aligned}
U_1 &= \alpha\ln\frac{\alpha w_i}{1+\alpha} + (1-\alpha)\ln\frac{1-\alpha}{1+\alpha} \\[2mm]
U_2 &= \alpha\ln\frac{\alpha w_1}{1+\alpha} > U_1 \\[2mm]
AU &= \alpha\ln\frac{\alpha w_1}{1+\alpha} + \frac{1-\alpha}{2}\ln\frac{1-\alpha}{1+\alpha}
\end{aligned}\right\} \tag{6.18}$$

These considerations remind us how unemployment can easily be a by-product of redistributive policies, a proposition discussed at length in chapter 5.

6.2.5 *Further Remarks on Corner Solutions*

Let us now go back to equation (6.1), which, as we saw, proved to make EAR and EDR incompatible. Equation (6.1) is of course closely related to (6.4): all we need to do to (6.4) is to replace the left-hand side of (6.4) with its logarithm, and we get (6.1) at once.

A utilitarian government in a society composed of individuals with differing abilities will find that average utility, its maximand, will reach a summit where rather odd things happen.

Suppose that abilities are distributed uniformly across the population, with a ceiling of 1 and a floor of 0. The best thing to do, it turns out, is to set one group of people (the more able) to work all the time, and for the rest not to work at all. Defining u as the unemployment rate (which conveniently can be identified with the ability level of the marginal individual on the borderline between the two groups, given our assumption on how w is distributed), this society will generate production of

$$\int_u^1 wh(w)\,dw^* = \frac{1-u^2}{2}. \tag{6.19}$$

This will be shared out equally among the unemployed. Social welfare, or average utility, will then be

$$AU = u\left[\frac{1-u^2}{2u}\right]^{\alpha} = u^{1-\alpha}\left[\frac{1-u^2}{2}\right]^{\alpha}. \tag{6.20}$$

Society's problem is then simply to choose the optimal unemployment rate that maximizes (6.20). This will be

$$u^* = \sqrt{\frac{1-\alpha}{1+\alpha}}. \tag{6.21}$$

In this society, the abler citizens are denied both leisure and consumption. It is efficient that they, rather than the less able, should work to the limit of their time endowment, since this will mean a higher aggregate output. There is no point in the abler individuals consuming anything, since their marginal utility of consumption will be zero anyway, when $h = 1$. So the entire proceeds of their work are confined to the unemployed. Reducing the unemployment rate has the advantage of raising the number at work, and hence aggregate output. It also means restricting this increased output to fewer individuals, so that each unemployed person will be much better off. But it has the drawback of lowering the number of individuals who gain positive utility. Equation (6.21) gives the point where the marginal advantage of reducing unemployment just balances the marginal cost.

This example paints a rather horrid and far-fetched picture. It will never prove the best policy when the individuals have a utility function such as (6.4), since the exploited, abler citizens will have utility of minus infinity if they consume nothing and retain no leisure time for their own enjoyment. Rather, the point of the example is to show how and why corner solutions can sometimes dominate the implication of following the EAR and EDR; and this can happen even when they are not incompatible.[1] Of course, the example in this section runs into very serious trouble on incentives. The temptation to play dumb could not be stronger.

6.2.6 *One Way Round the Incentive-Incompatibility Problem*

In section 6.2.3 we saw that the combined application of EDR and EAR could lead to the difficulty that some people have an incentive to lie. The abler individuals gain by lying because their utilities will be lower than for the less efficient workers. The more efficient will pretend to be less efficient, enjoy more leisure and have lost consumption made good by fiscal redistribution.

A possible answer to the incentive-incompatibility problem is to ensure that no one gains by lying in this way. This means that you should be no worse off by being honest, and declaring your true ability, than by playing dumb.

In what follows in this section, we therefore impose the constraint that utilities be equalized across the population. This is a simple rule to apply. It reduces the incentive to lie. We shall investigate the optimal distribution problem subject to this condition, within a model that combines the utility function (6.4) with the assumption on the distribution of abilities employed in section 6.2.5. Wage rates vary therefore, between a maximum of 1 and a minimum of 0, and are rectangularly distributed across this interval.

Allowing for the possibility of the corner solution (that h_i is constrained to be zero), (6.9) gives us

$$h_i = \text{Max}\left[0, \alpha - \frac{a_i(1-\alpha)}{w_i}\right]. \tag{6.22}$$

As before, we eschew marginal income taxation, and pay a lump-sum transfer of a_i to the person with ability w_i (and a_i can of course be negative). Using the budget restraint (6.8), and (6.22), the utility of each individual will be:

$$U_i = \ln(w_i + a_i) + \alpha \ln \alpha + (1+\alpha) \ln(1-\alpha) - (1-\alpha) \ln w_i \qquad (6.23)$$

when $h_i > 0$. For unemployed individuals, who supply no work, utility will be

$$U = \alpha \ln a_u \qquad (6.24)$$

where a_u is the lump-sum transfer to the unemployed.

The condition that utilities be common implies that (6.23) and (6.24) will be equal, and, furthermore, that (6.23) hold for everyone in work. This means that

$$\frac{w_i + a_i}{w_i^{1-\alpha}} = \text{constant } (z, \text{ say}) \qquad (6.25)$$

and also that

$$a_u = \alpha z^{1/\alpha}(1-\alpha)^{(1-\alpha)/\alpha}. \qquad (6.26)$$

Furthermore, (6.22) implies that $u = a_u^{(1-\alpha)/\alpha}$. Finally, the breakeven condition on transfer payments implies that $\sum a_i = 0$. Consequently,

$$0 = \int_0^1 a(w)\, dw = \int_u^1 \{w^{1-\alpha}z - w\}\, dw + ua_u$$

$$= u^2 \frac{\alpha}{1-\alpha} + u^\alpha \frac{1-u^{2-\alpha}}{(2-\alpha)(1-\alpha)} - \frac{1-u^2}{2}. \qquad (6.27)$$

If $\alpha = \frac{1}{2}$, for example, (6.27) establishes an unemployment rate of about 0.139. Everyone's utility will equal approximately -0.987.

By contrast, the optimal first-best distribution is given directly by the EAR and EDR. Consumption is equalized by the EDR at a value c, which incidentally also equals the unemployment rate, u, when $\alpha = \frac{1}{2}$ (see (6.22)). The EAR gives a condition on h_i which makes it possible to calculate the level of output per head in terms of c (and hence u). The resulting equation can be solved for unemployment at once: if $\alpha = \frac{1}{2}$, $u = 2 - \sqrt{3} \sim 0.268$, implying average utility, given now by the pleasantly simple result

$$AU = \frac{1-u}{2} + \log_e u \qquad (6.28)$$

at -0.951 or so. This calls for almost double the unemployment achieved under the previous system, and leads to a modest improvement in average utility.

Incentive-compatibility restrictions reduce optimal unemployment sharply, because they require that no one at work be worse off than the unemployed. This means raising the attractiveness of working, by tempering the higher lump-sum taxes that the abler must pay when both EAR and EDR apply.

Two qualifications should be made about this answer to the incentive-to-cheat problem: it fails to deal with the issue of training and education raised at the end of section 6.2.5, and, more importantly, it only avoids penalizing the abler members of society. It does not fully deal with the incentive-compatibility problem. It still pays to pretend to be less able than you are provided that the authorities cannot see the wage rate at which you are actually paid. If they can, it solves it, since you gain nothing by lying.

6.2.7 *The Rawlsian Objective*

The answer to the incentive-incompatibility problem that bedevils the complete utilitarian redistribution programmes (EAR plus EDR) studied in section 6.2.6 relied upon the device of equalizing utilities. It is rather odd that what began as a Benthamite exercise should end up with that.

Equalizing utilities is often (not always) equivalent to maximizing the utility of the least advantaged. This is the Rawlsian policy prescription, studied in chapter 5. The incentive-compatible scheme described in section 6.2.6 will therefore represent a Rawlsian optimum. It is interesting to note that in this context the Rawlsian objective does not lead to higher unemployment than the Benthamite. If the first-best incentive-incompatible Benthamite policy is brought back into play, the Rawlsian optimum will in fact call for less unemployment. The reason for this is that it is the abler individuals who are paradoxically the less advantaged members of society when EAR and EDR are in force together.

The Benthamite optimum happens to equalize utilities when this constraint is imposed to side-step the cheating problem. The first-best Benthamite optimum that ignores this equalizes incomes, but not utilities. It is sometimes thought that equalizing marginal utilities of income, typically, or often, calls for the equalization of utilities or incomes or both. This really is not true. In fact, a policy of utility equalization can often imply the opposite direction of transfer between individuals to that which follows from Benthamite policy. This is particularly true when individuals' utility functions differ. For instance, let

$$U_i = \beta_i f(c_i) \quad \text{where} \quad \beta_i > 0 \quad \text{and} \quad i = 1, 2$$

in a two-person society. Suppose that their aggregate consumption, $c_1 + c_2$, adds to a constant, y. Each utility function displays a positive but diminishing marginal utility of consumption.

The Benthamite policy is

$$\text{Max}_{c_i} \sum \beta_i f(c_i) + \lambda[y - c_1 - c_2]. \tag{6.29}$$

The solution to (6.29) is to equate the marginal utilities of consumption, so that

$$\beta_1 f'(c_1) = \beta_2 f'(c_2), \quad \text{or} \quad \frac{c_1}{c_2} = f'^{-1}\left[\frac{\beta_2}{\beta_1}\right]. \tag{6.30}$$

The person with the higher β gets more to consume: he is simply a better happiness machine. The absolute egalitarian, or in this case Rawlsian, policy will be

$$\text{Set } c_i \text{ s.t. } \beta_1 f(c_1) = \beta_2 f(c_2), \quad \text{or} \quad \frac{c_1}{c_2} = f^{-1}\left[\frac{\beta_2}{\beta_1}\right]. \tag{6.31}$$

Note that this time, the person with the *lower* β receives more consumption, in order to top his utility to match the other person's. Given that f is increasing and concave, (6.30) and (6.31) call for a different ordering of consumption levels between the two people.

6.3 The Linear Income Tax System

6.3.1 *General Discussion*

Systems of redistribution explored in the previous sections of this chapter are rather distantly removed from the fiscal systems currently employed in Western countries. The simplest reasonably satisfactory approximation to reality takes the form of a linear income tax rate. This is especially true of the UK, where a 29 per cent 'standard rate' of income tax is levied on every pound earned between about £3000 and £18,000 or so per year. The marginal rate of tax is constant over a very wide range, running from barely one-third, to more than double, average earnings. In what follows, we shall make the simplifying assumption that all earnings are subject to tax at a single rate, t. In this section, we shall assume that the proceeds of this tax are redistributed to everyone as a lump sum; in section 6.4, tax proceeds will be confined to the unemployed. In both cases, the budget will be deemed to balance.

A number of further assumptions simplify the analysis. A sketch of what may happen if they are relaxed will be given later, in section 6.5. The population is infinite. Individuals are selfish, and concerned only with their own incomes and utilities. Labour is the only factor of production. There are constant returns to scale, and only one good is produced. People are free to choose their hours of work, but cannot supply negative labour time. The government provides no public goods. Individuals have identical preferences. They have convex-to-the-origin, downwards-sloping indifference curves between the two goods in which they are interested (income or consumption, and leisure). Society's welfare maximand is some function, to be discussed, of the utilities of the individuals of which it is comprised. Lastly, the individuals differ in abilities, which are distributed uniformly between 1 and 0; and each person's ability to earn is a constant, independent of his work time, and accurately reflected in the wage rate he commands. These are essentially the same assumptions underlying the less formal analysis of chapter 5.

Each individual i will face a budget restraint

$$w_i h_i(1-t)+a-c_i = 0. \tag{6.32}$$

His work time, h_i, is constrained to non-negativity. In (6.33), a denotes the lump-sum transfer that everyone gets, and c_i denotes person i's consumption. He will optimize by maximizing

$$U(c_i, \ell_i)+\lambda\{w_i h_i(1-t)+a-c_i\} + \mu(h_i+\ell_i-T)+vh_i. \tag{6.33}$$

If ℓ_i represents leisure time, and T the endowment of time. λ, μ and v are Lagrange multipliers; the last of these expresses an inequality constraint (the fact that $h_i \geqslant 0$). The solutions to this Kuhn–Tucker problem include

$$h_i = \text{Max}\,[0, g(w_i, a, t, T)]. \tag{6.34}$$

The second branch of (6.34), the function $g(..)$, must respond *negatively* to a on the innocuous assumption that leisure is a normal good. A rise in the lump-sum payment can only reduce labour supply if this is so. g must increase in T on the equally reasonable assumption that income is a normal good: so increased life expectation, or a miracle drug enabling people to dispense with sleep, will stimulate labour supply. Compared with a, the role of T is rather uninteresting; it is exogenous to the system we are examining, and from now on we shall take it to be locked at the convenient value of 1. How w and t affect g is unclear; they each involve a clash of income and substitution effects, the resolution of which chiefly depends upon whether income and leisure are substitutes or complements. If substitutes, g generally rises with w and is cut by t; if complements, often the opposite. The qualification 'generally' and 'often' are used advisedly, since the presence of the term a modifies the familiar conditions.

The value of w, $\bar{w}$, at which both branches of (6.34) apply simultaneously, if there is one, will be identified with the unemployment rate. This follows, at least, if all those with $w < \bar{w}$ are unemployed, while those with higher efficiency are working. If this is so, we may write

$$g(u, a, t) = 0 \tag{6.35}$$

which defines a functional relation connecting the two fiscal policy parameters, a and t, to u. T has been dropped from (6.35), now that it has been locked at unity.

The next step is to explore the government's budget position. Tax receipts must balance lump-sum transfers. Consequently,

$$t \int_u^1 w g(w, a, t) dw = a. \tag{6.36}$$

The left-hand side represents the tax proceeds: the integral denotes the total original income per head in the society. Equation (6.36) follows (6.35) in assuming that the unemployed consist of all those and only those, with ability below the critical value of $\bar{w}$. It also reflects the simplifying nature of our assumptions on the distribution of income. Equations (6.35) and (6.36) are, respectively, the supply and demand curves for unemployment introduced in chapter 5. Linking (6.35) and (6.36) should (if these functions are sufficiently invertible) allow us to express a and t as functions of u:

$$\left.\begin{array}{l} a = \phi(u) \\ t = \psi(u) \end{array}\right\}. \tag{6.37}$$

The final step is to introduce a social welfare function. Suppose that we can write it, quite generally, as

$$S = S(U(u)) \tag{6.38}$$

where U is the vector of all individuals' utilities. The simplest form that (6.38) may take is the Rawlsian

$$S_R = \text{Min}_i \, U_i(u). \tag{6.39}$$

The Benthamite utilitarian social welfare function will be the sum of all individuals' utilities, or average utility:

$$S_B = \int_0^1 U(u, w) \, dw. \tag{6.40}$$

The Champernowne social welfare function is identifiable with the product, or geometric mean of all individuals' utilities; these can be transformed conveniently into

$$S_C = \int_0^1 \{\ln U(a, w)\} \, dw. \tag{6.41}$$

Equation (6.41) supplies the missing gap (by L'Hôpital's Rule) in the more general equation (6.42) which embraces both (6.39) and (6.40) as extreme special cases:

$$S_H = \frac{1}{1-\varepsilon} \int_0^1 [U(u, w)]^{1-\varepsilon} \, dw. \tag{6.42}$$

Equation (6.42) is known as the constant elasticity of substitution (or CES) function; its older name, homohypallagic, is commemorated in the subscript H, to

Table 6.1 *Six candidates for the role of social welfare*

Abbreviation	Name	Verbal form	Formal form	Shape of social welfare contours in utility space
S_R	Rawlsian	Minimum utility	$\mathrm{Min}_i\, U_i$	Rectangular (L-shaped)
S_B	Benthamite utilitarian	Average utility	$\int u(w)\,dw$	Linear (gradient 1)
S_C	Champernowne	Average log utility	$\int \ln U(w)\,dw$	Rectangular-hyperbolic
S_H	CES	Average Cox-Box transformed utility	$\dfrac{1}{1-\varepsilon}\int U^{1-\varepsilon}_{(w)}\,dw$	Downwards-sloping, convex, between extremes of S_B and S_R ray-homothetic
S_N	Negative exponential	Average exponentiated utility	$-\int e^{-\varepsilon U(w)}\,dw$	As S_N, except unit-gradient expansion paths
S_M	Median voter	Median utility	$U\left(\dfrac{N+1}{2}\right)$ for population of N ranked by ability	Horizontal if median utility on vertical axis

avoid confusion with (6.41). Equation (6.42) has been widely employed in this and similar contexts, first by Atkinson (1970). The significance of ε is that it measures society's coefficient of relative aversion to inequalities in utility.[2] The range within which ε may lie runs from zero to infinity.[3] In the former case, (6.42) reduces to (6.40); in the latter, to (6.39). Another function, very similar to (6.42), is (6.43):

$$S_N = - \int_0^1 \exp\{-\varepsilon U(u, w)\}\, dw \quad \varepsilon \geqslant 0. \tag{6.43}$$

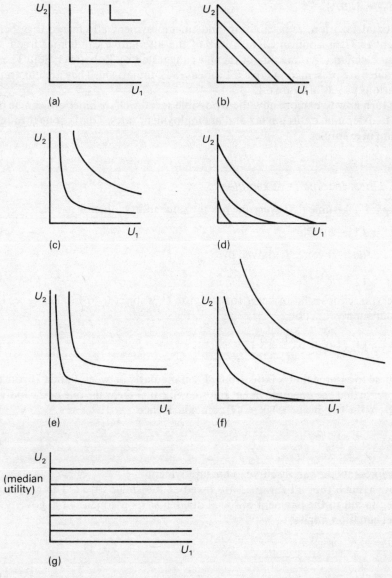

Figure 6.1 *The shapes of various social welfare functions in utility space: (a) the Rawlsian SWF; (b) the Benthamite SWF; (c) the Champernowne SWF; (d) the CES SWF, for $\varepsilon = \frac{1}{2}$; (f) the negative exponential SWF; (g) the median voter SWF*

This 'negative exponential' function kisses (6.40) when ε tends to zero; ε is, this time, society's *absolute* inequality aversion parameter.[4] Lastly, the political system may be such as to make the median voter a social dictator. This can easily happen in political duopoly, first considered by Hotelling (1929). The two political parties must compete keenly for the median voter's support; if they do not, they face defeat in a simple model where only one political dimension distinguishes electors' views, and voters always support the party nearest to their own position. The median voter in our case will impose the welfare function (6.44) upon society:

$$S_M = U(u, \tfrac{1}{2}). \tag{6.44}$$

Optimal taxation, redistribution and unemployment all emerge together, the moment (6.37) is confronted with one of the alternative candidates for a social welfare function (or some mix of them, as suggested by Roberts (1980)). These six candidates are presented in table 6.1 for ease of comparison. They are illustrated in the various panels of figure 6.1.

We turn now to explore how these possible social welfare functions can be put to work to determine optimum tax and unemployment rates. This is done through the medium of examples.

6.3.2 Linear Income Tax Examples

Example 1   Assume that everyone has the same utility function

$$U = I^\alpha (1-h)^{1-\alpha}. \tag{6.45}$$

Here, I denotes income. I_i is given by

$$I_i = a + w_i h_i (1-t). \tag{6.46}$$

Everyone chooses his or her h_i to maximize U_i, subject to (6.46). This gives rise to a labour supply function

$$h_i = \text{Max}\left(0, \alpha - \frac{a(1-\alpha)}{w_i(1-t)}\right). \tag{6.47}$$

Continue to assume that w is distributed rectangularly between 1 and 0. From (6.47) we observe that the unemployment rate, u, will equal the wage rate of the individual for whom the two branches of (6.47) coincide. Hence

$$u = \frac{a}{1-t} \frac{1-\alpha}{\alpha}. \tag{6.48}$$

This represents the supply curve of unemployment.

Now assume that all earnings are taxed at the single rate t. The proceeds are applied in full to the payment of social dividends. Consequently the government's budget equation implies

$$a = t \int_u^1 \{wh(w)\} \, dw$$

$$= \frac{\alpha t}{2}(1-u)^2. \tag{6.49}$$

This is the demand curve for unemployment.

Combining equations (6.48) and (6.49) to eliminate t, we find, when $\alpha = \frac{1}{2}$,

$$a = u\left(\frac{1-u}{1+u}\right)^2. \tag{6.50}$$

The *Rawlsian* optimum will be found by maximizing the utility of the least advantaged person. Such an individual will be unemployed, receiving an income of a. So his utility is simply a^α. Hence a Rawlsian government will optimize by maximizing a. The optimal value of unemployment that maximizes the utility of the least advantaged is $\sqrt{5}-2$, or approximately 23.6 per cent. This gives rise to a value of a of about 0.0906. The income tax rate in this position will be 61.8 per cent.

The *Benthamite* optimum is found by computing average utility, and maximizing this with respect to the unemployment rate. Substitution of (6.47) into (6.45) reveals that the utility of an employed person is $\frac{1}{2}(a+w(1-t))(w(1-t))^{-1/2}$, while for someone out of work it will simply be $a^{1/2}$ (when $\alpha = \frac{1}{2}$). The Benthamite utility integral will therefore be

$$S_B = \frac{1-u}{1+u}\left(u+\frac{1-u^{1.5}}{3}\right). \tag{6.51}$$

This reaches a maximum where $u \sim 0.096$, $a \sim 0.065$ and $t \sim 32$ per cent. So the Benthamite optimum prescribes an unemployment rate less than half the Rawlsian optimum. The tax rate is almost halved, and the lump-sum transfer payment, a, is cut by nearly 2/7.

The *median voter's* utility will reach $2^{-1/2}(u+\frac{1}{2})(1-u/1+u)$ when $\alpha = \frac{1}{2}$. This is maximized by setting u (and hence both a and t) equal to zero. Political competition between two parties will, therefore, at least in this example, lead to no redistribution and no unemployment.

The *Champernowne* optimum will occur where the geometric mean of utilities (or equivalently the sum of the logarithms of utility) is maximized. When $\alpha = \frac{1}{2}$, this prescribes unemployment of almost 16 per cent, with t at 48 per cent and a at approximately 0.076.

Example 2: Greater risk aversion Suppose that the utility function (6.45) now becomes

$$U = \alpha \log_e I + (1-\alpha)\log_e(1-h). \tag{6.52}$$

The effect of this is to leave the individual's indifference map unchanged, but to reduce the marginal utilities of both income and leisure. With (6.45), utility displayed 'constant returns to scale'. Now returns to scale are diminishing. The marginal utility of each good is inversely proportional to the amount enjoyed, under (6.52). It is tantamount to increasing the individual's risk aversion. Relative income–risk-aversion increases from $\frac{1}{2}$ (with (6.45)) to 1.

The new utility function (6.52) has no effect upon labour supply. So the demand and supply curves of unemployment are unaffected. The solution for a remains unchanged, as will the Rawlsian solution that depends upon it. But the Benthamite optimum is equivalent to the Champernowne optimum in example 1. Under (6.52), the Champernowne optimum unemployment rate advances to 19 per cent. The median voter optimum continues to give zero unemployment.

The implication of example 2 is that non-Rawlsian optima that place some weight upon the utilities of the employed are liable to register higher optimum unemployment and taxation, the more steeply the marginal utility of income diminishes. If (6.45) were transformed in the opposite direction, for example to $U = I(1-h)$, where the marginal utility of income is constant, Benthamite optimum unemployment vanishes.

Example 3: When labour supply curves can bend backwards   The Cobb–Douglas utility function with which we have been working so far – either (6.45) or (6.52) – has the property that (if a were set to zero) labour supply would be independent of the wage rate and the tax rate. The labour supply curve would essentially be vertical. This is clear from (6.47), the moment a is set to zero. This feature stacks the cards somewhat against redistribution, if we accept the rather strong body of evidence that labour supply curves probably bend backwards for many primary workers (Killingsworth (1983) summarizes evidence on this). For those with backwards-bending labour supply curves, higher income tax rates, taken by themselves, will imply longer work hours and higher tax receipts. If the size of the pie increases with the income tax rate, at least initially, the scope for redistribution will increase substantially.

One way of allowing for this is to amend (6.45) to read

$$U = (I-c)^{\alpha}(1-h)^{1-\alpha} \quad c \geqslant 0. \tag{6.53}$$

The role of c is to denote 'subsistence consumption'. Equation (6.53) is an example of the Stone–Geary utility function, which recentres the asymptotes of the indifference curves from $(0,0)$ with (6.44) to $(c,0)$. The new labour supply curve will be

$$h_i = \text{Max}\left[0, \alpha - \frac{(a-c)(1-\alpha)}{w_i(1-t)}\right]. \tag{6.54}$$

Equation (6.54) gives rise to a new supply curve of unemployment:

$$u = \frac{a-c}{1-t}\frac{1-\alpha}{\alpha}. \tag{6.55}$$

Equation (6.55) generalizes (6.48). It shifts the supply curve leftwards. If $a < c$, there will be no unemployment. The demand curve for unemployment remains (6.49). The resulting function giving a in terms of u alone, found by eliminating t from (6.55) and (6.49), will be

$$a = (c+u)\left(\frac{1-u}{1+u}\right)^2 \tag{6.56}$$

where $\alpha = \frac{1}{2}$. Equation (6.56) is a simple generalization of (6.50). Maximizing a with respect to u gives the Rawlsian optimum:

$$u = x-2; \quad a = (c+x-2)\left(\frac{3-x}{x-1}\right)^2; \quad t = 1 - \frac{(3-x)^2 - 4c}{(x-1)^2}$$

where $x = \sqrt{5-4c}$. We may infer that a rise in c reduces the Rawlsian optimum value of u, but increases those for both a and t. Similar results follow for the Benthamite and other optima. The same qualitative findings emerge if (6.53) is replaced by the CES function

$$U = \{\tfrac{1}{2}I^{(\sigma-1)/\sigma} + \tfrac{1}{2}(1-h)^{(\sigma-1)/\sigma}\}^{\sigma/(\sigma-1)} \tag{6.57}$$

when σ, the substitution elasticity between income and leisure, is less than unity. To repeat: making the labour supply curve bend back tends to increase optimum taxation, and reduce – possibly eliminate – the unemployment associated with this.

Example 4: Altering the ability distribution The simplest modification to the distribution of abilities assumed in example 1 is to displace it to the right by a positive constant, say z. So instead of lying on the interval from 1 to 0, w now ranges from $1+z$ to z. If the other assumptions of example 1 remain in force, the supply curve of unemployment will now be

$$u = \frac{a}{1-t} - z \tag{6.58}$$

when $\alpha = \tfrac{1}{2}$. As under example 3, this will tend to lower unemployment. The demand curve for unemployment, on the other hand, remains as in (6.49). The resulting equation for a will be

$$a = ((1-u)^2(u+z)/((1+u)^2+4z) \tag{6.59}$$

which also generalizes (6.50). It is clear that $da/dz > 0$. Furthermore, the value of u at which da/du vanishes (which defines the Rawlsian optimum) must fall as z increases. The effects of increasing the endpoints of the ability distribution must therefore be to lower, and perhaps to eliminate, optimal unemployment. The same tendency is observable for the Benthamite and other optima too. These conclusions are if anything reinforced if it is only the minimum ability level that is increased. Results are unaffected, on the other hand, if it is only the maximum which is changed.

If the rectangular distribution is replaced by other shapes that display one interior mode, the primary consequence is to alter the supply curve of unemployment. It develops an S-shaped appearance. Although it cannot slope down, it becomes flattest at the mode, and generally steeper at lower and higher values of a.

Example 5: Both preferences and abilities vary Suppose that people differ not just in ability but also in their preferences between income and leisure. Revert to the assumptions of example 1, except that α is now a variable, distributed uniformly between 3/4 and 1/4. Let α and w be uncorrelated.

Someone on the margin between employment and unemployment will now have α and w such that

$$w = \frac{a}{1-t} \frac{1-\alpha}{\alpha}.$$

The supply curve of unemployment will be given by

$$u = 2\int_{1/4}^{3/4} \frac{a(1-\alpha)}{\alpha(1-t)} d\alpha \sim 1.197\frac{a}{1-t}. \tag{6.60}$$

The demand curve for unemployment is derived as usual from the balanced budget equation, so that

$$a = t \int_{1/4}^{3/4} \int_{a(1-\alpha)/\alpha(1-t)}^{1} \left(w\alpha - a\frac{1-\alpha}{1-t} \right) d\alpha \, dw. \tag{6.61}$$

Eliminating t from (6.60) and (6.61) gives the function relating a to u:

$$a \sim \frac{u}{1.197} \left[\frac{4u(1.197)}{(1.197)^2 - u(2-u)} + 1 \right]^{-1}.$$

This reaches a maximum at $u \sim 0.34$, $a \sim 0.099$, $t \sim 0.651$. By contrast the Bethamite optimum occurs at $u \sim 0.12$, $a \sim 0.071$, $t \sim 0.292$.

Example 6: Introducing government spending   Suppose now that government tax revenue is applied to public goods spending (g) as well as social dividends. Then

$$a + g = ty(u). \tag{6.62}$$

Retain the other assumptions of example 1. The solution for $a(u)$ will now be

$$a = u((1-u)^2 - 4g)/(1+u)^2. \tag{6.63}$$

This reaches a maximum where $u = 2 - (5 - 4g)^{1/2}$. If g exceeds or equals $\frac{1}{4}$, therefore, optimum unemployment on the Rawlsian criterion of minimum utility will be zero. A lower threshold for g will make unemployment vanish on the Benthamite test of average utility. Whatever the social welfare function, as g increases, optimum u and a both drop while optimum t increases.

6.3.3 *Relaxing other Assumptions*

If the population size is finite, and reasonably small, individuals will notice that a fraction of their tax proceeds are returned to them personally. In general, marginal taxes on income make the individual's leisure a public bad. There is essentially a free-rider problem. But as the population size dwindles, the adverse incentive effects of income tax become (slightly) less acute.

Until now we have assumed that everyone is egocentric. If people are altruistic and public-spirited, they will derive satisfaction from the wider social benefits to which their tax payments are put. Output should respond less adversely to the income tax rate. This should increase the demand for unemployment, and could also reduce the supply of unemployment. It is also possible that individuals are envious, and attach significance to their relative incomes. If so, optimum income tax rates will probably increase. This argument is explored by Oswald (1983). If t is increased by this effect, higher unemployment could well emerge as a by-product.

The utility function with which we have been working has made the marginal utility of leisure unambiguously positive. This is a strong assumption. The extra leisure received by those out of work is widely thought to represent a reduction, not an increase in their utility. It seems more than possible that the marginal utility of leisure is positive over a range, but becomes negative, for many people at least, when h is low (close to zero, for example). The consequence of amending the utility function to allow for this is to remove social-dividend-generated unemployment completely, for those for whom this is the case.

6.3.4 *The Linear Income Tax Model: Summing Up*

Summing up the findings of the six examples studied, one can see that the optimal rate of unemployment, u^*, is sensitive to:

1 the wage distribution. Reducing the minimum reduces u^*, and can easily set it to zero. Optimum u^* will also fall, when already low, if the distribution becomes more clustered around its mean or mode;

2 how utility varies with income and leisure. Greater concavity, suggesting more aversion to risk, raises u^*. On the other hand, making leisure a 'bad' at the margin when h is low will remove unemployment completely;

3 the social welfare function. The greater the weight on minimum as opposed to average utility, or the greater the inequality aversion, the higher u^* will be;

4 preference differences, which may act to raise u^*;

5 the government's revenue requirement for public goods spending. This will lower u^*, and could eliminate it;

6 whether labour supply rises or falls with t. Optimal tax rates will be much higher in the first case than the second, and u^* may be much lower, too.

6.4 Unemployment Benefit Models

There is a close similarity between unemployment benefit models and linear income tax models of unemployment. The formal structure differs in one respect only: the social dividend is now restricted to those out of work. The supply curve of unemployment is governed by an indifference condition: those who elect for unemployment do so because the wage offered to them in the market place is so low that they are better off not working.

Begin by considering the set-up for the linear tax model in example 1 of the previous section. Replace the social dividend, a, by a benefit, b, which is confined to the unemployed. The supply curve of unemployment is deducible from the fact that the household's utility will now be

$$\text{Max}\,(b^{\alpha}, \text{Max}_{h}\,((wh(1-t))^{\alpha}(1-h)^{1-\alpha})). \tag{6.64}$$

Those for whom $b^{\alpha} > \text{Max}_{h}\,((wh(1-t))^{\alpha}(1-h)^{1-\alpha}) = \alpha^{\alpha}(1-\alpha)^{1-\alpha}(w(1-t))^{\alpha}$ are unemployed. Those for whom this inequality is reversed are employed, working for the fraction α of their one-unit time-endowment. The critical person, j, indifferent between working and not working will command a wage rate w_j that satisfies

$$b = w_j(1-t)\alpha(1-\alpha)^{(1-\alpha)/\alpha}. \tag{6.65}$$

Since w is rectangularly distributed between 1 and 0, we have

$$u = \frac{b(1-\alpha)^{-(1-\alpha)/\alpha}}{(1-t)}. \tag{6.66}$$

The amended balanced budget equation for the government gives

$$bu = t\int_{u}^{1} wh\,dw = \frac{\alpha}{2}t(1-u^{2}). \tag{6.67}$$

Equation (6.67) provides the demand curve for unemployment. Eliminating the tax rate, t, gives

$$b = \frac{u(1-u^2)\alpha A}{2(1+u^2(2A-1))} \tag{6.68}$$

where $A = (1-\alpha)^{(1-\alpha)/\alpha}$. When $\alpha = \frac{1}{2}$, (6.68) reduces to

$$b = u(1-u^2)/4. \tag{6.69}$$

The *Rawlsian* optimum in this case involves maximizing b. The resulting values of the parameters are: $u = 1/\sqrt{3} \sim 0.577$; $t = 1/3$; and $b \sim 0.0962$.

The *Benthamite* optimum can be found by computing average utility. This is

$$AU = \sqrt{b}(u + 2u^{-1/2})/3$$

when $\alpha = \frac{1}{2}$. The optimum unemployment rate falls to 35.2 per cent, and the benefit slips back to 0.0771. The income tax rate in this equilibrium is lowered to only 12.4 per cent. The *median voter* prefers $u = b = t = 0$, and achieves utility of $2^{-1/2}$. This is higher than in the Rawlsian optimum, where the median voter is unemployed (u exceeds $\frac{1}{2}$): here, his utility will be only 0.31. The *Champernowne* equilibrium is found by maximizing

$$\tfrac{1}{2}u \log_e b + \tfrac{1}{2}\log_e(b/u)\int_u^1 \log_e w \, dw = \tfrac{1}{2}(1+u)(\log_e b + \log_e u).$$

This prescribes unemployment at about 44 per cent.

As in the linear tax models, results change significantly if the assumptions are altered. Raising the minimum wage rate has the effect of lowering t and u (while raising b). Transforming the utility function to make the marginal utilities of income and leisure decline faster leaves the Rawlsian optimum unchanged, while bringing the other optima closer towards it. A government revenue requirement for public spending raises t, and lowers b and u in all optima. Replacing the rectangular distribution by something with smaller tails (such as the triangular distribution) will lower u under most conditions.

6.5 Another Approach to Optimum Unemployment

There are other ways of analysing the issue of optimum unemployment. It is more than possible that both individual job-seekers and particular job requirements are sufficiently heterogeneous for it to be thoroughly unwise for everyone to be induced to accept the first job offered. Efficiency calls for a balance to be struck between the benefit of increased search (better matching) and its costs (output sacrificed during search). There is also another way of looking at the issue of optimum unemployment, to which this section is devoted.

Suppose that there are product markets liable to random shifts in demand. Prices and capacity limits, let us suppose, have to be fixed ahead. Imagine that it is simply not possible to adjust capacity in the short run, and that transaction costs prevent firms from letting the price float to clear the market, as in an auction market. So both the price and the capacity level have to be predetermined.

An example will help to illustrate this. Suppose we are trying to choose how many seats there are to be in a theatre, and also to set the prices that these seats will command. We cannot predict exactly how much demand there will be. If demand is very high, there will be queues. Some of the people who want to come will be unable to buy tickets. On the other hand, there will be seats to spare when demand is low. The interesting question is this. What governs the *optimum* number of spare seats?

Suppose that we are interested in a social optimum, rather than the profit-maximizing outcome. Both p (the price) and x (the capacity ceiling) must be predetermined. The problem is that the demand, $p(q)+e$ let us say, is liable to disturbance. This is provided by the random term e. Imagine that this is rectangularly distributed between $+\frac{1}{2}$ and $-\frac{1}{2}$.

In a social optimum, we wish to maximize the sum of consumers' surplus and producers' surplus (in a partial equilibrium setting, with no relevant distortions in other sectors that impinge directly on the market in question). This sum can be broken down into

$$B = \int_{y}^{+1/2} \int_{0}^{x} (p(q)+e)\, de\, dq$$
$$+ \int_{-1/2}^{y} \int_{0}^{q(p)+e} (p(q)+e)\, de\, dq - \int_{0}^{x} C(q)\, dq. \tag{6.70}$$

The first term in (6.70) is the expected value of the consumers' total benefit when there is excess demand for seats. The variable y gives the value of e at which the market clears exactly, so that $y = x - q(p)$. The second term is the expected value of the consumers' total benefit when there is excess supply. The last term represents the costs of provision. We assume that the probability distribution for e is known for certain, and that there are no extra costs to queues.

Society will wish to choose p and x to maximize B. Consider the following example. Let $p(q) = 2.6 - 0.1648x + e$, and $C(q) = 1.053$. The optimum values of p and x will then be 2 and 3 respectively. y will equal -0.1056. So nearly 40 per cent of the time there will be some spare seats. The optimum expected value of these is 15.7 per cent.[5]

The analogy with labour is easily drawn. The labour force contains both 'bakers' and 'firemen'. Bakers produce a good – bread – for which demand is both regular and predictable. They never suffer unemployment. But there is also a need for firemen. The demand for firemen is substantial, but random. Society must choose how many bakers and firemen there should be. For various reasons, we have to predetermine the wages that each group will have, before we know exactly how much demand for firefighting there will be in a particular period. The transaction costs of operating an auction market for firemen will be prohibitive. When a fire has to be put out, we can surely not wait to bargain over wages and draw labour away from other uses. Some of the time, firemen will be on stand-by, waiting to be called out. Whether we call them unemployed is largely a matter of semantics. Even if formally classified as employed, many firemen will spend a high proportion of their time waiting to put out fires. There will typically be an inventory of spare labour. Car parks should be priced so that there are typically a few spare spaces to cope with random jumps in demand. Theatre tickets should be priced so that there are often a few spare seats. Labour should be priced so that there is often some reserve of spare labour ready to meet sudden jumps in demand. This will be especially true if the product they produce cannot be stored (as firefighting services clearly cannot) and demand is liable to substantial disturbance.

7 Shocks that can and may have Generated Unemployment, I: Monetary Shocks

7.1 Introduction

This chapter and chapter 8 are devoted to shocks that can help to explain short-term changes in the level of unemployment. They should be seen as an adjunct to chapters 3 and 4, on quantity-rationing models. It is in chapters 7 and 8 that we survey the factors that can precipitate changes in the demand for labour, in a macroeconomy where prices and wages are sticky enough for this to register in at least temporary changes in unemployment. Chapter 7 concentrates on various types of monetary shock, and 8 on shocks of a real nature.

7.2 Money Supply Shocks in a Closed Economy

If the prices of all goods and factors, including labour, are perfectly flexible, fully anticipated changes in monetary conditions should leave unemployment unaffected. A doubling in the supply of money will lead to a doubling of the money prices of every good, and the money wage paid to every kind of labour, all else equal. Real variables in the economy, such as quantities of output and employment, and relative prices, will not be affected; if they alter, it will be because of changes in real factors, such as preferences or technology, that happen to accompany the monetary increase.

When expectations are fulfilled and all prices are fully flexible, the money supply is 'neutral': real variables are independent of its level. This is not to say that they may not vary with the growth rate of the nominal money supply: money can be neutral and yet not 'superneutral'. (Money is superneutral if real variables are invariant to the speed with which the money supply increases.) The long-run growth rate of the nominal supply of money will affect the demand for real money holdings, for example. This in turn influences the real revenue the government earns on its monetary liabilities, and the budgetary consequences of this may lead to changes in tax rates which may bear upon the level of unemployment. Another argument for the non-superneutrality of money turns on the costs of changing the money prices of goods and factors increased. Real resources must be devoted to this if the inflation rate quickens, and relative prices may start to swing quite violently because nominal price changes are not simultaneous. The time pattern of production and employment in particular sectors may well be disturbed as a result, and increased frictional unemployment could ensue. These ideas are pursued further in chapter 12.

When price flexibility is imperfect, on the other hand, money will not be neutral. Neutrality will also fail if money supply changes occur unexpectedly. An unanticipated jump in monetary aggregates will tend to redistribute wealth from people with net nominal claims to those with net monetary liabilities. Unemployment could increase in these circumstances if the two groups of people affected differ in their spending reactions to the changes in their wealth, or, more important, perhaps, if some of the losers go bankrupt. But incomplete price flexibility poses a deeper threat to the level of employment.

Consider the case of an unexpected fall in the nominal money supply. The money market will tend to clear. If it does, the demand for money has to come down in line with its reduced supply. How is this to be brought about? Had prices and wages been perfectly flexible, the answer is clear-cut. Negative inflation would reduce the amount of nominal money that firms and households require in order to finance their transactions. The paper value of these transactions will fall along with the general reduction in prices, and so will their demand for money. But if we interrupt or suspend this process of price reductions for the time being, something else will have to give if the demand for money is to be brought down. Besides the level of prices, there are two critical variables upon which the demand for money is generally agreed to depend. These are individuals' real incomes, and the level of interest rates. The demand for money increases with real income, most obviously because real income will exert a powerful influence on the real expenditure which holdings of money are needed to finance. Interest rates matter because they represent the opportunity cost, or price of holding money. The interest rate that could have been earned on a bond, or an interest-bearing deposit with a financial institution is a measure of the cost of holding currency (or non-interest-bearing bank deposits) instead. An increase in interest rates on alternative assets must make holding money less attractive.

If the reduction in the money supply is to be matched by a fall in the demand for money, and price reductions are ruled out, the foregoing implies that monetary equilibrium has to be established by other means: interest rates must rise, or real incomes must fall, or both. Of these two variables, interest rates are the more likely candidate to bear the immediate, initial burden of adjustment. A jump in interest rates will tend to reduce the demand for labour in two ways. First, there is the direct effect upon firms which employ labour at one date to produce goods for sale later. A higher interest rate implies a reduced present value of future sales. The discounted value of labour's marginal revenue product comes down. The drop in this crucial variable will be reinforced if producers reckon that the money supply reduction will bring down the nominal price they can expect to receive on their future output, or make it harder for them to sell it. Since the profit-maximizing level of employment will be given by the point where labour's discounted marginal revenue product balances its marginal cost, in the form of wages, employers can be expected to lay off labour unless the current money wage rate can be lowered. Since we are assuming that this cannot happen quickly, employment will fall off. Higher interest rates also increase the probability of bankruptcy, and labour will be laid off as a result: Farmer (1985) provides a subtle analysis of this.

There is a second, indirect mechanism at work which will undermine aggregate employment. Higher interest rates reduce the profitability of current investment. They will also squeeze the demand for household durable goods, such as cars and dwellings, the acquisition of which is in any case typically financed by loans. Interest-sensitive components of aggregate demand will therefore fall. Corporate investment in plant and machinery may take several months, perhaps a year or more, to respond much; the impact on new house-building, and more particularly cars and other durables, will be felt more quickly, in a matter of weeks. The ensuing fall in output and employment will exert direct downwards pressure on economic agents' demands for money; this will gradually help to moderate, and probably reverse, the previous increase in interest rates. But this may not happen quickly, particularly if the real demand for money depends more upon people's perceptions of their long-run, or permanent income, than their current income.

A monetary squeeze will result in a state of Keynesian unemployment if it occurs in an economy previously in Walrasian equilibrium. Gradually goods prices will start to fall – or at least increase at a slower rate – and the economy will be driven towards the boundary of Keynesian and classical unemployment described in figure 3.13 in chapter 3. Later on, money wage rates should begin to respond. Falls in money wages, if they occur, will help to rebuild employers' demand for labour. Eventually, if this continues, Walrasian equilibrium should be re-established. Yet it is worth noticing that the final resting point will in all probability not be the same as it would have been in the absence of the monetary squeeze. The reduction in capital spending during the recession will leave the permanent legacy of a lower stock of capital. The real output generated from this shrunken capital base will be smaller, too. Lower output incidentally implies a higher price level, for a given supply of money, so the long-run reduction in prices should be somewhat smaller than the money supply cut that caused it. Worse still, at least under simple conditions, a lower stock of capital implies a reduced real wage rate paid to labour in equilibrium. If organized labour is not prepared to accept their real wage cut imposed by the long-run consequences of reduced investment, classical unemployment could last indefinitely.

Such is the gloomy tale of woe to which a monetary squeeze will give rise, in an economy suffering from imperfect wage and price flexibility. Perhaps a word or two needs to be said on the other side, since the picture painted above may be a little darker than the reality. First, if the money supply cut is announced far enough ahead and believed by everyone (this is an important qualification), its adverse consequences on output and employment will surely be neutralized to some extent by the fact that money wage rates should be renegotiated at lower levels. The prices of goods, too, will be reduced somewhat, as producers anticipate the dangers of setting prices too high. On the other hand, such developments would require people to hold forward-looking, rational expectations of future prices, and also to employ a theory of price and wage forecasting which relied upon the notion that nominal prices should respond one-to-one to money supply changes. Many economists (not all) would regard both these hypotheses as rather implausible. No less important, people must believe the authorities' claim that they will reduce the nominal money supply for the story to go through. History provides ample evidence that monetary aggregates often tend to increase faster than the average target growth rates declared by Central Banks. Observers may question the Central Bank's *ability* to restrain the growth of the money supply. They could also doubt their *sincerity*, or capacity to curb a government anxious to win votes by engineering the short-lived boom that frequently accompanies a sudden easing of monetary conditions. Below some point, government promises to reduce inflation may be downright incredible.[1] Output and employment may jump temporarily in response to surprise price increases, if producers can take advantage of unexpectedly low real wages and households fail to appreciate what is happening or to obstruct an increase in work time. Unexpected inflation also reduces the real costs of servicing the national debt – to the extent that government bonds are unindexed – and could therefore provide room for cuts in distortionary (and employment-reducing) taxation.

Another factor that may be set in the balance against the costs of disinflation is the gains in welfare, and conceivably also in employment, that are sometimes argued to accompany a lower rate of inflation. Such gains include the welfare effects of pricing money closer to its (negligible?) marginal cost, which should arise if once slower monetary growth is translated into lower nominal interest rates. One point in their favour is that they could be permanent. The output and employment losses from disinflationary policies on the other hand, painful as they may be, are largely transitional. There is also the chance that greater financial stability could strengthen aggregate demand in the short run. These arguments, and objections which may be levelled against them, are explored in Sinclair (1983a, chapter 9); we shall return to them briefly in chapter 12.

All this said, there is no denying that monetary squeezes are usually associated with substantial increases in unemployment. Ironically, these seem to be more serious when the rate of inflation is modest (Gordon (1982)) than when the authorities succeed in stopping hyperinflation (Sargent (1982)). An impression of this quantitative significance is provided by contributions to Argy and Nevile (1985). Simulations based upon the Federal Reserve Board's econometric model of the US economy by Clark (1985) reveal that a hypothetical 1 per cent cut in the growth rate of narrow money supply, M1, starting at the beginning of 1975, would have had the following effects. Two years later, after a spell of higher interest rates, unemployment would be nearly 0.6 per cent higher, while real output would have been almost 1.75 per cent lower than it actually was at the start of 1977; the rate of price inflation, measured by the annual change in the consumption deflator, would have been some 0.5 per cent lower. Two years after that, the decline in output is over 2.2 per cent, unemployment almost 1 per cent higher and inflation down, now by nearly 2 per cent, partly as a result of the delayed effects of a sharp appreciation in the exchange rate, and reduced interest rates. Over the longer term, the output effects go slightly positive for a while partly in response to a spending stimulus from interest rates, and unemployment and inflation come closer to their actual level. Eventually, output and unemployment will converge on their actual historical values, and inflation settles down to a permanent 1 per cent reduction. Estimates and assumptions by Fischer (1985) enable him to calculate that actual disinflationary (monetary) policies that began in the US in early 1980 will have led to a cumulative percentage loss of output some four or five times larger and an increase in unemployment 1.6 to two times higher, than the fall in inflation that has transpired. In other words, every 1 per cent reduction in inflation achieved over this period as a whole has a cost of roughly 1.5 million man-years of additional unemployment, and perhaps $150 billion in lost output. Fischer finds that these sacrifices paid for lowering inflation are somewhat smaller than the median estimates of this calculated for earlier periods by Okun (1978); but they are still very appreciable. This controversial and important topic receives further attention in chapter 12.

7.3 Money Supply Shocks in an Open Economy: Floating Exchange Rates

The previous section examined the effects of a money supply cut in a closed economy. This provides an illustration of what could happen in a worldwide monetary squeeze (such as occurred in 1969–70, and again in 1981–2), or in a large economy, such as the United States, where international trade and capital movements are relatively unimportant. But the economies of Western Europe and the Pacific Rim, for example, are essentially open, and even the United States is much less closed under present conditions than in the past. Many of these countries now employ floating exchange rates, either on their own or in concert with others. Another phenomenon that merits close attention is the increased international mobility of capital. This implies links between interest rates available on deposits, or bonds, denominated in different currencies. This contrasts powerfully with the analysis of the previous section, which treated interest rates as a purely internal variable independent of foreign influence.

This section will explore the consequences of a money supply cut in a small open economy with a floating exchange rate. The starting point remains the concept of monetary equilibrium within the country. This may be written in its simplest form

$$PM_d(r, q) = \bar{M}. \tag{7.1}$$

In (7.1), $\bar{M}$ denotes the nominal supply of money, P an index of prices and M_d the demand for real money ($\bar{M}/P$ in equilibrium). M_d varies positively with real income, q, and negatively with the domestic interest rate, r. In keeping with the analysis of the previous section, we assume that prices are temporarily sticky. The price index P is given in the short run, and let us suppose that the same is true, initially at least, of the real income variable, q. In these circumstances, a sudden unexpected fall in the nominal money supply, $\bar{M}$, must lead to a jump in the interest rate. This is the only way that monetary equilibrium can be preserved, and is exactly what happened under similar conditions in the closed economy of the previous section.

The significance of opening the economy is that domestic and overseas interest rates will be linked by international capital mobility. If this is perfect, funds lodged at home must bear the same prospective return as they would have earned overseas. We therefore obtain an equation connecting r with its foreign value, r^*:

$$r = r^* + \hat{R}^e. \tag{7.2}$$

The second term on the right-hand side of (7.2), $\hat{R}^e$, is the expected rate of depreciation of the home country's currency in terms of foreign exchange. Suppose that this is a pure number (so that exchange rate expectations are 'single-valued'). If everyone expects the home currency to fall by 2 per cent in the next year, they must anticipate a capital gain of 2 per cent or so[2] on foreign-exchange-denominated assets. So if the full yield on the home and foreign bonds is to be equal – and if it were not, a limitless flood of capital would leave the country in order to equalize returns – the difference between domestic and foreign interest rates must also be 2 per cent. Home-currency-denominated bonds have to carry an explicit yield 2 per cent above their overseas counterparts, in order to cancel the expected capital gain on the latter.

We began with the jump in r which followed on the heels of the cut in $\bar{M}$. Now (7.2) will tell us that if r^* is unchanged $\hat{R}^e$ must jump by the same amount as r. The home currency must now be expected therefore, to depreciate by an amount equal to the interest differential, $r - r^*$, if $\hat{R}^e$ were previously zero. It seems natural to relate expectations of future exchange rate changes to the model under examination. Suppose that people know and understand the model, and are convinced that there will be no more monetary disturbances at home or abroad. Suppose, too, that q (and its foreign counterpart) are static, that the foreign price level and money supply are given and that r^* will therefore be given. Assume that people know that it will take a specified time, say 3 years, for the domestic price level, P, to respond in full to the domestic money supply cut. In 3 years' time, the price level will have fallen in equal proportion to the present cut in $\bar{M}$. Lastly, suppose that there is a long-run association between the home and foreign price indices, P and P^*, given by

$$P = P^*/R. \tag{7.3}$$

In (7.3), R is the exchange rate, defined as the number of units of a foreign currency needed to buy one unit of domestic money. Equation (7.3) is a long-run purchasing-power-parity condition. Equation (7.3) tells us that when the 3 years are up, and P has fallen by the same proportion as $\bar{M}$ (say 5 per cent), R must be some 5 per cent higher than it was in the previous equilibrium before the money supply cut occurred. The long-run effect of the monetary squeeze will be to cause *appreciation* of the exchange rate.

We now encounter a paradox. The exchange rate must appreciate in the long run. Yet, because of (7.2), it must be expected to *depreciate* in the meantime, before the new equilibrium is reached. The paradox can be resolved, if exchange rate expectations are formed on the basis of complete understanding of the model itself, as we have assumed, by having the spot exchange rate jump initially by more than the 5 per cent long-run appreciation that people will be forecasting. This means that the exchange rate will overshoot. It must rise suddenly now, by more than the long-run change in order to create room for the depreciation anticipated. Suppose that the pattern of domestic price adjustments implies the following sequence of values for the domestic interest rate:

now: $r - r^* = \hat{R}^e = 2$ per cent
1 year's time: $r - r^* = 1$ per cent
2 year's time: $r - r^* = \frac{1}{2}$ per cent

The domestic interest rate will tend to drop back, since gradual falls in domestic prices must lower the domestic demand for money, and therefore release the pressure on r to preserve the monetary equilibrium condition (7.1). These numbers will imply a forecast depreciation of the exchange rate of roughly $3\frac{1}{2}$ per cent over the 3-year period. We solve back from the end of the price-adjustment period to the present, to obtain an equilibrium current exchange rate some $8\frac{1}{2}$ per cent above its old value, before the cut in M occurred. To repeat: an x per cent fall in the domestic money supply will cause a larger than x per cent jump in the exchange rate now, in order to create room for the anticipated depreciation implicit in the newly emerged interest differential between home and foreign bonds. Similarly, an x per cent money supply increase should cause a greater-than-x per cent depreciation of the country's currency now (since home interest rates will be temporarily reduced to prevent an excess supply of money), and this will entail expectation of future exchange rate appreciation.

This model of exchange rate overshooting was proposed by Dornbusch (1976). It can be extended in various ways. A distinction may be drawn between traded goods, exportables and importables upon which an 'arbitrage' condition such as (7.3) may hold even in the short run, and non-traded goods like haircuts or bricks or restaurant meals, the prices of which respond sluggishly to monetary conditions. Another amendment would be to introduce forecasts of *future* monetary policy. Newly formed beliefs that the money supply will be reduced next year, for example, should cause an exchange rate appreciation now, in anticipation of this event. This notion can be extended to consider changes in the expected future growth of monetary aggregates. If participants in bond and foreign exchange markets suddenly expect tighter restrictions on the growth of the money supply, as they presumably will have done both before and shortly after Mrs. Thatcher's General Election victory in May 1979, they will anticipate a spell of higher domestic interest rates while the new policy bites (and eventually lower ones, as inflation and inflationary expectations subside). If the exchange rate is forecast to depreciate (because of high domestic interest rates, and (7.2)) down to an appreciation trend, it must jump by a substantial amount now to create the room for this. 1979 and 1980 witnessed a steep climb in the effective exchange rate for sterling. Other factors, such as North Sea Oil and the second oil shock, undoubtedly played some part in this; but there are cogent reasons for attributing much of the appreciation to the monetary expectations mechanism described above. This is the story told in detail in a brilliant paper by Buiter and Miller (1981), extended in subsequent work of theirs (1982, 1983); variants on the theme appear in other interesting contributions to Eltis and Sinclair (1981). Figures 7.1, 7.2 and 7.3 sketch the Dornbusch and Buiter–Miller overshooting phenomena.

What implications do such exchange rate developments have for unemployment? The clue here is to examine what happens to the *real* exchange rate. This can be

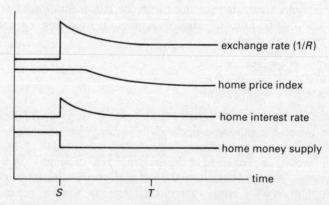

Figure 7.1 *The Dornbusch model: unexpected money supply cut at* S, *when the price adjustments are complete at* T

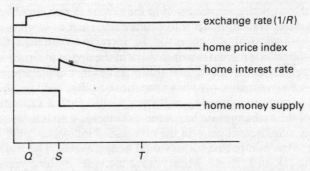

Figure 7.2 *The Dornbusch model: money supply cut at* S *anticipated at* Q

defined as PR/P^*, which is the ratio of the home price index, expressed in foreign currency, to the price index overseas. Consider the simple Dornbusch model depicted in figure 7.1. At date S, the exchange rate R jumps sharply, and P has yet to register any fall. Abroad, prices are given. So PR/P^* suddenly increases. As time goes on, it eases back, for two reasons: there is downwards pressure on the domestic nominal price index, P; and R itself slips back gently towards its new long-run equilibrium. But the initial effect will be goods for overseas or home markets which are reasonably close substitutes for foreign goods. In the numerical example constructed above, the real exchange rate rises by $8\frac{1}{2}$ per cent initially, and takes 3 years to return to equilibrium. Faced with a loss of competitiveness on this scale, domestic producers of tradable goods will suffer a serious erosion of profit margins; they will be forced to cut back output and employment; some may well founder on the rocks of bankruptcy. Exactly the same phenomenon would be observed if, as in figure 7.2, the money supply cut were anticipated ahead, or the change in policy took the form of a reduction in the growth rate of monetary aggregates, as in the Buiter–Miller case shown in figure 7.3.

It would be the tradables sector that bore the brunt of employment losses.

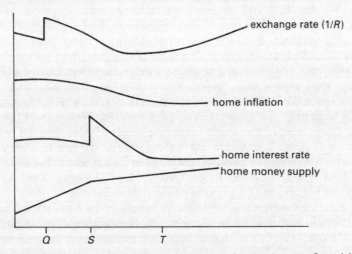

Figure 7.3 *The Buiter–Miller model: cut in the money supply growth rate at* S, *anticipated at* Q; *price adjustments completed by* T

Elsewhere in the economy, appreciation in the exchange rate could be far from an unrelieved disaster. Traded inputs into production, such as of oil, would become cheaper. Households' real wealth could be increased (although the monetary squeeze and interest rate increases would work in the opposite direction), at least in terms of cheaper, imported goods, and this might even stimulate some additional spending. To set against this, people whose incomes depended on the fortunes of exportables and import-competing industries would curtail expenditures. If the appreciation of the exchange rate happened to coincide with a sharp rise in money wage rates, any employment gains in the non-traded industries could be squeezed, and losses in the trade-impacted sector would be aggravated. This was exactly what occurred in the UK in 1979–80. Money wage increases in these years were of the order of 16 per cent per annum, some 7 per cent above the Organisation for Economic Co-operation and Development (OECD) average, at just the time when sterling rose sharply against almost every OECD currency. The increase in unemployment of $1\frac{1}{2}$ million in 1980 and 1981 can largely be ascribed to this unfortunate combination of events.

7.4 Money Supply Shocks in an Open Economy: Fixed Exchange Rates

The previous section explored the consequences of a tightening of monetary policy, actual or expected, in an economy with a freely floating exchange rate. This represents one end of a spectrum of possibilities. At the other end one could envisage the case of an immutably fixed exchange rate. Between these extremes will lie managed floats, where the Central Bank intervenes at times to stabilize the exchange rate or nudge it in a particular direction; exchange rate arrangements like the European Monetary System, where a set of countries restrict the variations in exchange rates between each other tightly, but float as a group against the rest of the world; a fixed exchange rate system that allows for periodic changes in parity; and other schemes, such as the declaration of fixed parities which allows for a time trend, or permits a substantial band around the par value within which the exchange rate can fluctuate, or multiple exchange rates for different types of transactions. There are examples of all these systems in the contemporary world. Overshooting could manifest itself, in an altered form, in all but the extreme case of an immutably locked exchange rate. The series of staggered devaluations by France between 1980 and 1983 is a case in point: foreign exchange market participants interpreted the expansionist policy proposals of the incoming Socialist administration as an indicator of future monetary and fiscal laxity, forcing the authorities to yield to exchange rate pressures that closely resembled the opposite of what had happened a little earlier to sterling. These devaluations did not prevent French unemployment from increasing in these years. But it rose much less than the OECD average. France's unemployment stood at 8.1 per cent at the end of 1983, as against 7.2 per cent in mid-1980. By contrast, the OECD average went up by much more, from 6.8 per cent to 10.1 per cent between these dates.

If exchange rates are irrevocably locked, changes in the domestic money supply of internal origin will tend to be absorbed by the balance of payments and the reserves. A money supply cut should create an initial excess demand for money. Capital will tend to flow in from abroad in response to any upward pressure on domestic interest rates, and as a direct consequence of domestic residents' attempts to liquidate interest-bearing assets in order to rebuild their money holdings. The trade balance could swing into surplus, too, in reflection of their likely wish to cut expenditure relative to income with the same end in view. There is no reason to expect adverse effects on competitiveness; if anything, any downwards pressure on domestic prices would ensure the opposite. Employment in the economy's traded sectors would be insulated against domestic monetary shocks originating at home. In marked contrast to what could occur under floating rates, however, the monetary squeeze might provoke temporary employment losses in the non-traded industries, where domestic producers would feel the full weight of reductions in demand. In the long run, domestic monetary equilibrium would tend to be restored as a result of the current and capital account surpluses. These would induce a rising level of reserves. Domestic residents would sell surplus foreign currency to their banks, who in turn would seek to exchange it for reserve assets at the Central Bank. Unless the authorities strove to perpetuate the shortage of domestic money, monetary aggregates would rise in line with the increased bank reserves.

A fixed exchange rate will tend to shield employment, at least in traded industries, from internal monetary shocks. But it will make it more vulnerable to changes in monetary conditions overseas. A tightening in the money supply in a large foreign country will induce deflationary effects elsewhere, particularly in countries that retain a fixed exchange rate against it. A country with a floating exchange rate should experience depreciation, and a consequent gain in competitiveness, which should serve to protect tradables employment against the worst of the recessionary pressures. As we saw in chapter 1, Britain's decision to abandon the Gold Standard in 1931, and allow sterling to drop by some 40 per cent against most other currencies, helped to ensure that unemployment climbed far more slowly in the UK than elsewhere during the Great Depression of the early 1930s. UK unemployment doubled to 22 per cent in 1933 compared with 1929, as against a tenfold increase to over 33 per cent in the United States between these years. A more recent, if less spectacular, example is furnished by the experience of 1981–2, when worldwide monetary restrictions dominated (if not initiated) by US policy helped to bring American unemployment up from 6.8 per cent at the end of 1980 to over 11 per cent at the end of 1982. Unemployment also increased in all West European economies between these dates, but in most cases considerably more slowly. Total EEC unemployment rose by only 3.5 per cent between these dates. This coincided with a 15 per cent depreciation of the European Currency Unit against the US dollar.

7.5 Demand for Money Shocks

A sudden increase in the demand for money will act just like a reduction in the supply of money. If wages and prices are fully flexible, there will be pressure on them to fall. If the demand for money rises and its nominal supply is fixed, society will achieve the higher real money holdings it seeks as a result of price and money wage declines. In the absence of wage and price flexibility, however, monetary equilibrium will be restored, in the short run, by a combination of interest rate rises and real output declines. Initially, it will be interest rates that carry most of the burden of adjustment; a little later, as a direct result of this, real expenditure will be squeezed as investment, and interest-sensitive components of consumer spending, are forced down. Any eventual tendency for prices and money wage rates to drop in the face of the Keynesian unemployment which emerges should help to stimulate a gradual return towards Walrasian equilibrium.

This is, at least, what will happen in a closed economy. An open economy with a freely floating exchange rate should undergo appreciation. If the demand for money jump is understood for what it is, and expected to last for good, the exchange rate path will look much as in figure 7.1, in section 7.3. This follows from the fact that there can be no real difference between a sudden increase in the demand for money and a sudden fall in its supply. When the exchange rate is frozen, as in section 7.4, a higher demand for money at home will induce the same effects as a domestic money supply cut: a tendency to surplus on the current and capital accounts of the balance of payments, growing reserves and (quite possibly) consequential increases in the money supply.

The demand for money might increase for a number of reasons. Perceptions of wealth could increase as a result of natural resource discoveries, for example: this phenomenon is studied in section 8.1 of the next chapter. The introduction of indirect taxation, or increases in the rates of existing indirect taxes (such as Value Added Tax) would tend to raise the demand for money, since the value of many transactions undertaken by economic agents will have to rise. In June 1979, the standard rate of VAT in the UK was raised from 8 per cent to 15 per cent. The sharp rises in the exchange rate and British short-term interest rates that occurred at the same time may be partly ascribed to this fiscal change. Another tax instrument which can cause major effects on the demand for money is income tax. Baba et al. (1985) have established that the demand for nominal money in the US can be closely linked to *after-tax* interest rates; some of the indifferent performances of previous demand-for-money econometric equations can be put down to their authors' failure to specify accurately the true opportunity cost of holding it. A rise in the income tax rate will lower net-of-tax interest rate, all else equal, and therefore tend to strengthen the demand for money (though there will presumably be income effects on the demand for money that run in the opposite direction: Sinclair (1983a)). Other variables that Hendry finds significant influences upon money demand include interest rate volatility (this is captured by the variance of bond yields in the previous 3 years, and raises the demand for money) and various measures of financial innovation and the time pattern of people's presumed reaction to it. Future studies might uncover the positive link between money demand and the variability of income, which theories of the precautionary demand for assets implies. A final potential cause of a jump in the demand for money that deserves mention is the old Keynesian hypothesis that a spontaneous fear of higher future interest rates – and the capital losses on illiquid assets to which they will give rise – would make money look a more attractive refuge and should therefore raise the asset demand for it at once. Relationships like this may help to explain the odd behaviour of the US dollar in 1983 and 1984, which rose sharply in international markets with every piece of bad news about the size of the prospective budget deficit, as will be seen in section 8.5 of the next chapter.

8 Shocks that can and may have Generated Unemployment, II: Real Shocks

8.1 The Nasty Side to Nice News: Natural Resource Shocks

The early 1970s saw substantial discovery and exploitation of natural gas finds in the Dutch sector of the North Sea. Much of the gas was exported to West Germany. Terms became increasingly advantageous in the wake of the 1973–4 oil shock, which raised the equilibrium prices of oil substitutes, of which gas was a prominent example. Dutch exports flourished. Her trade surplus improved sharply. Dutch residents' real income also rose strongly. One might have expected other sectors of the Dutch economy to boom as a consequence of its residents' increased wealth. But they did not. In fact the opposite occurred.

The competitiveness and profits of Dutch companies in other, non-energy, traded sectors were squeezed hard by rising wage rates and a strong exchange rate, which continued to mark time, more or less, with the German Mark (while Germany enjoyed much lower rates of price and wage inflation). Productivity stagnated. Unemployment climbed. Observers in the Netherlands and elsewhere alike mused at this mysterious phenomenon. It was christened Dutch Disease, suggestive of the tragic affliction killing many of the world's elm trees at much the same time.

Similar developments happened elsewhere. Iranian agriculture, for example, crumbled in the 1970s. The country had fed itself in the early 1960s; by the late 1970s, it was importing three-quarters of its food, and many farms lay abandoned. The growing wealth from oil production was the generally accepted reason for this. Probably no Canadian province or US state has richer reserves of natural resources per head than British Columbia, yet few have a higher average rate of unemployment. South and Western Australia provide another example. In Latin America, industrialization has often proceeded much more rapidly in relatively resource-poor economies, such as Brazil, than in others like Mexico or Venezuela which are blessed with vast oil endowments. The fastest economic growth rates in recent years were often to be found in countries like Japan or East Germany which enjoy a negligible natural resource base. Finally, North Sea finds in the early and mid-1970s ensured that Britain, almost alone among Western countries, would be more than self-sufficient in oil for two decades or more after 1978. In the 5 years that followed, unemployment trebled and the level of industrial production declined by over 9 per cent.

The mechanism by which favourable natural resource effects exert such unpleasant side-effects on an economy can be described in various ways. First, there is the exchange rate story. North Sea Oil might be thought to represent a jump of some $2\frac{1}{2}$ per cent in the permanent income of British residents.[1] Suppose that Britons' demand for money depends in part upon their permanent income. If the supply of money is given, and a floating exchange rate is assigned the task of preserving equilibrium in the market for money, there will have to be appreciation. A variant of this argument stresses the exchange rate as equilibrating the demands and supplies of all sterling-denominated assets, including bonds and equities. If British residents have a rather strong penchant for such assets, again one would expect appreciation. A further twist to the story would stress the importance of the government's tax revenues from North Sea oil production. These would create room for tax cuts, increasing the attractiveness (and worldwide relative price) of British equities if lower rates of corporation tax, for instance, were expected to ensue. Then there is the simpler point that replacing imported by home-produced oil has a major positive effect upon the trade balance, and this – or expectations of this – could help to strengthen the exchange rate directly. A final point would be that oil tax revenues would make it easier for the authorities to keep budget deficits down and hence, according to some economists,[2] to avoid the need for future increases in the money supply, that takes us back to the Buiter–Miller argument of section 7.3. If, for whatever reason, the nominal exchange rate jumps, other traded industries will suffer a reduction in competitiveness and profits, and losses in output and employment will follow.

The 'real' aspects of how natural resource discoveries could damage other sectors of the economy can be sketched out differently. The additional incomes generated as a result of them will be spent partly on traded goods, and partly on non-traded goods. The former can be shipped in easily from overseas, the latter not. So the relative price of non-traded goods increases. Wages are bid up. The non-traded sectors gain labour; the traded sectors release it, and contract. Overall unemployment may increase for a while in the wake of these structural changes, especially so if redundant ex-employees in the traded industries take time to be re-engaged elsewhere, perhaps because their skills are specific to the industries shedding them. Upwards pressure on the wage rate will be keen if labour as a whole reacts to the resources discovery by behaving as if it had gained a new source of unconditional, non-labour income: if leisure is counted as a normal good, the effective labour supply will tend to shrink if this is so. It is a sad and curious fact that the British government's yield from taxes on North Sea Oil is similar in magnitude to the increase in unemployment benefit payments that has occurred since 1978. Lastly, a noteworthy empirical phenomenon: natural resource industries, particularly those that are newly established, are typically much less intensive in the use of labour than the old manufacturing industries that contract as a result.

The economies of the Dutch Disease have been studied by numerous authors. Corden (1984) provides a most illuminating survey of the literature in this field; other important contributions include those of Bruno and Sachs (1982a), Buiter and Purvis (1982), Corden and Neary (1982) and Fender (1985). A common finding is that the unemployment effects of a natural resource boom depend very much upon how government reacts, how wage rates behave and what is assumed about the relative factor intensities of the different sectors.

Lastly, in this connection, it is worth citing one country which has conspicuously *not* suffered from Dutch Disease: Norway. Norway's current oil output is four times larger, per head of population, than Britain's; her recoverable reserves per head are thought to be some nine times greater. But Norwegian unemployment has averaged 2–4 per cent in the years 1975–85. At the time of writing (1985) it is 3 per cent, as against 13 per cent in the UK. Norway also managed to avoid, then and now, the crippling high real exchange rate which damaged the UK so badly in 1980–1. Norway's escape from Dutch Disease owes something to design, something to luck. She has deliberately chosen to extract her oil much more slowly than the UK; this will have helped to shield the exchange rate from some of the balance of payments pressures in early years that have afflicted the UK. Foreign capital is discouraged from entering Norway by a variety of factors including high taxes. Employment and production in Norwegian industry, much of which is oil-related, are insulated – implicitly subsidized – by import tariffs and other instruments.

8.2 Oil Price Shocks

The two oil shocks of the 1970s, in 1974 and 1979, exposed the fragility of economies built upon transforming energy inputs into manufactures and services. The two decades from 1951 had witnessed an actual slight *decline* in the nominal dollar prices of oil products, in a period where the prices of final goods were increasing in dollar terms at an average of 3 per cent per annum. The high ground of hindsight enables us to see now that some of the unprecedented economic growth in Western industrial economies in these years can be attributed to the favourable trend in the real price of energy. Bruno and Sachs (1982b) go further and claim that the estimates of growth in these years are overstated by the national income statisticians' failure to correct fully for this trend.

Theory suggests that the real price of oil should, if anything, increase over time. If oil-well owners are to be indifferent between investing in oil-in-the-ground and other assets, such as bonds, the prospective rates of return – adjusted for factors such as taxation and risk – should be equal. Setting the costs of extraction aside, this can only occur if the price of oil is expected to rise at the rate of interest. If the rate of interest exceeds the expected rate of oil price increase, few people will want to hold oil, and down its price must come; when oil prices are expected to rise faster than the rate of interest, the opposite will occur. So the nominal price of oil should be expected to rise at roughly the nominal rate of interest, the real price at the real rate. If expectations are to be fulfilled on average, and the real rate of interest is taken to be some $2\frac{1}{2}$ per cent, it might seem reasonable to predict a long-run trend in the real price of oil of between 1 per cent and $1\frac{1}{2}$ per cent per annum. The difference is explained partly by the presence of extraction costs, partly by the possibilities of new discoveries and oil-saving technological changes.

The actual price of oil may deviate sharply from this long-run trend. News of finds, or wars, or taxes, developments that could influence the growth in demand, or interest rates, could cause spot oil prices to shoot up or down violently, in much the same fashion – and for analogous reasons – as the exchange rate did in the overshooting model of section 7.3 of the last chapter. The economics of oil have been the subject of a powerful recent survey by Newbery (1984) which examines these issues in detail. One additional complicating factor described there and explored at greater length in Newbery (1981) is the question how competition evolves between the cartel of major oil exporters, OPEC, and the fringe of independent oil producers that have flourished in the after-glow of the two OPEC-led price hikes of the 1970s. Another interesting question is the effect of long-run changes in savings and demographic variables upon the oil market.[3]

These points are valuable, for they help to remind one that oil price shocks are not spontaneous. They happen for a reason. This is no less true of other shocks. For statisticians there is a clean conceptual break between the purely random, the white noise, in a variable, and the systematic variation which can be traced to changes in other variables. This simple distinction is carried over into econometric studies and theoretical inquiry. But in practical terms it is really very hard to swallow. Coups, elections, strikes, famines, fires and the like do not just happen on their own. Yet they are hard to predict in advance, especially as to timing. From that standpoint we can often quite properly deem them random. Furthermore, this curious status of an event, that it is random ex ante but explicable ex post, is not confined to oil price shocks. It is equally true of every shock examined in this chapter and the last one.

How does dearer oil affect the demand for labour? There are various channels. First of all, it raises producers' operating costs, because oil is a direct input, or indirect input (through electricity). Product prices rise, and output falls, bringing down the demand for labour. This effect will be most pronounced in energy-intensive industries, such as steel, facing elastic demand for their products. A second effect, which is favourable to the demand for labour, turns on substitution in production techniques: now that energy is dearer, and labour relatively cheap, it becomes profitable to make production less energy-intensive and more labour-intensive. But the second effect is slow. It typically has to await a new generation of more energy-efficient capital. It is also very likely to be dominated by the first, unfavourable effect, especially if demand is elastic and labour-for-energy substitution is weak. A third influence running from oil prices to labour demand works through wage rates: dearer oil raises the cost of living, and wage rates may increase because of explicit or implicit indexation mechanisms on pay. This will be adverse. A fourth is positive: labour demand will be stimulated in energy-extractive industries, and in their suppliers. The relatively low labour intensity in these sectors implies that the macroeconomic significance of this will typically be insubstantial, however.

Then there are likely to be repercussions on international exchange rates. Oil exporters experience an improvement in their terms and balance of trade. Direct upwards pressure will be felt on exchange rates if they are free to float. This will be strengthened by other considerations, such as the likely consequences for government tax revenues: equity market participants may forecast lower taxes on capital, and bond dealers may anticipate less danger of deficit-monetization. So the capital account of the balance of payments may improve at existing exchange rates, implying appreciation. For oil-importing countries, the picture is reversed. They are likely to experience downwards pressure on exchange rates. The consequential exchange rate re-adjustments will tend to squeeze the overall demand for labour in oil-exporting countries, and strengthen it for oil importers, as the pattern of international competitiveness for non-oil-trading industries alters. These mechanisms are explored in detail in Fender (1985), Sinclair (1983b), Wijnbergen (1985) and elsewhere.

8.3 Technology Shocks

How does technological progress affect the demand for labour? Can it generate unemployment? The short answer to these questions is that anything can happen. Improved technology reduces the labour required to produce a unit of output, particularly when it is labour-saving. This effect is obviously adverse for employment. On the other hand, the fall in costs may help to reduce prices, leading to higher demand and higher output. That effect must be positive. The net result depends upon which effect dominates. The greater the elasticity of demand, and the greater the flexibility of prices, the likelier it becomes that the demand for labour is strengthened rather than weakened.

Other considerations affect the repercussions on the demand for labour, too. We saw in chapter 4 that, when wage rates and prices are fixed, technical progress is certain to imply less employment in conditions of Keynesian unemployment, but likely to raise the demand for labour when unemployment is classical. If money wage rates are fixed and goods prices are flexible, everything turns on the price elasticity of demand for output: a higher elasticity implies a greater rise in output, and a large chance of employment increases. If both money wage rates and goods prices are perfectly flexible, the economy should adjust to a state of continuous full employment, at least under ideal conditions: in that case, technological change will exert its major impact upon the pattern of factor and goods prices, and not upon employment.

In an international setting, the picture becomes more complicated. If an industry in one country tries to resist technical changes adopted by its overseas competitors, it is almost certain to suffer. Foreign competition will drive prices downwards. If it fails to match this unit cost reduction, it will face falling sales, and even bankruptcy. When the domestic industry sells only to the home market, it may be saved by tariff increases, but the overall loss in consumers' welfare implied by this policy casts grave doubt over its merits.

Technical change is likely to raise the demand for certain types of labour and cut it for others. Whether unemployment increases as a result depends upon how relative wages, and the actors concerned, react. Retraining measures should soften the impact. But if wage rates for the adversely affected groups stay up, and no attempt is made to retrain them, severe unemployment may ensue.

The effect of technical progress upon employment and wages is an old question. The possibility of adverse changes was first explored in depth by Ricardo (1821). More recently macroeconomic models were set up to examine the issue by Neary (1981) and Sinclair (1981). It was also the subject of a detailed inquiry by Heffernan (1981). Stoneman (1983) presents a variety of approaches, extended subsequently by Venables (1985) and Stoneman and Ireland (1986). In the context of developing countries, Hall and Heffernan (1985) provide a valuable study, building upon Heffernan's earlier work.

8.4 Other Shocks

A country's demand for labour may fall victim to other types of shock, as well. The country may experience a violent change in its international terms of trade. A terms of trade deterioration means that the relative prices of its exports fall in terms of its imports. Such an event lowers workers' consumption wages, in comparison with their levels expressed in terms of producers' prices. It acts like a sudden increase in the income tax wedge between them levied by the fiscal authorities. If the consumption wage is slow to adjust, producers will experience a jump in product wages, and falls in output and employment will ensue. The 1973–4 oil and commodity prices shocks provide an illustration of this: at that stage, the entire OECD area, including the UK, was a substantial net importer of oil and many other primary commodities. Unemployment climbed with a speed and severity unparalleled since the Second World War. The pronounced differences in the unemployment experiences of the UK and the US in the early 1930s may also testify to the fact that while Britain's terms of trade improved sharply, those of the US suffered a marked deterioration in that period. The unemployment consequences of a worsening of the terms of trade turn critically upon the flexibility of wage rates. The 1979 oil shock provides an interesting contrast between Japan, where real wages fell by 6 per cent or so in the following 12 months and unemployment barely rose at all, and many Western countries, where real-wage stickiness led to a sharp rise in unemployment.

In the UK, on the other hand, the second oil shock brought an improvement, not a worsening, in the terms of trade. By this time she had become a major net exporter of oil. But that did not prevent a sharp jump in unemployment: in fact unemployment rose more swiftly in the UK from 1979 to 1981 than in almost any OECD country. The reasons for this paradox were twofold. First, it happened to coincide with a period when the UK was widely regarded to be undergoing or to be about to undergo, a period of sharp monetary disinflation. But, more interestingly for our purposes, the terms of trade improvement added to other forces inducing a jump in the exchange rate for sterling. When exchange rates are floating freely, the exchange rate tends to respond swiftly to terms of trade changes. Deterioration induces depreciation, which helps to insulate the demand for labour in exportable and importable industries. The opposite happens when the terms of trade improve.

A further set of shocks that can cause a sudden response in the demand for labour is fiscal. Tax cuts reduce the wedge separating employers' and employees' perception of wage rates. They also strengthen the personal sector's real income: consumption spending will increase, particularly when the tax cuts are unexpected, or when households have been constrained by credit restrictions. The sharply diverging unemployment experiences of the US and Western Europe since 1981 can be attributed in no small part to the fact that taxation has been lightened in the former and, broadly speaking, tightened in the latter. The US and Western Europe have also experienced different trends in central government spending. This has risen sharply in the US primarily under the impact of greatly increased military expenditure; the UK, France, West Germany and Spain, on the other hand, have witnessed varying degrees of retrenchment in government expenditures on goods and services. It is noteworthy that the rate of inflation in the United States has not deteriorated in comparison with the OECD average; if anything, the reverse has occurred. Much of the explanation for this lies in the fact that the combination of budgetary expansion and monetary tightness in the United States led, in 1981–4, to a pronounced appreciation of the dollar. This held down the prices of internationally traded goods and contributed to a sharp drop in the rate of inflation. Whether America's exceptional good fortune in improving her unemployment–inflation trade-off so dramatically will endure is a moot point. The mounting budget deficits to which her tax cuts and rising government expenditures have led should eventually induce a depreciation in the exchange rate for the dollar, through a variety of mechanisms (Sinclair (1983c)). Indeed, 1985 has already witnessed a sharp reversal in the dollar's previous climb. This will ultimately feed through into a (temporarily) increased rate of inflation. Budgetary expansion should not, therefore, be relied upon as a lasting cure for stagnation. But this is not to deny that it can exert powerful favourable effects for several years. When the restrictive consequences of higher debt servicing charges come to be felt, as eventually they must, one can only hope that the macroeconomy in question will have returned to lower general levels of unemployment. In that case, the fiscal boosts will at least have succeeded in reducing the swings in unemployment.

If the US response to the unemployment crisis of the early 1980s has proved remarkably successful in reducing both unemployment and inflation together within its national boundaries, it has brought one major threat to employment elsewhere in the world. Tight money and large deficits have combined to push real interest rates to unparalleled heights, not just in America but everywhere else, as well. Higher real interest rates exert downwards pressure on purchases of durable goods by firms and households alike. Investment outlays in dwellings, plant machinery, inventories and consumer durable goods will all tend to fall as a result. An increase in real capital rental rates squeezes the demand for other factors of production, including labour and primary materials. If the prices of these factors are flexible, they must tend to ease. The early 1980s witnessed rather pronounced declines in the real prices of oil and other material inputs into production; but real wage rates have held up, with a consequent squeeze in employment levels (at least in most West European countries).

8.5 Concluding Remarks

In this chapter, and the previous one, we have seen that the demand for labour is vulnerable to a large number of shocks. These shocks can be monetary or real. There are cogent reasons for believing that the last 5 or 10 years have witnessed an unfortunate coincidence of several unfavourable shocks, particularly in the UK. But a fall in the demand for labour at given wages and prices need not betoken an increase in unemployment. This can only happen if relative prices fail to adjust swiftly enough to the new situation. The recent climb in unemployment in the UK and elsewhere in Western Europe, must therefore be attributed to a *combination* of two sets of factors. First, there have been negative shocks on the demand for labour: tight money, high real interest rates, oil market developments, exchange rate appreciation and the like. But no less important, these have been translated into higher unemployment because labour markets, particularly in Western Europe, have been too inflexible. Constitutional weaknesses have impeded the relative price adjustments that could otherwise have saved the day. Unemployment has been contained, and later cut, in the United States, partly because of her unique (and impressively successful) budgetary stance, and partly because real wages have displayed flexibility. Japan has escaped by virtue of her system of wage flexibility. In the UK, and other West European countries where unemployment has continued to nudge upwards since 1982–3, real wages have proved almost impervious. Much of the explanation for this must lie in the nature of labour contracts prevailing on the Eastern shores of the Atlantic. Possible reasons for wage rigidities were discussed briefly in chapter 2; they also form the subject matter of the next chapter, which is devoted to the study of implicit contracts.

9 Implicit Contracts

9.1 Introduction

Why are wage rates often determined in advance, often before the employer knows what his exact demand for labour will be? Why is it that employment often varies so much more, in response to shocks of the kind studied in the last two chapters, than rates of pay? What difference does it make if the worker has less information than the firm about the environment affecting the latter, or if the firm is averse to risk? It is to these questions that this chapter is devoted.

The structure of this chapter is as follows. Section 9.2 presents a simple model, which is examined in detail in 9.3. The assumptions underlying the simple model are relaxed in 9.4. The analysis bears a strong resemblance to the study of optimum distribution explored in chapters 5 and 6. In fact, optimum tax theory under the Benthamite criterion of *average utility* is formally equivalent to implicit contract theory under the *expected utility hypothesis*. This hypothesis underpins much of the analysis of the present chapter. It states that, under uncertainty, people act to maximize the weighted average of utility in each 'state of the world', or outcome, where the weights are the perceived probabilities of the states in question. The hypothesis is unfortunately far more uncontroversial. The recent survey by Shoemaker (1982) presents arguments and evidence against it. The great virtue of the hypothesis, on the other hand, is that it provides a simple basis for analysis. There is no serious rival to it in this role.

9.2 The Simplest Model: Background and Assumptions

An implicit contract is an agreement between an employer and his employees about rates of remuneration, and hours of work, that will apply when particular circumstances arise. What makes such agreements interesting is the existence of uncertainty about the circumstances surrounding the employer's demand for labour. There is a random element, which cannot be predicted ahead. It may be the price of the product in the next period that is uncertain, or more generally the strength of demand for the good in question. Alternatively, the production function may be uncertain, because of randomness in technology; or the price of another factor of production, such as energy, may be subject to random shocks. In practice, all three types of uncertainty may be present.

Implicit contracts have been the subject of detailed scrutiny by numerous economists in the past decade. The first models, explored by Azariadis (1975) and Baily (1974), were concerned with explaining why employment levels seem to vary much more than wage rates in the face of random short-term shocks to the demand for labour, in several advanced economies, particularly in the United States. Subsequently models were devised to see whether contracts of this type would lead to more or less unemployment than spot-auction markets, where the wage rates and the employment levels were simultaneously determined in the period in question, rather than agreed ahead (in probabilistic terms). A frequent element in the story in these later models was an assumption that the worker(s) knew less about the state of the world governing the demand for labour than the firm. This asymmetric information twist was found to have important implications. Models of this kind have been the subject of an excellent recent survey by Hart (1983). For a general survey on all types of implicit contract models, the reader is warmly encouraged to consult Rosen (1985). What follows will provide a simple sketch of the central ideas, which are examined in greater detail in these two papers.

Models of implicit contracts can be taxonomized by the different answers that they give to certain questions. This defines the critical assumptions that underpin the various models. Probably the most important questions are:

Q1: How many employees does a particular contract cover?
Q2: How does the 'representative' worker's utility vary with his income and his leisure time?
Q3: What is the worker's attitude to risk?
Q4: What does the employer's utility function depend upon, and how?
Q5: How many products does the firm produce?
Q6: Does the firm operate in a competitive environment for its product(s)?
Q7: How is output related to the labour input?
Q8: Do non-labour factors also enter the production function(s)?
Q9: How does the state of the world govern the employer's demand for labour?
Q10: What does the probability distribution for states of the world look like?
Q11: Is the probability distribution known to everyone?
Q12: Is the state of the world visible to all parties, once it materializes?
Q13: Is the contract enforceable?
Q14: How many time periods does it cover?

The simplest model explores the implications of assumptions that give the following answers to these 14 questions:

A1: One worker only.
A2: The single worker has a utility function in which both consumption, c, and leisure time, l, play a role. Suppose that the worker will be endowed, in the next period, with one unit of time. His leisure will be the difference between this endowment and his time spent working for the employer, h:

$$l = 1 - h. \qquad (9.1)$$

Time spent not working for the firm is devoted to producing goods at home. Each unit of l can produce α units of consumption. We might

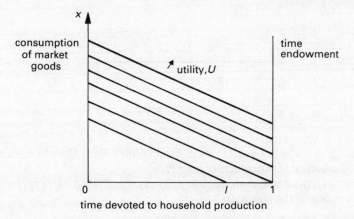

Figure 9.1 *Indifference curves between consumption of market goods and time allotted to household production*

think of him growing vegetables in his garden, painting his home, repairing his car or cooking meals. These activities are known as 'household production'. If he earns a wage rate of w, and wage income of wh, his total consumption will therefore be

$$c = wh + \alpha l = (w - \alpha)h + \alpha. \tag{9.2}$$

The simplest thing is then to assume that we can write his utility as

$$U(c) = U(wh + \alpha l). \tag{9.3}$$

Suppose x is defined as the consumption of 'market' goods bought out of wage income, so that $x = wh$. Equation (9.3) may be rewritten

$$U(c) = U(x + \alpha l). \tag{9.4}$$

Equation (9.4) gives a set of straight-line indifference curves between market goods consumption and time free for household production. They are illustrated in figure 9.1.

A3: The worker is averse to risk. This means that there is a diminishing positive marginal utility of total consumption: for $U(c)$, $U' > 0 > U''$.

A4: The employer's utility depends solely on his profits, and he is neutral to risk. This means that the firm will be concerned solely to maximize the mean expected value of profits, $E\pi$.

A5: The firm produces a single product.

A6: The firm is perfectly competitive. This entails that the price of its product, p, is outside its control. Perfect competition between firms can also be invoked to imply that the firm's expected profits will vanish, given neutrality to risk (A4).

A7: The simplest assumption would make output, Q, directly proportional to the labour input, h:

$$Q = \beta h. \tag{9.5}$$

There are constant returns to labour according to this production function. The productivity of labour, β, is a constant.

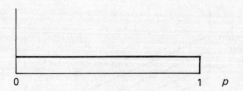

Figure 9.2 *The rectangular probability distribution to the state of the world and the price of the product*

A8:   Labour is the sole factor of production (this is already reflected by the absence of other factors from (9.5)).

A9:   The price of the product, p, is simply equal to an index representing the state of the world, θ:

$$p = \theta. \tag{9.6}$$

There is no technological uncertainty (β is not subject to random shocks), and since labour is the only factor of production (A8), the demand for labour cannot be affected by random changes in the availability or price of any other factor.

A10: The states of the world, and hence, given (9.6), the prices of the product, are uniformly distributed between a maximum of 1 and a minimum of 0. Figure 9.2 illustrates this probability.

A11: Yes: The probability distribution depicted in figure 9.2 is known to everyone.

A12: Yes: both the worker and his employer observe the state of the world accurately and costlessly once it materializes. There is no asymmetry of information.

A13: Yes. The contract can be enforced costlessly, and with certainty, by both parties.

A14: The contract agreed at one date specifies x and h, that is the total wage income and the level of employment, for the next date only.

9.3 Analysis and Implications of the Simplest Model

Begin by assuming that the worker and the firm agree to a contract that says the following. If the worker spends any time working for the firm, he will receive the actual value of the marginal product of his labour as a wage rate. If he does not supply any time to the employer, he will receive nothing. So, if $h = 0$, $x = 0$; but if $h > 0$, $x = wh = phm$, where m is the marginal product of labour. From (9.5), m will equal β. Hence $x = ph$. Call this contract A.

The worker will face a budget line between x and l. If $l = 1$, $h = 0$ and $x = 0$. This point is illustrated by point A in figure 9.3. At the other extreme, if the worker surrenders his entire endowment of time to the employer (so that $l = 0$ and $h = 1$), he will receive wage income of $p\beta$. This is shown at point B, in figure 9.3. But since p may lie anywhere between a maximum of 1 and a minimum of 0, with equal probability (recall A10), contract A provides the worker with a range of possible budget restraints. The steepest occurs when p is at its highest possible value, of unity; the flattest will be horizontal. Figure 9.4 depicts this.

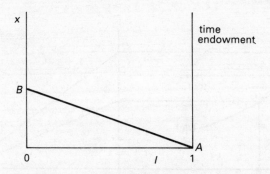

Figure 9.3 *The worker's budget restraint under contract A*

The worker's indifference curves, shown in figure 9.1, can now be superimposed upon the family of possible budget restraints. The indifference curves are drawn in figure 9.4 as dashed lines. What will the worker choose to do? When the budget line is *steeper* than the indifference curves, he will do best to devote his time to working for the firm full-time. When it is flatter, his best policy is to allocate all his time to household production, and reach point *A*. There is a critical value of *p* at which he will be indifferent between these two courses of action. When his budget restraint is given by *AE*, which is parallel to the indifference curves, points *A* and *E* (and anywhere in between) will be equally attractive. Point *A*, where the time endowment is retained in full for household production, will enable him to consume α units of consumption. Hence point *E* will be defined by the condition that total consumption will be the same as at *A*: hence, at *E*, $x = \alpha$. Label this critical value of the price of the product as p^*. Since the wage income at *E* is $p^*\beta$, and since $p^*\beta = \alpha$, we have

$$p^* = \frac{\alpha}{\beta}. \tag{9.7}$$

Wherever the price *exceeds* this critical value, household production will be

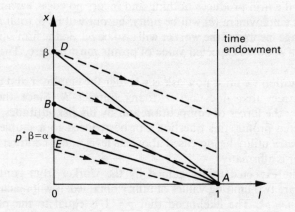

Figure 9.4 *The multiplicity of possible budget restraints under contract A*

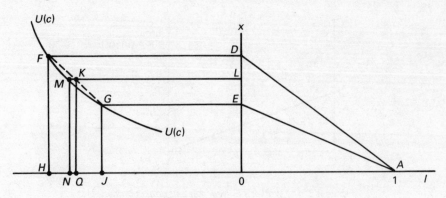

Figure 9.5 *The worker's utility under contract A*

replaced by full-time employment, and consumption will equal βp. Below p^*, time will be reserved fully for household production, yielding consumption of α. Hence actual consumption will be *either βp, or α*, whichever is higher:

$$c = \text{Max}\,[\beta p, \alpha]. \tag{9.8}$$

The utility level enjoyed by the worker will depend upon p. Figure 9.5 shows this. The curve in the left-hand panel of figure 9.5 depicts the utility function, which reflects the diminishing marginal utility for consumption stipulated in A3. The highest utility will be obtained when the price of the product is at its upper limit of unity: this is shown by point H. The worst that can befall is utility level J: this is what the worker gets when he devotes all his time to household production. The likelihood of this is given by the ratio OE/OD, given the rectangular probability distribution and price limits laid down in A10. The probability of non-employment is therefore $p^* = \alpha/\beta$ (from (9.7)). If the worker is employed, the chance of which will be $1 - p^* = (\beta - \alpha)/\beta$, he is exposed to randomness in both his consumption and his utility. Any point between H and J can arise. All, save J, are equally likely.

Finally, we should check these results under contract A for consistency with the other assumptions of the model. Does the firm have zero expected profits, as implied by perfect competition and risk neutrality on the part of the employer? Yes: when $p < p^*$, the firm produces nothing and incurs no costs, earning zero profits. When $p > p^*$, employment (h) will be unity; output will be β; total receipts will be $p\beta$; and the wage income of the worker will also be $p\beta$. So the firm earns zero profits at all values of p. So its expected value of profits must be zero. The model is fully consistent.

The key question we must now ask is whether the employer and the worker can devise a contract that does better than contract A. Since the employer is constrained by the forces of competition and by his risk attitudes to a vanishing level of expected profits, this question can be reduced to a simpler one: can the worker's *expected* utility be increased above its level under contract A? As we shall see, the answer is affirmative.

Consider the expected utility gained by the worker from contract A. When $p > p^*$, there are two limiting values of utility obtained: it will reach H when $p = 1$ and J when $p = p^*$. The likelihood that $p = 1$ is equal to the probability that $p = p^*$. So the *expected* utility from these two events alone is the probability that one of them will occur, multiplied by Q. Q is the mean of H and J; it is found by drawing a straight line between points F and G, and finding the midpoint (K).

Now the firm would be indifferent between (a) paying a wage of D when $p = 1$ and E when $p = p^*$, and (b) paying L (the mean of D and E) in both these eventualities. If it did this, the curvature of the utility function between F and G would enable the worker to increase his expected utility in the event that p was either 1 or p^*, from Q (corresponding to point K) to N (corresponding to point M). The worker would be unambiguously better off.

The argument can be extended. Suppose we consider a price slightly below 1, $1 - \varepsilon$ let us say. The probability that $p = 1 - \varepsilon$ and $p = p^* + \varepsilon$ are equally probable. The firm would be indifferent between paying L in both these events, and paying the wage incomes implied by contract A in the two cases ($\beta(1 - \varepsilon)$ and $\alpha + \varepsilon$ respectively). The worker would again prefer a sure income of L in either event to half a chance of $\beta(1 - \varepsilon)$ and half a chance of $\alpha + \varepsilon$. Getting L in each case would give utility N, rather than something smaller. This is true of *all* pairs of points between D and E symmetrically distributed around L.

Let us define contract B as a contract that will pay the worker the expected value of his wage income whenever $p > p^*$. Contract B will confer utility of N for certain if $p > p^*$, and J if $p < p^*$. This must be superior to the expected utility under contract A, which will be approximately equal to

$$Jz + (1 - z)(N + Q)/2$$

where z is the probability that $p < p^*$. What drives this result is the shape of the utility function. Had diminishing marginal utility of C (risk-aversion) been replaced by a constant marginal utility (implying risk-neutrality), the utility curve in the left-hand panel of figure 9.5 would have been linear. Then contracts A and B would have promised the household equal levels of expected utility. Points M and K (and hence N and Q) would have converged. Had the worker been a risk-lover, contract B would have been less attractive than A; M would lie to the right of K, not to the left.

In fact an even more attractive contract than B can be devised for the worker, which does not violate the zero expected profit constraint for the firm. Although B exposes him to much less risk than A, there is still uncertainty. The worker is better off when $p > p^*$ than when $p < p^*$. His utility is N in the first case, J in the second. So there is still room for the worker to gain by a further provision of insurance from the firm.

The optimum contract, let us call it C, will offer a guaranteed utility level, so that the worker will be indifferent between working and not working. It will consist of a two-part wage: a payment of y_1 if the worker works full-time for the firm, and a compensation payment, y_2, if it turns out that the firm finds it more profitable not to engage him. If the worker is to regard these two eventualities with indifference, $y_1 = y_2 + \alpha$, since total consumption, c, will be the same in each case. The firm will wish to employ the worker if the net rewards from doing so, $p\beta - y_1$, exceed the costs. The 'cost' is in fact negative: it is the saving of the unemployment compensation payment, y_2. Hence employment occurs if

$$p\beta - y_1 > -y_2 = \alpha - y_1, \quad \text{i.e.} \quad p\beta > \alpha.$$

The critical value of p below which the worker is not employed is the same, therefore, as under contract A. The firm's policy will be:

employ if $p > \alpha/\beta$;
not employ if $p < \alpha/\beta$.

We can now work out the size of y_1. It must be whatever is necessary to set expected profits to zero.

Expected profits will equal the expected value of total receipts, less the expected value of total wages paid. Total receipts will be $p\beta$, except when $p < \alpha/\beta$, in which case they will be zero. Hence expected receipts will be

$$\int_{\alpha/\beta}^{1} p\beta \, dp = \left(1 - \left(\frac{\alpha}{\beta}\right)^2\right)\frac{\beta}{2} = \frac{\beta^2 - \alpha^2}{2\beta}. \tag{9.9}$$

The expected value of costs will be y_1, multiplied by the probability of employment $(1-(\alpha/\beta))$, plus $y_2 (= y_1 - \alpha)$, multiplied by the complementary probability α/β, that the price of the product will be too low for employment to be worthwhile. This amounts to

$$y_1\left(1 - \frac{\alpha}{\beta}\right) + (y_1 - \alpha)\frac{\alpha}{\beta} = y_1 - \frac{\alpha^2}{\beta}. \tag{9.10}$$

If expected profits are to vanish, (9.9) and (9.10) must be equal. Consequently

$$y_1 = \frac{\beta^2 - \alpha^2}{2\beta} + \frac{\alpha^2}{\beta} = \frac{\beta^2 + \alpha^2}{2\beta}. \tag{9.11}$$

Since $y_2 = y_1 - \alpha$, (9.11) will also enable us to identify the optimal value of unemployment compensation

$$y_2 = \frac{\beta^2 + \alpha^2}{2\beta} - \alpha. \tag{9.12}$$

This optimum contract is depicted in figure 9.6. Under contract C, the worker gets a wage income of R if he is employed by the firm, and a payment of S if he is stood off. R and S lie on a line parallel to AE. The line connecting R and S therefore represents an indifference curve (recall figure 9.2). The certain level of utility enjoyed by the worker is V, in the left-hand panel, which corresponds to point R.

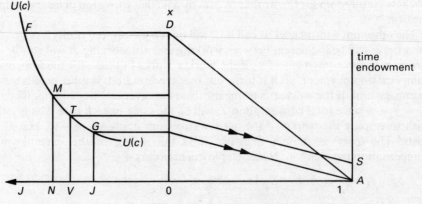

Figure 9.6 *Contracts B and C compared*

9.4 Generalizations: Relaxing the Assumptions of the Simplest Model

9.4.1 *More than One Worker Covered (Relaxing A1)*

The results obtained in section 9.3 carry over directly to the case where there are many employees, all of whom have the same preference (as given by A2). When the price of the product exceeds the value implied by point R in figure 9.6, everyone will be working full-time for the firm. When it falls below this, employment will be zero. When the price equals the value implied by R, there may be partial employment, with some people working and others not.

If the workers differ in their preferences, because their efficiency in household production, as captured by α, varies, the slopes of their indifference curves between x and 1 will differ. Those with the highest will have the steepest indifference curves. They will be engaged by the firm less often, since the price of the product has to jump a higher hurdle for it to be worth the firm's while to employ them. But when they are at work, they will receive a higher wage (as equation (9.11) testifies). Samuelson (1985) presents an analysis of the effects of heterogeneity among workers in a more complex framework with interesting results.

9.4.2 *Generalizing Preferences (Relaxing A2)*

Under assumption 2 of the simpler model, straight-line indifference curves were generated between x and l. We turn now to examine a case where the indifference curves between consumption and leisure time (time not spent working for the firm) take their more typical shape, downwards sloping and convex to the origin. This might be because there are diminishing returns to household production. Alternatively, we may assume that the worker enjoys both consumption and leisure, with a diminishing marginal rate of substitution between them.

It will help to work with a particular example of a utility function. This will illustrate the differences between various possible contracts, and enable us to see precisely what happens to consumption, labour supply and expected utility in the various cases. Accordingly, we replace (9.3) and (9.4) by

$$U = 2.5 + \log_e c + \log_e (1 - h). \tag{9.13}$$

Equation (9.13) generates indifference curves between consumption and leisure which are perfect rectangular hyperbole, depicted in figure 9.7.

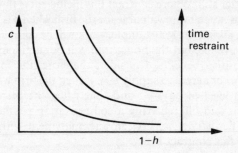

Figure 9.7 *Rectangular-hyperbolic indifference curves between consumption and leisure, implied by (9.13)*

We are now in a position to explore different possible contracts, carrying over the other assumptions of the simplest model. One possibility, call it contract D, is for both parties to agree to 'wait and see'. The wait-and-see contract will pay labour a wage rate equal to the ex-post value of its marginal product, βp. This means that the firm and the worker will wait until the value of p is known; the household will then choose its preferred work time, h, in full knowledge of the price of the product, and will receive a wage income of βph.

Under this wait-and-see contract, the household will select h to maximize

$$U = 2.5 + \log_e (\beta ph) + \log_e (1 - h).$$

Utility will be maximized where $h = \frac{1}{2}$. So leisure time will be $\frac{1}{2}$, and consumption will equal $\beta p/2$. In order to obtain precise numerical estimates, assume that $\beta = 1$ (the exact value of β makes no qualitative difference to the results). Consumption will then lie anywhere between a maximum of $\frac{1}{2}$ (when p is at its highest value, unity), and a minimum of zero (when p is its floor of 0). Expected utility will be given by

$$EU = 2.5 + \int_0^1 \log_e p \, dp + 2 \log_e \tfrac{1}{2} = 0.1137.$$

Contract D guarantees leisure at $\frac{1}{2}$, since the household's optimal work time does not vary with p under the particular utility function chosen. But consumption is random.

Contrast contract D with a different case, where *both* consumption *and* leisure are guaranteed. Call this contract E. Suppose the firm promises to engage the worker for a fixed time, $\bar{h}$, and to pay it a fixed wage, equal to the expected value of its marginal product multiplied by $\bar{h} (\bar{h} Ep)$. Utility will now be

$$U = 2.5 + \log_e (\bar{h} Ep) + \log_e (1 - \bar{h}). \tag{9.14}$$

The expected value of the price of the product, Ep, is $\frac{1}{2}$, by virtue of the assumption (A10) that p is distributed rectangularly between 0 and 1. The value of $\bar{h}$ that maximizes U will be $\frac{1}{2}$, as in contract D. Hence expected utility will be

$$EU = 2.5 + 3 \log_e \tfrac{1}{2} = 0.421.$$

It is clear that E is much more attractive than D. There is 'full employment' at $h = \frac{1}{2}$ under both contracts. But E scores over D in eliminating income-risk for the worker. The firm, which is neutral to risk, absorbs all the burden of uncertainty about the price of the product. E offers the household 100 per cent insurance, as under contract C in the simplest model.

But we can do better still. Where contract E is inefficient is that it fails to allow for the fact that labour is much more valuable for the firm when p is high than when it is low. When p is at its minimum, for example, work will be completely pointless, since it will generate no revenue; but the household will be sacrificing leisure time from which it derives positive benefits. Consider, therefore, the following possibility. Suppose that the worker agrees to supply $h = \frac{1}{2}$ when the firm wishes to engage it, in return for a certain level of pay, y_1; and that when the price of the product is sufficiently low, he is laid off, receiving a compensation payment, y_2, that is high enough for him to be *indifferent* between unemployment with y_2, and employed ($h = \frac{1}{2}$) with y_1. Call this contract F.

Indifference on the worker's part between these two cases means that utility must be equal:

$$U = 2.5 + \log_e \tfrac{1}{2} + \log_e y_1 = 2.5 + \log_e 1 + \log_e y_2$$
$$\Rightarrow \log_e y_1 = \log_e y_2 + \log_e 2$$
$$\Rightarrow y_1 = 2y_2.$$

Hence y_1 must be twice as large as y_2. The firm's expected profits must be zero. This enables us to find the highest values of y_1 (and hence y_2) that the firm can afford. The cut-off value of p, call this p^*, below which the firm makes a lower loss by setting $h = 0$, can be found by setting the profits from employment ($h = \tfrac{1}{2}$) by those from unemployment ($h = 0$):

$$\text{at } p^*: \frac{p^*}{2} - y_1 = -y_2 = -y_1/2$$

$$\Rightarrow p^* = y_2 = y_1/2.$$

The value of y_1 can now be found by setting expected profits to zero:

$$E\pi = \int_{y_1/2}^{1}\left(\frac{p}{2} - y_1\right)dp - \int_0^{y_1/2} y_1/2 \, dp = 0$$

$$\Rightarrow \boxed{y_1 = 0.536, p^* = y_2 = 0.268.}$$

Contract F therefore generates a probability of unemployment of nearly 27 per cent; this is also equal to the level of unemployment benefit (nearly 0.27), while income at work, which the worker has a probability of over 73 per cent of receiving, is nearly 0.54. Expected utility under contract F will be nearly 0.49, as compared with only 0.421 under E.

There is an important conclusion to be drawn from contrasting these three contracts. Workers can do better for themselves in an uncertain environment in which they are averse to risk, by agreeing hours and pay in *advance*. A policy of waiting and seeing (contract D) will expose them to avoidable risks. Furthermore, they can do still better by entering into an agreement that specifies that the employer lays them off in adverse circumstances, provided they are adequately compensated in that eventuality by receiving unemployment pay which makes them no worse off, in utility terms, than they would have been at work.

Yet, although F represents a considerable improvement over D and E, it is still not the best possible contract which can be devised. We turn now to the *optimum* contract between the firm and the worker. Call this contract G. Contract G will, in general, display two properties. These are:

Property I: Pareto efficiency: The worker's marginal rate of substitution between leisure and consumption equals the value of labour's marginal product, in every state of the world (for every p).
Property II: Optimum risk apportionment: given that the worker is averse to risk (A3), and the firm is risk-neutral (A4), the worker's marginal utility of consumption should be equal to all states (for every p).

Property I follows from an ex-post efficiency requirement. If it failed to hold, there would be circumstances in which it would be possible to increase both utility for the workers and profits for the firm, by altering the 'trade' (c, h) between the two. Property II calls for the worker's marginal utility of consumption to be the same in all states. If it failed, the worker could reach a higher level of expected utility by shifting consumption in some state (where MU was lower) to others (where it was higher).

What do these properties imply? The worker's marginal rate of substitution between leisure and consumption is simply the ratio of the marginal utility of leisure $(1/(1-h))$, given (9.13) to that of consumption $(1/c)$. Hence:

$$\text{Property I} \Rightarrow \frac{c}{1-h} = p. \tag{9.15}$$

Now the marginal utility of consumption equals $1/c$. Hence consumption should be stabilized at a particular value, c^*, no matter how high or low the price of the product:

$$\text{Property II} \Rightarrow c = c^*. \tag{9.16}$$

Combining (9.15) and (9.16) we have

$$h = 1 - c^*/p. \tag{9.17}$$

There is a problem with (9.17). If p is very low, c^*/p could exceed 1, this would be a nonsense, since it would imply that the worker should supply a negative labour input to the employer. So (9.17) should be amended to

$$h = \text{Max}\,[1 - c^*/p, 0]. \tag{9.18}$$

From (9.18) we see that if $p < c^*$, there will be zero employment.

Our next task is to calculate c^*. The firm transfers a flat rate of pay, c^*, to the worker, irrespective of how much labour is supplied (if any). So its costs are certain, at c^*. Since expected profits must vanish, costs must equal expected receipts. If $p > c^*$, when the worker will supply labour equal to $1 - c^*/p$, the firm's receipts will be $p - c^*$. Hence

$$E\pi = \int_{c^*}^1 (p - c^*)\,dp - c^* = \frac{1 - c^{*2}}{2} - c^*(1 - c^*) - c^* = 0.$$

This yields the solution $c^* = 2 - \sqrt{3} = 0.268$.

How much better off will the worker be under contract G than its predecessors? When he is unemployed ($p < 0.268$), he will supply no work time. So utility, in that event, will be $2.5 + \log_e(0.268) = 1.183$. When p exceeds the critical value of 0.268, the worker will supply work time of $1 - c^*/p$, cutting his leisure to c^*/p. Hence his utility will be $2.5 + 2\log_e(0.268) - \log_e P$. Expected utility will be

$$EU = \int_{0.268}^1 \log_e \left[\frac{0.268}{p}\right] dp + 2.5 + \log_e(0.268) = 0.598.$$

Contract G therefore represents a substantial gain in expected utility over F, and even more so over E and D.

All four contracts, D, E, F and G, are now summarized for comparative purposes in table 9.1. The inferences to be drawn from this table are as follows. First, to repeat, the optimum contract secures much higher expected utility than the others, while F and G also do much better than the wait-and-see contract, D. Second, the more efficient contracts (as measured in expected utility) are liable to display a positive probability of unemployment. It is simply silly for the worker to sacrifice

Table 9.1 *Four possible contracts, for utility given by equation (9.13)*

Contract	Description	Expected utility	Consumption		Work time		Unemployment possibility
			Mean	Variance	Mean	Variance	
D	Wait-and-see. Wage rate equals ex-post value of labour's marginal product	0.114	0.25	0.021	0.5	0	0
E	Pay and hours fully guaranteed against risk	0.421	0.25	0	0.5	0	0
F	Worker indifferent between working for guaranteed hours and pay, or unemployment with reduced pay	0.49	0.232	0.003	0.366	0.049	0.268
G	Optimal contract, obeying Pareto efficiency and optimal risk apportionment	0.598	0.268	0	0.353	0.072	0.268

valuable leisure time in circumstances where the value of labour is too low. Third, a more general point: hours of work vary positively with the price of the product, and the value of labour's marginal product, in the more efficient contracts. F and G display appreciable variance in work time. Lastly, expected utility tends to increase when the variance of consumption is reduced: E scores much better than D because of this, and similarly it is partly for this reason that G does so much better than F.

This example also serves to reinforce an important result obtained in the simplest model, which has considerable macroeconomic implications. The facts of the world, as seen in chapter 1, definitely suggest that booms and slumps have a stronger immediate impact upon levels of unemployment than on wage rates. Upswings, associated with favourable price or technology shifts that raise firms' demand for labour, lead to gains in employment, while wages tend to be sticky in the short run. Downswings take a considerable toll on jobs, while wages stay up. The implicit contract models studied in this chapter suggest a possible explanation for this phenomenon: it is simply more efficient for workers and firms to enter into contracts that pre-specify lower levels of employment, at unchanged or only slightly reduced rates of pay, in unfavourable conditions.

On the other hand, the reader is warned against placing too much reliance upon a particular example. Other utility functions generate different results. The author has shown elsewhere (Sinclair (1986c)) that the utility function

$$U = \sqrt{c(1-h)} \tag{9.19}$$

has some surprising consequences. Contract G is unattainable because properties I and II have incompatible implications. In this case, the optimal contract calls upon the worker to retain no leisure, and consume nothing, when the price of the product is sufficiently high, while he receives a large unemployment benefit, and supplies no work, when this is not so. This kind of contract, although optimal under (9.19), has no real-world counterpart, perhaps because it would be so hard to enforce, or because the firm has such a large temptation to lie about the price of the product (pretending that it was higher than its true value), or because (9.19) understates the degree of risk-aversion which workers typically display. By contrast, all the four contracts compared in table 9.1 do seem to co-exist in practice.

9.4.3 *Relaxing the Assumption that the Worker is Averse to Risk (Relaxing A3)*

The simplest model depended critically upon the premiss that the household was averse to risk. Risk-aversion also underpinned the model of the previous section (9.4.2): when utility is related to the logarithm of consumption as in (9.13), the marginal utility of consumption is inversely proportional to the level of consumption, and, with a utility function such as (9.13) successive increments to both consumption and leisure have a diminishing impact upon utility.

Had the worker been neutral to risk, the utility function (9.4) of the simplest model could be written

$$U(c) = ac + b$$

where a is a positive constant. In fact, a becomes the (constant) marginal utility of consumption. The utility curves in the left-hand panels of figure 9.5 and 9.6 become straight lines. The advantage of contracts that eliminate income risk vanishes at once. If we go further and assume that the worker positively enjoys risk, utility will be represented as a convex increasing function of consumption. The utility curves will be curved towards the vertical, consumption axis rather than the utility axis; point k would lie to the left of M in figure 9.5 and the worker would seek to avoid the tedium of predictability in his consumption. He would accept any fair bet that increased the spread of possible consumption values, for a given mean, and would even be prepared to take on some gambles that were unfair to himself.

The possibilities of risk-neutrality or risk-preference are maintained for formal completeness. But they do not seem sufficiently probable to merit further space.

9.4.4 *Relaxing the Assumption that the Employer is Risk-neutral (Relaxing A4)*

Everything up to now has been based upon the assumption that the firm is neutral to risk. This has meant that the firm is concerned only with its mean value of expected profits. Coupled with the assumptions about perfect competition and technology, it has enabled us to set expected profits to zero and compare contracts from the worker's standpoint simply on the criterion of his expected utility.

If both the worker and his employer are risk-averse, the latter will have a diminishing marginal utility of profits, resembling the former's diminishing marginal utility of consumption. It will cease to be true that the firm can be forced by competition to shoulder all the risks of production: in general, the burden of uncertainty will be shared between employer and employed.

Consider the following example, that retains the structure of the model set up in section 9.4.2, but simplifies the range of values that the price of the product can take. Suppose that p is known to have only two possible values, of $\frac{3}{4}$ and $\frac{1}{4}$, and that the two events are equally likely. The household's utility is as given by (9.13). But since the firm is also averse to risk, endow it with a utility function

$$U_f = \log_e(\pi + a). \tag{9.20}$$

Equation (9.20) displays risk-aversion, since the marginal utility of profits is $1/(\pi + a)$, which declines as a increases. Suppose that competition among firms sets the firm's expected utility to zero. Define y_1, h_1 and y_2, h_2 as the consumption levels and work time to be agreed upon in the two events. Subscript 1 refers to the favourable outcome, when p will be $\frac{3}{4}$.

Equation (9.20), and the restriction that the firm's expected utility vanishes, enable us to write

$$EU_f = 0 = \tfrac{1}{2}\{\log_e(\pi_1 + a) + \log_e(\pi_2 + a)\} \tag{9.21}$$

where $\pi_1 = \frac{3}{4}h_1 - c_1 + a$ and $\pi_2 = \frac{1}{4}h_2 - c_2 + a$. Using (9.13), the worker's expected utility will be

$$EU = 2.5 + \tfrac{1}{2}\log_e c_1 + \tfrac{1}{2}\log_e(1 - h_1) + \tfrac{1}{2}\log_e c_2 + \tfrac{1}{2}\log_e(1 - h_2). \tag{9.22}$$

The optimum contract maximizes (9.22) subject to (9.21). Optimizing with respect to c_1 and h_1 gives us

$$\frac{1 - h_1}{c_1} = \frac{4}{3} \tag{9.23a}$$

and, for c_2 and h_2,

$$\frac{1 - h_2}{c_2} = 4. \tag{9.23b}$$

Conditions (9.23a) and (9.23b) are the Pareto-efficiency conditions, obeying property I of the optimal contract, G, in section 9.4.2. They state that the worker's marginal rate of substitution between leisure and consumption should equal the value of labour's marginal product.

We can now substitute for h_1 and h_2 in (9.22) and (9.21), then reoptimize with respect to c_1 and c_2. This gives the condition

$$\frac{c_2}{c_1} = \frac{\frac{1}{4} - 2c_2 + a}{\frac{3}{4} - 2c_1 + a} = \frac{\frac{1}{4} + a}{\frac{3}{4} + a} \tag{9.24}$$

which describes the optimal trade-off between consumption in the two states. Note that if $a \to \infty$, the firm becomes risk-neutral, because the marginal utility of profits to the firm will then be insensitive to the level of profits. In this extreme case, (9.24) implies that $c_1 = c_2$; the marginal utility of consumption is equated in the two states, and, given (9.13), this calls for the same levels of consumption. But with finite a, this ceases to be true, and $c_2 < c_1$. The lower is a, the more risk-averse the firm, and the more c_2 drops below c_1, in proportionate if not absolute terms.

The characteristics of the optimum contract can be found, in terms of a, by substituting (9.24) into (9.21):

$$c_2 = \tfrac{1}{2}\left(\tfrac{1}{4} + a - \sqrt{\frac{\frac{1}{4} + a}{\frac{3}{4} + a}}\right). \tag{9.25}$$

Equation (9.25) enables us to find c_2, and hence, from (9.24), (9.23a) and (9.23b), c_1, h_1 and h_2, for a given value of a. Table 9.2 illustrates various cases. As the firm becomes more averse to risk, a falls; the levels of consumption that the firm can promise diminish at least in the unfavourable state subscripted 2 (when $p = \frac{1}{4}$); work hours increase in both states, especially the adverse one; and the worker's expected utility must drop.

Table 9.2 *The optimum contract between risk-averse firm and risk-averse worker*

a	c_1	c_2	h_1	h_2	Worker's expected utility
∞	$\frac{1}{4}$	$\frac{1}{2}$	$\frac{1}{2}$	0	0.767
0.994	0.28	0.2	0.626	0.2	0.456
0.769	0.149	0.1	0.801	0.6	−0.869

9.4.5 *Introducing a Multi-product Firm (Relaxing A5)*

If the firm can produce more than one product, and can switch labour costlessly and immediately from one product line to another, with the technology and competitive environment assumptions carried over from the simplest model, it will always allocate production to the most profitable uses. Less than perfectly positive correlation between the prices of the different products would imply a reduction in the probability of unemployment, since it becomes distinctly improbable that there is nothing in the firm's product range that is worth producing. If the firm is averse to profit risk, as in section 9.4.4, multi-production carries the additional attraction of allowing it to diversify and reduce overall risk. On the other hand transferring resources between different lines may be costly; diminishing returns may apply, and the firm may perceive some monopoly power which will limit the extent to which it can increase output on relatively profitable lines; and if the source of the disturbance to selling prices is essentially macroeconomic, there is a distinct likelihood that a low price for one product will be accompanied by low prices for others. Nevertheless, some of the risk in selling a particular product is liable to be microeconomic, and confined to that product. In such circumstances, particularly when the firm is averse to risk, there is a major opportunity to gain from diversification. We might think of large, diversified corporations in the US, Western Europe and Japan as little more than holding companies, or internal capital markets, whose function is to exploit the advantages of spreading risks. If formal, external capital markets were perfect, these gains could be secured by individual portfolio holders; no doubt this occurs to some extent. When the random variables (here, the prices of the products) are common knowledge, no informational asymmetries arise between the enterprise, its employees and its stockholders or holding company. So there will be no moral hazard problem (no incentive for the enterprise to behave differently when insured than when uninsured, and cheat the insurer). Consequently, when the enterprise itself is averse to risk, like the worker, both parties can gain by acquiring insurance against poor values of p from a third party. This third party may be the shareholder or the parent company. But under asymmetric information, the enterprise may be able to conceal the true value of p from the insurer, and, since the insurer will no doubt know this, actuarially fair insurance will be unavailable. Worse still, firms seeking insurance may be rationed or even unable to obtain any insurance at all.[1]

9.4.6 *Imperfect Competition (Relaxing A6)*

When the firm operates in a monopolistic, rather than a competitive environment, it will be able to exercise some control over the price of its product. The variable p

will no longer be given independent of its actions. But this does not mean, of course, that it is immune from uncertainty; the demand for its product will now slope downwards, but is just as capable of random shifts. A second implication of departing from a perfectly competitive framework is that we may no longer be able to appeal to the forces of competition to set expected profits to zero. Subject to these qualifications, however, the previous analyses carry over relatively unchanged.

9.4.7 *Diminishing Returns to Labour (Relaxing A7 and A8)*

Up to now we have assumed that labour is the only factor of production, and that there are constant returns to it. The marginal physical product of labour was set at β in the simplest model; in the model explored in section 9.4.2, β was restricted, for simplicity's sake, to unity. What happens if there are diminishing returns to labour?

We might imagine firms choosing their capital stocks in some previous period, so that capital becomes a fixed factor of production in the short run. If there are constant returns to scale, and convex-to-the-origin isoquants between labour and capital inputs, there must be diminishing returns to labour alone. This will make the labour demand curve slope downwards. In section 9.3 and section 9.4.2, it was (by contrast) horizontal. If we simultaneously repeal the first assumption of the simplest model, to allow for many workers (as in 9.4.1), the implications of this will be as shown in figure 9.8.

In the two panels of figure 9.8, the supply and demand for labour are drawn under two of the contracts studied in section 9.3. The simplest model continues to apply, but with two changes: the employer is endowed with a pool of labourers, of size N ($N > 1$); and there are diminishing returns to labour. In the left-hand panel, labour is hired in a spot-auction market, when both parties know the price of the product, p. The minimum wage payment is α; if the price of the product falls beneath this threshold, so that the value of the marginal product of labour falls beneath α even at a zero level of employment, everyone stays at home and concentrates on 'household production'. This is what happens when the demand curve for labour is given by ϕ_2, or below this (such as ϕ_1). When the price is high enough to push the demand curve of labour to ϕ_5, or above this point (e.g. ϕ_7), there is full employment.

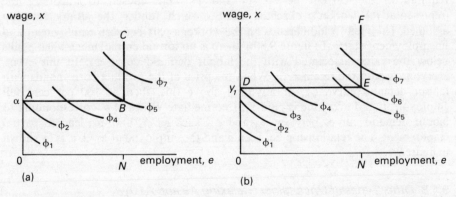

Figure 9.8 *(a) Labour supply and demand under contract A; (b) Labour supply and demand under contract B*

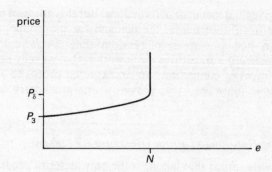

Figure 9.9 *The relation between product price and employment*

Everyone supplies his complete time endowment to the firm. The wage corresponding to any ϕ curve above ϕ_5 will be given by the point of intersection with the vertical full employment line, BC.

When the price of the product falls between these limits, contract A (the spot-auction market) will give a wage of α. Some of N workers will be engaged by the firm; others will devote themselves to household production. The labour demand curve ϕ_4 will, for example, generate a 'formal' employment level of about 50 per cent. Half the workers will be engaged by the firm. The other half will stay at home. Since the two groups of workers will enjoy the same level of consumption, there will be no incentive for them to shift in one direction or the other; it is easiest to imagine the formal sector employees, engaged by the firm, being chosen by lot. The interesting point about figure 9.8, and the assumptions on which it rests, is that they furnish an explanation of partial employment. By contrast, section 9.4.1 modelled employment as a binary variable, which would take on a value of 1 or 0, at least when workers' household productivities (α) do not differ. By contrast, figure 9.8 shows that there can be a wide range of values for the price of the product which give rise to partial employment.

The right-hand panel of figure 9.8(b) shows what happens under contract C. This took the form of a guaranteed employment wage, y_1, offered to everyone engaged full-time by the firm, and a stand-by retainer fee, of y_2, given to workers not required in the current period. y_2 and y_1 were chosen to maximize the (representative) worker's expected utility, which (under the utility function assumed, $U(c)$) led to indifference on the worker's part between employment and unemployment states. In figure 9.8(b), there is no formal employment when p falls below the value associated with the labour demand curve ϕ_3. In this event, everyone is paid the retainer y_2. When the price of the product corresponds with labour demand curve ϕ_6, or anything above this, there is 100 per cent full employment, and everyone is paid y_1. Intermediate values of p (corresponding to labour demand curves between ϕ_3 and ϕ_6, such as ϕ_4 and ϕ_5) lead to partial employment. The relationship between p and the employment level, e, is as shown in figure 9.9.

9.4.8 *Other Types of Uncertainty (Relaxing A9 and A10)*

Assumption 9 laid down that the price of the product was the only random variable affecting the firm; and A10 stipulated a particular probability distribution, according to which p was equally likely to fall anywhere between 0 and 1, but never outside this range.

The story up to now could carry over just as well to the case of technological uncertainty. The marginal physical product of labour, β, could have been a random variable, lying between 0 and 1, while the price of the product was locked at unity. Exactly the same results would have been reached in the model explored in section 9.4.2, and, subject to trivial amendments, for the simplest model examined in section 9.3. The only technical difference would be that expected profits and utility would have been integrated over the new random variable, β, rather than over p.

The qualitative results would also have followed, although only after a marked increase in computation and algebraic clutter, had the rectangular probability distribution $1 \geqslant p \geqslant 0$ been replaced by something less convenient. Perhaps the most significant implication of changing this distribution would be the change in the unemployment probabilities calculated under the optimal contract in section 9.4.2. Lifting the maximum value for p, while retaining the rectangularity property, has no effect, except to raise the values of c and expected utility in a rank-preserving fashion. But lifting the lower threshold above 0 has the important consequence of reducing the likelihood of unemployment in contracts F and G. Indeed, if the minimum value of p is high enough, the chance of unemployment is eliminated. If the rectangular shape is replaced by something more concentrated, such as an isosceles triangle peaking at the mean value of p, the chance that p is too low for positive production to be worthwhile is again reduced substantially.

9.4.9 *Uncertainty about the Probability Distributions for the Random Variables (Relaxing A11)*

Until now we have assumed that everyone knew the probability distribution from which the price of the product is drawn. This can be described as a situation of risk rather than uncertainty. Many economists have followed Knight (1921) and Shackle (1949, 1972) in stressing this distinction. Uncertainty is a state of affairs where you do not know the probability distributions for the random variables affecting you. Oswald (1986) advances this view in the context of labour contracts. Uncertainty, as opposed to risk, may also explain why contracts are so often incomplete, in failing to allow for all possible contingencies. Malcomson (1985) shows how contract incompleteness can lead to forms of involuntary unemployment.

Uncertainty of this type deprives the insurer of the basis on which insurance premia for random events can be calculated. There is simply too little information to go on. It also removes from the applicant for insurance any way of calculating his insurance demands. It destroys the market for insurance by leaving both the consumers and the suppliers too much in the dark. In the context of our model, it would create a strong bias in favour of 'wait-and-see' contracts, such as A in section 9.3 and D in section 9.4.2, which replaced promises and guarantees with a spot-auction market for labour.

A less radical and essentially destructive viewpoint would be to allow the probability distribution for p to evolve over time. This would mean that there was not a single probability distribution for p, but a family of distributions, which itself formed a probability distribution in its own right. For example, we might say the price level at date t obeyed

$$p_t = \mu_t + \varepsilon_t \tag{9.26}$$

where μ_t is the mean at date t, and ε_t is a 'white noise', purely random term; and further that

$$\mu_t = \mu_{t-1} + \zeta_t + a \tag{9.27}$$

so that the mean of the distribution has a central tendency to rise by a trend of a, and a second random element, ζ_t. We could go even further and replace a in (9.27) by a_t, laying down that

$$a_t = a_{t-1} + \eta_t \tag{9.28}$$

so that the growth trend was also random.

Suppose that the firm and the household are confronted with an unexpectedly low price at date t. This could be explicable in terms of a particularly low value of ε_t in (9.26). If this is all it is, there is at least the consoling thought that p_{t+1} is likely to prove much higher. But it might be a low value of ζ_t, in (9.27), that has caused the low realization of p_t. If so, (9.27) implies that future mean values of p will suffer as a result. Worse still, η_t in (9.28) could be very low. This has even worse implications, for it suggests that the future trend growth rate will be lower. The negative price surprise could equally well be explained by a one-off aberration, therefore, by an enduring shift in the mean level of p and by a lasting reduction in the mean growth rate of p.

In cases such as this, evidence must be assessed with care. Economic agents will adapt their expectations of the probability distribution for p in the light of experience. They will examine time series to see what can be gleaned from past data about the persistence of shocks, and how they affect levels and trends. They are also very likely to look behind the actual values of p, to search for explanations in terms of changes in such variables as preferences, technology and resources. They will try to determine whether p has fallen for supply or for demand reasons, and to judge what implications this has for the future. Economists are apt to draw a sharp distinction between 'adaptive' and 'rational' expectations. Adaptive expectations are formed on the basis of the time series; they involve changes in predictions as a response to revealed errors in previous predictions. Rational expectations are taken to look further at the series of numbers for p, at the fundamental forces of demand and supply that determine p; expectations are rational when all existing available information is employed to make optimum predictions for p. But this contrast between the two types of expectation can easily be pushed too far. When the 'model' determining p, and the probability distributions governing the random terms, are all known perfectly, the 'rational' expectation of p is a clear-cut concept. But uncertainty about the model, or about the probability distributions governing the random terms, is all too likely when the relationships that govern the model are themselves capable of changing and patently disputed by experts. In circumstances like this, rational expectations call for updating estimates of parameters in the light of new evidence, which is exactly what the adaptive expectations hypothesis suggests. For this, and for other reasons, adaptive and rational expectations may well overlap.

It is possible to interpret the evidence of the positive trend in unemployment since 1970 or so in the following terms. Many industries in Western Europe and the

US have experienced sharp profit downturns. Selling prices have dropped in relation to production costs. This has not happened everywhere, nor in every industry; but numerous sectors have experienced it at various dates. Vehicle assembly, steel, textiles, shipbuilding and even computers are celebrated examples. These negative price shocks have mostly come as an unwelcome surprise. The workers and employers concerned have had to make up their minds, as we saw earlier, about whether they are temporary aberrations or indications of a lasting reduction in the mean level or growth rate. Initially, they may well have inclined to the first view. If neither worker nor employer thinks that the probability distribution governing p has fundamentally changed for the worse, there is no reason to revise the way contracts are constructed. Real wages in the various eventualities and corresponding employment levels, are renegotiated along corresponding lines; all the real wage rates may simply be scaled upwards to reflect belief in an unchanged, underlying trend growth in the productivity of labour. The adverse price shock is countered by cuts in employment and production, which had been – hypothetically and 'implicitly', at least – allowed for in the quasi-contract agreed upon. The sharp reductions in employment and production throughout the OECD in the 1973–5 recession could be seen as an instance of this.

In the years that followed, real wages continued to rise. Some observers and some companies became increasingly aware that 1973–4 represented something of a watershed, with an unparalleled increase in energy costs and accumulating evidence of a reduced growth rate; but many labour market participants, on both sides of industry, still carried on much as before, and were to some extent sustained in their optimism by the recovery of output and profits between 1975 and 1979. Then came the second oil price shock, quickly followed by a concerted official attempt in leading financial centres, particularly the UK, the US, Japan and West Germany, to contain and reduce inflationary pressures by a programme of strict monetary restraint. In Japan, labour contracts in large companies resemble contract D: employment is effectively guaranteed, while pay includes a large and volatile bonus element which is directly related to profits. So the second oil shock was absorbed by a sharp cut in real wages. In the older industrial economies of Western Europe and North America, where contracts were more often closer to F or to G, real wages held up, or even advanced, and employment tumbled in the manufacturing sectors. This was particularly acute in the UK, where the oil price shock was accompanied and followed by a pronounced appreciation of the exchange rate. Unions may have seen themselves caught in a game of poker; they were used to companies 'crying poor' and to government threats not to accommodate wage pressures by easy monetary and fiscal policy; they may have been less than convinced that the other participants in the game were sincere.[2]

Since 1980–1, unemployment has fallen markedly in the US. It has dropped from over 11 per cent in 1981 to 7 per cent in 1985. Doubtless some of this can be attributed to the income tax cuts, and increases in government spending, that have marked Reagan's Presidency. But the downwards movement in real wage rates throughout much of American industry must also have played a part. In the UK, unemployment has risen rather than fallen between these years, and although the increases have fallen, unemployment still shows little sign of turning downwards. In contrast to the US, UK real wages for those in work have been remarkably buoyant, despite the large and rising levels of unemployment. It is tempting to conclude that the workers and employers that survived the 1980–1 epidemic of bankruptcies and redundancies have yet to accept that the demand for labour appears to have dropped permanently below the high-growth path it followed in the 1950s and 1960s. Alternatively, they have reconciled themselves to the disappearance of a large slice of manufacturing industry and employment, and those workers who remain 'in the game' have successfully contrived to insulate themselves from competition from the outsiders who have been forced out. At any event, it may take considerable time for workers and their employers to recognize an adverse shock to the level or growth in demand for labour for what it is. In the meantime, real wages will be higher, and employment levels lower, than they would have been had such developments been correctly perceived.

9.4.10 *Introducing Asymmetry in Information (Relaxing A12)*

Assumption 12 paints a view of the world where the employer and his employees can both observe the price of the product, and any other variables, such as technology levels and input costs, that govern the former's demand for labour. In such a world, the employer cannot cheat his employees by pretending that the demand for labour differs from its true value.

Much recent work on implicit contracts has started from the opposite assumption. Once date t arrives, the firm can see the price of the product, and know its demand for labour. But the employees, and the union representing them, cannot. One might think of the firm employing crafty accountants to dress up profit figures and sales returns in such a way as to imply that product prices were lower than their true magnitudes. In such a case, a contract such as D in section 9.4.2, which pays labour in proportion to the ex-post revealed value of the price of the product, gives the employer an incentive to lie. If it announces that p is below its true value, it can compress its wage bill, and increase its profits. Contracts F and G, by contrast, confer no such temptation upon the employer. They are 'incentive-compatible'. If the employer states that p is below what it really is, it is only he who suffers, because he is likely to be required to reduce employment, in circumstances where he will know that it is unprofitable for him to do so.

Asymmetric information cuts deeper than this. Akerlof and Miyazaki (1980) have established that, when information about the state of the world governing the firm's demand for labour is common knowledge to the employer and employee alike, efficient contracts that pre-specify levels of employment and pay as functions of the state of the world have no systematic tendency to generate higher unemployment than 'wait-and-see' (spot-auction market) contracts like D. In particular, they cannot generate involuntary unemployment: unemployment, if it arises, will have been allowed for as a contingency which frequently leaves the worker no worse off than he would have been at work. Indeed, if the marginal utility of consumption increases with leisure – this will not happen with the logarithmic utility function for the worker assumed in (9.13), but may well in other cases, as for example the Cobb–Douglas function (9.19) investigated in Sinclair (1986c) – the worker gets a higher level of consumption when he is unemployed than when he is at work. When out of work, he has, as it were, more time to enjoy it. Furthermore, if the firm is averse to risk, as it was in section 9.4.4, 'efficient' contracts can if anything give rise to overemployment. This is hinted at in table 9.2, where the worker's time at work, in both high-price and low-price states, rises as the firm becomes more risk-averse. This will also arise under conditions where the firm is prohibited from paying more than a fraction of the optimal level of unemployment compensation. In a sentence, with fully symmetric information, implicit contract theory can explain the fact that price shocks are accommodated by fluctuations in employment rather than in pay, but cannot explain any tendency to systematic or involuntary unemployment.

The picture changes quite dramatically once the worker is unable to observe p, or, more generally, the state of the world governing the firm's true demand for labour, in circumstances where both worker and employer are averse to risk. If the firm is averse to risk, it will seek to depress rates of remuneration in adverse states, where p is low. That way will enable it to escape some of the unwelcome tumble in profits that is associated with such events. But because the worker cannot see how low p truly is, and because he knows that the firm would otherwise have an incentive to state that p was below its real value, the contract to which he and his employer agree has the property that employment also falls when pay is cut. That will 'keep the firm honest'. The employer no longer has an incentive to lie about the state of the world, because the cut in employment and production will bite deeply into profits if p is actually higher than the employer claims. The involuntary unemployment generated is socially excessive; it would not arise if p were common knowledge; it typically violates property I (the Pareto-efficiency condition that requires equality between p and the household's marginal rate of substitution between leisure and consumption).

This ingenious twist to implicit contract theory can explain involuntary and socially excessive unemployment. But it cannot at the same time be invoked to explain 'wage stickiness', or the widely attested phenomenon of employment being much more responsive than pay to shocks in the demand for labour. The ideas themselves were first explored in detail by Grossman and Hart (1981); they are also the subject of powerful analytical surveys by Hart (1983) and Azariadis and Stiglitz (1983). One policy implication that can be drawn from them is that unemployment may be lessened by improving the flow of information about a company's financial position and sales to its workforce and the trade union(s) representing them. Hart has suggested that Joint Works Councils, and electing or nominating worker or union representatives to the boards of companies, may help to achieve this objective. High standards of auditing company accounts also assume greater significance. They too could help to increase the workers' trust in their employer's veracity. Another variant on the asymmetric-information theme is that workers may know more than their employer about what they could earn elsewhere: this case has been explored by Moore (1985).

The asymmetric-information versions of implicit contract theory are not without their critics, however. Prominent among these is Stiglitz. In Stiglitz (1985a), several arguments are advanced for treating such models with caution. Is it really so easy for the firm to conceal the facts from its workers? Even if the firm has some advance information about the state of the world, which it can obtain before its employees, surely the truth will out in the end? If a firm lies about its prices and profits, will it not acquire a reputation for duplicity, which will have adverse consequences in future wage negotiations?

9.4.11 *Difficulties Over Enforcement (Relaxing A13)*

So far we have assumed that neither party has any difficulty in enforcing the contract. Since it is described as an 'implicit' contract, this is surely problematical. It can hardly be enforced at law unless it is explicit. Furthermore, in some legal systems, such as that currently in force in the UK, there are strict limits on trade unions' liability for breach of contract. And can individual workers be required to work for what turn out to be rates of pay far below those prevailing in other, spot-auction labour markets, merely because they 'hypothetically' assented to a contract that predetermined pay before an unexpected jump in the economy-side demand for labour? Such a thing smacks of slavery. Still further, can the employer be forced to pay unemployment compensation in adverse states? What would happen, for example, if it went bankrupt?

It is not just the employer who may know something others do not. It may be that the worker knows more about what he can earn elsewhere than his employer. The 'external option' for the household examined in the simplest model, in section 9.3, took the form of household production, where the worker, or workers, had a known productivity of α. But household production is not the only external option; and even if it were, α could well be – presumably would be – unobservable by the firm. Hall and Lazear (1984) have recently examined the implications of this type of informational asymmetry, which had been first discussed by Mortenson (1982).

Employment separations can occur for either of two reasons. The employer may dismiss workers, on grounds of redundancy or for other causes. Alternatively, the worker can quit. Statistical evidence revealed in chapter 1 that the first of these was much the more frequent.

9.4.12 *Multi-period Contracts (Relaxing A14)*

Assumption 14 of the simplest model stipulated that the implicit contract agreed at one date governed pay and employment levels, in terms of the state of the world, only for the following date. Almost all the literature on implicit contracts adheres to this premiss. A rare and powerful exception is Stiglitz and Weiss (1983). This paper is concerned with contracts that cover two periods. Most of their analysis is devoted to the relationship between bank and borrower. The bank agrees at date t to give a borrower a contract that stipulates a credit limit and an interest charge for the loan repayment at date $t+1$, and for date $t+2$, a set of credit limits, interest charges and probabilities of renewal for the loan, all specified as functions of how much the borrower repays at $t+1$. The borrower applies the loan to an investment project, the outcome of which depends partly on his own actions (which the bank cannot observe) and partly on luck. If the project proves sufficiently disastrous, the bank impounds collateral and takes over ownership of the assets and liabilities associated with the project. This gives the borrower an incentive to gamble too much, because the downside risk is borne by someone else (the bank). In bad outcomes at date $t+1$, the borrower is faced with a high probability that his credit line will be switched off. Termination is punishment for the wicked. It also hits the unlucky, because the bank does not know enough to tell bad luck and bad project management apart.

Although the Stiglitz–Weiss analysis is formally couched in terms of the bank–borrower relation, this is essentially a metaphor for a more general relation involving a 'principal' and an 'agent'. The principal (the lender; the shareholder; the landlord; the insurer; and, for our purposes, the employer) has to devise a structure of payments between himself and his agent (the borrower; the manager; the tenant; the insured; and, in our case, the worker). These are likely to vary according to the 'outcome' (project returns; profits; upkeep of property, or yield from agricultural land; (non-)occurrence of event insured; output or sales revenue). The outcome is observable, and depends upon two factors; luck, and the agent's action (quality of project management; managerial effort; maintenance of property or labour input into farming; care; worker's effort) neither of which is visible to the principal. The agent is typically cowardly (averse to risk), lazy (disinclined to 'act'), and intelligent. In such circumstances, the best feasible contract that can be drawn up between the principal and his agent is highly likely to prove inefficient. Worse still, when applied to the two-period labour market, the Stiglitz–Weiss story implies that there will be people who are 'terminated' (i.e. dismissed) in the second period simply because of bad luck, and the fact that multi-period contracts become less inefficient when it is known that a bad first-period performance can have this outcome.

10 Search Theories of Unemployment

10.1 Introduction

The subject of this chapter is search. What determines how long people take to accept (or find) a suitable offer of employment? This is the central question to which this chapter is addressed. Section 10.2 presents a simple search model, the assumptions of which are relaxed in section 10.3. Section 10.4 is concerned with randomness in job offers, and its implications.

10.2 A Simple Model of Search

Probably the simplest model of search starts with the following assumptions:

1. Individuals seek to maximize their (discounted) lifetime income stream;
2. capital markets are perfect, and there is a unique rate of interest, r, at which everyone can borrow or lend, that does not vary with time;
3. searching for a new job is impossible if you are already working;
4. a job offer consists of a stream of wages, to be paid over an interval of time, T;
5. taxes are negligible, and no unemployment benefits are paid;
6. expectations of future job offers are held with confidence.

The first assumption implies that individuals do not care about leisure, and are not concerned with any risk to their income, either. The second ensures that future incomes are always discounted at a uniform, common rate of interest. The third provides the essential reason for staying out of work. This is in fact that it is the only route to the higher future income which may be had from a job that pays better than what you can earn at present.

Assumption (4) is important, too; if T, the duration of the job over which earnings are guaranteed, is high, you will be anxious to avoid being locked into a position which gives you less earnings than could be obtained elsewhere. The fifth assumption is imposed for the sake of simplicity, and the sixth sweeps away uncertainties that complicate matters in interesting ways. Section 10.3 investigates the effects of relaxing the first five assumptions and section 10.4 explores the implication of introducing randomness in job offers.

The implications of these assumptions are immediate and straightforward.

Unemployment is simply a form of investment. Current earnings are sacrificed now, in order to boost future income. The cost of unemployment is foregone earnings; its yield, the gain, is discounted lifetime earnings that will accrue from waiting for a better offer.

Suppose that you are now offered a job for 2 years that pays £200 per week throughout that period. Suppose the rate of interest is 0.2 per cent per week, which is equivalent to 10.95 per cent per year. The discounted present value of this is £18,800. Imagine that you know you will be able to obtain an offer of another job in a week's time that pays £210 per week for the remaining 102 weeks of the 2-year period. Should you accept the first job, or wait for the second? The second job has a discounted present value of £19,320. This is £520 higher than the value of the job on offer now. What you lose by waiting for the second job has a present value of £399.60 (since the second week's wages have to be divided by 1.002 to express them in present value terms). So the net return from waiting is £120.40. That is a measure of what you gain by waiting for the second job. You will therefore refuse the offer of £200 per week and wait for the second offer. Had the second offer been for £208.70 rather than £210 per week, you would be indifferent between accepting the first job and waiting for the second since both give the same discounted present value of £18,800.

There will be some people who stay out of work because the discounted value of their lifetime earnings increases as a result of turning down what is currently on offer. But the marginal individual should be indifferent between taking up the current offer and waiting. For him or her, the marginal return from 'investing' in unemployment will be zero.

What will determine the overall level of unemployment according to this theory? The critical variables will be three. First there is the difference in rates of pay between your present offer, and the most lucrative future offer you expect to receive. Then there is the interval of time for which you must remain unpaid in order to wait for the second offer. Finally, the rate of interest matters. The higher the rate of interest, the likelier you are to accept your present job offer, because the returns from delaying employment will be discounted at a higher rate.

10.3   Relaxing the First Five Assumptions of the Simple Model of Search

Begin with the first assumption. Suppose, now, that you derive positive pleasure from the additional leisure that unemployment brings. If leisure is treated as a good, the hours of work stipulated in a job offer will be relevant to your choice. It will no longer be a simple matter of calculating which offer gives you the highest discounted stream of income.

If the job on offer at present, and future job offers, all impose the same sacrifice of leisure time for each period of employment, the effect of making leisure desirable will be to increase the level of unemployment. The fact that extra leisure can be enjoyed during the unemployment spells is an advantage, to be placed in the balance of the purely pecuniary considerations of which job offers the highest discounted earnings. On the other hand, if leisure is a bad when one is unemployed, as a result of the boredom and loneliness to which it may give rise, we should see less unemployment than the simple model would predict.

Another possible way of relaxing the first assumption is to introduce risk-aversion. This is tantamount to assuming that the marginal utility of income decreases. By itself, this will not change the picture, unless assumption (7) is also amended in order to allow for income uncertainty. When future job offers are random, risk-aversion will imply a greater preparedness to accept current offers which are known for certain, in preference to speculative offers in the future.

Imperfect capital markets (relaxing assumption (2)) should also have the effect of lowering search unemployment. The reason for this is the fact that the unemployed are likely to be rationed in the amount they can borrow. The First Law of Credit Markets lays down that you can borrow what you like when you can prove that you do not need to. Prospective creditors are apt to ask for collateral for loans. Liquid assets which are sold easily for a predictable value, like deposits with financial institutions or bondholdings, are readily acceptable; other capital assets which are less liquid, such as shares or real estate, will be taken as collateral with rather more difficulty. But if the individual can only borrow against the promise of repayment from future labour earnings, he will seem a poor risk. This is, of course, precisely the situation in which he will most need to borrow, since he has no financial assets to decumulate.

The third assumption of the simple model stipulated that you can only search for, or obtain, new job offers if you are out of work. This is patently unreasonable. Empirical evidence on on-the-job search has recently been provided by Hughes and McCormick (1985). Job applications can be made by post; notwithstanding assumption (6), employers advertise for jobs in communications media accessible to people at work no less than to the unemployed; time off for job interviews can usually be arranged without difficulty. Labour-force turnover statistics reveal that about one in eight workers changes employer in any year, and of these, as many as 85 per cent are recruited directly from another job, with no intervening spell of unemployment. The technology of job-search is compatible with continuous employment. All this appears to deliver a death-knell to the empirical plausibility of search theories in explaining mass unemployment. On the other hand something can be salvaged from the wreck. Searching for jobs is certainly time-consuming, and time is one resource with which the unemployed are richly endowed. People may be reluctant to search for a change of employer when at work, for fear that this will signal dissatisfaction with their current job, and worsen their career prospects if they do not change. They may also have promised, or contracted, to work for a considerable period with their current employer, and the length of notice required for separation may preclude them from taking up new job opportunities. Yet for all this, the fact that search is not the exclusive preserve of the unemployed detracts seriously from the appeal of the theory.

Relaxing the fourth assumption goes a little way to repair the damage done by repealing the third. Taxes and unemployment benefits both tend to prolong unemployment spells. Tax rates matter because, in several countries (excluding the US and now the UK) unemployment benefits – unlike wage income – are exempt from income tax. Furthermore, if you leave a well-paid job in the middle of a tax year, some of the income tax already paid will be returned to you. Tax on earnings is deducted at source on the assumption that you will continue to be paid at the same rate over the year, and since income tax rates are progressive, you become entitled to tax rebates as soon as you leave employment. On the other hand, progressivity of income tax reduces the attractions of holding out for really lucrative offers. This argument is explored in detail by Pissarides (1985c). But most important of all, unemployment benefits are a direct subsidy to the unemployed. They will help to defray the earnings sacrificed during an unemployment spell.

10.4 Introducing Randomness in Job Offers

It is at this point that search models begin in earnest. The consequence of allowing randomness in job offers is the subject matter of this section.

The simplest set-up to envisage is a case where the job searcher does not discount future earnings or costs, and receives exactly one job offer per time period when he is out; wage offers are drawn randomly from a known and unchanging probability distribution, Φ; leisure has no intrinsic value; and job-search entails a constant cost of s per time period. A job offer consists of a wage rate, w, which is promised to the individual in return for employment over an indefinite time-span. Finally, assume the individual has no wealth and is risk-neutral.

In this case the individual does best by devising an optimum stopping rule. If the wage offered exceeds a critical value (called the 'reservation wage'), he accepts it. But when $w < z$, he carries on searching. The value of z is found by balancing the expected marginal benefit of continued search against its marginal cost. The marginal benefit of carrying on searching for one more period is either z, or the next wage offer (w_1), whichever is higher, minus z. The marginal cost is S. Hence the optimum stopping rule satisfies

$$S = E \max(z, w_1) - z. \tag{10.1}$$

Given the probability distribution (w), (10.1) can be rewritten

$$S = \int_z^\infty (w - z)\, d\Phi(w). \tag{10.2}$$

To see how (10.2) works, consider an example. Suppose that wage offers are known to be distributed evenly on the interval from 0 to 1. Consequently (10.2) will be

$$S = \int_z^1 (w - z)\, dw = (1 - z)^2 / z. \tag{10.3}$$

Equation (10.3) enables us to solve for the reservation wage in terms of the search cost S. If S is zero, the reservation wage is 1. It pays to carry on searching until you get the maximum wage offered. Anything less will be silly, because you lock yourself in a lower wage for ever than the highest wage that you know you must eventually find. If S is 1/20, (10.3) gives a reservation wage of 0.8. There is therefore a chance of one in five that you will search for only one period. The probability of your rejecting the next offer is 4/5. The chance of staying out of work more than two periods is $(4/5)^2$, and more than t periods $(4/5)^t$. The mean expected unemployment duration, from now, will be 5.

If S increases to $\frac{1}{2}$, the reservation wage drops to $\frac{1}{2}$, and the mean expected unemployment spell falls to 2. With S at 4/3, the reservation wage sinks to 1/3, and the mean spell of search of $1\frac{1}{2}$. Figure 10.1 illustrates the relation between s, z and the average unemployment duration in this case. The shape of the curve in the lower panel is highly sensitive to assumptions about the probability distribution, Φ, but it must have a negative slope. The curve in the upper panel of figure 10.1 is necessarily downwards sloping and convex to the origin.[1]

This basic framework can easily be extended to encompass other cases. Suppose that you do not necessarily receive a job offer each period. If, for example, there is a

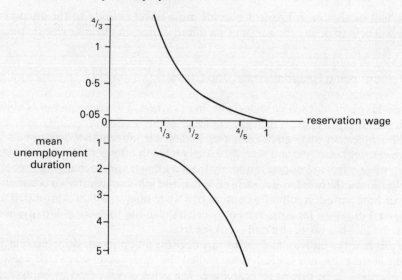

Figure 10.1 *Mean unemployment duration, reservation wage and the cost of search*

probability p of receiving one offer, and no chance of any more than that, the left-hand side of (10.1) becomes s/p. This implies that a reduction in the likelihood of receiving job offers (in slump conditions, for instance) acts just like a rise in the cost of search. It will lower the reservation wage. What this suggests for the mean duration of unemployment spells is unclear: the fall in z means that any given offer, if it materializes, is likelier to be accepted, but there is of course a lower probability that an offer will be forthcoming in any given period. These two effects may cancel. Alternatively you may be able to receive more than one job offer per period. If individuals can choose the intensity of search at any date, Morgan and Manning (1985) show that it may be wiser to adopt a 'fixed sample-size' strategy of sampling a cross-section of employers at one time, rather than following a sequential strategy with an optimum stopping rule of the type considered here.

Suppose now that future wage offers, and search costs, are subject to a discount rate of r. Let us assume both arise at the end of the period. In this case (10.1) is amended to

$$S = E \max (z, w_1) - z(1 + r). \tag{10.4}$$

The higher the discount rate, the lower the reservation wage and the more eager people will be to enter or re-enter the labour force. This effect will be neutralized if each wage offer, and the wage rate in each job, rise each period by the rate of discount.

If people have a finite horizon over which they expect to work, because of retirement or mortality, an important new phenomenon arises. The reservation wage ceases to be unchanging over time. At the horizon, it vanishes, because nothing is to be gained by turning down the wage currently on offer. It tends to fall over time as the horizon gets closer, although the picture becomes less straightforward if previous job offers continue to be available. With an infinite time horizon, it makes no difference whether job openings at given wages in earlier periods remain on offer, because the reservation wage is stationary. If you turned it down before, you won't accept it later. The reservation wage will also tend to fall over time if people tend to explore the most lucrative job opportunities first (see Salop (1973)).

Further extensions can be made to other cases. If the probability distribution $\Phi(w)$ is not known for sure, and can shift over time with the vicissitudes of the trade cycle, the reservation wage will be modified by news.[2] Morgan (1985) gives some interesting examples of how adaptive search with learning might proceed. The private benefit from search may be increased by the greater knowledge about $\Phi(w)$ which this gives. The introduction of wealth makes for longer search: the wealthier you are, the choosier you will be, and the higher your reservation wage. Risk-aversion usually has the opposite effect: a bird in the hand is worth two in the bush.

As we saw in section 10.3, allowing workers to search on-the-job may have rather destructive implications. On-the-job search allows you to retain your current earnings. On the other hand, it may be much easier to search full-time, when your full energies can be devoted to exploring possible job openings, approaching potential employers, studying advertisements and the like. So on-the-job search costs (s_j) could exceed the costs of search full-time. If they do not, it will always pay to accept the best current offer and (perhaps) continue searching on-the-job if the expected benefits from doing so exceed s_j. In this case, the analysis and results above continue to apply, with the important difference that the individual concerned is not unemployed. But if $s_j > s$, full-time search may be the best thing to do. Lippman and McCall (1976) show that different reservation wages may apply to on-the-job and full-time search. Call these z_j and z respectively. If z_j is high enough, the best policy is to discontinue search completely if the current job offer exceeds z_j, accept the offer but carry on searching if it lies between z_j and z, and otherwise stay unemployed. If z_j fails to reach a particular threshold, this threefold choice set collapses to a two-way option: stop searching completely if the current offer exceeds z, and stay searching full-time if not.

Search theory gives ample opportunities for government to intervene and affect overall unemployment. Unemployment benefits cut the cost of search. The relative cost of on-the-job and full-time search also changes. One should be wary of thinking that government should therefore cut unemployment benefits in order to bring down the level of unemployment, however. For one thing, considerable debate and doubt attaches to the magnitude of the fall in unemployment that would result. There are also two, perhaps more, important reasons. First, longer search can bring an externality gain from an improved assignment of people to tasks. If everyone accepts the first job offered to them, labour market allocation is likely to be much less efficient than if people (and firms) are choosier about accepting and making offers. Second, the loss in social welfare due to reduced incomes for those who will remain out of work, despite the cut in benefits, may well be regarded as excessive. This will be especially true if society is highly averse to inequalities in the distribution of utilities and incomes across the population, as was established in chapter 5.

Other ways in which government can affect search include subsidies to, or direct provision of, information about job vacancies; training subsidies; and measures to subsidize education or ability tests, which can serve to improve the accuracy of screening of job applicants. Some of these are discussed further in chapter 16.

11 Unions, Wages and Unemployment

11.1 Introduction

This chapter is concerned with the behaviour of trade unions, and their impact upon wages and employment. Section 11.2 explores a simple model, and section 11.3 generalizes it and examines its implications. Section 11.4 extends the analysis to the macroeconomy, reviewing a two-sector model where capital is either sector-specific (11.4.1) or mobile (11.4.2), describing recent attempts to integrate the behaviour of wage-setting unions with price-setting firms (11.4.3) and concluding with a brief survey of recent econometric evidence (11.4.4).

The economic analysis of unions is the subject of an excellent recent survey by Oswald (1985), to which the reader is referred for more detail on some of the issues explored in this chapter.

11.2 A Simple Union Model

We begin by setting out a simple model of how a union might determine an optimum wage rate for its members. Suppose that its total membership is given as N. Those of its members who are employed work for a single employer, who produces a single product under monopolistic conditions. Labour is the only variable factor he employs, and the union can prevent the employment of non-members. Every employed worker will supply a single unit of time to this firm, earn a wage of w and gain utility $U(w)$. If not employed, he will receive unemployment benefit b and receive utility $U(b)$. The proportion of the N union members that gain employment θ, varies negatively with the usage and positively with the price of the firm's product, p. The union chooses w so as to maximize the sum of the utilities of its members. Consequently its objective will be

$$\text{Max}_w \, N\{\theta U(w) + (1-\theta)U(b)\}. \tag{11.1}$$

An interior maximum (where $1 > \theta > 0$) will satisfy the first-order condition

$$0 = [U(w) - U(b)]\frac{\partial \theta}{\partial w} + \theta\frac{\partial U(w)}{\partial w}. \tag{11.2}$$

Equation (11.2) can be rearranged to give

$$1 - \frac{U(b)}{U(w)} = \frac{e}{\eta} \tag{11.3}$$

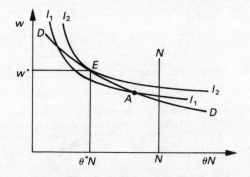

Figure 11.1 *The union's optimal wage and its implication for employment*

where e is the elasticity of the employed worker's utility to his wage, and η, defined as a positive number, is the wage elasticity of the firm's demand for labour. Equation (11.3) states that the proportionate gain in utility from a wage pitched above the level of unemployment benefit, must be balanced by the (relative) trade-off that a higher wage brings between utility for those employed, and the volume of employment. Equations (11.2) and (11.3) amount to the requirement that the marginal benefit from the wage set balance its marginal cost. The first term on the right-hand side of (11.2) constitutes the latter, once its sign is changed:[1] it gives the adverse effect upon average utility from the loss in employment. The second term states the marginal benefit, in the form of higher utility for those who remain at work for a higher wage.

A geometric portrayal of the union's wage decision, and its employment consequences, is given in figure 11.1. The vertical axis depicts the wage rate secured for the union's members, the horizontal the number who gain employment, θN (θ is the proportion of the N union members at work). The curve DD represents the monopolist's demand curve for labour (more on which below). I_1I_1 and I_2I_2 are union indifference curves between the wage rate and the employment level. These are drawn downwards sloping and convex-to-the-origin. They will slope down wherever the wage rate exceeds the unemployment benefit level, b (or more precisely, when the utility of the wage in employment exceeds the utility obtained when out of work and receiving b). Where the two utilities are equal, the union's indifference curve becomes horizontal. At a wage below this, it will slope upwards.

Convexity-to-the-origin (in the region where $U(w)$ exceeds $U(b)$) will follow if the marginal utility of the wage declines as the wage increases. I_1I_1 and I_2I_2 would be parallel straight lines if the marginal utility of the wage were constant. The more sharply $U'(w)$ diminishes as w rises, the more pronounced the curvature of the indifference curves.

The union optimizes in figure 11.1 by choosing a wage rate of w^*. This corresponds with the point E, where the highest indifference curve, I_2I_2 is attained, subject to the restraint DD provided by the firm's demand for labour. E will be preferred to any other point on DD, such as A. Point E gives an employment level of θ^*N.

Figure 11.1 depicts the straightforward case. In other circumstances, such a tangency point as E may be problematic. There are three possible reasons for this. First, it may not be unique. Although the curve DD may well slope downwards

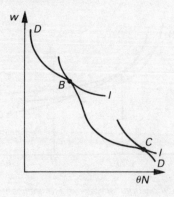

Figure 11.2 *Non-uniqueness of tangency point*

monotonically (even this is not guaranteed,[2] witness figure 2.8 in chapter 2), there is nothing to rule out a sequence of concave and convex jumps along it which gives rise to the possibility of multiple equilibria. Second, it may represent a pessimum rather than an optimum for the union. This happens if *DD* is more convex to the origin than the relevant indifference curve at the point of tangency. Again, there is nothing to preclude this possibility. Third, the point of tangency may be both unique and optimal, but it may break the bounds of feasibility. In figure 11.1, the vertical line *NN* depicts the given number of union members. Points on and to the left of this line are feasible; points to the right are not. θ cannot exceed unity. It could well be that *DD* is tangent to a union indifference curve to the right of this line. If so, all the union can do is to set the wage where *DD* cuts *NN*. These three problematic cases (non-uniqueness, non-optimality and infeasibility) are depicted in figures 11.2, 11.3 and 11.4. Points *B* and *C* are both equilibria in figure 11.2; it is even conceivable that they could be equally attractive. Point *F* in figure 11.3 represents a local pessimum along *DD*. Point *G* in figure 11.4 breaks the bounds of feasibility imposed by the number of union members, *N*. So the union will restrict itself to *H*.

If the three kinds of pathological tangencies depicted in figures 11.2, 11.3 and 11.4

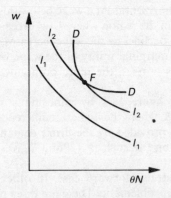

Figure 11.3 *Non-optimality of tangency point*

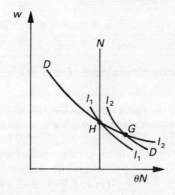

Figure 11.4 *Infeasibility of tangency point*

are ruled out, we return to the example shown in figure 11.1. What implications can we draw from this? First, the union's optimal wage will typically increase with the ratio of e to η. This means that a higher elasticity of $U(w)$ to w, or a lower elasticity of the curve DD, should be associated, all else equal, with a higher wage and a lower proportion of N employed. Second, a rise in the utility from unemployment, as a consequence of an increase in the rate of unemployment benefit, will have the same consequence for w^* and θ^*. Third, an elasticity-conserving shift in the level of demand for labour, occasioned by a change in the price of the monopolist's product resulting from a change in the level of demand for it, will leave w^* unchanged, and alter θ^* in the same direction. DD will move rightwards if demand for the product rises, and so long as the value of η is unchanged at the old optimal wage, w^* will not change either. Fourth, a change in N, the number of union members, has no effect upon w^* and simply alters θ^* in the opposite direction. This can be seen from the fact that N is a multiplicative term in equation (11.1), which can be made to vanish on differentiation.

We should examine e and η in a little more detail. The elasticity of $U(w)$ to w may be interpreted as a coefficient describing the worker's attitude to income risk. If e is unity (so that the indifference curves are horizontal), he or she will be neutral to risk. If e lies below unity, a requirement for the union's indifference curves to be convex to the origin, the worker is risk-averse. In fact, $1 - e$ represents the coefficient of relative risk-aversion. So much for e. Turning to η, the elasticity of the monopolist's demand curve for labour, we can interpret this parameter in terms of three others. η will be related to the elasticity of demand for his product (ε, defined as positive), the elasticity of substitution between labour and the fixed factor(s) employed by the firm (call this σ), and the elasticity of output to labour (define this as λ). If the monopolist has constant returns to scale, η will be related to ε, σ and λ by[3]

$$\eta = \left[\frac{\lambda}{\varepsilon} + \frac{1-\lambda}{\sigma}\right]^{-1}. \tag{11.4}$$

Equation (11.4) tells us that the elasticity of demand for labour will be increasing in the elasticity of demand for the product and the elasticity of substitution between labour and the fixed factor(s). Whether it rises or falls with λ depends on whether or not σ exceeds ε.

11.3 Further Implications and Generalizations of the Simple Union Model

11.3.1 *The Wage–Employment Relation is not Pareto-efficient in the Simple Model*

In the model described in section 11.2, the employer chooses the level of employment, taking the union's wage as given, while the union fixes the wage taking the employer's demand for labour as given. The employer's demand for labour is presumed to depend upon profit-maximization. This means that it chooses the level of employment, θN, where the horizontal wage line is tangent to the highest-valued attainable isoprofit curve. Figure 11.5 illustrates this.

The demand curve, DD, joins all points of tangency between horizontal wage lines and upside-down U-shaped isoprofit curves. The firm's profits increase as you move down the demand curve from left to right. The union's indifference curve, on the other hand, is tangent to DD at the union's optimum point (e.g. E in figure 11.1). Consequently the union's indifference curve is not tangent to the employer's isoprofit contour. The latter is horizontal along DD, while the former slopes down, since it must be tangent to the downwards-sloping demand curve. This implies that the union and the employer could both gain by increasing employment and lowering the wage somewhat. Any move from point E into the shaded area in figure 11.6 will bring gain to both parties.

By raising θ above θ^*, and reducing w below w^*, it is possible for the firm to increase its profits above π^* and the union to increase its utility above I^*. The shaded area in figure 11.6 Pareto-dominates point E: both the union and the employer gain, and no one loses from the change. Pareto-efficient bargains between union and employer are restricted to a contract curve where isoprofit and union indifference contours are mutually tangent. This is depicted by the curve ZZ in figure 11.7. It was Solow and McDonald (1981) who developed this piece of analysis; the idea was first proposed by Leontief (1946). Once on ZZ, the two parties will recognize that their interests are diametrically opposed. The firm's profits increase as one moves left along ZZ, while the union's utility increases in the opposite direction. One possibility is that the two will agree upon a point inside the shaded area in figure 11.6, that lies on the contract curve ZZ, which maximizes the

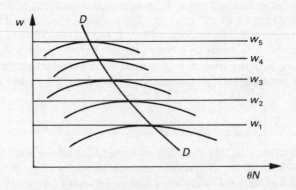

Figure 11.5 *The employer's demand for labour as a set of isoprofit tangencies*

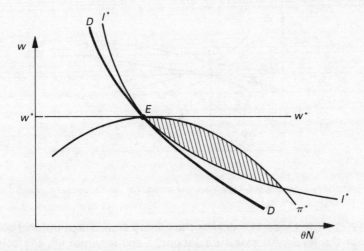

Figure 11.6 *The set of wage–employment combinations that Pareto-dominates the equilibrium at E*

product of profits and union utility. This would correspond to a Nash co-operative solution (Nash (1953)).

11.3.2 *Strategic Behaviour by the Monopolist*

Another possible outcome will arise if the monopolist perceives that the union's optimal wage, w^*, increases with the level of demand for labour. This should occur if the union thinks that the demand for labour becomes less elastic as it increases. In such a case, the firm will cease to regard w^* as given. Its demand curve will not be given by the locus of isoprofit curve maxima, as in figure 11.5.

Rather, the employer will perceive an upwards-sloping labour supply curve, which it will identify as the average cost of labour. The marginal cost will exceed this, by a proportion inversely proportional to the elasticity of the average curve. The employer will optimize by finding the point where the latter is tangent to an isoprofit contour. This will entail a deliberate restriction in the level of demand for labour. Figure 11.8 illustrates.

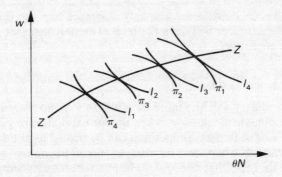

Figure 11.7 *Pareto-efficient wage–employment bargains*

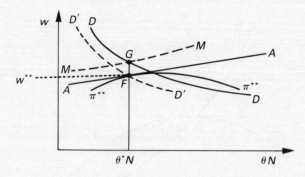

Figure 11.8 *The monopolist manipulates his demand for labour to achieve higher profits*

The curve AA in figure 11.8 depicts the union's conjectured optimal wage as a function of the level of demand for labour. Since it slopes up, the employer's perception of the marginal cost of labour, MM, lies above AA. Profits will be maximized by setting employment at $\theta^{**}N$. At this point, labour's marginal revenue product (given by DD) intersects MM at G, and point F, lying directly below G, is the tangency between AA and isoprofit contour π^{**}. The firm therefore reduces its demand for labour, as perceived by the union, to $D'D'$. Since, as we have seen, w^* declines with η (the elasticity of the demand for labour), the firm has a strong incentive to misrepresent this elasticity of demand. The greater the elasticity he can persuade the union that his demand curve possesses the more he can beat down the wage that the union sets. To counter the risk of this kind of behaviour, the union should recognize that its interests are served best by pretending that AA is as elastic as possible.

11.3.3 *Non-profit-maximizing Behaviour by the Firm*

Everything up to now has been built upon the premiss that the firm is a profit maximizer. Since he is a monopolist, likely to earn supernormal profits, one cannot easily invoke the Darwinian argument in favour of profit maximization that will apply under more competitive conditions. (That non-profit maximizers will be driven out of business by losses.) It is by no means impossible that a monopolist will be interested in sales revenue as well as profits. If so, his demand curve for labour will be higher (as observed in section 2.3.6 of chapter 2). Provided the elasticity of demand for labour, η, is unaffected, the only difference between this firm and the traditional profit maximizer will lie in the level of employment; the union-optimal wage, w^*, will be unchanged.

11.3.4 *Oligopoly and Competition*

An oligopolistic industry will hire more labour than a monopolized one, except in the limiting case of perfect collusion, when the formal difference between the two market forms dissolves. Perfect competition can be treated as another special case of oligopoly, reached when the number of firms is infinite and each acts independently in the belief that its decisions have no effect on its competitors. As the number of firms increases, industry output rises, bringing up the demand for labour. Provided that the elasticity of the industry's demand for labour is independently given, the effect of higher competition will simply be to raise the employment level; w^* will not alter. Increased competition has the same effect as a higher demand for, and price of, the employer's product in monopoly. It is possible, however, that a perfectly competitive or oligopolistic industry will pay a higher wage than its counterpart in monopoly. This is likely to happen if the elasticity of the demand for the product, ε, falls as price comes down, as for example when the product demand is linear. In that case, a union able to block entry by non-members into the industry's labour force will perceive a lower elasticity of demand for its labour (recall (11.4)); and w^*, which all else equal varies negatively with η, will therefore be higher.

11.3.5 *Re-examining the Union's Utility Function*

The union's objective function, (11.1), has been assumed until now to be synonymous with the sum total of its members' utilities. Just the same optimization conditions, (11.2) and (11.3), will emerge from choosing w to maximize their average utility; all this does is to divide (11.1) by N, which makes no difference to (11.2) or (11.3). Another way of interpreting average utility is to treat it as the representative union member's expected utility. This will be quite natural if unemployment for the fraction $1 - \theta$ who will be out of work is assigned by lot.

But the union may have other objectives. Instead of seeking to maximize the average utility of its members, a Benthamite utilitarian objective, it may wish to behave in a Rawlsian fashion. This would mean that it aims to maximize the utility of its least advantaged member. In that case, it would drive the wage down to the point where all its members were in work, such as point H in figure 11.4. This would follow, at least, provided that the full employment wage brought greater utility than the unemployment benefit, b. As things stand, those employed gain greater utility than the unemployed provided this is so, so the union's indifference curves effectively become vertical wherever $U(w) > U(b)$. The Rawlsian union would push the wage down to the point where everyone was in work, or where $U(w)$ equalled $U(b)$, whichever gave the lower level of employment.

There are, of course, countless intermediate possible union objective functions between the Benthamite and Rawlsian extremes. One example is the Champernowne function, which is equivalent to the product, or geometric mean, of its members' utilities. In our context, this would imply that the union choose w to maximize

$$NU(w)^{\theta(w)}U(b)^{1-\theta(w)} \tag{11.5}$$

which gives the solution

$$\log_e \frac{U(w)}{U(b)} = \frac{e}{\eta} \tag{11.6}$$

in place of (11.3). This will typically betoken a lower optimal wage, and higher employment level, than the Benthamite function (11.1). The Champernowne function will place greater emphasis on the utilities of the unemployed, and hence seek to lower their number.

Yet a further possibility is that the union acts to maximize the aggregate incomes of its members, and then redistributes between the employed and the unemployed to equalize their utilities (and incomes, if those out of work neither gain nor lose from their extra leisure). This amounts to maximizing

$$b(1 - \theta(w)) + w\theta(w). \tag{11.7}$$

This is achieved where $w = b\eta/(\eta - 1)$, assuming that $\eta > 1$. If the labour demand curve has a constant elasticity, so that

$$N\theta = aw^{-\eta} \quad a > 0 \tag{11.8}$$

there will be no differences in wage rates, employment levels or union utility levels so long as union members are neutral to income risk (so that $e = 1$). But when $e < 1$, so that individual workers are taken to be risk-averse and the marginal utility of w declines as w rises, the following differences emerge. The aggregate-income maximizing union sets a lower wage rate, leading to higher employment, than its Benthamite counterpart which follows (11.1); and it will also achieve a higher aggregate level of total utilities for its members. This finding is rather important; it casts a considerable shadow of doubt upon why a union should ever behave as the simple model suggests. One way round the problem is to argue that income redistribution between union members is simply infeasible. In that case, the Benthamite union will reject the idea of following (11.7), since it will fail to strike the optimal balance between the marginal benefit and the marginal cost of the wage. There is a second difficulty with the income-maximizing approach. If the demand for labour were everywhere inelastic, it would lead to infinitesimal employment at an infinite wage; this would be distinctly disagreeable for the overwhelming proportion of union members out of work, unless they could gain a share of the bloated wage bill confined to the tiny few employed. If labour demand were inelastic at higher levels of employment, and the Benthamite equilibrium fell in that range, the income-maximizing union would employ fewer of its members than the Benthamite, and serious difficulties would arise in the absence of appropriate compensation for those out of work.

11.3.6 *When Workers' Work Time is an Endogenous Variable, Affecting Utility*

Until now, we have assumed that each person employed supplied an exogenous single unit of time to his or her employer. Utilities, for those in work and out of work alike, have been expressed simply as functions of the income they receive. It is the purpose of this section to see what happens when those assumptions are relaxed.

Suppose, instead, that the demand for individual workers, N, varies not just with the wage and the price of the firm's product, but also with the duration of the time each spends at work, h. Let h represent the fraction of the individual's time endowment, of 1, devoted to employment. The utility of an employed worker becomes $U(w, 1 - h)$; someone out of work gains utility $U(b, 1)$. Let the union choose w and h, leaving the firm free to set θ to maximize profits. The other assumptions of the simple model remain in force. What happens now?

The union's objective will be to select w and h to maximize

$$N\{\theta(w, h)[U(w, 1 - h) - U(b, 1)] + U(b, 1)\}. \tag{11.9}$$

Denote the marginal effects of w and h upon θ by θ_1 and θ_2 (θ_1 and θ_2 will both be negative). Let U_1^w and U_2^w denote the employed worker's marginal utilities of income and leisure, and U^w and U^b the utilities of the employed and the unemployed respectively. A maximum for (11.9) with respect to w and h gives rise to the two conditions

$$\left.\begin{array}{l} 0 = \theta_1[U^w - U^b] + \theta U_1^w \\[2mm] 0 = \theta_2[U^w - U^b] - \theta U_2^w. \end{array}\right\} \tag{11.10}$$

The first of these restates condition (11.3), while the two together imply that the employer's trade-off between wage and work time, θ_1/θ_2, equals the employed workers' marginal rate of substitution between income and leisure.

11.3.7 *Introducing Alternative Employment Opportunities*

When union members fail to secure employment with the firm or industry under scrutiny, we have assumed until now that they must be out of work. There is another possibility. They may gain another job, for example in a competitive sector where entry into employment is not blocked by other unions. Suppose that there is a probability β of gaining employment elsewhere, at a wage w_c. Assume, further, that $U(w_c)$ is not less than the utility of being unemployed $U(b)$. How will this affect the union's behaviour?

Assuming that all other assumptions of the simple model remain in force, the union's objective will now become

$$\text{Max}_w\, N\{\theta(w)U(w) + [1-(w)][\beta U(w_c) + (1-\beta)U(b)]\}. \tag{11.11}$$

An interior solution to (11.11) will obey, in place of (11.3)

$$\left[1 - \frac{\beta U(w_c) + (1-\beta)U(b)}{U(w)}\right] = \frac{e}{\eta}. \tag{11.12}$$

Previously we found that an increase in the level of unemployment benefit would raise the union's optimal wage. We can now expand this statement. The expected utility foregone by employment is transformed from $U(b)$ to $\beta U(w_c) + (1-\beta)U(b)$. This implies that an increase in the competitive wage, w_c, or an increased probability of gaining it conditional upon non-employment in the 'home' industry, β, both tend to raise w^*. The latter statement is true, at least, if $U(w_c)$ exceeds $U(b)$. We have now identified a reason for thinking that the union's optimal wage will drop as overall unemployment increases, since this could only be expected to imply a reduced value of β.

There may be other reasons for expecting w^* to react negatively to aggregate unemployment. The looser the labour market conditions in other sectors, the greater the danger that the union's monopoly power could be undermined by cheaper labour outside the union's control. Other firms producing relatively close substitutes for the 'home' industry may be able to expand production at lower cost.

11.3.8 *Open Shops and Closed Shops*

When a business operates a closed shop, it is restricted to employing members of a particular union. The enterprise's employees must all join the union; if they do not, they face dismissal. But not all shops are closed. In Western Europe and North America, shops are more often open than closed. This means that workers are free to choose whether or not they join a union; they can also, within limits, select which union to join. In such circumstances, the union's members will no longer be an exogenous number, N. The union will be anxious to increase membership. This can only increase membership dues, and spread the fixed costs of the functions provided by the union over a larger number of workers.

It seems likely that the propensity to join a union will increase with the wage that the union appears to negotiate for its members, and decrease with the dues charged. If this is so, it is by no means unthinkable that closed shops lead to lower wage rates than open shops. The greater the weight that membership dues have in the union's objective, and the more sensitive the membership propensity to the wage rate achieved, the greater the benefit the union will perceive from increasing the wage, where possible, in the open shop. In a closed shop, membership is mandatory; the case for a higher wage to stimulate membership disappears. The reader is referred to Sinclair (1980) for a formal demonstration of this proposition. A second argument for expecting higher wages in open shops turns on the notion that employers may wish to discourage union membership by paying sufficiently high wages to non-members.

Concern with membership dues may have other effects, too. Unemployed workers are all too likely to drift away from their union. They are also likely to be exempted from some or all of their membership charges. If this is so, the union will be inclined to place higher weight upon employment, as opposed to wage rates. The fact that the demand for labour is so strongly correlated, positively, across sectors suggests that the union may respond to news of growing unemployment elsewhere in the economy by moderating their conception of an optimal wage rate. One factor that could inhibit this tendency is that the union will be reluctant to convey the impression to the firm that its optimal wage increases with the strength of the demand for its labour; it would then expose itself to the dangers depicted in figure 11.8. There are also other considerations. Once unemployed workers have left the union, if leave they do, their preferences will cease to count. Despite the implications of the simple model, which makes w^* independent of the number of members the union has, the disappearance of the unemployed may make those that remain more prepared to gamble on a higher wage. Lastly, existing employees' fears of losing their job may be much more sensitive to the change in unemployment than to its level. When unemployment is rising, jobs may look increasingly vulnerable. Once it has stabilized, albeit at a high level, workers and the union representing them, may see little reason to alter their wage-setting behaviour.

11.3.9 *Responses to Fiscal Parameters*

The only point at which the government's fiscal behaviour has impinged upon the union thus far is through its payment of unemployment benefit, b. As we have seen, the level of b has an unambiguously positive effect upon the union's optimal wage. This is as true of the income-maximizing union, obeying (11.7), no less than the simple model.

But there are other ways in which the government's fiscal environment can affect the union's behaviour. Oswald (1985) demonstrates that w^* is increased (reduced)

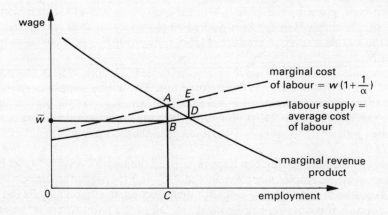

Figure 11.9 *Employment under monopsony*

by subsidies (taxes) upon the employment of labour levied on the firm. A lump-sum income payment to households in work will lower w^*, since it reduces the marginal utility of the employed worker's income (assuming $U(w) < 0$). Changes in the standard income tax rate are ambiguous, since they induce the usual conflict between income and substitution effects which point in opposite directions (the former raises w^*, the latter reduces it).

11.3.10 *Why Unionization Could Even Increase Employment*

There are circumstances where the impact of unions will be to raise rather than reduce employment. Consider a firm facing an upwards-sloping supply curve of labour; assume that its objective is to maximize profit, and that it has no power to discriminate between its employees by paying them different wage rates. As figure 11.9 shows, it will set employment at the point where the marginal revenue product of labour just balances labour's marginal cost (provided that the latter cuts the former from beneath). This occurs at A.

The labour supply curve will represent the average cost of labour. Increasing employment implies paying a higher wage, and not just to the new recruits. Because the employer cannot discriminate in wage rates, the existing employees must be paid more, too. So the marginal cost of labour exceeds the labour supply curve, by an amount inversely proportional to α, the elasticity of labour supply. The wage

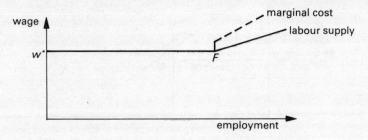

Figure 11.10 *A union-imposed minimum wage*

paid will be $\bar{w}$, given by the point where the employment level OC intersects the labour supply curve. Had the firm pushed employment up to D, where the wage equals the marginal revenue product of labour, its profits would have fallen by the area AED.

Suppose our firm's labour force is now unionized. The union fixes a minimum wage of w^*. We assume that it can enforce this. The labour supply curve is now horizontal at w^*, up to the point F where the old curve is reached; beyond that, it follows the latter. Figure 11.10 illustrates the firm's new marginal cost curve is coincident with w^* up to point F. Then it jumps to the old marginal cost curve, as in figure 11.9.

There are three things that can happen. First, if the union's wage w^* is set below $\bar{w}$, it has no effect; employment remains at OC, and the wage remains at $\bar{w}$. The union's constraint upon the firm does not bind. Second, the union may fix the wage above point A. If it does so, employment will fall to the point where w^* intersects the marginal revenue curve. Employment drops, and the wage increases sharply.

It is the third possibility that offers greatest interest. If the wage w^* is set between $\bar{w}$ and point A – anywhere in the vertical gap between points A and B in figure 11.9 – employment will go up. Figure 11.11 depicts the case of a small rise in the wage, to w_1^*, which is less than point D; a higher wage than this (w_2^*) is shown in figure 11.12.

In figure 11.11, the new wage of w_1^* creates a marginal cost curve that is horizontal up to point G, then vertical to M and finally follows the old curve to the right of that. Employment is determined where this new curve cuts labour's marginal revenue product, at H. The wage is of course w_1^*. Employment has risen from OC to OJ, despite the higher wage. In figure 11.12, the union's wage, w_2^*, is rather higher than in figure 11.11. The marginal cost of labour becomes w_2^*KNP. This cuts the marginal revenue product at K, fixing employment at OL. Employment rises from OC to OL. The union does much better for its members in figure 11.12 than figure 11.11. What is unfortunate from their standpoint about figure 11.11 is that the wage can be pushed up by the amount GH at no loss in employment. Alternatively, further increases in the wage as far as D will occasion further increases in employment. The wage that maximizes employment is given by point D. If the union is fully appraised of the position it must seek to fix w at or above D, never below. Where it does so will be determined, for example, by the point

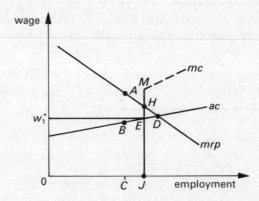

Figure 11.11 *A modest wage increase and the resulting rise in employment*

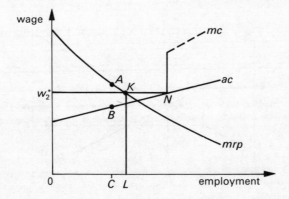

Figure 11.12 *A larger wage increase and the resulting rise in employment*

of tangency between the marginal revenue product curve and its indifference curve, if we apply the principles of the simple model of section 11.2.

In sum, then, the union's imposition of a minimum wage will lead to increased employment and higher wages if it lies between the limits set by *A* and *B*; to greatly increased wages but reduced employment if above *A*; and to no effects if it is set beneath *B*. Exactly the same consequences follow from minimum wage legislation, assuming, again, that it is enforceable. It is simply not true that higher minimum wages must undermine employment. Beyond some point, they must; up to that point, they will increase both employment and wages.

11.3.11 *Unions and Skill Differentials*

Until now, labour has been assumed to be an entirely homogeneous factor of production. There have been no differences in ability, no distinction drawn between experienced and inexperienced, or skilled and unskilled.

With the introduction of ability differences between individuals, the trade union may start to act like the government in chapter 5. It may impose taxes of its own upon its members' earnings, and redistribute the proceeds as a lump sum to everyone, including those out of work. Alternatively, it may tax the earnings of those in work to subvent transfer payments to the rest of the membership. If it allows its members freedom to choose their hours of work, the analysis of chapter 5 will carry over lock, stock and barrel.

One important implication of such an approach is that the level of unemployment (which will be concentrated among the less skilled) will be positively associated with the union's aversion to inequality among its members. The Benthamite union will experience less unemployment than the Rawlsian. This contrasts sharply with what we found in section 11.3.5 above.

11.4 General Models of an Economy with Unions

11.4.1 *The Two-sector Model with Sector-specific Capital*

One way of capturing the general economic effects of labour unionization is to split

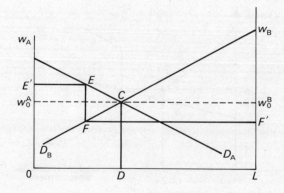

Figure 11.13 *The allocation of labour in the two-sector model: the zero unemployment case*

up the economy's labour markets into two sectors. One, sector A, is unionized; the wage rate there is determined by the union along the lines of the simple model in section 11.2. Sector B, on the other hand, is fully competitive, in the sense that entry into employment there is unconstrained. Each sector has a fixed, sector-specific supply of capital (and any other factors, for that matter). The total potential labour force, L, is split between these two sectors. Initially, we ignore the possibility of unemployment, so that L will equal the sum of the levels of employment in A and B. Each sector's demand for labour declines as the wage paid there increases.

Figure 11.13 illustrates all this.[4] The base of the diagram is given by the total labour force, OL. Employment in sector A is measured rightwards from the origin; sector B gets what is left. If labour market equilibrium prescribes a common wage in the two sectors, this will be given at point C, so that A employs OD and B, DL. If the union(s) controlling employment in A should now enforce a wage of E' there, employment in that sector will decline by DG. Sector B will take up this slack, but the wage in B must fall to F' for full employment to be maintained. In figure 11.13, the union or unions in A will affect the distribution of income and employment, but they do not cause unemployment.

But what will happen if the wage in B cannot fall as far as F'? Suppose now that the government provides unemployment benefit, b; the utility obtained when out of work, $U(b)$, is equal to the utility gained from working a wage of $\bar{w}$. If the extra leisure, or household production opportunities that unemployment provides contribute positively to utility, $U(b)$ and $U(\bar{w})$ can be equal despite the fact that $\bar{w}$ exceeds b. If the additional leisure is positively disliked, b must exceed $\bar{w}$ for $U(\bar{w})$ and $U(b)$ to be equal. Figure 11.14 shows the effects of introducing unemployment benefit and its utility-equivalent wage, $\bar{w}$.

Now, it will not be possible for the wage in B to fall below $\bar{w}$. Unemployment benefit provides a floor to the wage rate. If the wage sinks to $\bar{w}$ there, sector B will employ JL units of labour. Employment in A remains restricted to OG. The residue of the labour force, GJ, will be out of work. Both they, and those working in B, gain a common utility $U(\bar{w})$; but the utility of the unemployed is below the average utility of those in work, $\{(OG)U(E') + (JL)U(\bar{w})\}/(OG + JL)$. The diagram abstracts from certain complexities, such as individual workers' choices of hours of work, ability differences, the quality of competition in the two sectors, the relative prices of their

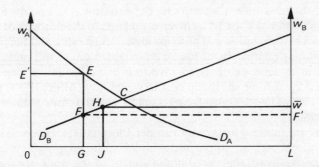

Figure 11.14 *Employment and unemployment in the two-sector model*

outputs and the question of where and how taxes are imposed to balance the cost of unemployment benefit payments. It is also silent on the possibility of involuntary unemployment. But its message is simple and rather persuasive. Unemployment can arise as a consequence of the interaction of union behaviour and unemployment benefits. Note that without union monopoly power in A, so that wage rates fell into equality in the two sectors, there would be no unemployment in figure 11.14. The common wage at C exceeds $\bar{w}$, so everyone would be better off in work than out of it.

11.4.2 *The Consequences of Allowing Capital to Migrate Between the Sectors*

In the previous section, capital was specific and its stock in each sector was fixed. It is the purpose of 11.4.2 to see what may happen when capital is allowed to switch between sectors, as eventually it must. Machinery will not be replaced when it wears out unless it earns a sufficiently high return.

In the context of figure 11.13, once the union in sector A imposes a wage of E' in place of the original common wage w_0, the return on capital will fall in A. The earnings of capital will fall by the area $E'ECw_0^A$. In sector B, on the other hand, they will rise, by the amount $F'FCw_0^B$. Capital rentals sink in A and go up in B. So capital must eventually transfer from A to B. As it does so, sector A's labour demand curve, D_A, will be pushed leftwards, as will D_B. The union will then be faced with a quandary. Either it will accept the new division of labour between the sectors, in which case it must acquiesce in a gradual erosion of the wage differential between them; or alternatively, if it insists on continuing to impose the wage rate of E', it will suffer continuing reductions in employment. In a particularly simple model, where the two sectors employ labour and capital in equal proportions in the absence of distortions, and the two industries' outputs are sold internationally at fixed relative prices, the union's long-run predicament is stark and uncomplicated. Its effect on the wage in A will either be completely undone as a consequence of capital migration, or output and employment in A will eventually collapse to zero.

When capital becomes a variable factor of production in the long run, the demand for labour facing a firm becomes steadily more elastic. This introduces an interesting conflict between short-run and long-run objectives for the union. The critical result obtained under the simple model, equation (11.3), points to the notion that the union's optimal wage, w^*, is inversely related to the elasticity of the demand for labour. So a myopic union will push for higher wage rates, and suffer in the long run from continuing employment losses; a farsighted union will press for a lower wage, which in a sense amounts to investing in higher future demand for its members' services at some short-run cost in wages now. Miller (1984) provides an interesting sketch of this dilemma facing a union, and the consequences of different courses of action.

These ideas are pursued further by van der Ploeg (1985). He considers a world where the firm chooses an employment and investment programme, and faces sharply increasing (quadratic) costs of adjustment of the stock of capital, up and down, in the short run. Its aim is to maximize the discounted present value of its profit stream. The labour it hires is monopolized by a union, which sets wages to maximize a dynamic version of (11.1). The central problem is that the union has an ex-ante incentive to promise a modest wage rate, and an ex-post incentive to push up wages unexpectedly once the firm has committed itself to a large capital stock. Disinvestment is costly in the short run, so the firm's profits can be squeezed hard, at what is initially only a small loss in employment. But the firm knows this so it underinvests in the first place, to protect itself against the blackmail to which it would subsequently have become vulnerable had the capital stock been larger. The union's promise of low wages is not credible. There are a variety of escape routes from this awkward conundrum. The union may try to abandon its power to set wages; the firm and the union may co-operate, to achieve a superior, Pareto-efficient outcome on the contract curve in figure 11.7; or the government may intervene by a judicious blend of unemployment benefits and investment subsidies.

11.4.3 *Integrating Wage-setting Unions with Price-setting Firms*

Layard and Nickell (1985) and Nickell (1985) have presented a very attractive model that combines the wage-setting actions of unions and price-setting by firms. It consists of three equations. The money wage rate is determined by trade unions, in the light of three variables: the level of unemployment (which has a negative influence, reflecting unions' perceptions of the danger posed to their members' jobs by the existence of a large pool of unemployed workers); exogenous 'pushfulness' variables, that might respond to the level of unemployment benefits, and the density of union membership; and either current, or expected future, retail prices (this will have a positive effect, possibly one-to-one). The second equation relates the demand for labour by firms to money wage rates (a negative influence), to current or expected future selling prices (positive), and, in recognition of the possibility that many imperfectly competitive firms may practise some form of mark-up pricing, to the level of demand in the macroeconomy (again, a positive or at least non-negative effect). The third equation connects selling prices set by firms to the money wage rate, prevailing and/or expected to prevail in the future, and also to output or employment (there are diminishing returns to labour, and, to the extent that firms maximize profits, the mark-up of prices on wages will therefore vary positively with the level of output).

This thumbnail sketch of the Nickell/Layard–Nickell set-up abstracts from a number of important dynamic features, and the longer term influences of changing technology and capital stocks, as well as employment taxes levied on both firms and workers (that tend to inhibit employment by driving a wedge between the two groups' perceptions of the wage rate). The full picture is therefore rather more complicated than the simple account of their model presented above, and the interested reader is warmly encouraged to consult their papers to gain a full impression of its subtler features. We return later, in chapter 16, to their framework, in the context of unemployment policy. But what is perhaps their most important conclusion deserves emphasis here. In their view, a lasting reduction in unemployment at no cost in additional inflation requires a combination of *two* things: a fall in the union pushfulness variable *and* an expansion in aggregate demand. One of these on its own is unlikely to be enough.

11.4.4 *Some Evidence on the Effects of Unions*

Carruth and Oswald (1985) present an econometric test of variants of the model examined in this chapter on data for wages and employment in the UK coal-mining industry. The results are encouragingly consistent with the theory. Their estimates of the elasticity of employment to the wage vary between -0.6 and -0.85 in the short run, building up to between -1 and nearly -1.4 in the long run. Somewhat larger elasticities result from treating the union as optimizing a dynamic, long-run objective, than when it is given a static objective. Miners' wages turn out to be positively related to unemployment benefit and wages earned elsewhere in the economy (although their tests do not allow one to disentangle these two effects separately). The price of oil is shown to have a large positive effect upon the demand for labour in coal mining, with a long-run elasticity of nearly 1. The workers' implicit risk-aversion coefficient is also approximately unity. The period studied is 1950 to 1980, during which the National Union of Mineworkers enjoyed an unassailable monopoly position. The Carruth–Oswald results are in many cases similar to the findings of an earlier study on wages and employment in the US mining industry (Farber (1978)), and also to those of other studies (such as Pencavel (1984) on the US printing industry).

Aggregate studies have been conducted which allow us to draw some inferences about the impact of unions on wages and unemployment. Andrews and Nickell (1982) find that a variable reflecting the density of union membership appears to have been responsible for about one-quarter of the rise in UK male registered unemployment between 1953/7 and 1971/6. The union/non-union wage differential also increased over this period, and seems to have contributed nearly one-tenth of the unemployment rise. In a second study (Nickell and Andrews (1983)), these authors inferred that these two indicators of union pushfulness were responsible for the loss of some 400,000 jobs in the UK between 1951 and 1979. Minford (1983) estimated the elasticity of unemployment to trade-union membership at $5\frac{1}{2}$, again on British data, this time for the period 1964–79. We do not yet have econometric tests that include the period of the 1980s. The recent past has witnessed a sharp fall in union membership figures in the UK. Probably the greatest single cause has been the steep decline in employment in manufacturing. The service sector has by contrast displayed quite a buoyant demand for labour (but insufficiently so to compensate for anything more than a tiny proportion of employment losses in manufacturing); and unionization levels in services are much below those in the manufacturing sector. The crude negative correlation between unemployment and union membership figures in the early 1980s is also reflected by inter-war experience in the UK. Union membership advanced rapidly in the first two decades of the twentieth century, and especially during the First World War. This growth was checked in the 1920s, when unemployment climbed, and reversed in the severe recession of the early 1930s. It is of course possible that multiple regression of unemployment on other variables besides unionization might still recover evidence of a positive association between the two, either for the 1980s or for the inter-war years, but this seems improbable.

The inferences to be drawn from the econometric evidence, then, are twofold. First, the micro data that have been examined are pleasingly consistent with the models of union behaviour studied in this chapter. Second, trade unions seem to have been responsible for some, but not all, of the rising trend of British unemployment in the 1960s and 1970s. Whether this is true of other periods, and in particular of the early 1980s, is much more doubtful. Higher unemployment may follow higher union membership, because this causes them to push for higher wages; but higher unemployment will tend to erode membership subsequently. The dynamics of this two-way mechanism may be protracted and intricate. Pissarides (1985a) explores some aspects of the subtle dynamics of unemployment, vacancies and real wages in an economy with trade unions.

12 Inflation and Unemployment

12.1 Introduction

This chapter is concerned with the links between inflation and unemployment. Section 12.2 analyses evidence and explanations for the association between these variables. Section 12.3 is concerned with the implications of rational expectations for the authorities' ability to stabilize unemployment. In section 12.4, attention turns to the costs and benefits of (policies that generate) inflation, while section 12.5 is devoted to two specific issues of dynamic adjustment: the question of *how quickly* inflation should be lowered, if it should be brought down at all; and the phenomenon of hysteresis in the unemployment–inflation relationship.

12.2 Evidence and Explanations for the Inflation–Unemployment Link

12.2.1 *The Phillips Curve*

Irving Fisher (1926) was perhaps the first economist to examine the statistical association between the level of unemployment and the rates of wage and price increases. But it is Phillips (1958) who became the eponymous hero of the relationship. His celebrated study of money wage increases in the UK between 1861 and 1956 established a well-defined negative association between this variable and the rate of unemployment, which appeared to change little over the 95 years. The rate of change of unemployment was also found to exert a significant impact on money wage increases. The money wage increase–unemployment rate relation was found to be curved, steepest when unemployment was very low, and steadily flattening as unemployment rose. The evidence suggested that money wages would be constant over time when unemployment had stabilized at a range between 7 per cent and 11 per cent, depending upon the period in question.

The Phillips curve was soon verified econometrically for other countries. The explanation usually offered for the phenomenon followed Lipsey (1960) and ran like this. Walras (1870) had hypothesized that there would be pressure for the price of a good or factor to be bid up when it was in excess demand, and to drop when in excess supply. Unemployment, or more strictly the excess of unemployment over unfilled vacancies, could be taken as an index of the excess supply in the market for labour. If and when unfilled vacancies exceed the number of those seeking work, labour as a whole could be regarded as experiencing a state of excess demand. In the latter case, there would be pressure for money wage rates to increase; in the former, they should tend to fall. Walras had invented the convenient device of an auctioneer, whose job it was to 'turn price in the direction of excess demand'. As with goods, so with labour. But it was recognized that the invisible auctioneer's mechanism worked rather slowly, particularly when unemployment was high and labour was in substantial excess supply. The macroeconomic relationship between national unemployment and wage increase averages aggregated over countless individual micro markets for different kinds of labour in different regions and sectors of the economy; this might account for non-linearities and other peculiarities in the data.

The 1960s witnessed an increasing awareness on the part of policy makers about the inflation–unemployment trade-off, for it was soon seen that price and money wage inflation rates were closely linked; money wage increases outpaced price rises by a margin that appeared to fluctuate somewhat over the business cycle (it was highest in upswings, reflecting labour-hoarding, and the fact that unit costs would drop, relative to trend, as the 'fixed' element in wage costs were spread over higher volumes of output) and to approximate the growth of labour productivity over the long run. The positive trend in real wage rates would equal the pace of labour productivity growth if labour's share in the value of output had no trend. Writing this latter variable as s, we have

$$s = \frac{w}{P} \frac{N}{Q} = \frac{w}{Px}. \tag{12.1}$$

In (12.1), w is the money wage rate, P the price level, Q and N the levels of output and employment and x the average product, or productivity, of labour. Equation (12.1) is only a definitional truism, but a helpful one. In proportionate rates of change (denoted by a hat ($\hat{\ }$) over the variables), (12.1) implies

$$\hat{w} - \hat{P} = \hat{x} + \hat{s}. \tag{12.2}$$

The left-hand side of (12.2) is the growth of real wages. This must equal the sum of the rate of labour productivity increase ($\hat{x}$), and the increase in labour's share of output ($\hat{s}$). If s is trendless in the long run, $\hat{s} \sim 0$ and $\hat{w} - \hat{p} \sim \hat{x}$.

12.2.2 *The Expectations-augmented Phillips Curve*

Unfortunately, policy makers' attempts to exploit the inflation–unemployment trade-off in the 1960s seemed to break down. The decade saw a gradual upwards trend in the rate of inflation in many Western countries, particularly in the UK, Italy, France and the United States; and unemployment if anything began to edge upwards rather than downwards. The 'price' of cutting unemployment was perceived as a higher rate of inflation; but the trade-off between these two variables seemed to become increasingly unfavourable as the decade proceeded. Phelps (1967) proposed that the trade-off should be expressed as a relationship between unexpected inflation and the rate of unemployment, u:

$$\hat{P} = E\hat{P} + f'(u) \tag{12.3}$$

where f' (the marginal effect of unemployment on the rate of inflation) was negative. This view was repeated forcefully by Friedman (1968).

The Phelps–Friedman argument ran as follows. Expectations of inflation $(E\hat{P})$ were formed adaptively, on the basis of previous evidence of the rate of inflation. The simplest form this could take would be

$$\Delta E\hat{P} = \alpha(\hat{P} - E\hat{P}) \qquad \alpha > 0. \tag{12.4}$$

The term in brackets on the right-hand side of (12.4) is the inflation prediction error. When the current rate of inflation was unexpectedly high, $(\hat{P} - E\hat{P})$ would be positive. Hence expectations of future inflation would increase. Inflation expectations could only be reduced by negative 'surprise' inflation $(\hat{P} < E\hat{P})$.

The relationship between inflation expectations and the history of inflation implied by (12.4) could be found by repeated substitution, on the assumption that (12.4) remained constant over time. This is

$$E_t\hat{P}_{t+1} = \alpha[P_t + (1-\alpha)\hat{P}_{t-1} + (1-\alpha)^2\hat{P}_{t-2} + \dots]$$
$$= \alpha \sum_{i=0}^{\infty}(1-\alpha)^i\hat{P}_{t-i}. \tag{12.5}$$

In (12.5), $E_t\hat{P}_{t+1}$ is defined as the expectation at date t of inflation at the next date $(t+1)$, and $\hat{P}_{t-i}$ is the inflation actually observed at date $t-i$. The parameter α measures the sensitivity of inflation expectations to inflation surprises, while $1-\alpha$ is the coefficient of inertia in expectations of inflation. Rewriting (12.3) as

$$\hat{P}_t - E_{t-1}\hat{P}_t = f(u) \tag{12.5'}$$

and substituting into (12.5) reveals

$$\hat{P}_t = f(u_t) + \alpha \sum_{i=0}^{\infty}(1-\alpha)^i\hat{P}_{t-1-i}. \tag{12.6}$$

The difference between the simple Phillips curve and its Phelps–Friedman 'expectations-augmented' version is depicted in figure 12.1. The left-hand panel shows the former, unique negative association between inflation $\hat{P}$ and the unemployment rate, u. The right-hand panel presents a family of 'short-run' Phillips curves, each given for a particular expected rate of inflation. When the previous rate of anticipated inflation is $\hat{P}_3$, for example, the economy's short-run trade-off

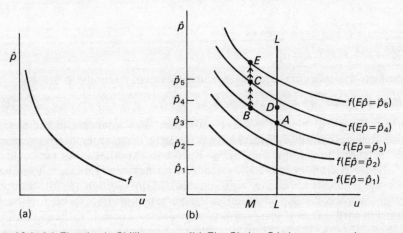

Figure 12.1 *(a) The simple Phillips curve; (b) The Phelps–Friedman expectations-augmented Phillips curve*

between $\hat{P}$ and u is given by the curve $f(E\hat{P} = \hat{P}_3)$. Expectations of inflation are fulfilled if the level of unemployment is at L, since point A represents the point where $\hat{P}_3 = E\hat{P} = E\hat{P}_3$.

If the authorities expand aggregate demand, and thereby lower unemployment from L to M, inflation will be given by point B. But there is now a positive inflation surprise. So, from (12.4), subsequent inflation expectations increase. If unemployment is to be held at M, inflation must increase. The short-run inflation–unemployment trade-off deteriorates. The economy adjusts to a higher short-run Phillips curve, such as $f(E\hat{P} = \hat{P}_4)$. Unemployment at M entails inflation at C. But this point cannot last either, since inflation is still higher than its previously anticipated value. In short, figure 12.1(b) suggests that the cost of lowering unemployment is not faster inflation but rising inflation. Unemployment at M will generate an inflation time-path from B to C and E and beyond. If inflation is stabilized at its level at B, unemployment must drift up to point D. Substitution of (12.3) into (12.4) reveals that the crucial relationship is between unemployment and the change in inflation expectations:

$$\Delta E\hat{P} = \alpha f(u). \tag{12.7}$$

The level of unemployment at which inflation expectations are unchanging, and hence perfectly fulfilled, is known as the 'natural rate' of unemployment. It is the value of u at which $\Delta E\hat{P} = 0$ in (12.7). In figure 12.1(b), it is presented as the vertical line, LL. If the natural rate is vertical, there is no permanent trade-off between inflation and unemployment. In Phelps' original paper, LL was presented as a negatively sloped curve; it was drawn much steeper than the short-run f curves, but still suggested that there would be some enduring gain in the form of reduced unemployment if the rate of inflation was permanently increased. Friedman, on the other hand, has argued that the long-run natural rate curve could slope upwards. Faster inflation, in Friedman's view, is associated with increased variability in relative prices, increased uncertainty and inter-sectoral shifts in output and employment, and hence, perhaps, in higher overall unemployment. It is easy to allow for both these possibilities by postulating a link of indeterminate character between the natural rate of unemployment, u_n, and the rate of inflation:

$$u_n = g(\hat{P}) \tag{12.8}$$

whereupon, if (12.3) is rewritten as

$$\hat{P}_t = E_{t-1}\hat{P}_t + f(u_t - u_n) \tag{12.3'}$$

the complete dynamics of the inflation–unemployment relationship become

$$\hat{P}_t = f(u_t - g(\hat{P}_t)) + \alpha \sum_{i=0}^{\infty} (1-\alpha)^i \hat{P}_{t-1-i}. \tag{12.9}$$

Perhaps the three most important subsequent developments in the study of inflation–unemployment dynamics have been these. First, econometric evidence in the 1970s tended to confirm the Phelps–Friedman hypothesis that the coefficient on inflation expectations in (12.3) was, indeed, insignificantly different from unity. Studies that indicated this are well summarized in Gordon (1976). Second, a powerful microeconomic basis for a short-run unemployment (or output) relationship with inflation surprises was provided by Lucas (1972) and confirmed on evidence (Lucas (1973)). Third, the Phelps–Friedman assumption of adaptive inflation expectations was confronted with a new rival: the premiss that inflation expectations are formed rationally. This had some intriguing implications for policy (Lucas (1976), Kydland and Prescott (1977)).

12.2.3 *Lucas' Explanation for the Phillips Curve*

The Lucas story is this. An economy is composed of numerous consumer–producers, who specialize in the production of particular goods. They know the current price of their own product, but cannot perceive accurately the current prices of other goods. They know the history of all prices. The nominal price of any good is known to vary with sector-specific microeconomic shocks that take the form of unexpected movements in preferences and technology. But it is also affected by economy-wide macroeconomic shocks, such as unexpected changes in the supply of money. When the price of their product is unexpectedly high, they have to decide whether this is due to micro or macro shocks. If disturbances to preferences or technology are responsible for it, they should respond by increasing production: their 'terms of trade' have improved. Now is a good time to work harder and sell more, since the price of their product could easily fall back later. Alternatively, if the higher nominal price of their product has been caused by a macro, monetary shock, their best policy is to carry on as before, since it will presumably tend to raise all prices equiproportionately, and leave relative prices unaffected.

Since they cannot be sure what has caused the unexpectedly high price of their product, they will probably do best by acting as if both micro and macro shocks have affected it. So output will tend to rise. If the authorities have engaged in an unexpectedly rapid increase in the nominal money supply, all prices will be bid up (since Lucas assumes a full market-clearing set-up), and the output levels of all producers are likely to be higher than they would have been. But they will subsequently discover that their higher nominal prices did not (on average) betoken improved relative prices. In the meantime, they may well have committed themselves to investment decisions, in plant, machinery, labour training and the like, that have some positive effect upon production in immediately subsequent periods. But the macro price shock that provoked these responses will be revealed for what it is, and economic agents will regret their decisions to expand production.

The simplest version of the Lucas story establishes a link between aggregate output at date t, Q_t, and the relationship between the current average price of the products, P_t, and its previously expected value, $E_{t-1}P_t$. A linearized version of this could be written as

$$Q_t = Q_n + \beta(P_t - E_{t-1}P_t) + v_t. \tag{12.10}$$

Equation (12.10) is known as a 'surprise supply curve'. The parameter β is the reciprocal of the slope of the surprise supply curve. Q_n denotes the 'natural' rate of output, the average value of output when price expectations are fulfilled. The term v_t is a random variable, most conveniently assumed to be independently and identically distributed and drawn from a known probability distribution with zero mean and given variance. If output is related linearly to unemployment, for example by

$$u_t = \gamma_0 - \left(\frac{1}{\gamma_1}\right)Q_t \qquad \gamma_1 > 0 \tag{12.11}$$

$$\Rightarrow u_n = \gamma_0 - \left(\frac{1}{\gamma_1}\right)Q_n$$

we can now use (12.10) and (12.11) to derive an expectations-augmented Phillips curve:

$$P_t - E_{t-1}P_t = [P_t - P_{t-1}] - [E_{t-1}P_t - P_{t-1}]$$

$$= -\frac{v_t}{\beta} + \frac{\gamma_1}{\beta}[u_n - u_t]$$

or

$$P_t - P_{t-1} = [E_{t-1}P_t - P_{t-1}] - \frac{\gamma_1}{\beta}(u_t - u_n) - \frac{v_t}{\beta}. \tag{12.12}$$

When P_t is defined as the logarithm of the price level at date t, (12.12) gives us an equation for inflation in terms of three variables:

1   the previous anticipation of inflation, $E_{t-1}P_t - P_{t-1}$, which has a one-to-one effect on current inflation;
2   the difference between actual and natural unemployment, $u_t - u_n$, which has a negative effect on inflation; and
3   the random disturbance term, v_t.

12.2.4 *Rational Expectations and the Expectations-augmented Phillips Curve*

The third major development in the study of the inflation–unemployment trade-off described at the end of section 12.2.2 was the challenge posed by the assumption of rational expectations.

The traditional approach to macroeconomic model building was to assemble a set of behavioural equations and identities linking economic variables. When economic agents' expectations of some of these variables played a role, they were typically modelled as responding to previous forecasting errors. The hypothesis of adaptive expectations was an example of this. In the context of expectations of inflation, this meant that people would raise their forecasts of inflation when they saw that they had underpredicted it, and lower them when inflation turned out to be less than they had expected. The linear adaptive expectations equation, (12.4), was the most convenient form to assume.

The major problem with the adaptive expectations hypothesis was this. The rate of inflation was actually determined by a set of relationships, governing such variables as aggregate demand, unemployment, output and the demand and supply of money. But people's expectations of inflation were evolving in an ad hoc, mechanical manner that took no account of these relationships and such information about the relevant macro variables as might be publicly available. The adaptive-expectations economist was asserting that the actual evolution of the macroeconomy behaved in one fashion, and yet the thinking human beings, whose economic actions were being described, formed their expectations quite differently. The rational expectations hypothesis stipulated that, when an economic model was common knowledge, then expectations of economic variables determined by the model must be based upon that knowledge. If expectations were to be consistent with such knowledge, there could not be systematic forecasting errors. Systematic forecasting errors could have been avoided, and would have been avoided under rational expectations if the relevant model was 'stationary' and known in full. If the model allowed for random elements in the system, errors would have been unavoidable. But such errors would be purely random.

It was a short step from this to the claim that deviations in unemployment and output from their natural values were random, and could not be affected by systematic intervention on the part of the government, if agents' expectations were rational. Systematic action by the government would become known to everyone. So long as the government lacked an informational advantage, its responses to observed phenomena would be built into people's expectations. If output and unemployment deviations from their natural magnitudes followed the 'surprise supply curve' described in section 12.2.3, systematic responses by the authorities would not come as a surprise. So they could not affect output. This claim is the subject of section 12.3.

12.3 Do Rational Expectations Nullify Systematic Policy Intervention by the Authorities?

12.3.1 *How they Might Nullify it*

Suppose the relationship between output and prices follows the surprise supply curve, (12.10):

$$Q_t = Q_n + \beta(P_t - E_{t-1}P_t) + v_t. \tag{12.10}$$

In (12.10), Q and P are in logarithms; the subscript n denotes the 'natural' output level, which represents average output in the absence of forecasting errors for prices; $P_t - E_{t-1}P_t$ is the difference between the current price level (at b) and what people had expected it to be, one period ago; and v_t is a random variable, identically and independently distributed with a mean of zero and a given variance, σ_v^2.

This sums up the supply side of the economy; assume that Q_n is exogenously given by unchanging technology, labour force and other factors of production.

Now to the demand side. Imagine that the demand for money (m_t^d) and supply of money (m_t) evolve as follows:

$$m_t^d = c + P_t + \gamma Q_t + w_t \qquad \gamma > 0 \tag{12.13}$$

$$m_t = d + m_{t-1} + \delta(Q_n - Q_{t-1}) + y_t \qquad \delta \geqslant 0. \tag{12.14}$$

Equation (12.13) is a demand-for-money equation, in nominal (logarithmic) magnitudes. The elasticity of the demand for money to the price level is unity, while the income elasticity of demand for money is γ. There is a constant term, c and a random variable, w_t, which resembles v_t in (12.10) in having zero mean, finite variance σ_w^2 and in being identically and independently distributed. y_t has the same properties (and variance σ_y^2) in the supply-of-money equation (12.14). The three random variables, v, w and y, are all independent of each other.

The money supply equation tells us that there is a trend growth rate of money, d, and a feedback coefficient, δ. When output drops below its natural rate, the authorities respond by raising the money supply in the following period. The parameters d and δ reflect the 'political humidity' of the monetary authorities. A 'wet' Keynesian government will respond to unexpectedly high unemployment and low output by expanding the money supply relative to trend. It might also be expected to allow a high trend growth rate for the money stock. A 'drier' government might set d and δ at lower levels, possibly even zero.

The system is closed by a money-market clearing condition

$$m_t^d = m_t. \tag{12.15}$$

We assume that the system (12.10), (12.13), (12.14), (12.15) forms a model about which all is known to everyone, apart from the future values of the random variables, v, w and y. If we are interested in the behaviour of output, Q_t, (12.10) tells us that we must first solve for the price prediction error, $P_t - E_{t-1}P_t$. This is done, in terms of Q_t, by first finding P_t, then computing the previous period's expectation of P_t, and finally taking the difference between them.

From (12.13), (12.14) and (12.15), we have

$$P_t = d + m_{t-1} + \delta(Q_n - Q_{t-1}) + y_t - c - \gamma Q_t - w_t. \tag{12.16}$$

Equation (12.16) is understood by everyone, given rational expectations; hence the previous period's expectation of P_t will be based upon it:

$$E_{t-1}P_t = E_{t-1}[d + m_{t-1} + \delta(Q_n - Q_{t-1})]$$
$$- E_{t-1}[c + \gamma Q_t] + E_{t-1}(y_t - w_t). \tag{12.17}$$

Subtraction of (12.17) from (12.16) gives

$$P_t - E_{t-1}P_t = \{d + m_{t-1} - E_{t-1}(d + m_{t-1})\}$$
$$+ \{\delta(Q_n - Q_{t-1}) - E_{t-1}\delta(Q_n - Q_{t-1})\}$$
$$- \{c + \gamma Q_t - E_{t-1}(c + \gamma Q_t)\}$$
$$+ \{(y_t - w_t) - E_{t-1}(y_t - w_t)\}. \tag{12.18}$$

Equation (12.18) can be simplified considerably. If we assume that the information set available to everyone at date $t-1$, call this I_{t-1}, contains all variables dated $t-1$ and all non-random parameters in the system, the first two expressions in curly brackets on the right-hand side of (12.18) simply vanish. Furthermore, since y and w have mean actual, and hence expected, values of zero, $E_{t-1}(y_t - w_t)$ also disappears. This leaves:

$$P_t - E_{t-1}P_t = -\gamma(Q_t - E_{t-1}Q_t) + y_t - w_t. \tag{12.19}$$

Meanwhile, (12.10) implies

$$E_{t-1}Q_t = Q_n \Rightarrow Q_t - E_{t-1}Q_t = Q_t - Q_n \tag{12.20}$$

so that (12.19) and (12.20) yield

$$(Q_t - Q_n)(1 + \beta y) = v_t + \beta(y_t - w_t). \tag{12.21}$$

The most significant fact about (12.21) is that it leaves out so much. We search in vain for any effect of systematic monetary policy upon Q_t. Q_t is completely independent of the trend growth of the money supply, d. More important, it is also independent of the size of the feedback parameter, δ, which reflects the sensitivity of the money supply to previous output. Output reacts to contemporaneous shocks in the product market (v), the money supply (y) and the demand for money (w). The income elasticity of the demand for money (γ) and the elasticity of the supply curve (β) both influence the responsiveness of output to these shocks. But d and δ have no effect. It is because the systematic elements in monetary policy are known, and predictable in advance, that they are built into the price forecast; consequently they cannot come as a surprise. The parity of information between the public and the monetary authorities is reflected in the fact that the latter cannot react to contemporary events when setting the current value of the money supply: m_t reacts not to Q_t in (12.14) but to Q_{t-1}.

It may help to provide an intuitive account of what is going on behind the scenes in (12.21). Imagine a negative product market supply shock: v_t is negative. Equation (12.10) suggests at once that Q_t, likelier than not, will be low. A low value of income implies a low nominal demand for money (see (12.13)). But the nominal money supply is evolving independently, according to (12.14), and (12.15) requires the money market to clear. Hence something has to boost the nominal demand for money to preserve monetary equilibrium. According to (12.13), the only variable capable of doing this is the price level. So the adverse product market shock is likelier than not to be accompanied by an unexpectedly high price level, and this will help to prevent output from falling as far as it would have done otherwise (since a positive price surprise induces a favourable response in output). A negative v will depress output, but by a multiplier $1/(1 + \beta y)$ which is less than unitary. A positive money supply shock ($y > 0$) or a negative demand for money shock ($w < 0$) both imply a tendency to excess supply of money, which only an unexpected jump in the price level can remove; and since output responds favourably to this, Q_t increases in $(y_t - w_t)$, as (12.21) shows. Only when the supply curve is very steep, so that β becomes close to zero, will this effect not be perceptible.

The simple model described in equations (12.10), (12.13), (12.14) and (12.15) deprives the authorities of any power to stabilize output, and, by implication, employment or unemployment either. The conditions given in these equations are sufficient for this result. But they are not necessary; the assumptions can be modified in numerous ways, without altering the result that systematic monetary policy is impotent in affecting the level or variance of unemployment. For example, we can introduce serial correlation in output, the well-attested phenomenon that associates above average (below average) output in one period with above average (below average) output in the next. It will still be true that systematic monetary policy cannot affect output, since the serial correlation by itself has no effect on the surprise element in prices, assuming that the public and the monetary authority are equally aware of it. We could go further and add an interest rate term to the demand for money equation, (12.13), and expand the model by introducing an equation for aggregate expenditure in terms of the rate of interest, and other variables. Provided that the two rates of interest in these two equations were the same, or differed by only current or past inflation levels, the impotence results would carry through unscathed. But there are circumstances in which systematic monetary policy can affect output and unemployment. The following section reviews some of them.

12.3.2 *Why Rational Expectations do not Necessarily Destroy the Case for Stabilization Policy*

One way of restoring potency to monetary policy and enabling systematic monetary rules to affect real macro variables such as output and unemployment, is to make output depend upon a richer set of variables than those given in equations

(12.4) or (12.10). For example, suppose that output depends partly upon one-period price forecasting errors, as in (12.10), and partly upon the error in forecasts made two periods ago:

$$Q_t = Q_n + \beta\{\theta(P_t - E_{t-1}P_t) + (1-\theta)(P_t - E_{t-2}P_t)\} + v_t. \tag{12.22}$$

The most natural value for θ to take is $\frac{1}{2}$. An equation like (12.22) could be justified on the following grounds. Suppose that money wage rates are not renegotiated continuously, but set for two periods, in the light of information available to the relevant parties when they strike their bargain. If prices turn out unexpectedly high, real wages will be unexpectedly low, and it will pay firms to expand employment (assuming that workers are willing to supply extra hours, or required by their contract to do so). If prices are unexpectedly low, on the other hand, real wages confronting employers would be correspondingly high, and employment offers will be curtailed.

The significance of adding the two-period forecasting error for P_t is this. Information might become available at one date which implied that market clearing money wage rates at the following date were very different from what had been previously anticipated. Examples of this, in a more realistic setting than the simple framework described in section 12.3.1 might be a sudden appreciation of the home country's foreign exchange rate, or a fall in the overseas prices of its labour-intensive exportables, or a permanent increase in domestic residents' demand for money. Had labour contracts been continuously renegotiated, events like this would very probably induce immediate money wage cuts. But money wage rates cannot suddenly go down. They are held rigid over two periods. At any one time, half the workers are bargaining with their employers over money wage rates to rule in the following period. The other half, meanwhile, know that their money wage rates are predetermined, both for this period and the next.

In conditions such as this the authorities can intervene to reduce the threat of unemployment that hovers in the next period over the second group of workers. By planning to increase the following period's money supply above the level it would have reached anyway, it will be able to bid up next period's price level, and make the money wage rates bargained for in the last period look more 'realistic' in real terms. Several authors have examined formal models that capture these ideas. Interesting examples include Phelps and Taylor (1977), Fischer (1977) and Begg (1982). The literature as a whole is summarized and surveyed in Taylor (1985). These papers share an assumption that money wage contracts in the economy overlap, and display the common finding that this can give the government an opportunity to control the aggregate demand for labour. The essential idea is that the authorities can react to newer information than that underlying the price expectations reflected in money wage contracts. The appeal of this owes much to three observed facts. First, in contemporary Western economies, hardly a week goes by without some important groups of workers agreeing rates of pay with their employers. Second, the interval of time over which these contracts run is rarely less than 1 year, and often, especially in North America, as long as 3 years. Third, the interval of time needed for the authorities to alter fiscal policy variables such as tax rates, or monetary policy instruments like open market operations in government debt, is very much shorter than that. A few days, at the most, are needed; some monetary instruments can be adjusted in a few minutes if needs be. All this said, however, the duration and character of labour contracts are themselves endogenous variables: in periods of inflation, for example, money wages may be set more frequently, or tied to an agreed price index. If the authorities suddenly decide to exploit the power to influence output that overlapping wage contracts give them, it is hardly likely that the nature of those contracts will remain unchanged.

A second line of counterattack on the impotence results of section 12.3.1 consists of introducing a nominal rate of interest that includes an allowance for current expectations of future inflation. To be precise, amend (12.14) to

$$m_t^d = c + P_t + \gamma_1 Q_t - \gamma_2 (R + E_t P_{t+1} - P_t) + w_t \qquad \gamma_1, \gamma_2 > 0 \qquad (12.23)$$

where R is, by assumption, an exogenously given real rate of interest. Equation (12.23) extends (12.14) in a wholly uncontroversial direction, since it is now common ground among monetary economists that the demand for money is affected negatively by nominal interest rates, inflation expectations or both. One significant point to notice is that (12.23) implies that asset-market participants choosing how to divide their portfolios between money and interest-bearing assets are assumed to have current information about the price level, and expectations of next period's price level that reflect all currently available expectations.

The implication of replacing (12.14) by (12.23) is that output does now depend on the systematic monetary policy feedback coefficient, δ. Solving for $Q_t - Q_n$ we have, in place of (12.21),

$$(Q_t - Q_n)\left(1 + \frac{\beta(\gamma_1 + \gamma_2 \delta)}{1 + \gamma_2}\right) = v_t + \beta\left(y_t - \frac{w_t}{1 + \gamma_2}\right). \qquad (12.24)$$

Equation (12.24) is in fact a generalization of (12.21). If $\gamma_2 = 0$, (12.24) reduces to (12.21). The important new element in (12.24) is that δ does have a role to play. It reduces the value of multiplier, $[1 + \beta(\gamma_1 + \gamma_2 \delta)/(1 + \gamma_2)]^{-1}$, that determines the sensitivity of output to the shock variables, v, w and y.

It is not immediately obvious how our modified demand for money equation, (12.23), restores an output-stabilization role for systematic monetary policy. The reason behind it is this. Consider, as in section 12.3.1 above, a negative product market supply shock ($v < 0$). As we saw, this tends to depress output, and therefore to raise the price level in order to preserve money market clearance. But this time a rise in the price level is not the only way of bringing up the demand for money in line with its supply. The nominal rate of interest can fall. And fall it will, at least when δ is zero. Downwards pressure on the rate of interest comes about because the product market supply shock is essentially a one-off incident. It is not likely to recur. The shortage of goods in the current period is firmly expected to be temporary. So prices must be expected to fall back, relative to trend. Expectations of reduced inflation, or even negative inflation, in the next period boost the demand for money, with a consequent lowering of the nominal rate of interest. The important point about a reduced rate of interest is that it implies that the current price level does not have to go up so much. This means that there is a smaller positive price surprise now, and therefore a reduced increase in output to soften the blow of the negative value of v.

When δ is zero, or low enough, therefore, the effect of introducing the nominal rate of interest, with its forward-looking inflation term, into the demand for money equation is to increase the variance of output in the face of product market shocks. The same goes for money supply shocks ($y \neq 0$), but not for demand for money shocks ($w \neq 0$), which are somewhat contained. The sensitivity of Q to v and y

increases with γ_2, as (12.24) shows. But how can a positive value of δ help in these circumstances?

Consider two economies, A and B. Suppose these economies are alike in all respects, save that δ is zero in A and positive in B. A has a 'dry' government, which refuses to loosen the money supply when output is below average (or restrict it in opposite circumstances). But B's government is wet, and always responds by expanding the money supply in the next period when output is low now. In A, output becomes more sensitive to v and y shocks than it would have been had γ_2 been zero. But in B, when output is depressed by negative product market or money supply shocks, everyone knows that monetary policy will be more expansionary in the next period. So they will forecast higher inflation than A's residents. So the nominal interest rate in B will be higher than in A. This means that the current price level will jump more in B than in A, and, since this price increase comes as a surprise, output will hold up better in B than in A. Unemployment will rise more in A than in B.

This mechanism is explored in more detail in Sinclair (1986a). Similar arguments are advanced by Buiter (1981) in the context of an open economy, and by Turnovsky (1980). It is worth stressing that the output and unemployment stabilizing role of δ, the money supply feedback rule, does not occur despite rational expectations, but because of them. There is a widespread but erroneous belief that rational expectations deprive the authorities of the power to stabilize output and unemployment. This is not true. Rational expectations alter the character of optimum stabilization policy. But they need not destroy the case for it. Whether monetary feedback rules help to stabilize output and unemployment does not turn on the issue of whether expectations are rational. Everything depends upon the assumptions of the model into which rational expectations are inserted.

The conclusion we have reached in this part of section 12.3.2 bears repetition. When the demand for money is sensitive to a nominal interest rate that incorporates forward-looking inflation expectations and all currently available information (and the money supply does not respond to output in the previous period, so that δ is zero), output becomes more sensitive to certain shocks than if it

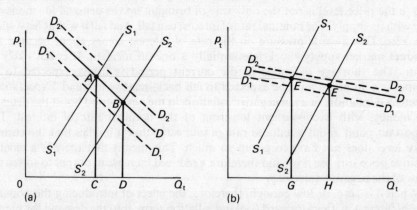

Figure 12.2 *(a) The output effects of supply shocks in the absence of demand shocks, when the demand for money is independent of nominal interest rates; (b) The output effects of supply shocks when aggregate demand is more elastic because the demand for money depends on the nominal interest rate*

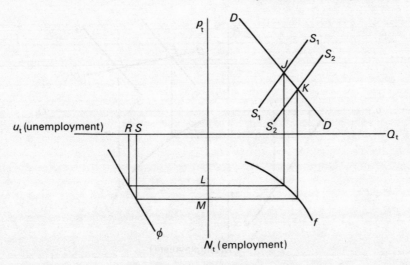

Figure 12.3 *The effect of a high feedback from output to the next period's money supply in steadying output and unemployment*

is not. The latter case, explored in section 12.3.1, is illustrated in figure 12.2(a); the former, which stems from the modified money demand equation (12.23), is shown in figure 12.2(b). In figure 12.2(b) aggregate demand is more elastic than in figure 12.2(a). Setting the demand shocks y and w to zero, aggregate demand will be given by the solid lines DD. Product market shocks ($v \neq 0$) generate supply curves between S_1 and S_2. When demand is more elastic, as in figure 12.2(b), the range of output values widens from CD in figure 12.2(a) to GH.

A high value of δ, the sensitivity of next period's money supply to current output, makes aggregate demand less elastic again, when the demand for money varies negatively with the nominal rate of interest. It means that output and unemployment will tend to be steadier as a result. Figure 12.3 shows this. The less elastic demand curve implies a narrower range for output (between L and M) and unemployment (between R and S) than in figure 12.4, where the money supply feedback parameter, δ, is zero. The curve f in the lower right panel is a production function linking output, Q_t, to employment, N_t; the curve ϕ in the lower left panel associates employment with unemployment, u_t. In figure 12.3, where δ is high, the range of unemployment (between R and S) is considerably lower than in figure 12.4 (where the corresponding range runs from T to U). The effect of demand shocks, shown in figures 12.2(a) and 12.2(b) by the dotted lines D_1D_1 and D_2D_2, is not drawn in figures 12.3 and 12.4 to save clutter.

This way of rebuilding a role for stabilization policy under rational expectations has much to commend it. It warns us against the lazy fatalism with which it is all too easy to regard the problem of excessive and volatile unemployment. It reminds us that it is not necessarily true that we have to live with large swings in unemployment. We may be able at the least to temper them by appropriate monetary and budgetary policy. But the line of argument we have just examined is not entirely immune from objections. It is open to criticism at two points in particular. One, it allows portfolio holders a complete set of current, up-to-date information when making their inflation forecasts (which in turn determine the

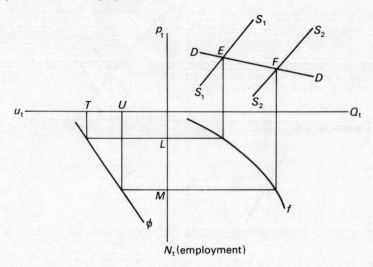

Figure 12.4 *The high sensitivity of output and unemployment to supply shocks when the money supply feedback parameter is zero, and aggregate demand is therefore more elastic*

nominal rate of interest, and hence the demand for money and the price level). This is in contrast with the information set available to product and labour market participants, who (according to the Lucas account, at least) only know the current price of their own product, and can only guess the current prices of other goods. Such a disparity in information sets is a little curious: it may not be wholly implausible, but it has to be admitted that it is a crucial assumption, in that the result (that stabilization policy is not impotent) will not follow without it. Secondly, there may be problems in making the money supply highly sensitive to the previous level of output. What happens if there are measurement errors in output? Is it feasible or desirable for banks to expand and contract loans and advances quickly (for this is what a high value of δ must entail in practice)? Will not the increased variability of prices, which will follow if δ is increased, bring disadvantages of its own, possibly even including higher unemployment as a by-product of increased bankruptcies and uncertainties? Finally, if monetary policy results in higher variance of prices, will not producers react by reducing their output responses to price surprises, so that β falls, the surprise supply curve steepens and output becomes more sensitive to product market supply shocks again?

There are other ways, too, of restoring some form of potency to monetary policy under rational expectations. A faster trend growth rate of the money supply (a higher value of d in the money supply equation (12.14)) could imply a higher long-run value of natural output, by raising the investment share of national income if households react to faster inflation by saving more. This effect had first been proposed by Tobin (1965); Begg (1980) showed how it would continue to apply in a rational expectations set-up not dissimilar to the one we have been examining. If wages and prices are given exogenously, as in chapter 3, Neary and Stiglitz (1983) show that rational expectations of the resulting rationing constraints faced by households or firms in particular markets can make the output effects of monetary or fiscal policy changes larger than they would otherwise have been. Furthermore, even in the market-clearing framework proposed by Lucas, if producers' output decisions respond to expectations of real interest rates (as argued first by Lucas and Rapping (1969)), there will be circumstances in which monetary rules can be designed to stabilize output and unemployment: these have been well summarized by Minford and Peel (1983). Then there is the distinct possibility that some of the model's equations will be non-linear. Snower (1984) has shown that the impotence results will typically fail to hold. Lastly, in a complex multi-sector economy, there can be no guarantee that the so-called 'natural' rates of output and (un)employment are uniquely given. Indeed, chapter 13 below is devoted to exploring several reasons for suspecting that there may be multiple unemployment equilibria. If this is so, the door is opened to the possibility that the government may be in a position to design its policy instruments to achieve one unemployment equilibrium path rather than another.

Rational expectations do not necessarily imply, then, that the authorities are powerless to affect the variance or mean level of unemployment. The Phillips curve is not necessarily a vertical line as far as systematic demand management policy is concerned. Yet whatever the trade-off between inflation and unemployment, especially if it is not just a given vertical line, it is important to ask what should govern society's preferences between the two ills of unemployment and inflation. It is this issue to which the next section is devoted.

12.4 The Costs and Benefits of Inflation (or Policies that Generate Inflation)

Chapter 1 contained a brief analysis of the costs of unemployment. It is therefore timely to examine the costs and benefits of inflation. In a sense, this is a rather fraudulent concept, since inflation is best seen as an endogenous variable determined along with everything else, and not an exogenous parameter. Consequently, the costs and benefits really attach to the policies that generate inflation, rather than inflation itself.

Some of the effects of inflation depend on whether it is wrongly predicted, and some do not. Into the first category falls the redistribution of wealth from lenders to borrowers, and old to young, to which unexpectedly rapid inflation typically leads. Such redistribution can have serious aggregate effects, not just because of spending, and factor supply patterns of the relevant groups may differ. Unexpected wealth redistribution – in any direction – may trigger bankruptcies, disrupt trading and investment and place strain upon the harmony of social relations. But these effects are just as likely if inflation is unexpectedly slow as if it is unexpectedly rapid. They may be quite independent of the trend level of inflation. No less important, they can usually be avoided by indexation. Indexing pensions, loans and other contracts to a mutually agreed price index should remove the adverse effects of unexpectedly fast or slow inflation.

Then there are effects stemming from inflation when some important macroeconomic variable is rigid in nominal terms. If a country with a fixed exchange rate for its currency against other countries inflates more rapidly than they, its trading industries will suffer deteriorating international competitiveness. The levels of profit, output and employment in import-competing and exporting sectors will be subject to an increasing squeeze. If income tax brackets or indirect tax rates are frozen in nominal terms, inflation will alter real tax rates and real tax receipts. Investment may suffer from an interaction of inflation and taxation on corporate profits that fails to correct for inflation in its depreciation and stock appreciation provisions (Feldstein (1982) provides evidence that this effect has been serious in the United States, although British evidence (Edwards and Keen (1985)) fails to confirm its existence in the UK context). The simplest way out of such problems is to remove the offending nominal rigidity: allow exchange rates to adjust to international inflation differences, or tie income tax brackets and indirect taxation to an appropriate price index.

Indexation will neutralize the effects of both unexpected inflation and the interaction of inflation with nominal rigidities in the tax system or exchange rates. This leaves us, then, with the effects of fully anticipated or 'equilibrium' inflation. Perhaps the most important of these is the fact that inflation is a tax on cash balances. Cash balances carry a zero nominal rate of interest; other nominal assets such as unindexed time deposits with banks or other financial institutions, or unindexed government bonds, carry an explicit interest yield. The nominal rate of interest. This proposition was first advanced by Friedman (1969). If inflation runs at rate of interest, and an allowance for expected inflation. Expected and actual inflation will be equal when expectations are fulfilled. If the marginal cost of providing real money balances is negligible, then, at least in an undistorted economy, so should the 'price' of money be (the nominal rate of interest should be zero). Hence actual and expected inflation should equal minus the real rate of interest. This proposition was first advanced by Friedman (1969). If inflation runs at any higher level than this, potential welfare losses arise. As a rough rule of thumb, they will increase with the square of the difference between actual and optimal inflation rates. This will be true, at least, when the demand for real money is a linear function of the nominal rate of interest.

Inflation is a tax on money holdings. The government saves some of the debt servicing charges it would otherwise incur. This can be made the basis of an argument that suggests that modest inflation may be rather advantageous (Sinclair (1983a) chapter 8). If the government relies on distortionary taxes, on income for example, for much of its revenue, the revenues earned by taxing money holdings through inflation will be very welcome. The optimum tax on holdings of money cannot be dissociated from the broader question of optimum tax rates on all incomes and goods. But it seems most unlikely that equalizing the marginal cost of distortions imposed by taxes on money, incomes and other goods, will not entail some element of tax on money. This will be especially true if, as Friedman has traditionally claimed, the interest elasticity of the demand for money is small, since that suggests that the deadweight loss from taxing money at a modest rate will be trivial.

Finally, there are costs associated with changing the nominal prices of goods and factors. The faster the rate of inflation, the greater the real resource loss represented by this. Further, relative prices will tend to swing about more violently as the rate of inflation rises (Cukierman (1984)), and this, too, may well entail some efficiency losses. Yet even when all these factors are taken into account, the net welfare costs of equilibrium inflation seem slight. They are a recurrent cost, as against the costs of reducing inflation (which largely take the form of output losses and additional unemployment during the transition to lower inflation). If inflation is above its optimal value, and can be cut costlessly, this is what should be done. But the public finance argument considered above suggests that the optimum rate of inflation may well lie in the range 3–8 per cent, and recent evidence on the sacrifice ratio (see chapter 16 below) shows that the costs of cutting inflation appear to be substantial. This does not suggest that the balance of advantage lies with policies designed to eliminate inflation, at least in the UK. In the section that follows, on the other hand, we shall assume that inflation should be cut, and turn to the question of how quickly this should be done.

12.5 Two Issues of Dynamics

12.5.1 *How Quickly Should Disinflation Proceed?*

Let us assume that the present rate of inflation is too high. Suppose that everyone agrees that it ought to fall from y per cent to x per cent, let us say, as a long-run policy objective. How quickly should inflation be brought down? Sinclair (1985) attempts to answer that question. What follows is based in part upon that analysis.

Five arguments can be adduced for gradual disinflation, and five for achieving the target of x per cent quickly. The arguments in favour of rapid disinflation are:

1 Cross-sectional justice. Slow disinflation may involve protracted unemployment for small minorities. It is unlikely to be spread evenly across the population. Older men and women are liable to suffer, because they find it particularly hard to find jobs. Those just about to enter the labour force when the policy is implemented; blacks and other minorities are especially at risk. Imagine, for simplicity's sake, that we can choose between calling a national holiday for a month, which will involve 100 per cent unemployment, and keeping 2 per cent (often the same 2 per cent) of the labour force out of work for 4 years; and also that both will bring about the new x per cent inflation rate when these periods have expired. The first of these at least has the merit of spreading the unemployment burden evenly over the current labour force.

2 Large negative inflation surprises may be disproportionately successful in lowering expectations of inflation. This argument relies upon the hypothesis of adaptive expectations, with an assumption of 'increasing returns' in the inflation surprise. Small surprises may be disregarded as random blips; a really sharp unexpected drop in inflation may knock expectations of subsequent inflation much more effectively.

3 The gains from permanently lower inflation accrue sooner.

4 If a programme of slower monetary growth is announced ahead, and people believe it and form inflation expectations 'rationally' on the basis of a simple monetarist theory, the economy should be spared at least some of the pain of abnormally high unemployment.

5 A government cannot bind its successors. Pre-announcing policies of gradual disinflation may be less credible than short-term policy commitments. Early evidence that inflation is falling quickly should in any case help to strengthen the belief that a promise to continue the policy will be honoured.

By contrast, the five arguments that favour gradualism are:

6   Intertemporal justice. Why should the present generation pay the whole cost of disinflation, with all the loss in employment, consumption and income that this must entail, when it is future generations that reap the benefits?

7   Diminishing returns in the production function. If there are diminishing returns to labour, small, lengthy employment cuts will involve a smaller total output loss than a brief substantial cut.

8   Convexity of the short-run Phillips curves. Evidence suggests that the short-run trade-off between inflation and unemployment is curved, not linear (see for example Coe and Gagliardi (1985)). The marginal effect of higher unemployment in cutting inflation falls off as the level of unemployment increases.

9   Diminishing marginal utility of income and leisure. The welfare cost of departing from the 'optimal' long-run trade-offs between leisure and income may increase with the *square* of the magnitude of the departure, at least as a local approximation.

10   Old contracts. Money wage rates are largely unindexed. They may be negotiated over intervals of up to 3 years; at least when inflation is modest, annual or 2-year contracts seem to be the rule. Loans are often made for much longer periods. The structure of contracts in force today reflects the inflation expectations of those that entered into them at the time when the bargain was struck. Unexpectedly slow inflation makes real wages unexpectedly high for a while, squeezing the demand for labour. When contracts overlap, it will take a long time for things to settle down to the new long-run equilibrium (Begg (1982)). There is also sudden redistribution from debtors to creditors. Bankruptcies are likely to ensue. Rapid cancellation of loans and overdraft facilities already promised by banks is inescapable if broad money aggregates are suddenly to grow more slowly. This could cause havoc.

Of the arguments for gradualism, (10) really constitutes a case for indexation, or for a pre-announced disinflationary programme with a delayed start, rather than a continuous process of slow disinflation initiated at once. (7), (8) and (9) are rather compelling; yet they depend upon some version of adaptive expectations, which is at best a controversial hypothesis that would command somewhat less support among academic economists today than a decade or two ago. (6) and (1), the first argument in favour of rapid disinflation, are nicely counterpoised. Reasonable men may differ on what is essentially an issue of ethics. (2) is perfectly plausible. But it has yet to be demonstrated empirically. Like (7), (8) and (9) it relies on adaptive expectations. There is no reason in principle to think that there are likelier to be increasing than decreasing returns to inflation surprises. (3) is undeniable, but is balanced by the fact that the costs will be borne earlier, too: Sinclair's (1985) model emerges with the result that the optimum speed of disinflation increases with the discount rate, in fact. (4) fails if the announced monetary programme is not believed, or if people do not forecast future prices on the basis of future money supply expectations. Presumably observers are likelier to expect a one-to-one link between the money supply and the price level over long than short periods; this is at least what the evidence seems to point to: the shorter the time period, the worse the empirical association between money supply changes and inflation. The rather poor association between targeted and actual growth of monetary aggregates, especially in the UK since 1979 – not to mention the general tendency for targets to be overshot – would encourage people to take official pronouncements of future monetary growth with more than a grain of salt. (5), on the other hand, is rather more convincing.

The conflict between these arguments is probably best resolved in the following fashion. The higher the initial level of inflation, the greater the case for speed in cutting it. This has some consistency with the Sargent (1982) and Gordon (1982) results that the costs of lowering inflation seem to be greatest when inflation is modest. The steadier inflation has been in the past, the stronger the case for delay (with pre-announcement), and also for gradualism. If inflation has recently shot up to its current level, on the other hand, the smaller the damage done by reducing it swiftly, before expectations of rapid inflation have had time to become ingrained. Widespread indexation should help to lower the costs of disinflation, whether fast or slow, and may tip the scales in favour of doing it more quickly. There is some attraction in announcing an ogive-shaped time path for the growth of monetary aggregates: initially, a very slight deceleration in the rate of monetary growth, or even a once-and-for-all jump in the nominal money supply to meet the rise in the demand for money that should attend a fall in inflation expectations; then, after a year or two, quicker declines; lastly, a gradual asymptotic convergence on the long-run optimum. The reduction in inflation may be assisted, especially in its early stages, by direct and indirect tax cuts (Buiter and Miller (1985) provide a detailed analysis of the merits of these in the context of a disinflationary programme).

12.5.2 *Hysteresis*

Hysteresis means 'turning up late' in Greek. In electromagnetism, it refers to the phenomenon of lagged adjustment: it implies that the state of a variable may become arbitrary, and dependent upon the history of how it has moved in the past. In the context of unemployment, it can be thought of as a type of inertia. There are many reasons for thinking that the 'natural' rate of unemployment is far from unique, and could settle down in a variety of places. Several of these arguments are presented in detail in chapter 13. But there is one issue that calls for mention now.

Unemployment may have a corrosive effect on the abilities and the attitudes of those that experience it. The very long duration of unemployment spells suffered by older workers who lose their jobs – already examined in chapter 1 – may testify to this. So does the alarming fact that inflation and unemployment seem to have stabilized in the UK in the period after 1982. Inflation has settled down to the 4–5 per cent range, while unemployment remains obstinately stuck at over 3 million. If inflation and unemployment are both steady over a period of 3 years or more, one is tempted to conclude that a point of equilibrium has been reached. Perhaps the 'natural' rate of unemployment is now stuck at 13 per cent. But how can this be? This is two and a half times as large as the long-run average rate for Britain since 1851, when hard, albeit narrowly based, statistical evidence first becomes regularly available. It contrasts even more sharply with the 2 per cent average unemployment rates recorded in the 1950s and 1960s, when inflation undulated gently around a trend level of $3\frac{1}{2}$ per cent per annum.

The answer may be that money wage increases respond to the *change* in unemployment at least as much as to its level. When unemployment is rising, fear restrains those in work from demanding large pay rises. Once unemployment has stabilized, even at a high level, the danger of further job losses recedes. Those still in work have no personal incentive to sacrifice their own living standards to rebuild employment opportunities for others. This view is propounded by Morris and Sinclair (1985). It is also discussed more formally by Buiter and Miller (1985). It carries with it the worrying implication that unemployment reductions, however achieved, must threaten to provoke a rise in rates of pay and price inflation, even if the level of unemployment remains quite high. There can be a silver lining, however. Once unemployment has stopped falling, wage pressures should slacken off.

13 Unemployment Breeds Unemployment

13.1 Introduction

The aim of this chapter is to examine various reasons for thinking that unemployment can feed on itself. Unemployment equilibria may well not be unique.

The evidence suggests that this is a serious possibility. British unemployment between 1921 and 1940, for example, seems to have been stuck in a 'high groove'. It averaged over 12 per cent in these years, and only barely and briefly fell as low as 9 per cent. The next three decades saw the average down to under 2 per cent and almost all annual observations between $\frac{1}{2}$ per cent and $3\frac{1}{2}$ per cent. In the past decade, international comparisons of unemployment are just as startling. Unemployment in eight countries (Austria, Greece, Japan, Luxembourg, New Zealand, Norway, Sweden and Switzerland) averages under $2\frac{1}{4}$ per cent with no annual observations for any country higher than 4 per cent. For another eight (Australia, Belgium, Canada, Ireland, the Netherlands, Spain, the UK and the US), the 10-year average has been four times as large as this.

This chapter examines five possible mechanisms that could account for non-uniqueness in equilibrium unemployment. The relationship between spot hiring and pre-empting labour, and its implications for unemployment, are scrutinized in section 13.2. Section 13.3 investigates imitation by employers while 13.4 is concerned with the possible effect of unemployment upon household preferences and what can follow from it. Section 13.5 examines non-uniqueness in search models, and 13.6 in quantity-rationing theory. Section 13.7 concludes.

13.2 Pre-empting and Spot Hiring

This section investigates a firm's choice between two ways of recruiting labour needed for a future project. Labour can be hired when production actually commences. Alternatively, it can be pre-empted. Hiring in advance is more expensive in one way: wages have to be paid out for a longer period. Pre-empted workers must be paid before production begins, as well as while the project is under way. But there are extra costs in spot hiring too. Last-minute recruitment involves more advertising and a much more active search on the part of the employer. It also carries the disadvantages that employees hired in this way may not be as skilled or productive, or as accurately screened, as those selected at an earlier stage.

In conditions of low unemployment, last-minute recruiting will be particularly expensive. The search for workers able to start work at once will be very demanding. The average quality of those hired in this fashion is also likely to be lower, since good workers could be extremely hard to find. When the overall level of unemployment is high, on the other hand, there should be a ready supply of talented, able workers seeking work, who can be engaged quickly, and the employer will find it cheaper to search for them.

The general level of unemployment will have an important bearing, then, on the employer's perceptions of the costs and benefits of hiring labour at the last minute. There is less reason to think that recruitment costs, and the average quality of workers recruited, are as sensitive to unemployment for pre-empted employees. It is quite possible to imagine that the greater freedom pre-emption offers to the firm brings recruitment costs down to a negligible level in comparison with last-minute hires, and that the firm can effectively guarantee the quality of the workers it engages in this way.

Suppose, then, that there were no costs of recruiting pre-empted workers, but that the costs of recruiting labour in the spot market, C, increase with the square of labour obtained in this way, (H_s), and fall with the overall level of unemployment, u:

$$C = \frac{a}{2} H_s^2 \phi(u) \quad \phi' < 0 < \phi, a. \tag{13.1}$$

Suppose, too, that the average quality of H_s (defined as q) increases with the overall unemployment rate. This means that the 'effective' labour force the firm hires will be $qH_s + H_p$, if H_p is the level of pre-empted labour. Assume for simplicity's sake that the firm inherits no labour from the past, operates in perfectly competitive conditions and will produce output in the next period subject to a production function, f, which depends only upon the effective labour force it employs:

$$f = f(q(u)H_s + H_p) \quad q', f' > 0 > f''. \tag{13.2}$$

The restriction that $q' > 0$ reminds us that the quality of spot hires rises with the unemployment rate, while $f' > 0 > f''$ states that there are positive but diminishing returns to labour. Call p the price that the firm will receive for its product, and let w_0 and w_1 represent the wage rates that the firm must pay any worker before production occurs, and during production, respectively. Perfect competition implies that p, w_0 and w_1 lie outside the firm's control. Finally, let r represent the rate of interest; suppose that a single time period elapses between pre-empting H_p and the date of production; and assume that the firm aims to maximize its profits, with no uncertainty about the value of future variables.

Viewed at the date of production, profits (π) will consist of the value of output, pf, less total wages: $((w_0(1+r)+w_1)H_p + w_1H_s)$ and recruitment costs, C:

$$\pi = pf(q(u)H_s + H_p) - H_p(w_0(1+r)+w_1) - H_s w_1 - \frac{a}{2} H_s^2 \phi(u). \tag{13.3}$$

The first term on the right-hand side of (13.3) stands for total revenue; the second is the wage cost of pre-empted labour (the value of w_0 must be multiplied by $(1+r)$ to express it in present-value terms); the third is the wage bill for the spot hiring and the fourth is the cost of recruiting them.

Profit maximization implies that the firm will select both H_p and H_s up to the point where the marginal revenue from each type of labour just balances its marginal cost. In the case of H_p, this will be where

$$pf' = w_0(1+r) + w_1 \tag{13.4}$$

and, for H_s:

$$q(u)pf' = w + aH_s\phi(u). \tag{13.5}$$

The second-order conditions that guarantee a maximum for profits will be met since $f'' < 0 < a\phi$.

Combining (13.4) and (13.5), we can obtain a solution for the firm's demand for spot labour:

$$H_s = \frac{1}{a\phi}\{qw_0(1+r) - w_1(1-q)\}. \tag{13.6}$$

To ensure that H_s will be positive, (13.6) tells us that q must be sufficiently large:

$$q > \frac{w_1}{w_0(1+r) + w_1}. \tag{13.7}$$

We shall assume that condition (13.7) is always fulfilled, no matter what the level of unemployment.

We can now examine the variables that determine H_s. The rate of interest is a positive influence. A higher interest rate increases the incentive to delay engaging labour, because it raises the relative cost of wages in the pre-empting period. Similarly, w_0 raises, and w_1 reduces, the demand for spot hires. Finally, the variable of most direct interest to us: the level of unemployment. Not surprisingly, higher unemployment unambiguously increases the demand of H_s. The variable q rises with u (to which H_s is negatively related) and decreases in u. Additional unemployment increases the attractiveness of spot hiring for two reasons: recruitment costs come down, and the quality of workers obtained goes up.

So much for H_s. What determines the level of pre-emptive hiring? We know that the marginal revenue product of H_p, pf', must equal its marginal cost. This is given by (13.4). So we can differentiate (13.4) totally to obtain an equation linking changes in H_p to other variables. Holding p, w and r constant, we obtain

$$f''H_sq'\,du + q\,dH_s + dH_p = 0. \tag{13.8}$$

Since $f'' < 0$, (13.8) implies

$$dH_p = -q\,dH_s - H_sq'\,du. \tag{13.9}$$

From (13.9) we infer that H_p reacts negatively to changes in H_s. There is also a direct negative influence from the level of unemployment. So it is clear that H_p must go down if the unemployment increases, both from this direct effect, and as a result of the fact that increased unemployment must raise H_s. Pre-empting labour will be attractive when labour markets are tight, and much less so in conditions of high overall unemployment.

Diagrammatically, the story can be presented as follows. The firm will have a series of linear isoquants between the two kinds of labour, since output is held to depend only upon their weighted sum, $qH_s + H_p$. Its isocost restraints will be concave, to reflect the fact of increasing marginal recruitment costs. In conditions of

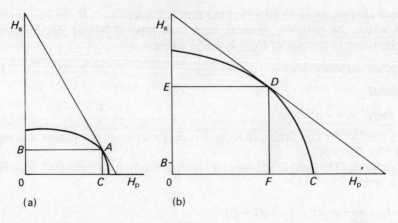

Figure 13.1 *Pre-emptions and spot hires in conditions of (a) low and (b) high unemployment*

low unemployment, the isoquants are steep because q is not high. The isocost curves will be quite flat, reflecting the high costs of recruiting labour in the spot market. This is the position illustrated in the left-hand panel of figure 13.1. Profit maximization takes the firm to a point of tangency between the two, at point A. Little labour will be hired on the spot market (OB). Pre-emptions will be high (OC, on the horizontal axis).

The right-hand panel of figure 13.1 depicts what could happen when unemployment is high. The increased productivity of spot hires means that isoquants will be flatter. Reduced costs of recruiting labour on the spot market makes the isocost curves steeper. The point of tangency, at D, implies a greater level of spot hiring (OE on the vertical axis), while pre-emptive hires go down (to OF).

How can this analysis be applied to explain changes in British labour markets? In the 1950s and 1960s, unemployment was very low. It averaged barely 2 per cent in these two decades. Interest rates were modest, while wage rates were starting to climb rather rapidly. Labour hoarding was widespread. In the terms of the analysis of this section, employers will have been anxious to pre-empt labour for new projects, since the tight conditions in national labour markets must have made last-minute recruiting decidedly unattractive.

Thus far, the 1980s have been characterized by high nominal and real interest rates, a slackening in the pace of money wage increases and, above all, a much higher average level of unemployment (11 per cent for 1980–5). Employers now have every incentive to adopt a 'wait-and-see' attitude with respect to recruiting labour. Workers are easy to find; talented experienced workers can be engaged quickly; and the interest costs involved in pre-empting labour are appreciable. No wonder, then, that the hoarding of labour has become far rarer.

The transition between a low-unemployment world with substantial labour hoarding, to a case of high unemployment and little pre-empting of workers, has been gradual. But while it has occurred, Britain has experienced a switch, as it were, from the left-hand to the right-hand panel of figure 13.1. National labour markets have displayed a major, once-and-for-all reduction in pre-emptive employment. During this transition, the total demand for new labour has fallen substantially. In addition to the factors already mentioned, a further influence has been at work.

There is another advantage of spot hiring which we have not yet considered. If uncertainty is introduced into the story, the employer will have an incentive to delay hiring labour until more is known about the prices at which he can sell his product, and other relevant variables. Pre-emption implies commitment. When p is subject to random swings, there is the grave danger that it will turn out unexpectedly low, and that the firm will be saddled with an excessive labour force, upon which heavy wage costs have already been incurred. Spot hiring gives greater flexibility, and reduces risk. Here again, the contrast between the early post-war decades and the 1980s is revealing. The former were characterized by little structural change. It was a relatively safe environment. The variance of selling prices which a firm could reasonably expect was not high. But all that had changed by the 1980s. Oil and primary commodity markets had become subject to huge price changes. Markets for particular manufactured goods became vulnerable to exchange-rate swings, and sudden import penetration from overseas. The amplitude of the business cycle had increased, as did the volatility of interest rates. Finally, to cap it all, employers began to think that dismissing labour in adverse conditions was expensive and difficult. Spot hiring became the order of the day.

To return to the model examined above, it is interesting to note that the sensitivity of ϕ and q to the overall unemployment rate raises the possibility of multiple equilibria for the level of unemployment. Suppose that the single competitive firm we have been examining is in fact a microcosm of the whole economy. Suppose that the total labour engaged at one date consists of labour hired spot at the time, labour pre-empted for the following period and labour pre-empted in the previous period. Assume that the latter two are equal. Setting aside any other labour inherited from earlier periods, the total labour force engaged will be $H_s + 2H_p$. How does this vary with the overall level of unemployment?

We have already seen that H_s rises, and H_p goes down, when the unemployment rate increases. It is therefore a simple matter to see how the aggregate $X \equiv H_s + 2H_p$ behaves from (13.9):

$$dX = dH_s + 2dH_p$$

$$= (1 - 2q)\, dH_s - H_s q'\, du$$

$$\Rightarrow \frac{dX}{du} = \left((1 - 2q)\frac{\partial H_s}{\partial u} - H_s q' \right). \tag{13.10}$$

13.3 Imitation by Employers

A firm which declares some of its labour redundant is making a public act. Labour shedding is well reported. Releasing labour can be taken as a signal. The firm anticipates deterioration in the selling conditions for its products, perhaps, or some other shock that makes it advisable, even imperative for it to reduce wage costs quickly.

The outside observer cannot know exactly why the firm has made some of its labour force redundant. But he or she can tell when it has happened, that something is amiss. The firm might be responding with a delay to events in the recent past, possibly events which have had widespread effects upon other firms as well. But it is just as likely that it is reacting to recent information about probable developments in the near future, information which may be known only to the firm's managers themselves. If so, the employer who dismisses labour publicly – and he cannot do so in any other way – is telling the world something about his own perceptions of his future economic environment.

Information about likely future changes in the economic or commercial environment facing companies is scarce and valuable. Profits depend much less on what you do than when you do it. Timing is all. Advance warning of an important event can earn you a fortune; lack of it may bring ruin. If you saw an army of depositors besieging your bank and demanding to get out their funds, you would ask yourself 'What do they know that I don't?' It could only be prudent to withdraw your own funds as well, if you could. The very fact that depositors were trying to withdraw their funds would itself increase the risk of the bank's collapse. Even if rumours or impressions of insolvency were originally quite ill-founded, they could turn into a self-fulfilling prophecy.[1]

Dismissing labour may be more common and less dramatic than a bank run. But there are parallels. Managers who see other firms releasing labour will ask themselves, 'What do they know that we don't?' Employers declaring redundancies may be taken to signal hitherto privy information about future adverse shocks to demand. It should cause the other firms' managers to become more pessimistic in their own forecasts. Furthermore there is even an element of self-fulfilment. A society can talk itself into slumps. Investment programmes are curtailed and orders cancelled; workers fearing that they may lose their jobs, not to mention those actually dismissed, will reduce their consumption expenditures. These reductions in aggregate demand will be translated into actual job losses when there is insufficient flexibility in prices and wages. Neary and Stiglitz (1983) show how the extent and character of unemployment in the current period depends on people's expectations of being constrained by disequilibrium in the next, and by the form that the disequilibrium is expected to take. Imitation of one firm by others can lead to multiplicity of equilibria in similar ways to the effects of expectations.

13.4 Household Preferences may Vary with Unemployment

If you are out of work when your friends and neighbours are all fully employed earning good incomes, the attractiveness of your leisure will be severely limited by the embarrassment you are likely to feel at your condition. But when others around you are out of work too, the stigma attached to unemployment will be softened. You are less likely to be blamed for your predicament. Society is kinder to conformists. The greater the incidence of unemployment among those near you, the less unpleasant your own unemployment may be.

If people's preferences between income and leisure vary with the overall level of unemployment, we encounter another possible reason for suspecting that 'unemployment equilibrium' can be non-unique. Consider the following model, modified from the unemployment benefit model of chapter 6. Suppose that everyone has the utility function

$$U = (1-h)I \tag{13.11}$$

if he is at work. $(1-h)$ denotes leisure, and I after-tax wage income, $wh(1-t)$. If you are out of work, your utility function is

$$V = \psi(u) \cdot b \tag{13.12}$$

where b stands for the level of unemployment benefit, and ψ is an increasing function of the unemployment rate. Abilities to earn are distributed evenly between 1 and 0. Taxes are levied on wages at the rate t so as to defray the total costs of unemployment benefits with a balanced budget. Consequently

$$bu = t \int_u^1 \frac{w}{2} \, dw = t \frac{1-u^2}{4}. \tag{13.13}$$

Suppose the income tax rate is 20 per cent. In that case (13.13) will yield a demand curve for unemployment

$$b = \frac{1-u^2}{20u} \tag{13.14}$$

while the indifference principle gives a supply curve of unemployment

$$b = \frac{u}{s\psi(u)}. \tag{13.15}$$

If, for example, $\psi(u)$ takes the form

$$\psi = \text{Max}[0.014, 0.01682 - 2775u + 5.134u^2] \tag{13.16}$$

there will be three possible equilibrium rates of unemployment: 10 per cent, 20 per cent and 30 per cent.

Figure 13.2 illustrates this. Introducing the notion that the utility enjoyed by those out of work increases with the unemployment rate makes it possible that the supply curve of unemployment bends back over part of its length. With the example given by (13.16), this is indeed what happens. There will be not one but three intersection points between the demand and supply curves at an income tax rate of one-fifth. If it be assumed that an intersection is stable when the supply curve crosses the demand curve from beneath, points A and C are stable equilibria, and B is unstable. The form that ψ takes in (13.16) ensures that the utility of unemployment increases with the level of unemployment when $u > 0.03$ or so, and is independent of u below that.

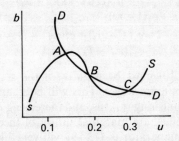

Figure 13.2 *Multiple intersection between the demand and supply curves of unemployment, which can arise when preferences vary with unemployment*

13.5 Unemployment Increases the Costs, and Lowers the Chances of Success, of Searching for Another Job

When labour markets are tight, it is easy for someone out of work to find another job. Search is cheap, and likely to succeed. But when the overall rate of unemployment is high, the tables are turned. There will be long queues of job applicants. You must be prepared to travel further, and spend more time, in the search for a job; and the chances of finding anything are slim. It seems likely that an increased general level of unemployment reduces the incentive for a jobless worker to conduct searches for employment opportunities.

It is not difficult to model this. Let c stand for the total costs of search, s. It makes sense to assume that c depends upon both s and u, the overall unemployment rate: if $c = c(s, u)$, we should expect $c_1, c_2, c_{12} > 0$. Let π denote the probability of success in search. Presumably this also varies with s and u, so that if $\pi = \pi(s, u)$, $\pi_1 > 0 > \pi_2, \pi_{12}$. The signs on the cross partials c_{12} and π_{12} reflect the principle that the marginal cost of search and the marginal product of search – the effect of increased search upon the probability of success – both respond adversely to higher unemployment. Let w denote the wage the worker expects to earn if he finds a job, b the rate of unemployment benefit and f and g his utility levels in employment, and when out of work, respectively. Finally, assume that g depends upon the higher leisure time available to the worker if he is out of work, which becomes more attractive (or less unattractive) as the overall unemployment rate goes up. Denote this by $\phi(u)$, and assume normal, convex indifference curves between income and leisure, so that $g_{12} > 0$.

The individual unemployed worker has the optimization problem

$$\text{Max}_s\, \pi(s, u) f(w - c(s, u)) + (1 - \pi(s, u)) g(b - c(s, u), \phi(u)). \tag{13.17}$$

The first-order condition for this, if we restrict attention to an interior solution, will be

$$\pi_1(f - g) = C_1(f'\pi + g_1(1 - \pi)) \tag{13.18}$$

Equation (13.18) states that search should be conducted up to the point where its marginal benefit, in terms of income enhancement, just balances the extra costs involved.

We can differentiate (13.18) totally to obtain the effect of an increase in the level of unemployment upon the individual's optimal search activity, s^*:

$$\frac{ds^*}{du} = \frac{\begin{array}{c}(f' - g_1)(\pi_1 c_2 + \pi_2 c_1) + g_{12}\phi'((1 - \pi)c_1 + \pi_1) - \pi_{12}(f - g) \\ + c_{12}(f'\pi + g_1(1 - \pi)) - c_1 c_2[\pi f'' + (1 - \pi)g_{11}]\end{array}}{\begin{array}{c}\pi_{11}(f - g) - 2\pi_1 c_1(f' - g_1) + c_1^2(\pi f'' + (1 - \pi)g_{11}) \\ - c_{11}(\pi f' + (1 - \pi)g_1)\end{array}}. \tag{13.19}$$

The denominator of (13.19) must be negative if the second-order condition for (13.18) to describe an optimum holds. This will be guaranteed if, as seems quite reasonable, there are diminishing returns, and increasing marginal costs, for search ($\pi_{11} < 0 < c_{11}$), and diminishing marginal utility of income when in and out of work ($f'', g_{11} < 0$). The numerator of (13.19) will very likely be positive; the only ambiguity stems from the term $\pi_2 c_1$, which will be negative given the assumptions made earlier. It is sufficient, but not necessary, for a positive numerator for (13.19) that $\pi_1 c_2 + \pi_2 c_1 > 0$. In this event, it is clear that higher unemployment must make the unemployed search less. The greater the general level of unemployment, then, the less productive and the more costly search will be. Unemployment is a trap. Escape is easy when everyone else has a job. But in conditions of substantial mass unemployment, looking for employment becomes a very laborious activity with minimal chance of success.

13.6 Multiple Unemployment Equilibria in Quantity-rationing Models

We saw in chapter 3 that unemployment could arise when wage rates, and/or prices, were frozen at non-Walrasian levels. Three kinds of unemployment might occur: underemployment or voluntary unemployment, in repressed inflation, when there is excess demand for both goods and labour; involuntary unemployment due to deficient aggregate demand, known as Keynesian unemployment; and involuntary unemployment resulting from excessive wage rates, termed classical unemployment. In this section, we explore the implications of certain kinds of fiscal reaction by the government which could give rise to multiple unemployment in the latter two regimes.

Consider Keynesian unemployment first. Suppose that the production function linking output, Q to employment, N, is $Q = \sqrt{N}$, so that $N = Q^2$. Let aggregate demand depend linearly upon government spending, G, and the level of real balances, $\bar{M}/p$:

$$Q = a\bar{M}/p + G. \tag{13.20}$$

In Keynesian unemployment, employment is determined by aggregate demand through the production function. So

$$N = (a\bar{M}/p + G)^2. \tag{13.21}$$

Assume that the government always balances its budget, and adjusts the ratio of G to Q (denoted by γ) to achieve this. The balanced budget equation will be

$$\frac{t-\gamma}{1-\gamma} x = b\left(\bar{N} - \left(\frac{x}{1-\gamma}\right)^2\right) \tag{13.22}$$

where $x \equiv a\bar{M}/p$. If the total labour force, $\bar{N} = 1000$, $t = 0.1066$, the unemployment benefit rate, $b = 0.0151$ and $x = \sqrt{800}$, there will be two possible equilibrium levels for unemployment, at 4 per cent and 20 per cent. The low unemployment equilibrium will see government spending at almost 2/23 of national income. Employment of 960 will be generated. In the high unemployment equilibrium, where employment will be available for only 800, the higher level of unemployment benefit payments will have squeezed government spending out completely, and γ will be zero. The moral of this example is that if government responds to higher unemployment by reducing its direct expenditure to preserve budgetary balance, in conditions of Keynesian unemployment, the equilibrium level of unemployment will go up. If, instead, it reacts by raising tax rates and holding government spending at its previous level, multiple equilibria will not occur in this example.

Multiple equilibria can arise in classical unemployment, too. Suppose that the real after-tax wage rate, y, is exogenously fixed, perhaps as a result of trade union target-wage setting. The production function is $Q = N^{2/3}$. If firms set employment where the real wage rate, grossed up for tax, equals the marginal product of labour, employment and output will be given by

$$N = \left[\frac{2}{3} \frac{1-t}{y} \right]^3, \quad Q = \left[\frac{2}{3} \frac{1-t}{y} \right]^2. \tag{13.23}$$

Suppose that the rate of unemployment benefit is set at 76.4 per cent of y, the real after-tax wage rate, and that the total labour force is 1000 as before. This time, assume that total unemployment benefit payments are financed by income tax receipts, with a balanced budget that leaves no room for direct government spending. The income tax rate is adjusted to ensure that tax receipts equal total benefits. The balanced budget equation will be

$$tQ = t \left[\frac{2}{3} \frac{1-t}{y} \right]^2 = \left[1000 - \left(\frac{2}{3} \frac{1-t}{y} \right)^3 \right] (0.764y). \tag{13.24}$$

If y equals 0.0637, unemployment equilibria can again be found at 4 per cent and 20 per cent. The low unemployment equilibrium calls for an income tax rate of 2 per cent, while the 20 per cent unemployment rises when income tax equals 11.3 per cent.

Classical unemployment can display multiple equilibria, then, when it is the real post-tax wage that is sticky, and the government aims to maintain a balanced budget by pushing up the income tax rate when unemployment threatens to increase. The higher income tax drives up the employers' perceptions of the costs of hiring labour, and the demand for labour falls as a result. This is a case where the demand for labour is lowered by unemployment, as a consequence of the additional taxation levied to defray the fiscal costs of unemployment benefits. Multiple equilibria could not arise in the example considered if the government locked the income tax rate and reacted to higher unemployment by cutting the rate of benefit instead.

13.7 Conclusion

This chapter has investigated a number of different reasons for thinking that unemployment equilibria can be non-unique. The evidence suggests that unemployment rates can differ markedly between countries and from period to period in the same economy. For 30 years after 1940, British unemployment averaged 2 per cent, never rising above 3 per cent. For the two decades before that, it averaged 12 per cent and never fell below 8.5 per cent. Since 1980, Britain has returned to this inter-war range in common with most West European countries. Meanwhile, some economies, such as Austria, Japan, New Zealand, Sweden and Switzerland continue to enjoy unemployment rates of between 1 per cent and 4 per cent. Unemployment in one year generally differs very little from the last. Many countries appear to get stuck, for a decade or more, at either high or low unemployment rates. The object of this chapter has been to explore possible causes for this.

We have seen that firms' overall demand for labour can depend on the general unemployment rate, at a particular real wage. High unemployment encourages them to postpone hiring labour until the last moment, if they can be reasonably sure of attracting high-quality labour cheaply in the 'spot' market. When labour markets are tight, on the other hand, they will be keener to pre-empt and hoard labour, which will make for even lower unemployment in the economy as a whole. Other reasons for suspecting non-uniqueness in the equilibrium unemployment rate include the tendency for employers to dismiss labour when they see other companies doing the same, and the fact that high unemployment may make the individual worker more prepared to acquiesce in unemployment himself, either because the disutility of unemployment drops when overall unemployment increases or because higher unemployment makes searching for another job costlier and less fruitful. Lastly, multiple unemployment equilibria can easily arise in quantity-rationing models, if government responds to higher benefit payments which increased unemployment brings by raising tax rates or cutting expenditure.

The policy implications of this analysis are intriguing. The equilibrium or 'natural' rate of unemployment is quite possibly non-unique. If there is more than one unemployment rate that can arise, it is surely open to government to try to select the lowest unemployment level available. The idea that heavy unemployment is inevitable becomes highly questionable. Unemployment can be caught in vicious and virtuous circles.

Perhaps the best prospects for stabilizing unemployment at a low level could be had by relating certain fiscal instruments to the rate of unemployment itself. Unemployment benefits could be made more generous in low unemployment, and a little less so when unemployment was high. Employment could safely be taxed quite heavily in low unemployment conditions, and marginal employment subsidies could be brought into play once unemployment had increased above a certain critical level. Bounties could be paid to private employment agencies which succeeded in placing unemployed workers in exceptionally severe conditions. Above all, government should refrain from reacting to increased unemployment by cutting its direct spending or raising income taxes. It should aim to budget on the basis of a very long-run historical average for the unemployment rate, such as the $5\frac{1}{2}$ per cent average recorded for the UK over the past 135 years. Surplus should be accumulated when unemployment fell below this figure, and run down deliberately when it rose above it.

14 Is a Share System Preferable to a Wage System?

14.1 Introduction: The Questions

Should workers work for a specified wage, or should they work for a share in their company's total earnings? Should profits and risks be shared with employees, or is it more efficient for the firm to absorb the burden of unforeseen shocks? What type of contract offers the greatest expected benefit to the worker? How do share and wage systems differ in the average level and variance of unemployment?

14.2 The Contrast Between Japanese and Western Payments Systems

This chapter is devoted to answering these questions. Their importance is underscored by the remarkable contrast between Japanese and Western labour markets. In Japan, workers change employer only very rarely. Employees in large companies typically stay with the same firm throughout their working lives. Employment is, as it were, guaranteed. What is not guaranteed is the worker's earnings. Frequently one-third, sometimes up to one-half of a worker's pay comes in the form of bonuses. The bonuses vary year from year, according to the firm's overall profit performance, and sometimes other considerations, such as the profitability of the particular division in which the worker is employed. This makes the employee into a kind of equity holder.

In advanced Western economies, on the other hand, payment conditions could hardly be more different. Profit-sharing is rare. Workers in industry receive a stipulated wage, which is set for a period of a year or more, and does not vary with the state of business. In hard times, the employer may put his workers on short time, or even dismiss them. When conditions are favourable, there will be overtime, and even recruitment. But the wage rate is effectively independent of profits and turnover. The Japanese arrangements may be termed a 'share system', while the Western pattern of remuneration conforms to a 'wage system'. In the share system, employment is impervious to the vagaries of market forces, or almost so; earnings bounce up and down to absorb them. Under the wage system, it is the wage that is sticky, and employment that responds to unforeseen shocks. The second oil shock in 1978–9 provides an excellent instance of the difference in how the two systems respond to a major disturbance that cut the demand for labour unexpectedly. Japanese real wages fell sharply. In the UK, money wage rates grew rapidly in this period, quite unaffected by the energy shock, and real wage rates were increased by the rise in the external values of sterling that accompanied it. Meanwhile, profits fell heavily. Unemployment rose in the ensuing 2 years nearly 15 times as much in the UK as in Japan. Grubb et al. (1983) find that the UK suffers from high real wage rigidity, and the US from high money wage rigidity, while Japan suffers from neither.

This evidence constitutes a powerful prima facie case for thinking that UK employment would have been far steadier had workers' contracts followed the share system practised in Japan, rather than the wage system actually in force. The arguments in favour of a share system have recently been given further publicity and impetus by Weitzman (1984, 1985). Weitzman maintains that employment tends to be both higher and steadier under a share system than a wage system, largely as a result of the fact that companies will become enthusiastic rather than indifferent employers of labour.

If workers are paid a lower fixed wage of w_0, for example, rather than w_1, and earn a share of profits in lieu of this sacrifice, the employer will maximize his share of profits by equating labour's marginal revenue product to w_0 rather than w_1. This is bound to imply a higher demand for labour. Both output and employment will go up. Furthermore, at least in the deterministic case where random influences on the demand for labour are swept away, the values of w_0 and the worker's profit share can be chosen to ensure that both the workers and their employer are better off than before.

All this makes Weitzman's case for profit-sharing highly appealing. But it also prompts one to ask why profit-sharing schemes are not commoner than they are. This form of industrial organization is not new; Britain's *Ministry of Labour Gazette*, for example, carried detailed analyses in the nineteenth century of how many schemes had started, how long they ran, how many workers they covered and why they failed if and when they did. Yet only a very small fraction of the national labour force ever seems to have been employed under systems of this kind. Recent empirical investigations into profit-sharing schemes, surveyed and discussed by Blanchflower and Oswald (1986), are no less disappointing. If profit-sharing is seemingly so attractive, at least under conditions of certainty, why is it so relatively rare? One possible explanation is that it is an inefficient way of dealing with uncertainty, particularly if workers are averse to risk, or suspicious that the boss knows something they don't. It is to the issue of uncertainty that much of the rest of this chapter is devoted.

14.3 Analysis: The Wage and Share Systems Compared When Both Parties are Neutral to Risk

In what follows, we shall examine how wage and share systems differ in essential respects through a series of examples. It is easiest to begin with a very simple case. Suppose each firm hires just one worker. Suppose that there are constant returns to labour in the production function, and that labour is the only factor that matters. If q represents the firm's output, and h the labour input supplied by the household in units of time, let $q = h$. Assume, too, that the selling price of the firm's product is random, rectangularly distributed between a minimum of zero and a maximum of one. Suppose that the household's utility, U, is some function ϕ of the product of its retained leisure $(1-h$, if it is endowed with a single unit of time) and its income, y: $U = \phi(1-h, y)$.

Assume, initially, that the firm is neutral to risk. Its utility function can then be written $V = \pi$ where π represents profits. Suppose, too, that the household has constant returns to scale in its utility function, so that it, too, is neutral to risk. Hence $\phi((1-h)y) = \sqrt{(1-h)y}$. Imagine that there is perfect competition among firms, so that the *expected* value of V is driven to zero. This corresponds with the notion of a zero-mean-value of profits, given that the firm is neutral to risk.

Consider the following wage system in this case. The employer promises to pay a wage rate w for the labour the household promises to provide, when the price of the product turns out to be high enough for it to be profitable to employ it. When the price is too low, on the other hand, the firm pays the household a 'retainer' or stand-by, unemployment fee of b, and no work is done.

The firm will wish to employ labour when the profit from employment is not less than the unemployed benefit payment, b. With the household utility function under consideration, labour supply will be $\frac{1}{2}$. The firm's profit from employment (π_e) will equal its total revenue from production, pq, less wage costs:

$$\pi_e = pq - wh = h(p - w) = \frac{p - w}{2}. \tag{14.1}$$

Labour will be engaged when

$$\frac{p - w}{2} > -b, \quad \text{or} \quad p > w - 2b. \tag{14.2}$$

Call z the critical value of price at which the firm is indifferent between producing and not producing:

$$z \equiv w - 2b. \tag{14.3}$$

Now the firm's expected level of profit will be

$$E\pi = -b\int_0^z dp + \int_z^1 \left[\frac{p - w}{2}\right] dp$$

$$= -bz + \frac{1 - z^2}{4} - \frac{w(1 - z)}{2}. \tag{14.4}$$

Since the firm is risk-neutral, $E\pi = EV$, and (14.4) will vanish.

Competition among firms in this position will bring about contracts that maximize the household's expected utility. Since $U = \sqrt{(1-h)y}$, we may write

$$EU = z\sqrt{b} + (1 - z)\sqrt{w}/2. \tag{14.5}$$

The first term on the right-hand side of (14.5) is the household's utility when unemployed (when $h = 0$ and $y = b$), multiplied by the probability of its occurrence, z. The second is its probability-weighted utility from employment. The household will therefore wish to pick b and w so as to maximize (14.5) subject to (14.3) and the condition that (14.4) vanishes. It transpires that the optimum results in a wage rate, w, of 0.518, and an unemployment benefit payment of nearly 0.1624. The average level of unemployment will therefore be $z = 0.194$. The chance of being employed is approximately four in five. From (14.5), the household's expected utility will reach

0.3685 in this case. One curious aspect of this equilibrium is that the household will actually prefer being out of work to being employed. Utility is 0.403 in the first case and only 0.36 in the second. If the wage system is revised so that the household's expected utility is equal in the two states the results will be: expected utility is 0.366, the wage rate equals 0.5359 and b is one-quarter of this; and unemployment averages 26.8 per cent.

Now contrast this with the share system. Suppose, instead, the household is paid a constant sum, b, and a share, s, in the firm's total revenue from production; and that it is always fully employed with a preferred labour supply of $\frac{1}{2}$. The firm, since it is neutral to risk, and perfectly competitive, must expect to break even, so that

$$b = (1-s)\int_0^1 ph \, dp = (1-s)\int_0^1 \frac{p}{2} \, dp = \frac{1-s}{4}. \tag{14.6}$$

The left-hand side of (14.6) represents the unconditional constant term in the household's remuneration, while the right-hand side is the firm's expected profit from production. The household, meanwhile, will receive a random income of $b+(sp/2)$. Household expected utility, $\sqrt{(1-h)y}$, will be

$$EU = \sqrt{\tfrac{1}{2}}[\int_0^1 (b+sp/2)^{1/2} \, dp] = \sqrt{\tfrac{1}{2}} \frac{1}{6s}[(1+s)^{1.5}-(1-s)^{1.5}]. \tag{14.7}$$

The household will wish to pick b and s so as to maximize (14.7) subject to the break-even constraint for the firm, that $b = (1-s)/4$. It turns out that the optimal value of s is zero. The firm absorbs all the risk. Had the utility function been $U = y(1-h)$, on the other hand, the household would be completely indifferent between any set of b and s at which $b = (1-s)/4$. Mathematically this follows from the fact that expected utility would now be a simple linear function, $\frac{1}{2}(b+(s/4))$. Equilibrium is indeterminate in such a case. Substitution would guarantee a particular value of expected utility, come what may: $EU = \frac{1}{8}$.

How do the wage and share systems differ in this example? The wage system exhibits a positive average level of unemployment (19.4 per cent), as against continuous full employment under the share system. The variance of unemployment is 0.16, compared with zero. The firm is indifferent between the two, since it breaks even on average in both. So far, so good. But the share system has a fatal flaw in this particular case. It offers the household less expected utility than the wage system: one-eighth, as against over five-thirty-sevenths, if $U = (1-h)y$; and 0.353, as against 0.366, if $U = \sqrt{(1-h)y}$.

So much for what happens when both the firm and the household are neutral to risk. This is the subject of the next section.

14.4 The Wage and Share Systems When One Party (or Both) is Averse to Risk

This section examines the implications of risk-aversion for the wage and share systems. Suppose, first, that the household is averse to risk (but that the firm remains risk-neutral for the time being). A convenient way of representing this will be to transform the utility function ϕ, so that

$$U = \phi(y(1-h)) = \log_e (1-h) + \log_e y. \tag{14.8}$$

The marginal utility of income, $\partial U/\partial y$, will now be inversely proportional to y. The household displays a coefficient of relative risk-aversion of unity. The wage system turns out now to give the household the best deal it can obtain when $b = 0.181$ and $w = 0.511$. The household's expected utility is -2.006. By contrast, the optimal share system, which maximizes EU subject to $E\pi = 0$, gives an unconditional payment of $\frac{1}{4}$ and a zero share for the household. Since the firm is neutral to risk and the household averse to it, it is efficient for the former to insure the latter fully against any income disturbance. The household's expected utility, when $b = \frac{1}{4}$ and $h = \frac{1}{2}$, will be -2.079. Again, the share system avoids unemployment (which will average 14.9 per cent in the wage system); but again, the wage system outperforms the share system in the crucial characteristic of promising higher expected utility. The consequence of introducing household risk-aversion, then, is not to reverse the superiority of the wage system by the criterion of the household's expected utility. In fact, it would reinforce it if the household were constrained to a positive share of the firm's total revenue.

Suppose, now, it is the firm rather than the household that is averse to risk. The most convenient form to assume for the firm's utility function, V, is quadratic:

$$V = \alpha\pi - \frac{\beta}{2}\pi^2 \quad \alpha, \beta > 0. \tag{14.9}$$

For simplicity's sake, set α and β to unity. Making the firm averse to risk has an important consequence. The firm now has an incentive to pass the risk, or some of it, to the household. This will be particularly true if the household is favourably disposed to risk. As an example of this, assume that $U = (1-h)y$.

Under the share system, it turns out best for the worker to absorb all the uncertainty of the price level. The optimum values of b and s are zero and one respectively. The household's expected utility remains what it was under the earlier case when $V = \pi$, namely one-eighth. There will be no unemployment. These results are found by maximizing $\frac{1}{2}[b + (s/2)\int_0^1 p\, dp]$ subject to the condition that $EV = 0$ in (14.9).

What about the wage system in this case? It transpires, perhaps surprisingly, that the optimal wage system now loses to the optimal share system in terms of expected utility, but only by a hair's breadth. When (14.5) is maximized subject to (14.3) and $EV = 0$ in (14.9), the preferred solutions are $w = 0.49$, $b = 0.12$. Unemployment averages 25 per cent. Expected utility reaches 0.122, which is very slightly lower than under the share system.

So far, the share system has consistently delivered lower and steadier unemployment, at zero, than the wage system; but, except in the last case, it has fallen down on what perhaps is the more telling test, namely which system delivers the higher expected utility for the household. Consider, now, a further case where the share system is again outperformed by the wage system, on the criterion of expected utility. This arises when *both* the household *and* the firm are averse to risk. Combine (14.9), with $\alpha = \beta = 1$, with (14.8). The optimal share system yields solutions $a = 0.159$, $s = 0.318$, $EU = -2.1457$ and again zero unemployment. By contrast, the optimal wage system again gives $b = 0.12$, $w = 0.49$, with unemployment of 25 per cent and expected utility at -0.2105. The share system may win over the wage system when the household is a risk-lover, but not otherwise. It is interesting to note, too, that the optimal share system displays a lower share than when the household was a risk-lover (31.8 per cent as against 100 per cent).

14.5 The VHGU (Variable Hours, Guaranteed Utility) System

The wage system considered up to now has been very simple. The firm either employs the worker for a period of one-half, which is the labour time the household will choose to work, or it shuts down and offers no employment at all. The second of these possibilities arises when the price of the product turns out to be so low that the firm loses less by shutting down than it would by continuing to produce. Sinclair (1986c) has investigated the properties of contracts of this kind, and compared them with various alternatives. One alternative stands out in offering higher expected utility, under almost all circumstances, than the wage system examined so far. We might call it the variable hours, guaranteed utility wage system, or VHGU for short.

The VHGU works like this. The employer pays a retainer of b in states which are so bad that it is better to produce nothing. In this, it resembles the wage system we have been considering. When the price level is high enough, there will be positive production. But the hours of work in this case are not given at one-half. Instead, the employer offers the worker an income level, y, which exactly offsets the loss of utility suffered as the employee's leisure time recedes. Consequently, if the utility function ϕ is simply $\sqrt{y(1-h)}$, the level of y will be given by

$$y(h) = \frac{b}{1-h}. \tag{14.10}$$

When (14.10) holds, the worker will be indifferent between working and being unemployed. Utility in unemployment is simply $\sqrt{b}$.

The firm chooses h, and hence $y(h)$, once it knows the value of p. Profit maximization will imply that h, and y, should be chosen to maximize

$$ph - y(h) = ph - \frac{b}{1-h}. \tag{14.11}$$

Equation (14.11) reaches a maximum where $1 - h = \sqrt{b/p}$. The resulting level of profits will be

$$\pi = p - 2\sqrt{bp}. \tag{14.12}$$

Now the firm cannot make a larger loss from production than when it does not produce at all. Consequently, we must impose the restriction

$$p - 2\sqrt{bp} \geqslant -b \tag{14.13}$$

since losses will be $-b$ when no employment is offered. Equation (14.13) implies that

$$p \geqslant b \tag{14.14}$$

is the condition for positive employment and production. When $p < b$, the plant will be closed, and the firm will pay the worker the amount b.

If the firm is neutral to risk, its expected profits will vanish. This implies

$$0 = E\pi = b\int_0^b dp + \int_b^1 [p - 2\sqrt{bp}]\, dp. \tag{14.15}$$

The value of b at which (14.15) vanishes is 0.1389. The employee's utility will therefore be guaranteed at a value of 0.373. This is some 2 per cent higher than the expected utility enjoyed in the optimal wage system when both firm and household are risk-neutral, and nearly 4 per cent above its value when b and w are chosen so that the household is indifferent between employment and unemployment. It is also noteworthy that VHGU offers a lower average level of unemployment than the optimal wage system, although the variance of work time is increased.

The superiority of VHGU over the optimal wage system is not affected by household risk-aversion. Indeed, it is strengthened, because the VHGU system protects the household against any change in its utility. Only when the household is strongly risk-loving can the optimal wage system promise higher expected utility.

What happens to VHGU when the firm is averse to risk? Suppose the firm's utility function is quadratic in profits, as in (14.9), with α and β again both set to unity. The expected value of the firm's utility will be given by

$$EV = -b\int_0^b dp + \int_b^1 [p - 2\sqrt{bp}]\, dp$$
$$\qquad -\tfrac{1}{2}(-b)^2\int_0^b dp - \tfrac{1}{2}\int_b^1 [p - 2\sqrt{bp}]^2\, dp. \tag{14.16}$$

Now (14.16) vanishes when b equals 0.1344. So introducing risk-aversion on the part of the firm will lower the retainer that it pays the worker in unemployment states, and hence his utility level both in and out of work. It also reduces the average level of unemployment, since the border condition for profitable production ($b \leqslant p$) drops one-for-one with b. Yet the employee's utility still remains higher than under the share system (0.367 as against 0.353), when $\alpha = \beta = 1$.

If the firm's utility function displays a still higher degree of risk-aversion, it is possible for VHGU to offer the employee less expected utility than the share system. If $\beta/\alpha = 2.8624$ in (14.9), the firm's expected utility, EV, vanishes at a value of 0.125 for b. This is the borderline at which the household will be equally well off under two systems. If $\beta > 2.8624$, it will gain more from the share system. We can conclude from this that the marginal utility of profits for the firm must be sharply downwards sloping for the share system to offer the household greater expected utility than the variable hours, guaranteed utility system. This is true a fortiori if the household is also averse to risk.

Essentially the reason for VHGU's relative success, when compared with alternatives, is that it gives the employer much-needed extra degrees of freedom in picking a level of employment. Hours of work, h, are highest when the price of the product is at its most favourable. They decline monotonically with p until the cut-out point of b.

The fact that employment and output vary continuously and positively with the price of the product above this point is important, because it means that the average value of output will be a good deal greater than it would have been, had they been frozen at their fixed 'full employment' value of $\tfrac{1}{2}$ in the wage and share systems. It is clearly efficient for output to peak when it is most valuable, and to reach its minimum when least. This is precisely what VHGU achieves. Variance in total output and employment should not necessarily be seen as undesirable. Provided that there is positive covariance with prices, it will bring efficiency gains. There must be a really very high degree of risk-aversion on the part of the firm to offset this advantage which the VHGU has over the share system that we have compared it with. The simple wage system only beats VHGU when, improbably, the household has a sharply increasing marginal utility of income (and hence a high preference in favour of income risk).

14.6 A Fundamental Flaw in the Share System

So far we have considered three systems: the wage system, the share system and the VHGU system. We have not asked what would constitute the *optimal* system. It is the purpose of this section to explore its properties. Unfortunately, we shall find that it is likely to be far removed from the share system.

An optimal system, when the firm is risk-neutral, perfectly competitive and hence constrained to breaking even, has essentially two properties. First, it will equalize the household's marginal utility of income across all states of the world. At least, it must do this if the household is averse to income risk, with diminishing marginal utility of income. The second property is Pareto efficiency: this entails that the marginal wage rate that the household faces (that is, the marginal rate of substitution between leisure and income) must equal the value of labour's marginal product in each state.

When the household's utility function is given by (14.8), the first of these two properties imposes the simple result that the household's income must be the same in all states. (This is a happy accident: if relative risk-aversion had taken some value other than unity, the optimal income would differ across states, depending on the size of h to be selected.) Since work hours will be higher in better states, the combined effect of this and the Pareto-efficiency condition will be to dictate a rather curious pattern of pay. Pay will consist of a state-specific lump sum and a marginal wage element. In good states, when p is high, the lump-sum element will have to be negative. Only this will permit a high enough marginal wage to meet the Pareto-efficiency test and induce the worker to supply a large time input. With his income in this case the same in all states, and with leisure time decreasing as p increases, the worker will be *worse* off when p is high than when it is low. Exactly the opposite of this is implied by the share system. This optimal system may have its drawbacks: the firm has an incentive to lie about p, for example, and pretend that it is larger than it really is; if the household is less risk-averse, it may be dominated by a 'corner solution' which has the worker earning nothing and working all the time when p is high, and unemployed and rather well paid when not. But one thing is clear: the share system is very far from optimal, at least in the context of the examples studied here.

14.7 Some Further Benefits of the Share System

There are other circumstances, however, under which the share system's relative performance improves. Dropping leisure from the household's utility function is an important instance: this has quite a dramatic effect. Suppose that h remains equal to one-half, as before, dropping to zero when the employer prefers to shut down in the wage system. The optimal share and wage systems now deliver the same expected utility to the household when both parties are neutral to risk, and the share system consistently beats the wage system when the household is neutral and the firm averse to risk. Removing leisure from the household's utility function destroys the basis of the VHGU, which collapses into a version of the wage system.

The share system has other potential advantages. Advocates point to the possibilities that workers' productivity and morale may improve as a result, and that employees will be less prepared to interrupt the continuity of production by engaging in strikes or working-to-rule during protracted wage negotiations. Grout (1985) has shown that even very small employee shareholding – at as little as 1 per cent of the total equity of a company – can lead to a considerable increase in employment. The average utility of existing employees drops fractionally, as a consequence of a slight reduction in wage rates, but the gain in numbers employed can be very much larger than this in proportionate terms.

Morale and productivity effects could be rather important. One instance of this is the case of asymmetric information. Suppose that the worker dislikes effort, and that his effort cannot be observed directly by his employer but has a positive effect on output. Since the firm can undoubtedly observe its output level, this means that output must be subject to two unobservable influences: the worker's effort, and an exogenous random variable of some kind (call it a 'gremlin'). The informational asymmetry is the fact that the worker can see (and choose) his effort level, while his employer cannot. A wage system will be inefficient in these circumstances. The worker recognizes that his pay is independent of his effort. All he does by working harder is to boost the profits of his boss. If he slacks, output should fall, but the employer will be unable to tell poor workmanship apart from hard luck. By contrast, the share system has the advantage of giving the worker a personal incentive to work harder, since reward and effort will be linked. The greater the worker's share of incremental profits, the stronger this incentive will be. On the other hand, if the worker is averse to income risk, he will dislike having his income destabilized by the gremlin. If the firm is less averse to risk than the worker, it is more efficient for the firm to insure the worker against this. But since the observable variable, output, is subject to influence from *both* effort *and* the gremlin, insurance is inevitably going to have the unwanted side-effect of 'moral hazard'. It will create an incentive for the worker to change his behaviour and supply less effort.

When the firm hires several workers, and not just one, the efficiency gains brought about by a share system tend to be squeezed. It is the individual worker who chooses his level of effort. The greater the number of his colleagues who participate in profits, the more thinly the fruits from his additional effort are spread, so the less in it there will be for him. It is the size of the individual's marginal share in profits that governs his incentive to supply effort. The more numerous the workers who enjoy a share of profits, the weaker this incentive will be. This is an example of the 'free-rider' problem. The individual worker is tempted to ride free upon the effort of others. This is not to say that a share system may not bring benefits; rather, we must expect those benefits to be greatest when the scale of the division or organization, which is sharing its profits with its employees, is small.

14.8 Summary and Conclusion

A share system has certain undoubted advantages over a wage system. It will always tend to reduce if not eliminate unemployment. Unemployment should vary less, if indeed at all. But the share system will not always promise greater expected utility for the employee. On the contrary, unless the employer is sufficiently averse to risk, the wage system will generally win on this all-important test. The wage system that we have compared with the share system displays two possible employment levels: a 'full employment' value, where hours of work are given thanks to the utility function assumed, and a zero employment value. The latter arises when the price of the product turns out to be so low that the firm minimizes its losses by shutting down. This contrasts with a third payment system, which guarantees utility but allows hours to vary in the former case (positive production). This 'VHGU' will always outperform the wage system, unless the household is an extreme risk-lover, on the expected-utility criterion. It will also tend to offer lower unemployment, but with an increased variance of hours worked. When the VHGU and share systems are compared, the firm has to be very risk-averse before the share system can hope to offer as much expected utility as the VHGU.

The share system has further advantages, in the form of enhanced productivity effects and the like. But these may be small if worker shareholding is widely dispersed, and could be outweighed by expected utility losses if the representative worker is averse to risk. Worker shareholding could also cause unions to bargain for slightly lower wage rates (and therefore higher levels of employment), and to be more reluctant to strike.

Share systems have much to commend them, particularly when the firm is taken to be averse to risk, and its employees less so. They also promise to reduce both the mean and the variance of unemployment. They surely merit closer scrutiny; certainly there seems to be some case for sharpening the fiscal incentives for worker shareholding, a proposal to which we shall return later (on p. 284). But they are not a panacea; workers could well be better off without them, especially when they are highly risk-averse. As compared with the VHGU, at least, they would sacrifice the efficiency gains accruing from positive covariance of employment with prices. Their champions are enthusiastic, but to the point of one-sidedness.

15 Does Steadier Employment Mean More Employment?

15.1 Introduction

It is the purpose of this chapter to see whether there are reasons for thinking that the mean level and variance in employment are associated. One such link is obvious. Increased structural change in the economy, caused by changes in technology, demand patterns or world prices, will cause more labour to switch between sectors of the economy. If the average interval of time between leaving one job and going to another is given, greater structural change will mean that more people will show up as unemployed when a still photograph is taken of the labour force at any moment in time. The stock of unemployment will go up.

This chapter proceeds to examine other, less obvious reasons for expecting an association between the steadiness and the average level of employment. We start, in section 15.2, with the demand for labour on the part of a risk-averse firm, faced with uncertainty in the price of its products. Aggregate demand uncertainty is the central issue in sections 15.3 and 15.4 where further reasons for a positive link between the mean and variance of employment are identified. In both section 15.4 and 15.5, we find that increased uncertainty could tend to mean a higher wage rate and a lower mean level of employment. Section 15.6 recalls the significance of different contract systems, and 15.7 discusses a selection of factors that could work to create a positive association between the mean and variance of employment. Section 15.8 concludes.

15.2 The Demand for Labour on the Part of a Risk-averse Firm

Suppose that a firm's objective is to trade-off the mean value of its profits against the variance of those profits. The mean of profits is a good, the variance a bad. This provides a convenient illustration of risk-aversion. The firm's utility function can thus be captured by

$$U = \alpha\Pi - \frac{\beta}{2}\Pi^2 \qquad \alpha, \beta > 0. \tag{15.1}$$

In (15.1), Π denotes profits. The ratio of β to α determines the extent of aversion to risk: if β/α is negligible, (15.1) shrinks to $U = \alpha\Pi$ and the firm is effectively risk-neutral.

Profits may be uncertain for a variety of reasons: technology may be subject to random shocks; the prices of labour, and other factors, may be uncertain; and the price of the product(s) which the firm produces may be unpredictable. Suppose that the third of these is the sole source of uncertainty. Assume, for simplicity's sake, that the firm is perfectly competitive. So it acts as a price-taker in both product and factor markets. Suppose that there is just one product produced, and that homogeneous labour is its only input; and let the price of the product, p, be drawn from a distribution with mean $\bar{p}$ and variance σ_p^2. Let the price of labour be certain, at w; and let q and q' denote the level of output, and the marginal product of labour, respectively. Assume that q' is positive but diminishing in n, the level of employment.

Profits, Π, will be $pq(n) - wn$. Substituting this into (15.1), taking expectations and maximizing with respect to n implies

$$(\bar{p}q' - w)\left(1 - \frac{\beta}{\alpha}\bar{\Pi}\right) = \frac{\beta}{\alpha}qq'\sigma_p^2. \tag{15.2}$$

In (15.2), $\bar{\Pi}$ is the mean expected level of profits.

Equation (15.2) tells us that if the firm were neutral to risk (β/α disappears), or the variance of the price of the product were negligible, employment would be taken to the point where the marginal product of labour balanced the real wage. But when β/α and σ^2 are both positive, the value of labour's marginal product will exceed the wage rate, at least when $(\beta/\alpha)\bar{\Pi} < 1$. The right-hand side of (15.2) will be positive, ensuring that the left-hand side must be positive, too. Now if labour's marginal product, q', is to stand above the mean real wage, $w/\bar{p}$, employment must be lowered in order to achieve this, by virtue of diminishing returns. Visually, the variance of p, and the firm's aversion to risk, displace the demand curve for labour leftwards. At any given (mean) real wage, the level of employment will decrease if the variance of the price increases.

Similar results emerge when the source of uncertainty relates to the wage rate, or to technology, rather than the price of the product. Suppose that the wage rate has mean $\bar{w}$ and variance σ_w^2, while p is known and unique. Taking expectations of (15.1) and maximizing with respect to n will give something very like (15.2):

$$(pq' - \bar{w})\left(1 - \frac{\beta}{\alpha}\bar{\Pi}\right) = \frac{\beta}{\alpha}n\sigma_w^2. \tag{15.3}$$

Since q' is related negatively to n, given that $1 > \beta\bar{\Pi}/\alpha$, an increase in the variance of the wage rate σ_w^2 (or the degree of risk-aversion, as captured by β/α) must lead to a drop in the level of employment. Indeed, the presence of n on the right-hand side of (15.3), in comparison with qq' in (15.2), which need not change much with n, gives grounds for suspecting that wage-rate uncertainty has more serious adverse effects on employment than price-level uncertainty.

Finally, technological uncertainty. Assume that $q(n) = Tf(n)$, with T randomly distributed around a mean of $\bar{T}$, with variance σ_T^2. Let w and p, on the other hand, be determined uniquely. The demand for labour can be observed implicitly in another variant of (15.2):

$$(p\bar{T}f' - w)\left(1 - \frac{\beta}{\alpha}\bar{\Pi}\right) = \frac{\beta}{\alpha}p^2 f(n)f'\sigma_T^2. \tag{15.4}$$

Yet again, risk-aversion and uncertainty, this time about technology, combine to squeeze the firm's demand for labour.

This is the first reason for expecting steadier employment to be associated with higher employment: steadier employment reflects less uncertainty for risk-averse firms, whose output, and demand for labour, should correspondingly be stronger.

15.3 Random Disturbances and the Quantity-rationing Model

We turn now to consider how the mean level and variance of employment may be associated in quantity-rationing models, which were the subject of chapters 3 and 4.

The simplest quantity-rationing model relates to a competitive, closed economy, with only one good and one type of household, where the government conducts no fiscal policy, all profits are paid directly to households and explicit household and producer choices are confined to just one period. Suppose that the household's utility and the firm's production function are both Cobb–Douglas:

$$U = (1-h)^\alpha \left(\frac{M}{p}\right)^\beta c^\gamma \qquad \alpha, \beta, \gamma > 0 \tag{15.5}$$

$$q = Tn^\delta \qquad\qquad 1 > \delta > 0. \tag{15.6}$$

In (15.5), $1-h$, M/p and c denote leisure (the household has an endowment of one unit of time), real money balances and consumption while a and T retain their definitions in the last section.

This economy displays a Walrasian equilibrium (where $q = c$ and $n = h$) where the levels of employment and the money wage are

$$n = \gamma\delta\mu \tag{15.7}$$

$$w = \bar{M}/\beta\mu \tag{15.8}$$

with $\mu \equiv [\alpha + \gamma\delta]^{-1}$. When both w and p are exogenously imposed, the resulting levels of employment will depend on the regime encountered:

Classical unemployment $\qquad n = [\delta PT/w]^{1/(1-\delta)}$ $\qquad$ (15.9a)

Keynesian unemployment $\qquad n = [\bar{M}\gamma/\beta PT]^{1/\delta}$ $\qquad$ (15.9b)

Repressed inflation $\qquad\qquad n = 1 - \alpha\bar{M}/\beta w.$ $\qquad$ (15.9c)

Suppose now that the price is perfectly flexible, and adjusts at once to eliminate effective excess demand in the goods market. But the money wage rate, let us assume, is imposed one period ahead, as the optimum forecast of what the Walrasian money wage rate would turn out to be from (15.8),

$$w_t = E_{t-1}(\bar{M}_t/\beta_t\mu_t). \tag{15.10}$$

For simplicity's sake, assume that β and μ are known, so the only uncertain variable relevant to the determination of next period's Walrasian equilibrium for the wage rate is the nominal money supply that will prevail then. We can rewrite (15.10):

$$w_t = (E_{t-1}\bar{M}_t)/\beta\mu. \tag{15.11}$$

There is no guarantee that this period's forecast of next period's money supply will be correct. It could well be wrong, possibly badly wrong. If it turns out to be

incorrect, there are two possibilities. The money supply may be overpredicted: $\bar{M}_t < E_{t-1}\bar{M}_t$. Alternatively, the money supply may turn out higher than expected: $\bar{M}_t > E_{t-1}\bar{M}_t$.

The overprediction case is straightforward. The money wage rate turns out to be too high. The economy is placed on the borderline between Keynesian unemployment and classical unemployment, since we have assumed that p is perfectly flexible. In fact, p adjusts to set (15.9a) equal to (15.9b), and the resulting level of employment will be

$$n = \gamma\delta\mu\bar{M}_t/(E_{t-1}\bar{M}_t). \tag{15.12}$$

The smaller the actual money supply, the lower employment will be. Employment falls in proportion to $\bar{M}_t$.

When the money supply is unpredicted, the nominal wage rate turns out too low. Two things can happen. One possibility is that firms whose demand for labour will now be large, will be able to satisfy their needs by enforcing contracts on households. But this will happen only if the contract specifies that firms can obtain as much labour as they wish at the prevailing wage rate, and if firms can succeed in enforcing this. If, as seems rather likelier, firms are unable to get the labour they would like to hire in such circumstances, the second possibility arises. This allows households to pick their hours of work at the prevailing money wage rate. The problem is here that when the ratio of the money to the money supply is low, the hours they will wish to supply will be low, too. This is clear from (15.9c), which gives the volume of employment in circumstances where it is supply-constrained (repressed inflation).

In the first case, where firms have no trouble getting all the labour they want (15.12) continues to apply. Since employment bears a constant proportion to the ratio of the actual to the anticipated money supply, variance in money has no effect on the mean level of employment. But in the second, (15.12) only applies when there is excess supply of labour. In conditions of excess demand, it is the repressed inflation relationship (15.9c), that takes over. Combining (15.12), (15.9c) and (15.11), we obtain

$$n_t = \text{Min}\left[\frac{\gamma\delta\mu\bar{M}_t}{E_{t-1}\bar{M}_t}, 1 - \frac{\alpha\mu\bar{M}_t}{E_{t-1}\bar{M}_t}\right]. \tag{15.13}$$

The employment level is now caught in a bind. Positive and negative errors in predicting the money supply both squeeze employment, though for different reasons. When the money supply is overpredicted, money wages turn out too high relative to the price level, and firms react to the unexpected jump in real wages by cutting back output and employment. When the money supply is underpredicted, households react to their unexpectedly high financial resources, in relation to the inappropriately low money wage rate, by cutting back their hours of work. It is this that reduces output and employment.

When (15.13) applies, it is obvious that the mean level of unemployment is negatively related to the absolute value, or the variance, in the money-supply prediction error. Noise in the money supply increases the variance of employment, and lowers its average value. This conclusion emerges when households can set a ceiling on their hours of work. But it does not depend in fact on their all doing so. All we need is for a few households to be able to insist on shorter hours under repressed inflation conditions, for employment to be less than implied by (15.12)

when $\bar{M}_t > E_{t-1}\bar{M}_t$: n_t will then be a concave function of $\bar{M}_t$, so that increased variance in the actual money supply will lower the mean value of employment. Results such as these do vary according to the character of the model and functions assumed, but this is at least what will happen in the simple case considered.

This, then, constitutes the second principal reason for expecting mean level of employment to decline as its variance increases. The greater the variance in the money supply (and by extension in other variables that influence aggregate demand), the lower the average level of employment, when employment is held back by the labour supply in situations of excess demand, and by the demand for labour in those of excess supply. Excess demand then leads to voluntary underemployment, excess supply to involuntary unemployment. Employment is maximized when there is no variance in aggregate demand.

15.4 Erring on the High Side: The Quantity-rationing Case

We have seen that deficiencies in aggregate demand lead to unemployment in the quantity-rationing model, while excess demand is liable to squeeze output for the quite different reason that the supply of labour is discouraged. Are households likely to be as badly off in these two situations, or are there grounds for thinking that one may be worse for them?

The answer turns out to be that excess demand is quite likely to do more damage to utility than excess supply, at least in the circumstances of the model considered in the previous section. Assuming that households cannot be forced to work longer than they wish, we can derive solutions for the household's utility under both excess supply and excess demand. Along the classical unemployment–Keynesian unemployment boundary, where there is excess supply, we can solve for utility to find

$$U = (1-p)^{\alpha} T^{\beta+\gamma} \left(\frac{\beta}{\gamma}\right)^{\gamma} \rho^{\delta(\beta+\gamma)} \tag{15.14}$$

where $\rho \equiv \gamma\delta\bar{M}/\beta w$. Under excess demand, when the economy adjusts to the Keynesian unemployment–repressed inflation boundary, utility will be

$$U = \sigma^{\alpha} \left(\frac{\beta}{\gamma}\right)^{\beta} \tau^{\beta+\gamma} \tag{15.15}$$

where $\sigma \equiv \alpha\bar{M}/\beta w$ and $\tau \equiv (1-\sigma)^{\delta}$. Investigation reveals that utility will probably decline more sharply as $\bar{M}/w$ increases away from Walrasian equilibrium along the second boundary, than when it falls along the first. (Figure 15.1 illustrates.) The condition for this to happen is that $\alpha > \gamma\delta$ (which in turn implies that leisure time exceeds work time in Walrasian equilibrium).

In figure 15.1, point A represents Walrasian equilibrium, where all markets clear. To the left of A, the ratio $\bar{M}$ to w is below equilibrium; firms cut back employment, since product real wages turn out too high as aggregate demand deficiencies depress the price of goods. This corresponds to the Keynesian unemployment–classical unemployment boundary. To the right of point A, the economy is forced to the boundary between repressed inflation and Keynesian unemployment. Households react to an excessive ratio of money balances to the

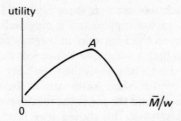

Figure 15.1 *Utility and the money supply/money wage ratio, when the price level is flexible and the money wage is given*

money wage by working less. Output, and the supply of consumption goods, are squeezed.

This asymmetry, in what might be called the disutility of disequilibrium, is certain to arise when utility is more elastic to leisure than to consumption (given that $\delta < 1$). It has important consequences. Suppose the next period's money supply is random, that the money wage rate must be determined one period ahead and that the price level adjusts instantaneously to remove excess effective demand or supply in the goods market. Imagine, further, that the money wage rate is chosen to maximize the household's expected utility.

If $\alpha > \gamma\delta$, it will be worse to underpredict the money supply than to overpredict it. It is better to be left of point A than right of it, all else equal. So the money wage rate should be pitched *above* the mean forecast of its Walrasian value. This will aggravate the consequences of excess supply, but reduce the damage done by the more worrying eventuality, excess demand.

It will help to look at a simple special case. Let $\alpha = \beta = \gamma = \frac{1}{3}$, $\delta = \frac{1}{2}$, $T = 1$ and the mean value of $\bar{M}$ be 1. If $\bar{M}$ were not subject to any variance, utility would be maximized by locking w at its Walrasian value, which will be $1\frac{1}{2}$. Utility reaches $2^{1/3}, 3^{-(2/3)} = 0.6057$. Employment will be $\frac{1}{3}$. But if $\bar{M}$ is known to be either $1\frac{1}{4}$ or $\frac{3}{4}$, both events equally probable, the optimum value of w will be increased to 2. The mean value of employment sinks to just 0.281, and it will be 0.1875 under excess supply (to the left of A), and 0.375 under excess demand. Expected utility reaches 0.5753. With a further increase in variance, so that $\bar{M}$ is equally likely to be 1.5 and 0.5, the optimum money wage rises to 2.41. Expected utility will be 0.5351 and the mean value of employment sinks further, to less than 0.241. These results are gathered in table 15.1 for ease of comparison.

Table 15.1 *Optimal wage, expected utility and employment with various values for the money supply*

	Optimal wage	Expected utility	Employment		
			CU/KU	KU/RI	Mean
Money supply					
Given at 1	1.5	0.6057	$\frac{1}{3}$ (Walrasian equilibrium)		
Either $\frac{5}{4}$ or $\frac{3}{4}$, equiprobable	2	0.5753	0.1875	0.375	0.2813
Either $\frac{3}{2}$ or $\frac{1}{2}$, equiprobable	2.41	0.5351	0.1037	0.3776	0.2407

The conclusion to which this example leads is clear. If excess demand is more damaging to utility than excess supply, and it may well be, workers and unions should be inclined to 'err on the high side' in wage negotiations when aggregate demand is uncertain. Too high a wage rate will be less damaging than a wage rate which turns out to be too low. The greater the variability of aggregate demand, the greater the amount by which wage rates are likely to exceed their average Walrasian values, if this is so; and the lower the mean level of employment is likely to be. The circumstances in which this should arise bear repetition: we have been investigating a world where prices of goods are flexible, but money wage rates are set one period ahead in ignorance of the exact character of future demand; where firms cannot force workers into working longer than they wish; and where, in Walrasian equilibrium, utility is at least as elastic to leisure as to consumption. These are perfectly plausible conditions, and provide yet a further reason for expecting variability in employment to be associated with a lower average level of employment.

15.5 Erring on the High Side: Labour Monopsony

In the last section, we saw that uncertainty could lead to wage rates being set above their Walrasian values. The essential reason for this was a possible asymmetry in the disutility brought about by disequilibria. If more damage is done by the distortion induced when the wage rate is too low, than when it is pitched too high, it is wise to err on the high side.

Exactly the same principle may apply to firms. Suppose that the firm must set next period's wage rate now. It does not know what the labour supply will be then. Imagine that next period's supply of labour will increase with the wage rate set now, but also vary with random factors about which the firm is now ignorant. Suppose, for simplicity's sake, that the production function and the demand for the good next period are known.

Had there been no uncertainty about next period's labour supply, fixing the wage rate w would have been straightforward. If the firm is to maximize profits, and cannot practice any form of discrimination, its objective will be

$$\text{Max}_w \, p(q(n(w))) \cdot q(n(w)) - wn(w). \tag{15.16}$$

The solution to this will obey

$$w = pq' \left(\frac{1 - \frac{1}{\varepsilon}}{1 + \frac{1}{\beta}} \right) \tag{15.17}$$

where q' is the marginal product of labour and β and ε represent the elasticities of labour supply and average revenue. Here, $1/\beta$ is a measure of the employer's monopsony power in the labour market, and $1/\varepsilon$ his monopoly power is the market for his product.

But uncertainty about next period's $n(w)$, the labour supply function, is likely to alter the profit-maximizing wage rate in comparison with the mean value implied by (15.16). When the labour supply proves to be higher than expected, the employer is always free to employ less than the full number of workers who offer their services. But he cannot employ more than are available when the labour supply is

Table 15.2 *Wage rate, and employment levels, set by a firm with monopsony and monopoly power, for different spreads of the labour supply shock*

Spread labour supply shock, $|\beta|$	Wage rate (pre-set to maximize expected profits)	Level of employment			
		Positive shock	Negative shock	Mean	Variance
0	5	10	10	10	0
1	5	11	9	10	1
2	3.2	6.8	4.4	5.6	1.44
3	3.8	6.2	4.6	5.4	0.64

unexpectedly short. He is constrained to employ no more than the number of those available.

An increase in the variance of next period's labour supply, around a given mean, has no direct consequences for the firm when labour supply is high anyway. But when it is low, it must lead to a still smaller level of employment and output. It is perfectly possible for the firm to react to this, the increase in the variance of labour supply, by deciding to raise the wage rate. Admittedly this will raise costs, and bite into profits, when labour supply is high; but in the opposite conditions of a tight labour market, a higher wage will at least ensure a larger level of production and employment.

How the expected-profit-maximizing wage and employment levels behave as the variance in labour supply increases is far from clear. Almost anything can happen. Table 15.2 presents a set of results for a simple, linear particular case, which gives an impression of the variety of possible effects. The labour supply is $2w \pm \beta$, where β is the labour supply shock, which may be positive or negative, with equal probability. The production function is simply $q = n$, and the average revenue curve is $p = 10 - q/2$.

In this case, as the spread of the labour supply shock increases from zero, the firm responds at first by keeping its wage rate unchanged, and letting employment reflect the increased volatility of the supply of labour at that wage. But when a critical value of β is reached, it becomes worthwhile for the firm not to employ all the people who offer themselves for work when $\beta > 0$, and it would much rather compress its wage bill. Hence the fall from 5 to 3.2 in w, as $|\beta|$ rises from 1 to 2. The lower wage rate means that employment will be considerably reduced taking $\beta < 0$ (4.4 for $|\beta| = 2$, as against 9 when $|\beta| = 1$). This also helps to drag down the mean value of employment, which drops heavily. As $|\beta|$ increases further, the wage rate starts to climb somewhat.

This reflects the firm's anxiety to secure enough labour when the labour supply is tight. The higher wage reduces the mean value of employment slightly, since, in this example, its depressive effect upon the demand for labour when $\beta > 0$ outweighs the boost it brings to the supply of labour when $\beta < 0$. The higher wage rate as $|\beta|$ increases gradually brings the levels of employment in the two states closer together. It is this that explains the decline in the variance of employment, from 1.44 to 0.64, as $|\beta|$ rises from 2 to 3.

In sum, then, when a firm with the power to set its wage rate, and the need to do so one period ahead, faces uncertainty in the supply of labour available to it, variability in labour supply will probably be reflected in variability of employment. As the volatility of labour supply increases, the wage rate which the firm wishes to set may fall discontinuously at the point above which the firm decides it does not need to employ everyone when labour supply is high. Beyond that, the wage rate may go up somewhat as the variability of labour supply increases still further. The association between the variance and mean level of employment is rather complicated, but there may well be a range over which they vary negatively with each other, as table 15.2 shows.

Uncertainties of themselves do not necessarily cause firms to 'err on the high side'. If it is future demand that is uncertain, and the price of goods that has to be set ahead, the price may rise or fall with the variance of future demand. It is likeliest to rise (suggesting a fall in the mean level of employment) when the firm's marginal costs are convex. When marginal costs accelerate with output, their mean value increases with the variance of output. Similarly, if the firm's marginal revenue is downwards sloping and concave, uncertainty about the level of marginal costs is likely to have similar consequences when the price level has to be fixed ahead, before the exact values of marginal costs are known. If both marginal revenue and marginal costs are convex, as seems rather plausible, whether a firm's mean level of employment rises or falls with its variance depends chiefly upon whether it is cost conditions, or demand, that is more volatile (and how they covary).

15.6   The Mean and Variance of Employment under Different Contract Systems

This section explores the link between the mean and the variance of employment in the various contract systems investigated in chapter 14. Three particular systems were scrutinized in some detail in that chapter. These were, first, a wage system that gave the firm the right not to employ the worker when conditions were sufficiently unfavourable for him to prefer this; a share system, which gave the worker some linear function of the value of the employer's output; and the VHGU, or variable hours, guaranteed utility system. As its name implies, the last of these guarantees the employee's utility at a particular value, and allows the employer to pick the combination of work time and pay that suits him best once he knows the price for which he can sell his product. The framework of assumptions in that chapter included perfect competition, and a Cobb–Douglas utility function for the employee.

The second of these three, the share system, displayed invariance of employment to the price of the firm's output, and the highest mean level of employment (one-half). The wage system displayed a somewhat reduced mean employment level, and increased variance. In the third system, the mean fell further and the variance rose further. In each case, the price of the firm's product was assumed to be distributed uniformly between a floor of zero and a ceiling of one.

What does all this suggest that one might find in empirical, cross-section inquiries into the relation between the mean and the variance of employment levels? Suppose that different firms in a particular industry practice each of the three systems. There would be a negative correlation between the mean and the variance of employment across such firms. Then imagine a comparison of firms in different industries. Those selling products subject to high price volatility would tend to employ fewer on average, and with greater variability than those in safer markets where the price moved in a narrower range. At least, this is the picture that would emerge unless the firm in question adopted the share system.

15.7 Factors that Could Create a Positive Association Between the Mean and Variance of Employment

Thus far, our study of the possible links between the average level and variability of employment has consistently, or at least usually, pointed to a negative association. Mention should be made of a couple of factors which could at least in principle, help to create a positive relationship between these two variables.

One is analogous to Stiglitz's ingenious argument (Stiglitz (1983)) against horizontal equity in taxation. 'Horizontal equity' is the principle of taxing people in like circumstances alike. Suppose everyone faces a random element in their tax bill. There is a finite probability of receiving a large tax demand, considerably greater than what would normally be charged on the basis of income. People are risk-averse. They are therefore frightened of this possibility, and take more precautions to guard themselves against it happening to them than they would had they been neutral to risk. The obvious precaution is to build up a balance of savings that could help to defray the random tax demand, should it materialize. But the only way to do this is to earn more, by working harder or longer. If the supply of labour time or efforts in any case has been reduced as a result of distortionary features in the tax system, this effect will be favourable. The receipts of the random tax should also allow the authorities to set a lower marginal tax rate on incomes. The end result could involve – it does not have to, but it could – an increase in the average utility of members of the society. This would mean that a Benthamite social welfare function, which is equivalent to the sum of everyone's utility, could register an improvement. Horizontal equity would be infringed; two people with the same income would pay different amounts in tax, if one of them is unlucky enough to get the random tax demand and the other is not. But social welfare could go up. Furthermore, this is not just a special feature of the Benthamite function for social welfare so long as the least advantaged member of society is exempt; a Rawlsian function should react very favourably to it, too. Enhanced tax receipts will permit a more generous transfer payment to him.

The analogy with unemployment would run like this. Nasty surprises can be good for you. At least, they can achieve benefits for an average member of society if not for their actual victims. The fact that you are vulnerable to random, unjustified dismissal or redundancy makes you and everyone else work harder. Distortionary tax rates can be reduced, and average utility could go up. More importantly, increased variability of employment would go hand-in-hand with an increased level of labour supply. As often as not, this should be reflected in a higher mean level of employment.

A second factor that could make for a positive link between the mean and the variance of employment is the possibility of positive covariance between employment and prices. Suppose output and employment are highest when the price of goods produced is also at its highest. The long-run, average product of labour will be boosted when price and output co-vary positively. An economy where this is a widespread phenomenon will be richer than one where it is not. If higher average output is translated into more capital accumulation, the demand for labour at any real wage rate will be higher too. It is worth stressing that if steadiness in employment is bought by official government action to stabilize prices for example, there might be serious losses in efficiency as a result. The Common Agricultural Policy of the EEC has stabilized agricultural employment. But it has done so by a system of price controls which entail massive financial losses which have to be made good by distortionary taxation which is hardly likely to increase employment elsewhere in the economy.

A third way in which greater variability could be associated with an increased average level of employment might be as follows. Imagine a large, spontaneous rise in the labour employed in a closed, perfectly competitive economy. In the simplest cases, at least, this should bring downwards pressure on real wage rates, but tend to increase the return on capital. If interest rates go up, companies will tend to hold smaller inventories. Inventories of working capital normally insulate employment and production, to some degree, from the vagaries of sales. So reduced inventories would make employment more vulnerable to shocks in the demand for output.

One could add to this list of qualifications the basic principle that steadier employment should mean higher employment. But the three already mentioned should serve to warn us that they are all, essentially, rather minor qualifications. They are hardly likely to subvert the various more powerful arguments for expecting a negative association between the mean and variance of employment, examined in earlier sections of this chapter. Only in special circumstances, such as the case where the source of particular threats to the stability of employment is contained by expensive, inefficient government action which entails a heightened burden of distortionary taxation, is there any serious ground for expecting this pattern to be reversed.

15.8 Summary

There are numerous reasons for thinking that increased variability of employment will be associated with a lower average level. Risk-averse firms will demand less labour, and produce less, when susceptible to increased variability in the price of their product; and greater price variability should imply greater employment variability, too. In cases where wage rates are predetermined, increased volatility in aggregate demand will imply increased variance of employment, and the mean level of employment should suffer when workers can exercise discretion in their hours of work in situations of excess demand. In such circumstances, it will often be in the interest of workers, and trade unions representing them, to 'err on the high side' when negotiating money wage rates, if the damage done to utility by re-pressed inflation would otherwise tend to be worse than that experienced under unemployment. Firms facing uncertainty in labour supply may also respond to increased variance by raising the wage rate at the expense of lower mean levels of employment. Finally, there are some counterarguments to throw in the balance, none of them particularly telling with the possible exception of government intervention to iron out price and employment variability, which could result in wasteful losses defrayed from job-threatening increases in taxation.

16 Policies to Combat Unemployment

16.1 Introduction

Previous chapters have been concerned with data on unemployment, and with why it occurs. It is now time to examine measures to reduce it. Several have already been mentioned in the context of discussions about how particular policy instruments affect unemployment. At this point we build upon the various strands of the analysis of previous chapters in order to debate the advantages and drawbacks of various possible 'solutions' to the unemployment problem.

Section 16.2 is devoted to exploring the effects of employment subsidies. These will be seen to offer substantial hope as an unemployment-reducing device, particularly if related to the *change* in employment, and even if – perhaps especially if – financed by a tax on wages. Section 16.3 investigates a number of popular policy recommendations which are flawed, or at least highly problematic: import restrictions, benefit cuts, a deliberate increase in the long-run growth rate of monetary aggregates, cuts in hours of work, and incomes policy. Then, in section 16.4, a number of detailed policy recommendations will be proposed. These offer distinct promise as methods of reducing unemployment. Finally, section 16.5 concludes.

Before turning to the policy issues, it is important to try to take stock of the central conclusions of the theoretical analysis of the previous chapters. How do the various theories of unemployment relate to each other? The short section that follows attempts a brief answer to this question.

16.1.1 *Resumé: The Theories in Perspective*

Changes in unemployment are essentially the outcome of two sets of forces. Short-term shocks with adverse effects upon the demand for labour (studied in chapters 7 and 8) act upon a system that is predisposed to the risks of unemployment, largely as a result of the structure of contracts (studied in chapter 9) and the behaviour of trade unions (chapter 11). How much unemployment results depends upon the behaviour of the demand for labour (examined in chapter 2) and also the nature of the quantity-rationing regime (chapters 3 and 4). Temporary wage rigidities that underlie such regimes are explained by a number of factors, considered in chapters 2, 9 and 11. In the longer run, equilibrium unemployment levels are governed by the features of the tax and benefit system (chapters 5 and 6), the formal analysis of which bears a strong resemblance to that of implicit contracts; levels are also affected by search behaviour at the individual level (chapter 10) and by unions' actions (chapter 11). The authorities' opportunities to affect unemployment depend critically upon the unemployment–inflation relationships (the subject of chapter 12). On the other hand there are good reasons for thinking that there could be multiple unemployment equilibria (chapter 13). Some have argued that the best cure for unemployment problems lies in replacing the wage system with profit sharing (chapter 14), which might help by reducing both the mean and the variance of unemployment rates. Yet these last two variables could well be related (chapter 15).

All these ideas play some role in the policy analysis that follows. We should proceed to explore this without further ado.

16.2 Employment Subsidies

16.2.1 *General Observations*

When something is in excess supply, the most natural cure for the problem is to increase the demand for it. As with other cases, so with labour. But how is the demand for labour to be increased?

If firms have been knocked off their labour demand curves by a sudden contraction in the demand for their products, we find ourselves in a state of Keynesian unemployment. This was examined in detail in chapter 3. In such circumstances, the most appropriate policy response for the authorities was seen to involve attempts to rebuild the demand for goods. Increases in government spending, cuts in direct and indirect taxation and easier monetary policy will all help in this regard.

When unemployment is classical, on the other hand, firms need the incentive of lower perceived real wage rates in order to be induced to raise output and employment. Shortage of demand is not an obstacle; firms are in equilibrium; something must be done to lower employers' perception of labour costs relative to the prices of their products.

If money wage rates are sticky, but goods prices adjust to remove imbalances between effective demand and effective supply in product markets, unemployment will be both classical and Keynesian. Raising aggregate demand will rebuild jobs if real wage rates can be squeezed (assuming that there are diminishing returns to labour). But there are other ways of achieving this. A reduction in the employer's perception of real wage rates will be no less effective.

Unless unemployment is unambiguously Keynesian, therefore, subsidies on employment will be an effective means of raising the demand for labour. This will follow except in the extreme case where the workers raise their wage rates to appropriate all the employment subsidy themselves. If at least part of the subsidy is passed on to firms, labour demand must increase. The greater the employer's share of the subsidy, the larger the effect.

Subsidies on employment merit close scrutiny, therefore. They would seem to offer a promising escape route from the grave unemployment conditions now afflicting so many Western countries. But they could be expensive. How are they to be financed? Under what conditions will they have maximum favourable impact? It is to these questions that we must turn.

16.2.2 *The Financial Implications of Across-the-board Employment Subsidies*

If employment subsidies increase employment, they could be at least partly self-financing. Newly engaged workers will cease to draw unemployment and other associated welfare benefits. Instead, they will draw wage income, and pay income tax and national insurance contributions. In contemporary Britain, each person transferred from the unemployment register to full-time work will lead to an average improvement in the central government's budget of some £6400 per year. The more effective employment subsidies were in generating additional jobs, the less they would cost in financial terms. Against this, across-the-board employment subsidies involve a large, direct, gross financial cost.

Suppose a subsidy paid at the rate on every job s, generates ΔN new jobs. These jobs are filled by people who would otherwise have been unemployed. Assume that each placement of an unemployed person saves the public authorities x. The net effect on the public finances will be

$$(x-s)\Delta N - sN.$$

This can be positive or negative. The net gain is maximized when the subsidy is set at the rate

$$s^* = \frac{\alpha x}{1+\alpha}$$

where α is the elasticity of employment to the subsidy. Assume that the demand for labour depends negatively upon the excess of the wage over the employment subsidy, $w-s$, with elasticity β. We can then find α:

$$\alpha = \frac{s\beta}{w-s}(1-w')$$

where w' is the marginal effect of the subsidy on the worker's wage. When $w' = 1$, the employer gains nothing, and will consequently leave employment unchanged. Substituting the last result into its predecessor, we obtain

$$\left(\frac{s}{w}\right)^* = \left(\frac{x}{w}\right) - \frac{1-\left(\dfrac{x}{w}\right)}{\beta(1-w')-1}. \tag{16.1}$$

This expression tells us that if the authorities are to maximize the financial gain (or minimize the financial cost) of an across-the-board employment subsidy, the rate of subsidy they should select will increase with the financial cost of unemployment relative to the wage (x/w) and the elasticity of the demand for labour (β), and decrease with the share of the subsidy diverted to labour in the form of higher wages (w').

For example, suppose that firms all employ a Cobb–Douglas production function under competitive conditions, and that two-thirds of the value of output is paid out in wages to labour (the only variable factor of production). Then β will equal 3 (see Sinclair (1983a) chapter 2). Suppose that w' is $\frac{1}{3}$. Take the current value of (x/w) to be 0.64 (we have already seen that x is approximately £6400 per year, and average full-time earnings, w, are close to £10,000 per year). Our formula for $(s/w)^*$

gives an optimum employment subsidy of some 28 per cent of w. This will be close to £2800 annually, or some £56 per week.

Several caveats must be expressed at this point. Equation (16.1) can be relied upon to give an explicit solution for the ratio of s to w only when the right-hand side variables $((x/w)$, w' and $\beta)$ can be taken as given. Unfortunately they generally cannot: all three may well depend upon s. Second, the formula can give nonsense results, for example when $\beta(1-w')$ is less than 1. Third, the net financial revenues must be compared with the policy of doing nothing (setting $s = 0$). It can easily occur that a zero across-the-board subsidy will be cheaper in financial terms than any positive subsidy. Fourth, the analysis depends on an assumption that firms are on their demand-for-labour curves, and would give very different results under conditions of Keynesian unemployment. Finally, two really important points: maximizing benefit to the government's finances is emphatically not the same as maximizing social welfare; and there can be ways of reducing the financial costs of employment subsidies far below what is implied by (16.1). It is these last two points that are explored in the next two sections.

16.2.3 *The Socially Optimal Across-the-board Employment Subsidy*

Suppose our Constitution requires us to subsidize all jobs, if we subsidize any. What level of employment subsidy should we decide upon? The objective is no longer the mere maximization of net gain to the government's budget. A social optimum requires us to examine real social benefits and resource costs, and strike the balance where the gap between them is as great as possible.

There is literally no end to the list of possible complications that one can introduce into such a problem. Questions of distribution, justice, dynamics, uncertainty, rationing restrictions and microeconomic interdependency all suggest themselves. Rather than try to deal with any of these formidable issues here, it is better to obtain some impression of what a social optimum might look like in very simple conditions. Suppose we are concerned with the welfare of a single 'representative' individual at one moment in time. His utility depends upon average real income (q) less employment subsidy costs, and upon the average level of employment (n):

$$U = U(q(n(s)) - ns, n(s)).$$

Choosing s to maximize this gives us the rule

$$s^* = \frac{\alpha}{1+\alpha}\left(q' + \frac{U_2}{U_1}\right). \tag{16.2}$$

Here, α is (as before) the elasticity of employment to the subsidy; q' is the marginal product of labour; and (U_2/U_1) is (minus) the marginal rate of substitution between leisure and real income. Equation (16.2) tells us at once that if the economy is Pareto-efficient, the individual's trade-off between leisure and income $(-U_2/U_1)$ will already equal the marginal product of his labour. So s^* is zero. The argument for a positive employment subsidy rests on the hypothesis that it can help to bring these two variables together. If unemployment is so serious that the marginal 'leisure' it allows is deemed to have a negative social value, U_2 becomes positive, and the case for an employment subsidy is reinforced. Strictly speaking, (16.2) only characterizes a relationship for the optimum employment subsidy. Substitution into our earlier equation for s^* gives us a result very similar to (16.1):

$$\left(\frac{s}{w}\right)^* = \left(\frac{y}{w}\right) - \frac{1-\left(\frac{y}{w}\right)}{\beta(1-w')-1} \tag{16.3}$$

where $y \equiv q' + (U_2/U_1)$. The only difference between (16.1) and (16.3) is that y has replaced x. Which of these two variables, y or x, is higher, is a moot point. If the leisure provided by unemployment has a negative marginal value, $U_2 > 0$ and y will be correspondingly increased. The higher the replacement ratio, on the other hand, the greater the level of unemployment benefits in relation to income in work, and the greater x will be. Under perfect competition, ignoring taxation and setting U_2 to zero, the ratio of x to y is simply the replacement ratio. It is not unreasonable to treat y as greater than x, therefore; but this can easily be overturned by introducing even a modest positive marginal utility of leisure.

Equation (16.3) has rectified one shortcoming of (16.1): at least we have progressed from the relatively minor question of revenue maximizing to the grander issue of a welfare-maximizing employment subsidy. But the other caveats noted at the end of the previous section remain in force, and must be supplemented by the qualifications relating to the simple utility function already noted above. Subject to these reservations, we note that the prime function of an employment subsidy, from the welfare standpoint, is to remove a distortion splitting households' trade-offs between leisure and income from the marginal product of their labour. An appropriately selected employment subsidy will restore the marginal efficiency conditions which would ideally have prevailed anyway. The focus on the marginality of these conditions suggests that what is really needed is a marginal employment subsidy. Why pay out scarce funds to subsidize jobs that would have existed anyway? The next section is addressed to this question.

16.2.4 *Incremental Employment Subsidies*

Employment subsidies can be confined to additional jobs. Subsidizing jobs which would have existed without the subsidy has no merit: it is a lump-sum payment, with no beneficial incentive effects, which will presumably have to be financed out of distortionary taxation. Hence the attraction of limiting the subsidy to incremental jobs.

One way of running a scheme of this kind would be to reward firms solely for increases in the number of full-time equivalent employees over the same period in the previous year. The financial gain from this policy would simply be

$$(x-s)\Delta N.$$

If the subsidy were anything below the financial cost of unemployment, x, a net gain in revenue would accrue to the Exchequer. This would be vastly cheaper (or more remunerative) than an across-the-board subsidy on every employee.

Yet there could be drawbacks. A firm would have an incentive to keep raising and lowering employment in alternate years. Every other year it would gain a subsidy, and lose nothing by reducing employment in the next. Two firms could keep swapping labour between themselves in such a fashion. Some firms would have increased employment in any case, so there would still be some element of deadweight loss. Many employers have come to regard hiring decisions as long-term commitments. If an employee is to be retained throughout his working life, a subsidy received in the year he is hired pales into insignificance when compared with the discounted present value of his life-time earnings. Lastly, the policy could lead to an excessive tightening of labour markets when and where unemployment was low; and furthermore, it must be admitted that a successful attempt to reduce unemployment in this way will tend to add to inflationary pressures.

How can these objections be met? One way of solving the problem of annual employment cycling is to pay a subsidy on each person employed above, say, 80 per cent of the previous year's employment level. A firm that cuts its labour force by anything up to 20 per cent per year will sacrifice the subsidy on each worker lost. Another could be to pay the subsidy on the difference between the current number on the pay roll and the average of, perhaps, the previous 3 or 4 years: that would not remove the incentive to employment cycling entirely, but it would make it much more gradual. There is no practical way of avoiding the problem of paying subsidies on additions to employment that would have occurred anyway; but the subsidy should surely have some marginal effects on top of the intramarginal rents bestowed in such cases. The 80 per-cent-of-previous-year's-employment rule would help to strengthen the incentive to employ 'lifetime' labour.

The problem of what to do when unemployment is low is unfortunately irrelevant in contemporary conditions in most Western countries. One can only hope that the time will come when it assumes more importance. The answer must surely be to taper the subsidy to the national unemployment rate itself. For example the subsidy could be paid at a rate of $x(u-\bar{u})$ or £$y(u-\bar{u})$, where u represents the unemployment rate and $\bar{u}$ the minimum sustainable level of u (which might be estimated on historical evidence at, perhaps, 3 per cent). The size of the subsidy would then be directly proportional to the 'excess' unemployment in the country as a whole. Variants on this idea would include the possibility of regionally differentiated job expansion subsidies: the relevant value of u might be taken to be the mean of the regional unemployment rate and the national rate, for example.

How could the system of incremental employment subsidies be tailored to minimize the risks of additional inflationary pressure? There are two attractive ways of helping to achieve this. One is to pay higher subsidies on the engagement of the long-term unemployed. This proposal is considered further below (pp. 281–3). The second is to recoup the cost of the subsidies by placing a tax on the wage bill. This is the subject of the next section.

16.2.5 *A Subsidy on Numbers and a Tax on the Wage Bill*

It might seem that taxing a firm's wage bill will undo all the benefits of subsidizing the number of employees, whether on an incremental or across-the-board basis. It turns out that this is not so. A subsidy on numbers pushes the employer's demand for labour upwards; a tax on the wage bill will make the demand curve more elastic. The net effect will be to raise employment.

Consider, first, the case of a firm that sets employment to maximize profit and a union that sets the wage to maximize its members' average utility. Recall the simple model of the union presented and discussed in chapter 10.

Suppose the firm takes the wage as given. It receives a subsidy s on each employee, so sN in all. Its wage bill wN is taxed at the rate t. If R is its total receipts, profit (π) can be written

$$\pi = R(N) + sN - w(1+t)N. \tag{16.4}$$

Profit maximization entails

$$R'(N) = w(1+t) - s. \tag{16.5}$$

Equation (16.5) states that N will be set so as to equate labour's marginal revenue product (R') with the marginal cost of hiring it.

The union has M members, let us assume. N of these will be employed (depending on $w(1+t) - s$, given (16.5)). Those in work gain utility $U(w)$ which depends upon the wage; the unemployed will have utility $V(b)$ where b denotes the unemployment benefit (or earnings that can be obtained elsewhere). The average utility of the union's members will be

$$AU = U(w) - V(b)N(w(1+T) - s) + MV(b). \tag{16.6}$$

The union picks w to maximize (16.6) subject to (16.5). An interior solution must obey

$$NU' + (U - V)(1+t)/R'' = 0. \tag{16.7}$$

The second-order condition for the firm's maximization problem guarantees that $R'' < 0$. A similar condition for the union will tell us that

$$A \equiv NU'' + \frac{1+t}{R''} U' - (U - V)\frac{(1+t)^2}{(R'')^3} R''' < 0. \tag{16.8}$$

Equation (16.5) and total differentiation of (16.7) now establish at once how N, the level of employment, responds to s and t:

$$dN\left\{U' + \frac{AR''}{1+t}\right\} = -dt\frac{U-V}{R''} - \left[\frac{ds - w\,dt}{1+t}\right]\left[NU'' + U'\frac{1+t}{R''}\right]. \tag{16.9}$$

From what has already been said, the coefficient $\{\ldots\}$ on dN is positive. If the wage bill tax rate, t, is adjusted so that the overall scheme breaks even, $s = wt$ and the second term on the right-hand side of (16.9) vanishes. Because people are better off in work, $U > V$, and since $R'' < 0$ (see above), (16.9) tells us that an increase in both s and t to keep $s = wt$ *must increase the level of employment.*

It is illuminating to consider an example. Suppose $U = \sqrt{w}$, $V = \sqrt{b}$ and $b = 1$. Let $R(N)$ be $2e^{\sqrt[2]{N}}$. In that case the union's optimum wage will be

$$w = \left[1 - \frac{1}{4(1+t)}\right]^{-2}$$

while the firm's optimum employment level satisfies

$$\ln N = 4 + 4\ln\left[1 - \frac{1}{4(1+t)}\right].$$

With no subsidy or wage bill tax, the wage is 1.7, and employment, 17.28. A subsidy of 0·72, fully financed by a wage bill tax of 50 per cent, will lead a wage of 1.44. Employment will climb to 26.33. Multiply w and s by £100 to give weekly values, and N by 1 million, and the numbers become extraordinarily realistic to British readers. A subsidy of about 0.2 (i.e. £20 per week) offset by a wage bill tax of some 16 per cent, would be sufficient to remove 3 million from the unemployment register, if the model could be accepted as an accurate picture of British labour markets.

A firm–monopoly union interaction model shows clearly, then, that a subsidy on numbers accompanied by a wage bill tax could offer a powerful stimulus to employment. To show that a similar finding emerges in other circumstances, too, I present an extended version of a model of wage-setting by firms provided by Blanchard et al. (1986, chapter 3, appendix 4).

Suppose firms set their wage rates to equate the marginal gain that the wage brings, due to reduced turnover and training costs, with the marginal cost. This captures the central idea in the Stiglitz (1985b) model examined in chapter 2. To be specific, let profit per employee for firm i be

$$\pi_i = a + s - w_i(1+t) - c\phi \tag{16.10}$$

where ϕ represents the proportion of its labour that quits. Suppose ϕ depends upon the ratio of the worker's utility, $U(w_i) = w_i^{1-\varepsilon}$, to his expected utility if he quits, $(1-u)w^{1-\varepsilon} + ub^{1-\varepsilon}$. Here, w denotes the wage prevailing elsewhere in the economy, b is the unemployment benefit, u the unemployment rate and ε the coefficient of relative risk-aversion for the worker. If the firm maximizes π_i, we can derive

$$w_i(1+t) = \frac{c\phi'(1-\varepsilon)(w_i/w)^{1-\varepsilon}}{1 - u(1 - r^{1-\varepsilon})}. \tag{16.11}$$

In (16.11), r is the replacement ratio b/w. Assume that competition between firms sets $w_i = w$ and $\pi_i = 0$. We then find that

$$s = c\left[\phi - \frac{(1-\varepsilon)\phi'}{1 - u(1 - r^{1-\varepsilon})}\right] - a. \tag{16.12}$$

Differentiating s with respect to u in (16.12) establishes that

$$\frac{du}{ds} = \frac{1}{c}[(1 - r^{1-\varepsilon})^{-1} - u]^2\{\varepsilon\phi' - (1-\varepsilon)\phi''(1 - u(1 - r^{1-\varepsilon}))\}^{-1}. \tag{16.13}$$

The second-order condition for the firm tells us that the term $\{\ldots\}$ on the right-hand side of (16.13) will be negative. Hence a higher subsidy must reduce unemployment, at least when $\varepsilon < 1$ (and a trivial recalibration of the utility functions will allow us to extend this finding to the case where $\varepsilon > 1$ as well). It is noteworthy that (16.12) makes u depend upon s, but not t.

16.2.6 *An Employment Subsidy-cum-sales Tax*

Another possibility would be to combine a specific subsidy on labour with a proportionate sales tax (or increase in the rate of value added tax), designed to finance it. Let s denote the subsidy, as before, and v the rate of sales tax.

Consider, first, a profit-maximizing monopolist, facing a given wage rate of w. His profit function will be

$$\pi = \frac{P(Q(N))Q(N)}{1+v} - wN + sN. \tag{16.14}$$

Setting N to maximize π yields

$$PQ' \frac{1 - \dfrac{1}{\varepsilon}}{1+v} = w - s \tag{16.15}$$

where Q' is the marginal product of labour, and ε, defined as a positive number, the elasticity of demand for the monopolist's product. If the employment subsidy is to be financed exactly by the sales tax ('the breakeven condition'),

$$sN = \frac{vPQ}{1+v}. \tag{16.16}$$

Substituting (16.16) into (16.15), and differentiating, yields

$$\frac{dN}{N}\left[\phi(N) - \frac{v\pi}{N}\right] = -\frac{\pi}{N}\frac{dv}{1+v}. \tag{16.17}$$

Equation (16.17) establishes that a rise in v, accompanied of course by a rise in s in obedience to the breakeven condition (16.16), *must increase employment*, given that $\pi > 0$ and the second-order condition for a profit maximum (which guarantees $\phi < 0$).

When the firm faces a given wage rate, therefore, the policy of s-cum-v will raise employment. The reason it does so turns on the fact that the specific subsidy boosts employment by more than the proportionate sales tax reduces it. Had the sales tax been specific, and the employment subsidy been tied to a proportion of w, the opposite would have happened. If the wage rate is controlled by a trade union, on the principles examined in chapter 11, there emerges a further reason for expecting employment to go up. The s-cum-v policy will make the firm's demand for labour more elastic, just as it did in 16.2.5. An increase in the elasticity of the firm's demand for labour all else equal, will lower the union's optimal wage. Figure 16.1 depicts these effects for the special case where the firm's demand for labour is linear.

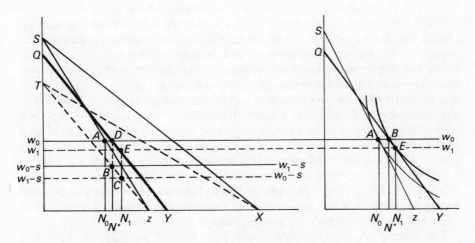

Figure 16.1 *The effects of an employment-subsidy-cum-sales tax*

16.2.7 *A Bibliographical Note on Employment Subsidies*

The seminal paper on employment subsidies is Kaldor (1936). Subsidies have been the subject of numerous theoretical and empirical studies. Many of these are discussed in Boltho et al. (1979), which examines various employment subsidy schemes operating in Belgium, France, the UK and West Germany. The arguments in favour of an incremental employment subsidy were first considered in detail by Layard and Nickell (1980). They are explored further in Oswald (1984). The proposal for an employment subsidy on numbers financed by a wage tax, is examined by Jackman et al. (1983). Many of the ideas explored there are discussed in the previous two sections.

16.3 Some Less Advisable 'Solutions' to Unemployment

16.3.1 *Mercantilist Policies: Tariffs and Quotas on Imports*

Limits on imports often seem a promising device to boost employment. A tariff levied on an imported good leads to an increase in its domestic price. Home producers of close substitutes should respond by raising production. This entails a rise in employment in the domestic industries in question, since real wage rates expressed in terms of such products will have fallen.

The simplest linear Keynesian macroeconomic model generates the result that equilibrium real national income (Y) is the product of two numbers:

$$Y = Bm. \tag{16.18}$$

B stands for autonomous expenditure[1] on goods produced at home; m denotes the multiplier. Import tariffs affect Y in two ways. They raise B, all else equal, by switching some autonomous expenditure from imported to home-produced goods. They also raise m by reducing the marginal propensity to import. If Y is related positively to total employment by an aggregate production function, therefore, import tariffs offer two positive influences upon employment. It is some version of this model which advocates of import tariffs usually have in mind.

There are two major objections to this argument. One stresses international repercussions and their likely consequences; the other develops the proposition that import tariffs are an inappropriate and largely misdirected instrument for increasing employment. The first objection is that import tariffs merely export unemployment. They are a 'beggar my neighbour' policy. Unemployment increases abroad because foreign countries must experience a reduction in their exports. This cuts their values of B, and hence Y and N. If the home country is large, its own value of B may be undermined by a consequential fall in exports (a slump abroad must tend to lower the home country's exports). Whether large or small, the home country is likely to face retaliatory action which must tend to squeeze B at home. A tariff war will merely squeeze international trade levels; gains from trade will be sacrificed; the fall in living standards entailed by this may lead workers to try to bid for higher wages; it is not impossible that unemployment could increase both at home and abroad as a result of all these pressures.

The second objection is rather different. A tariff on imports acts as a simultaneous consumption tax and production subsidy on importable goods. The latter can be broken down into an employment subsidy on labour, and a subsidy on other factors, confined to these domestic industries. The ideal policy response to economy-wide unemployment is an economy-wide employment subsidy. Notice how import tariffs differ from this. First, they involve a tax on importables consumption. Second, they impose a subsidy on the employment of other factors in importables industries, which should lead, sooner or later, to a diversion of such factors away from other sectors. Third, the employment subsidy element implicit in import tariffs is confined to the importables industry. All three effects will impose unnecessary and indeed distorting changes (if the economy is not suffering from other problems besides excessive unemployment). A nationwide employment subsidy does not suffer from these deficiencies. It is a direct solution to the problem, not an indirect device which leads to a separate set of distortions. Admittedly, an import tariff brings in revenue to the government, while a nationwide employment subsidy has the opposite effect. On the other hand, we have already seen in the previous section that the costs of an employment subsidy can be limited if it is applied to incremental employment only (on some compromise, such as the 80 per cent formula suggested on p. 264). Furthermore, it can be financed by an off-setting wage bill tax which, as we saw, will still leave room for a cut in overall unemployment. A final point about import tariffs: if they succeed in improving the balance of trade, which seems rather probable in the short run unless retaliation is substantial, upwards pressure on exchange rates may result. This will squeeze employment in other traded industries (particularly in exporting sectors). All in all, therefore, import tariffs should not be seen as a reliable general method of reducing unemployment in an economy. They are much likelier to redistribute employment, away from industries in which the home country enjoys a comparative advantage, towards those in which it does not.

What of quota limits on imports? Under certain conditions, an import quota will have exactly the same effects as a tariff. These conditions are: (a) import licences are auctioned by the government; (b) no uncertainties; (c) a large number of domestic firms produce the importable good at home, and act independently. If the government does not auction import licences, it will fail to gain the revenue which would accrue under an otherwise equivalent tariff. Under uncertainty, quantity restrictions (like quotas) may be preferable to price restrictions (such as a tariff) under particular conditions and less so in others (this was shown by Weitzman (1974)). Finally, if the domestic supply of the importable is controlled by a single firm, or a group of firms acting in concert, a quota will offer opportunities for price-setting power which a less than prohibitive tariff would not. Such a firm or group of firms will be tempted to cut back production, as compared with what happens with a tariff that has similar effects on the volume of imports, in order to equate marginal cost with marginal revenue. A quota will then be more damaging to employment than a tariff. The fact that import quotas have been used as a method of safeguarding employment in particular importables industries beset by foreign competition testifies to the weakness of government in capitulating to special interest pressure groups. A quota brings large rewards to the owners of factors specific to the protected industries. But such rewards are essentially transferred from the rest of the nation, and in particular domestic consumers of the goods in question: a large gain to the few, and a loss suffered by almost everyone else which is sufficiently widely dispersed, and small enough when expressed in individual terms, for the political system to fail to respond adequately to prevent it. Furthermore, when one industry's representatives see import quotas conferred upon others, this can only heighten their incentive to ask for similar favours. There may be a strong case for temporary employment subsidies to soften the blow of increased import competition afflicting the demand for labour in particular sectors, especially when these are concentrated in regions of high unemployment. But such subsidies should be provided to all firms in those regions, not confined to the threatened sector. This would allow a smooth, distortion-free transfer of labour from the ailing industries to other sectors where prospects of long-term employment are brighter.

In sum, therefore, mercantilist reactions to unemployment are inefficient on many scores. Strenuous attempts should be made to avoid them, and to eradicate the distortions already in place. International co-ordination, through the General Agreement on Tariffs and Trade, will be needed to ensure the effective removal of these highly unsatisfactory features of the contemporary world. If only one country removes its trade barriers, and others fail to follow suit, the former's import-competing industries may be even more vulnerable, since suppliers in the rest of the world will divert exports to them away from countries to which access is denied.

16.3.2 *Lowering Unemployment Benefit*

A fall in the level of unemployment benefit would exert some downwards pressure on unemployment rates. This, at least, is the implication of the analysis of chapters 5 and 6. It was also supported by the results of the simple model of union behaviour in chapter 10. This predicted that higher benefit would lead to a higher union-optimal wage rate, and consequently to a fall in levels of employment. Does econometric evidence confirm or cast doubt upon the theoretical prediction that unemployment benefit should give a positive impetus to unemployment?

There are two kinds of evidence, micro and macro. The first relates to tests on samples of individuals, or to cross-section tests on groups of individuals. The latter consists of aggregate tests, such as regressions of national average unemployment rates upon benefit levels (or replacement ratio) and other variables for a span of years. (The replacement ratio is the level of unemployment benefit, expressed as a proportion of after-tax earnings.)

United States micro evidence points to a significant positive association between unemployment and unemployment benefit. Feldstein (1978) examined temporary lay-off unemployment among 25,000 individuals. He was concerned with the rate of unemployment, rather than the duration of the unemployment spell for those out of work. He found that approximately half the temporary lay-off unemployment could be attributed to the legal provision of unemployment benefit, on a linear extrapolation of its apparent effects over a narrower range. Raising the replacement ratio from 40 per cent to 60 per cent increases the temporary lay-off unemployment rate by about one-third (or just over 0.5 per cent at the time he wrote). He also compared union with non-union members. He found that of people in the 25–55 age bracket in the experienced labour force, the incidence of temporary lay-offs was more than twice as frequent among union members as non-members. Part of the explanation for this could be that workers in trades with strong swings or seasonality in demand are more likely to join unions to protect their position. But the finding is also consistent with the notion that where the union has greater control over the wage, it responds to higher benefit by pushing wage rates up somewhat, and exposing workers to greater unemployment risks. It conforms with one of the predictions of implicit contract theory, too: the provision of unemployment benefit by the State creates an incentive for firm and workers, especially unionized workers perhaps, to enter contracts that exploit the subsidy in adverse states.

Moffitt and Nicholson (1982) look at another aspect of the effect of unemployment benefit: the impact upon the duration of unemployment spells on the part of those out of work. If you take a still photograph of the labour force at a single date, the unemployment rate you infer is really the product of two numbers—the proportion that have recently lost or left their jobs, and the average interval of time they take to regain employment. Benefits may affect overall unemployment by operating on the latter, and this is what Moffitt and Nicholson examine. They investigate a sample of individuals collecting unemployment insurance benefits in 1975 under the Federal Supplemental Benefits Programme (which extended the period of eligibility to federal unemployment benefits). Their results suggest that a 10 per cent increase in the net replacement ratio increases the average duration of unemployment spells by about 0.4 weeks for the workers in this sample, and by up to 1 week for workers in what they consider to be a more representative sample. Further, they suggest that lengthening the period of benefit eligibility by 1 week will result in an increase in the mean duration of unemployment spells of about one-tenth of a week. Solon (1985) calculates that the 1979 decision to subject unemployment benefits to income tax reduced the mean duration of unemployment spells of higher income workers by about 1 week.

The United States system of unemployment compensation has many interesting features, not least the fact that it varies substantially between different states. In addition to federal benefits, there are state-provided benefits. There is no significant association between state unemployment rates and state-provided benefits. But when the former are corrected for differences in racial balance and the latter expressed as a proportion of average earnings in the state in question, the picture changes. A simple linear regression for 1983 data, for example, suggests that an increase in this definition of the replacement ratio by 10 percentage points is associated with a rise in the corrected unemployment rate of almost 1 percentage point. But it is worth stressing that higher unemployment might cause higher benefits, through the political mechanism; there could be a two-way interaction between the variables. Furthermore, within Western Europe, there is very little apparent cross-sectional association between the variables. Belgium and the Netherlands have much higher replacement rates *and* unemployment than Greece or Portugal, but unemployment in Norway and Sweden is currently one-seventh of Spanish levels, despite much higher replacement rates.

United Kingdom micro evidence also points to a positive effect of benefits on unemployment. Nickell (1979) found an elasticity of spell duration to the replacement ratio, in household terms, lying between 0.6 and 1. The earnings related supplement to unemployment benefits, introduced in 1965, was found to have raised overall unemployment by one-tenth. Another of Nickell's results was that the long-term unemployed (out of work for 6 months or more) were apparently much less sensitive to benefit rates – their probability of leaving the unemployment register responded much less to the replacement ratio than that for those only recently out of work. Narendranathan et al. (1985) disaggregate by age cohort, and examine a large group of unemployed men in 1978. They find that young men's average duration of unemployment spells is markedly sensitive to their replacement ratio. But this is not true for older workers, for whom the probability of leaving the register in any given week is both much lower, and much less responsive to benefit payments. Atkinson et al. (1984) also finds a weak positive association between unemployment benefit rates and various dimensions of unemployment.

Turning to macro evidence, most investigations find a significant positive effect of benefit levels, or replacement ratios, on the unemployment rate. But there is considerable dispute about the magnitude of the effect. Andrews and Nickell (1982), for example, find that changes in the replacement rate were responsible for about 35 per cent of the predicted rise in unemployment between 1953–7 and 1971–6 in the UK on the basis of their reduced-form equation, and somewhat under 20 per cent for their structural equation for unemployment. Testing for the effect a third way, relying on an imperfect-competition framework similar to that developed later by Layard and Nickell (1985), just under one-quarter of the predicted unemployment increase is attributed to the rising replacement rate.

In another UK study, these authors (Nickell and Andrews (1983)) find that 'the level of unemployment benefits has only a marginal impact on employment'. By contrast, employment taxes, union power proxied by membership density and union/non-union wage differentials, are found to be far more important factors behind adverse movements in the demand for labour in the UK in the period 1951–79. On the other hand, Minford (1983) finds an elasticity of unemployment to real unemployment benefits of almost $+3$. Minford's estimate of the impact of increased union power is even higher than Nickell and Andrews' (an elasticity of unemployment to the unionization rate of $5\frac{1}{2}$, as against a loss of jobs due to unions of 400,000), and of employment taxes, relatively somewhat lower. The discrepancies between the Minford and the Nickell–Andrews results on the effect of unemployment benefits are due to a number of factors. First, Minford uses quarterly data for 1964 to 1980. Nickell and Andrews use annual data for 1951–79. Unfortunately, complete quarterly statistics for the relevant variables are unavailable before 1964. Second, there are some differences in their measures of unemployment benefits. The antilog of the log R column in Nickell–Andrews (Data Appendix, p. 258) does not correspond perfectly with the real benefit index in Minford (figure 9, p. 565). The latter includes local authority rents and school meals for example (these are rents rebated to the unemployed) and the former does not; they employ slightly different weights for the effect of the earnings-related supplement; Minford nearly always regresses upon a benefit-plus-income tax term, found to be more significant than the two variables on their own, but the Nickell–Andrews tests are generally based on real benefit by itself. Lastly, most of the Nickell–Andrews inferences are drawn from tests where lagged unemployment does not enter as an exploratory variable, unlike in Minford's results. Nickell (1984) argues that this last point leads Minford to exaggerate the long-run effect of unemployment benefit (and union power), in the latter's influential book (Minford et al. (1983)). Nickell claims that the absence of additional terms as possible influences upon unemployment, such as relative raw materials prices, indirect taxation and the capital stock, in the equations Minford uses as tests of his theory, leads to an over-attribution of long-run influences to the remaining variables, particularly since lagged unemployment is also present as a regressor. Minford (1984) reponds to this by saying that he has to limit the number of potentially important influences on the demand for labour somewhere, and that it is possible that the evolution of the capital stock in industry is itself responsive to wage rates and other variables (leading to an underestimate of the long-run unemployment effects of benefits).

Minford et al.'s book (1983) advocated capping unemployment benefits so that they never exceed 70 per cent of net income in work. This proposal has commanded widespread attention. Since it is based upon econometric work contained in the book, it is important to discuss these tests, and the points at which they diverge from others, in some detail. In the present author's opinion, Minford is clearly right to allow for the school meals and housing element in benefits to the unemployed, but he must subtract something to reflect the fact that they might well have continued to obtain some part of these benefits in work, had their incomes been low enough. Minford is also right to argue that union pressure to push up wages, perhaps in response to the stimulus of higher benefits to the unemployed, should ultimately lead to a relative outflow of capital from the sector in question. This was the result we obtained in chapter 11, pp. 203–4. On the other hand, Nickell's complaints about the combined effects of *both* omitting variables which he finds significant *and* using lagged unemployment as a regressor are well taken. Yet it is unfortunate that the econometric testing of employment and unemployment equations – despite the fact that it has become vastly more sophisticated in recent years – has yet to match the intricacy of the dynamic specification techniques developed and applied by Hendry and his collaborators on other macro issues (e.g. Davidson et al. (1978), Davidson and Hendry (1981) and Hendry (1983) on consumers' expenditure and Baba et al. (1958) on the demand for money). A Hendry approach would consist of testing a long-run model of 'core' or 'long-run' unemployment, embedded in a set of empirically based networks of lagged relationships, in levels, differences and changes in differences, to capture the complex dynamics of short-term movements. This is not to deny that the short-run pattern may be responsive to economic variables too. The central point in the Minford–Nickell dispute about just how powerful unemployment benefits are as an influence upon unemployment concerns the treatment of lagged unemployment in the econometric equations. Its final resolution can only await the full application of dynamic specification techniques. More research on this vital question is urgently required. But the present author hazards the guess that these would reveal long-run estimates much closer to Nickell's than to Minford's.

Let us sum up. Lowering unemployment benefit levels would undoubtedly reduce unemployment. Unions would gradually adjust wage demands downwards. People who left or lost their jobs would take a little less time, on average, to find their way back into employment. But this would be much more noticeable for young people out of work for a short period than for older workers or the long-term unemployed. There are also considerable grounds for suspecting that the most influential work pressing for cuts in, or limitation on, unemployment benefits, Minford (1983b), is based upon overestimates of their unemployment-reducing effects, although this cannot be proved beyond doubt until we know more about the exact timing patterns of unemployment relationships when these have been specified in fully dynamic terms. But this is no excuse for not attempting certain policy changes now. Recommendations on changes in unemployment benefit levels and regulations are presented below (pp. 279–81). They do not involve across-the-board cuts in unemployment benefit. What is proposed essentially involves a twist in the time structure of benefits, in favour of older workers and the long-term unemployed, coupled with other measures designed to lower the poverty trap for all low-paid workers. This should be a more humane and ultimately more effective method of combatting unemployment.

It must be remembered that there are major social advantages of paying unemployment benefit, as well as disadvantages. By allowing those who have lost their job to take longer to find a new one, they reduce the chances of the serious mismatches between people and tasks that would inevitably result if everyone were forced to accept the first offer available. More important, they prevent the unfortunate job loser from suffering really serious financial distress. Even utilitarian, let alone Rawlsian, arguments can be constructed for redistribution in favour of the less advantaged members of society, as we saw in chapter 5. Such redistribution may well involve higher unemployment as an unwanted by-product. Unemployment benefit cuts could lower unemployment, yes; but there is much uncertainty about precisely how much it would fall by, and when; and there would undoubtedly be greater suffering on the part of many poor people, especially older workers unemployed for long periods, who would simply have even less to live on and remain out of work. General unemployment benefit cuts should not be implemented. To reinforce this conclusion, two simple facts. Replacement rates have *not* risen in the UK in the period of massive unemployment increase (after 1979) and they have *not* fallen at all substantially in the US in the recent period of falling unemployment (after 1982).

16.3.3 *Faster Long-run Expansion of Monetary Aggregates*

Disinflationary monetary policies applied in the UK in the past decade, and more particularly since 1979/80, are undoubtedly to blame for at least some of the deterioration in Britain's *relative* unemployment position over this period. Unemployment has risen almost everywhere, but rarely more so than in Britain, where these policies have been applied with particular ferocity. Does this suggest that we should seek to return to easier monetary conditions as an act of deliberate long-run policy? I think not.

Most good recent studies of the inflation–unemployment trade-off (e.g. Lucas (1973)) emerge with one inescapable conclusion. This is that faster inflation does next to nothing for unemployment in the long run. It would be foolish to ignore this evidence. A deliberate return to a policy of rapid and sustained increases in monetary aggregates would quickly get translated into expectations, and hence into wage settlements, interest rates and other variables. The additional uncertainties introduced by such a policy could actually make things worse. Faster growth of monetary aggregates may well mean *unsteadier* growth, a drunken lurch between credit crises and plenty, and sudden swings associated with expectations of policy changes. The British disinflationary programme may well have brought large costs in terms of faster increases in unemployment than would have occurred otherwise. But this is not to say that there have not been benefits from a stabler financial environment, some of which could show up ultimately in the form of lower unemployment. Reversing the policy now would involve sacrificing whatever gains have been painfully secured. And even if the British disinflationary experiment was misconducted or ill-conceived, that does not prove that it should now be reversed. In the present author's opinion, a policy of indefinitely faster growth in monetary aggregates would bring negligible long-run gains to aggregate employment.

16.3.4 *Shorter Hours of Work*

It is tempting to think that the unemployment problem could be solved by reducing working hours. If there is a fixed amount of work to 'go round', to be shared among workers, a more even sharing of the burden of recession would lead to fewer people wholly unemployed. If average hours at work fell by one-tenth, or approximately 4 hours per week per person at work, would this not allow for a 10 per cent increase in the numbers of people who would work at least 90 per cent of 'standard' hours?

There are unfortunately several reasons for thinking that this would be a *non sequitur*. Labour is not homogeneous. The unemployed come disproportionately from the unskilled. Such experience and skills as they have were often derived in particular industries where the demand for labour seems to have fallen irretrievably (steel, vehicle assembly and component production, shipbuilding, textiles, coal-mining). They cannot be transferred with equal or immediate success to other sectors where future employment prospects are better, where labour shortages are often restricted to certain specific categories of skill.

Another problem relates to the curious phenomenon that hourly productivity appears to rise sharply when hours at work are reduced. Productivity per hour seems to have gone up by over 20 per cent in many industries in the first quarter of 1974 in the UK, when many workers were restricted to working for only 3 days per week during the fuel shortages caused by the 1974 coalminers' strike. Whether this higher level of hourly productivity could have been sustained is of course open to doubt. But the evidence of 1959–60, when the official working week fell permanently in many British industries by some $3\frac{1}{2}$ hours, suggests that the hourly productivity gains (which almost offset it) proved durable.

These two observations cast doubt on the notion that a shortening of hours for those in work would lead to anything like a commensurate increase in the demand for the labour of the unemployed, but perhaps the most important reason for suspecting that such a policy could founder turns on the question of pay. If weekly wage rates were kept up despite the fall in hours, firms would face an increase in labour costs per unit of output. If governments responded to the once-and-for-all inflationary pressures to which this would give rise by tightening aggregate demand, the reduction in the numbers unemployed would be correspondingly lowered. It is noteworthy that when West Germany attempted to counter rising unemployment in 1983 by a package involving a cut in the length of the working week, many unions organized a protracted and ultimately successful strike in protest against reductions in weekly earnings. The lesson of the West German experiment is that shorter hours are likely to increase producers' unit labour costs. This makes it a cumbersome, unreliable and inefficient method of trying to lower unemployment.

16.3.5 *Incomes Policy*

The basic argument in favour of pay controls and guidelines, or any other label attached to incomes policy, is that it seems to offer a direct way of containing wage inflation which avoids the pain associated with restrictive demand management policies. A corollary is that it may offer a route to lower real labour costs, which are necessary on many interpretations to secure increases in employment. Inflation may simply register incompatible claims on the national product. It is in one union's interest to press for high wages, despite the fact that this will lower the real wages of other workers; all might agree that they would be better off with less wage and price inflation, but a Prisoners' Dilemma prevents such a superior equilibrium being attained. By changing the rules of the game, incomes policy advocates maintain, private and social interest may be brought into harmony.

The central difficulties with all this are twofold. First, history suggests that pay controls become progressively harder to enforce the longer they are applied. Secondly, fossilizing relative wages, at what may initially be inappropriate levels, can become increasingly inefficient: unforeseen changes in tastes, technology and world prices call for structural changes in the distribution of labour between sectors that relative wage flexibility will be needed to ensure. Moreover, expectation of *future* pay ceilings goads unions into pressing for higher wages than they would otherwise have sought, given the in-built asymmetry that will allow them to lower their members' relative pay much more easily than to increase it. This is not to say that governments do not have a direct responsibility for pay-setting within the public sector. They clearly have. The point is whether they should attempt to apply this to private-sector earnings.

The present author has discussed elsewhere, with Derek Morris (Morris and Sinclair (1985)) the advantages and drawbacks of various ingenious proposals to remedy these dilemmas. The arguments do not need to be repeated here. There are many attractive features in two particular proposals; Meade's suggestion (1983, 1984) for pendular wage arbitration on the criterion of which pay increase, the union's claim or the employer's counter offer, is likelier to increase employment, and Layard's call (1982) for a special tax on inflationary wage increases. But the practical difficulties of implementing them are legion, and there are grounds for fearing that they would prove unworkable. They may be worth attempting, on the argument that little is lost if they fail, while the gains from any enduring success in improving the unemployment–inflation trade-off could be very valuable. The present author is convinced that greater chances of success lie with other policies, however. It is to these that we now turn.

16.4 Policy Recommendations to Lower Unemployment in the UK

16.4.1 *Introduction*

In what follows, certain policy recommendations are proposed in the context of the UK. Some apply specifically to Great Britain, while others have more general application to other countries as well. We begin, in section 16.4.2, with fiscal reforms. Later sections explore proposals for reforming unemployment benefits; combating fraud; employment subsidies; a Job Guaranteee Scheme; boosting jobs for minority workers; policies for improving intra-firm flows of information and extending profit-sharing; exchange rate policy; public sector infrastructural expenditure; and current public expenditure programmes.

16.4.2 *Fiscal Reforms*

The proposals set out below have one major end in view: to reduce effective marginal tax rates on the low paid. These recommendations are designed to alleviate the poverty and unemployment traps afflicting many workers who currently straddle the borderline between low-paid jobs and unemployment.

The rates can be lowered at the margin with no loss in tax yield if the tax base for income tax is widened. In the UK and the US, the income tax base is narrowed artificially by the favourable tax treatment of interest payments. In the UK, interest payments on house mortgages of up to £30,000 are tax deductible. If the rate of interest is 11 per cent, someone with a house mortgage of £30,000 or more can therefore deduct £3300 from his income before tax is assessed. If he or she pays income tax at the standard rate (currently 29 per cent), this is equivalent to a lump-sum subsidy of £957 per year. Those on higher incomes, facing higher marginal tax rates, receive an even greater subsidy. Lump-sum subsidies do not favour incentives to work: on the contrary, if leisure is a normal good, they will undermine it. The mortgage interest deductibility provision does not really make the house-buyer much better off: the price he must pay to buy a new or existing dwelling is boosted by the capital value of the fiscal privileges implicit in it, so much of what he gains from the subsidy he is likely to lose in the form of a higher mortgage incurred. The phased removal of mortgage interest relief would permit a cut in the standard rate of income tax of approximately 2 per cent, to 27 per cent.

If mortgage interest relief were abolished overnight, on the other hand, many unpleasant consequences would follow. Those who had recently purchased a house at a high price, reflecting everyone's expectation that the fiscal subsidy would continue, would suffer a sharp diminution in their living standards. There would be a major redistribution of net income from recent mortgages to other sections of the community. The inevitable fall in house prices, while it would greatly soften the blow to new buyers, would undoubtedly cause distress in the building trades. So it makes sense to adopt a gradual, phased withdrawal of the fiscal privileges attached to mortgages, which is announced well-ahead to allow people to plan accordingly. The policy recommended here, therefore, is as follows:

1   limitation to standard-rate deduction: immediate;
2   tax deductibility of mortgage interest to be reduced, on both existing and new mortgages, in steps by one-seventh each year for 7 years, to start 1 year from the announcement of the change.

The reduction in the standard rate of income tax, to 27 per cent, should take effect immediately. This would deliver a powerful, short-term fiscal stimulus to consumption, and a greater long-term incentive to labour supply and investment.

Dwellings and durable goods yield a flow of imputed income. Their owner does not have to pay rent to enjoy these assets, if he owns them himself. Imputed income from owner-occupation of dwellings is at present subject to a form of taxation, through the medium of property rates. There are proposals, issued by the UK government in January 1986, to replace these ultimately by a 'community charge', or poll tax. Such a policy change suffers from numerous disadvantages. It is regressive, since the poll tax will bear no relation to ability to pay. It also involves the removal of a valuable counterdistortionary device: property rates are the only instrument that combats the damaging distortion favouring capital accumulation in dwellings as against industrial capital. Capital employed in industry is taxed through the medium of Corporation Tax; capital gains on equities are liable to tax; no interest relief is available to individuals borrowing to finance equity purchases or loans to industry. Capital gains tax is not levied on gains on disposals of owner-occupied dwellings; imputed rent is not taxed, save through rates; and the interest costs of borrowing to finance house purchase are tax-deductible. Efficiency prescribes that the marginal product of capital should be made as close to equal as possible, in various uses to which capital may be put. The wide unevenness in the fiscal treatment of capital-in-dwellings, and industrial capital, will undoubtedly have undermined the capital stock in industry, which in turn lowers the demand for the labour it employs. It is imperative that this distortion should not be aggravated further. Indeed, it would be highly desirable to adopt steps to try to lower it. The abolition of property rates therefore would be a highly retrograde step. One fervently hopes that this ill-advised policy will never be implemented.

Turning to the imputed rent from other durables, one notices that only private motor cars are subject to a special tax, in addition to VAT at the point of purchase (the current rate is 10 per cent). From 1974 to 1979, other durables were subject to higher rates of VAT. A 'super-VAT' on durables can be defended on the ground that it compensates for the non-taxation of the imputed rent stream gained by their owners. The removal of this device in 1979 was unfortunate. Accordingly, I recommend the imposition of a new high rate of VAT at 25 per cent, on such goods as television sets, video recorders, cookers, refrigerators, carpets, watches, jewellery, motorbicycles and furniture, with a 5 per cent increase in the special tax on motor cars. These changes would bring in additional fiscal revenue of approximately £1.9 billion in a full year at 1986 prices. They would allow a further cut in the standard rate of income tax of nearly $1\frac{1}{2}$ per cent. In order to ease adjustment on the sectors affected, it would be wise to stagger the changes over a period of 3 years or so. Knowledge that tax rates were to rise further in future would help to strengthen demand in the short run. If excise duties on alcohol, gasoline, tobacco and vehicle licences were increased slightly faster than warranted by inflation over a 2-year period, the additional revenues would allow a further standard rate income tax cut of $\frac{1}{2}$ per cent. All these measures, taken together, would permit the standard rate to be lowered to 25 per cent.

The next step in the attempt to widen the tax base would be to halve personal allowances for income tax. Under the present UK tax system, the first £3000–£4000 of income is usually exempted from tax (how much depends upon marital status, mortgage interest and other factors). This would be lowered to £1500 for single persons and £2000 for married couples electing for joint taxation. In place of this, a new low rate of income tax of 12 per cent would be introduced on the first £5000 of taxable income. The net effect of these measures would be to lower the marginal rate of tax faced by most low-paid and unemployed individuals by a full 17 per cent (from its present rate of 29 per cent). Given the wide prevalence of means-tested benefits, such as rent and rate rebates, school meals reductions, Family Income Supplement and the like, the effective marginal income tax rates at present in force in the UK can exceed 75 per cent, and even 100 per cent for some groups (Dilnot and Morris (1983), and Dilnot et al. (1984) provide graphic illustrations of this). The proportion of an increase in income that such households can retain would rise quite dramatically if these proposals were enacted. A cut in the marginal rate of income tax from 29 per cent to 12 per cent in this range (on incomes up to £6500 or so) would also lead to a large fall in the replacement rate.

One disadvantage of the fiscal changes suggested here is that the number of individuals subject to income tax would increase sharply by some 3 million or so. It has to be accepted that this would involve extra work for the tax authorities, and impose burdens on the taxpayers themselves. Extra resources would have to be devoted to the processing and collection of income tax. But in the author's view, these would be minor when compared with the efficiency gains of lower marginal income tax rates, and the increases in employment and income that would ensue.

Higher up the income scale, above £5000 of taxable earnings, the standard rate should be lowered to 25 per cent on the next £4000, but kept at 29 per cent above that. At the point where higher marginal rates become payable, there is some case for a gentler, more staggered progression than the 10 per cent jumps currently in force. These increases might with advantage be lowered to 5 per cent or 6 per cent, with somewhat narrower bands before each higher step is reached.

The fiscal reforms outlined above have much to commend them. They would lower replacement rates and effective marginal tax rates at sensitive points in the income scale. They would also make the British income tax system less anomalous from an international standpoint, and move closer to that in force in many other countries that have enjoyed greater success in containing unemployment, particularly the United States.

16.4.3 *Unemployment Benefit Reforms*

We have seen that general cuts in unemployment benefits would cause widespread and serious suffering for what is probably a relatively small gain in reduced unemployment. Such a policy is therefore to be rejected, at least in the context of the UK at the time of writing. But it should be recognized that the halving of income tax allowances, combined with a new initial marginal income tax rate of 12 per cent above that, might bring some reduction in net-of-tax benefits received by some of the unemployed (but others with total incomes of $1\frac{1}{3}$ times personal allowance levels or more, would be better off). Unemployment benefits are currently liable to income tax in the UK (and the US).

To alleviate this, and to try to reduce the suffering experienced during unemployment of particular groups who, evidence cited above (pp. 271–2) suggests, are least sensitive to replacement rates and most at risk from lengthy unemployment spells, the following changes are recommended:

1 A new special age-related redundancy benefit. This could be set at 0.6 per cent of present basic benefit levels, for each year's age above 30, payable to workers declared redundant. This would be payable until re-employment or retirement age. A married unemployed person at age 50 would receive an extra £5 per week or so after being declared redundant, above current benefit levels. It would not be payable to people who had left their job voluntarily or been dismissed.
2 An additional long-term unemployment benefit of 5 per cent of current benefit levels for anyone unemployed for more than 6 months. This might be withheld if no evidence of continued job-search (such as rejection letters) could be provided.
3 A 100 per cent increase in the earnings limit for individuals receiving unemployment benefit.
4 The continued payment of unemployment benefit for the first week of paid work, on the first occasion of re-employment in a 2-year period.

Proposal 1 is designed to alleviate the plight of older individuals experiencing redundancy. Their subjection to unemployment is demonstrably not attributable to any fault on their part. UK evidence suggests that the older the worker suffering this, the lower his likelihood of securing rapid re-employment. Older workers are also much less sensitive to replacement rates than the young (Narendranathan et al. (1985)).

Proposal 2 can be supported by two observations: first, wage equations show greater sensitivity to short-run unemployment rates than to the levels of long-term unemployment; and second, the long-term unemployed are much less sensitive to replacement rates (Nickell (1979)). The condition that evidence of continued job-search may have to be provided in order to qualify should strengthen the resolve of the long-term unemployed not to acquiesce in their unfortunate position, and would provide a modest stimulus to keep looking for other jobs.

The argument for 3 is that it will encourage the unemployed to search for casual jobs that will help to keep their job skills from stagnating. It might be advisable to introduce a 'block-averaging' rule for casual earnings to protect them from falling foul of benefit entitlement when these were liable to sharp fluctuation.

The case for 4 is that it provides a further carrot to secure re-employment, and some compensation for the costs of search. The restriction to the first occasion of re-employment is designed to prevent fraudulent abuse of the system.

Taken together, these four policies would increase the total financial cost of unemployment benefits by approximately 16 per cent if the pattern of unemployment spells remained unchanged, and before allowing for the effects of income tax changes in the previous section. The income tax changes would cut the net cost to about 11 per cent. The reductions in replacement rates, especially for the younger and the short-term unemployed, could be expected to lower the duration of unemployment spells of these groups by an amount which is hard to predict, but could easily outweigh the increase in benefit levels. The major advantage of all these recommendations is that their combined impact will be to increase the relative rewards from employment, as compared with unemployment, for all those whose behaviour seems most sensitive to that comparison, while alleviating the suffering of those for whom it is not. It is surely worth experimenting with these changes, and examining their effects. If they fail to moderate unemployment, little will have been lost, and older and long-term unemployed workers will have benefited from a modest improvement in their distressed condition. If they succeed, as the present author firmly believes they would, in combating suffering *and* reducing unemployment, it is little short of criminal folly not to implement them.

16.4.4 *Combating Benefit Fraud*

Those claiming unemployment benefit are not a homogeneous group. The earliest inquiries, such as those by Rowntree and Lasker (1911) and The Pilgrim Trust (1938), testify eloquently to this. The overwhelming majority of those out of work are found to be looking for work. Yet there is a minority (Rowntree and Lasker estimated this at less than 8 per cent) who are deemed to be workshy. Such people are unambiguously unemployed by choice, claiming benefit while deliberately choosing not to search for opportunities for employment. There will also be a second group, an unquantifiable but probably much smaller minority, who are fraudulently receiving benefit while in receipt of pay for regular employment. The suffering of so many of those out of work must not blind us to their existence.

A recent incident in Bedfordshire provides some disagreeable evidence on this. Benefit recipients in some Bedfordshire and Thames Valley towns were informed that their circumstances were to be investigated in detail by officials from the Department of Health and Social Security in 1985. Nearly 1000 of them promptly discontinued their claims for benefit. This occurred in an area where unemployment was barely half the national average, and may therefore prove to be unrepresentative. Some of them may have been lucky enough to find employment soon after hearing about the investigations; others may have been frightened into stopping claims for benefit to which they were actually entitled. But a crude extrapolation to the rest of the country would suggest that there could be as many as 100,000 benefit recipients who are obtaining benefit illegally. This would still amount to barely 3 per cent of those unemployed, but it is not a negligible figure. There is clearly some merit in repeating the Bedfordshire experiment elsewhere.

16.4.5 *Employment Subsidies and Incentives*

On pp. 264–8 we saw that unambiguous reductions in unemployment could result from introducing a self-financing system of subsidies on numbers employed, recouped by an appropriate tax on wages, or the value of sales.

The scheme proposed here consists of a payment of £10 per week for all full-time equivalent employees in addition to 80 per cent of the number of full-time equivalent workers on a firm's payroll at the same period in the previous year. The gross annual cost of this measure would be somewhat in excess of £2000 million. It could be financed by a 1 per cent special tax on firms' wage bills, or a 2 per cent tax on that part of the wage bill that exceeded £4000 per annum per full-time employee. The latter would have a greater effect on increasing the elasticity of the demand for labour perceived by workers and unions, while at the same time increasing the incentive to provide less well paid jobs. It is this proposal that is recommended here. Such a policy has not been attempted before, so that history provides no guidance on its likely effect. But theory can come to our rescue. As we saw above, it should certainly succeed in reducing unemployment.

It is not clear that this policy should be implemented indefinitely. If applied in conditions of low employment, it could lead to excess demand in labour markets, and consequent inflationary pressures. It would be inadvisable in such circumstances to reward firms at the margin for not releasing labour which might be badly needed elsewhere in the economy. Hence, as a long-term measure, it might be wise to tie the subsidy to the national average level of unemployment. At 1986 prices, £1 per week for each percentage point in the unemployment rate above 3 per cent would do the trick. If unemployment fell to 8 per cent, the subsidy would be halved and the special wage tax on wages over £4000 per year would fall to 1 per cent.

16.4.6 *A Job Guarantee Scheme*

In January 1986, there were 700,000 individuals who had received unemployment benefit for more than 2 years. This constitutes some 3 per cent of the labour force. Would it be possible to all but eliminate this form of long-term unemployment? The experience of Sweden, which has offered employment guarantees to people unlucky enough to be in the position, suggests that it is.

If this group is to be re-employed with no loss in employment for others, employment will have to increase by some 3 per cent. This could not be achieved overnight. But progress towards this objective over a period of 2 years or so is perfectly achievable. Every employing organization, public and private, would have to increase numbers at work by an average of 3 per cent.

Within the local authorities, the nationalized industries and central government, a policy of this kind merely requires the courage to impose it and the will to ensure that it is carried out. Elsewhere in the economy, and within the public sector too, perhaps, incentives are required. How could a scheme of this kind operate?

The first thing to determine, at least within the public sector, would be rates of pay. These should perhaps best be set as a multiple of the married person's long-term unemployment benefit, plus other relevant allowances and supplementary benefits. A figure of 130 per cent of this total, or perhaps £6000 per year, appears reasonable. The gross financial cost of the scheme, if it were to absorb all the 700,000 people out of work for over 2 years, would reach nearly £4¼ billion. The net cost would be less than £1 billion, however, once allowance is made for the saving in benefits and the additional receipts of income tax.

Employers would need an incentive to create jobs for the 700,000. Perhaps the best balance between incentive benefits and costs might be struck by giving them a subsidy of £4000 per person per year taken on in this way. This would cover two-thirds of the 'target wage' (£6000), and, from the Exchequer's standpoint still fall below the savings in unemployment and other benefits. The net cost to an employer would then be only £40 per week. Employers who wished to pay higher wages would still be free to do so, but at a direct cost to themselves.

Within the public sector, one envisages the possibility of substantial numbers of auxiliary police officers, traffic wardens, hospital porters, nursing assistants, park attendants, cleaners, school messengers and other staff. Local authorities could be enabled to reduce their appalling backlog of housing repairs and renewals. Apartment blocks would gain concierges and porters to combat vandalism, and improve security and assistance to residents. There is patently no lack of such work to be done. A decade of tightening financial restrictions and excessive pay settlements has created a vast excess demand for unskilled labour of this kind (at a marginal wage, after all, of only £40 per week). The areas of highest long-term unemployment also often happen to be those where the needs are most acute.

To work effectively, such a policy would need sticks to reinforce the carrot of a large wage subsidy. Perhaps the most direct type of stick would take the form of a penalty on the employees of organizations that failed to participate in the scheme. They could be surcharged on their national insurance contributions. The justification for doing this is simple and compelling. By refusing to allow the employment of the long-term unemployed, they are imposing a substantial negative externality on the rest of society: everyone else has to pay higher taxes, now or eventually, to meet the extra costs of unemployment benefits. Employees in organizations that failed to meet the target of a 3-in-100 employment of the previously long-term unemployed could have a surcharge of 30 per cent or so on their national insurance contributions. They would then bring substantial pressure on their employer to participate in the scheme. Indivisibilities would make this an awkward scheme to administer for small companies; one imagines that organizations with fewer than 25 employees would be exempt, while those with 25–54 employees would have a target of one extra person, 55–84 two, 85–109 three and so on. Incomplete participation in the scheme could be discouraged by a reduced penalty rate, and overfulfilment of targets rewarded by a cut in national insurance contributions.

As time went on, the population of those who had passed the threshold of 2 years' unemployment would increase. Target employment figures would therefore have to be revised upwards. One hopes that the large employment subsidy would create a spontaneous incentive to offer more jobs to this group, but it might not; in such a case, the targets would have to be increased. Rates of pay would be tied to benefit levels, and therefore would increase roughly in line with average wages. The incentive on employees could easily be supplemented by surcharges on Corporation Tax to non-participating firms, while judicious manipulation of central government subventions to local authorities and external financial limits on nationalized industries, could be used to enforce compliance there. All these policies involve a regrettable degree of intervention, but they can be defended on the ground that they internalize a glaring externality: everyone else suffers higher taxes if organizations fail to offer jobs to the long-term unemployed. The scheme would have the additional merit of reversing the trend for low-paid jobs to disappear, under the combined impact of union pressures, the benefit-and-tax system and macroeconomic and structural shocks. It does not amount to an attack on natural economic forces. It does not work against the grain of the price system. It works with it.

One potential drawback with the Job Guarantee Scheme for the long-term unemployed is that it could encourage firms to divert job offers away from those out of work for shorter periods, and from school-leavers and others entering the labour force for the first time. This can be countered by increasing the incentives to engage such people. A way of doing this is to offer a bounty on each job offered to, and accepted by, a school-leaver or unemployed worker. This incentive could be strengthened by exempting the employer from his national insurance contributions on such employees, or part of them. A bounty could be set at perhaps £1000, which would be forfeit if the individual were dismissed or declared redundant in the ensuing 2 or 3 years. A 2-year holiday on the employer's contributions for national insurance, of up to perhaps £600 in total, would reinforce this. Although the gross financial cost of such measures might seem high, it should be stressed that they pale into insignificance in comparison with the Exchequer cost of unemployment (some £6400 per year per person).

16.4.7 *Creating More Jobs for Minority Workers*

The UK exhibits disproportionately high unemployment figures for non-white workers, as we saw in chapter 1. Those of West Indian origin are particularly prone to unemployment. Young West Indians suffer unemployment rates many times the national average. Urgent steps are required to improve the position.

It is tempting to suggest that racially discriminatory employment subsidies and taxes should be introduced. This would certainly help to reduce the imbalance. But they would strike most people as decidedly unfair, and could hardly be expected to receive widespread support. There are two other measures which would stand greater chance of political approval, and are conspicuously more easily justified on equity grounds. There are:

1   special measures to boost the demand for labour in regions of high black unemployment; and
2   stimuli to firms to offer employment opportunities to blacks and whites in proportion close to the population averages in their travel-to-work area.

The first of these could take the form of Enterprise Zones, which have been established in areas with high unemployment since 1981 in the UK (and since 1983 in the US). So far, Britain's Enterprise Zones have been confined to places such as Corby and the Isle of Dogs where unemployment is exceptionally high because of the collapse of a local industry (steel and docks, respectively), but not to areas with high *black* unemployment. They could easily be extended to the latter. The essential principle is that firms in the area get exemption from property taxes, reduced red tape and interference by public agencies and certain tax privileges on investment outlays.

They are not free of objections. In a perfectly functioning market, these benefits will be captured, in whole or at least large part, by those lucky enough to own land within them. They lead to a diversion of economic activity from adjacent areas. The boost to jobs may be largely temporary (when new investment expenditure is undertaken). Employment generation may attract migrants or commuters into the area, but do little for local residents. Lastly, it is not clear that the diversion from other regions is ultimately justified on efficiency grounds, because it could, for example, perpetuate a permanently higher structure of transportation costs.

Despite these disadvantages, it clearly seems worth attempting a widening of the scope of the Enterprise Zone schemes, to include inner-city deprived areas in London, Birmingham, Liverpool, Manchester and elsewhere suffering from high levels of black unemployment. A further possibility would be to extend the employment subsidy scheme proposed in section 16.6.2, by increasing subsidy rates within such areas.

The second proposal, would involve, first of all, gathering accurate statistics on the ethnic balance of the different travel-to-work areas, particularly for the school-leaving population. The next step would be to furnish local employers with the relevant data. Finally, firms that persistently hired fewer young blacks than local demographic data would warrant, could face the risk of being excluded from public-sector purchasing. In doing this, Britain would only be copying the Affirmative Action Program applied in the United States. Evidence certainly suggests that this programme has succeeded to some degree in evening up job opportunities for the different ethnic groups: see, for example, Leonard (1984) and Smith and Welch (1984).

16.4.8 *Improving Information within the Firm and Profit Sharing Incentives*

We saw in chapter 11, the chapter on implicit contracts, that a tendency to unemployment could be explained by asymmetric information. If workers think that the employer can conceal or disguise data pertaining to his true demand for labour, such as figures on profits, productivity or selling prices, they may feel impelled to enter contracts that give rise to unemployment in adverse states of the world. Chapter 14, on the share system, explored the recent recommendation by

Weitzman (1984) that if workers were paid a share of profits, rather than by predetermined wage rates, the demand for labour would increase.

Unfortunately, there are objections that can be levelled against both these arguments. The first is questionable on several grounds, particularly the fact that externally monitored accounts are produced, and that the employer's ability to withhold relevant information from the workers is ultimately rather weak. The Weitzman argument suffers, as we saw, from the fact that contracts which specify the wage are likely to dominate those with profit-sharing, especially if the worker is averse to risk.

Nonetheless, despite one's feeling that no panacea for reducing unemployment can be found in improving the quality of information to workers or adopting profit-sharing systems of remuneration, it does seem likely that they could play a role of some value as part of a wider attempt to meet that objective. A future Companies Act might prescribe disseminating information on profits and other relevant financial data to employees, on the same basis as it does at present for shareholders. Summarized, unaudited quarterly data could also be provided in the same way. Firms can only lose by creating suspicion on the part of their workforce. The marginal cost of giving such information to employees when it is already printed for shareholders is trivial. If it leads to more efficient bargains between employer and employee, both will stand to gain, and the levels of employment would be likely to rise in this event (Solow and Macdonald (1981)). Greater use of Joint Works Councils, and worker representation on company boards, should be encouraged. A start on this, and on parallel measures to decentralize decision taking as far as possible should be made with those industries that remain in public hands. But the present author stops short of suggesting that such changes be mandatory within the private sector. Spontaneous evolution in this direction is preferable, partly because private sector firms are too diverse to legislate for the particular form that the changes should take.

Turning to profit sharing, the natural device would be to confer fiscal privileges to employee equity participation, on a greater scale than hitherto. Rather than allowing purchases of equity on advantageous terms, or income-tax deductibility on share acquisitions, perhaps the most effective way of doing this would be to exempt dividends from Corporation Tax or standard-rate imputed income tax. This would solve the greatest problem experienced with worker shareholding schemes – that the worker often sells his shares soon after acquiring them. The continuing tax privilege of dividend tax deduction would discourage this. A ceiling of perhaps £300 per year per employee might be placed on dividend income that qualified for this deduction. The exemption would doubtless have to lapse when the employee left or retired.

16.4.9 *Exchange Rate Policy*

The British Government has moved gradually in recent years away from targets on monetary aggregates towards targets on exchange rates. The two exchange rates currently watched most closely are the trade-weighted Effective Exchange Rate against all major currencies, and the exchange rate for sterling against the European Monetary System's European Currency Unit (ECU). After the painful experiences of 1979 and 1980, when perceptions of a tightening of British monetary policy combined with other factors to induce a sharp exchange rate appreciation these changes are both explicable and wise. Serious consideration is now being given to joining the European Monetary System, by adopting a pegged exchange rate against Britain's partners in the European Community (EC). Indeed, Britain has already become a de facto participant in this system. Now that sterling has declined so much from the peaks it reached in 1980–1, this policy has much to commend it. The only real danger is that any protracted slide in oil prices will tend to depress sterling, and hence the authorities may be induced to raise interest rates to defend current parities more vigorously than Britain's long-term interests warrant.

Exchange-rate depreciation is not an unmitigated blessing. It tends to raise the sterling prices of all traded goods, and hence to worsen – albeit only temporarily – the short-term rate of inflation. There are industries that rely on traded inputs to produce for the domestic market; for them, depreciation will tend to weaken rather than strengthen the demand for labour. But for traded industries, whether selling exportables in world markets or producing close substitutes for imported goods, depreciation is favourable: as we observed in chapter 7, their demand for labour will increase, along with profits and production, at least if money wage costs are rising sufficiently slowly at the same time. On balance, the short-term effect of devaluation should be positive on the overall demand for labour in the economy, particularly if it induces a contraction of product real wages in the traded sectors, and if these sectors are large and flexible employers of labour. For these reasons, it is to be hoped that spontaneous market forces or government action will succeed in lowering both nominal and real exchange rates somewhat further in relation to our EC partners. If another 5–8 per cent depreciation in the latter statistic can be achieved, this should provide a welcome impetus for employment in the UK at the time of writing (January 1986). If a somewhat lower set of exchange rates involves a temporary relaxation of monetary policy under present conditions, that would also be welcome. But a move to a permanently more expansionary monetary policy would be inconsistent with attempts to peg exchange rates at such levels, and would in any case be undesirable on other grounds, as argued in section 16.3.3 above.

16.4.10 *Public Sector Infrastructure*

The United Kingdom does not suffer from an overall shortage of structures in several major areas. There is no longer an overall excess demand for dwellings, although there are shortages in particular regions (such as the home counties surrounding London) and in particular types of housing (such as small flats for the increasing numbers of older people, and one- and two-person households). There is if anything an excess supply of schools. Hospital provision is greatly improved compared with earlier decades: the real problem is shortage of funds to run them. Capital equipment in the defence sectors seems far from meagre in comparison with Britain's West European NATO partners (if not with the US). It is hard to offer any convincing argument for major increases in public investment expenditure in any of these areas. But there is one important exception. The network of major roads in the UK could benefit from substantial expansion.

Road-building budgets have been squeezed by successive governments since the early 1970s. Environmental and financial pressures took their toll. The two oil price hikes in 1974 and 1979 cast a question mark over previous extrapolations of the likely future growth in vehicle travel. Most important of all, governments anxious to contain the growth of financial deficits responded by imposing cuts where the immediate political pressure would be least acute. This meant insulating current expenditures, and the public sector payroll they represented, from the brunt of the reductions. Investment is always a more flexible budget item than consumption. This is especially true with construction, where the government is only an indirect employer, and can largely escape from the odium it might otherwise incur.

It is all too easy for an economist to talk in broad generalities, and avoid issues of detail. In order to defend himself against this charge, the present author offers some specific road-building programmes for Britain which seem, on limited personal inquiry, to merit close consideration. Table 16.1 gives a list of suggestions for dual carriageway (divided highway) new roads, broken down into regions.

These schemes amount to a total of 1495 miles of new or improved trunk road. The total cost might be estimated tentatively at approximately £10 billion in 1985 prices. The aims of the programme as a whole include the provision of improved roads to some isolated areas of high unemployment (such as Thanet in Kent, Cornwall, Central Scotland, South Wales, Humberside and West Cumbria); to relieve some roads which have become grossly congested with recent changes in the geographical pattern of economic activity (in East Anglia, for example); to increase the number of fast trans-Pennine roads from one to four; to provide rapid, continuous highways on certain at present ill-served routes, such as from Humberside and the East Midlands to both Southern England and South Wales, from Bristol to the Hampshire and Sussex coasts, Aberdeen and Dundee to the Clyde, and along the North Wales coast.

The microeconomics of road programmes merit a brief examination. Consider a road improvement with a financial cost of £1 million, all incurred at the stage of construction. Suppose that the real interest rate is 3.5 per cent (the yield on UK long-term indexed bonds at the date of writing). Suppose the new road has a life of 40 years. If its average annual benefit exceeds £45,243 in present prices, it is worth undertaking. This means that only 482 vehicle drivers need to experience an average delay of 5 minutes during each working day, at an average hourly cost of £4.50 at current prices, which the road improvement would avoid, for it to make a profit on social terms. If real growth is built into the hourly value of time savings, or traffic volume, or both, the critical figure for the time-saving in the first year, needed for the project to be worth undertaking, will fall. If any value is placed, as surely some must, on faster journeys at other times, the social net gain increases. If allowance is made for the fact that some of the labour and other resources expended in road construction would otherwise have been idle, the road programme looks even cheaper in both Exchequer and real resource terms.

Some of the particular suggestions made may well prove inadvisable on closer analysis of traffic flow data and costs. Perhaps some other road improvements could be identified with a higher prospective social return. But these points, freely admitted, do not weaken the thrust of the general argument. An additional £10 billion spent on major road schemes over a period of 10 years would cost less than two-thirds of the revenues collected on vehicle licence duty, and less than 16 per cent of the proceeds of taxes on gasoline. It would do no more than restore the ratio of road construction expenditures to total government outlays observed in the 1960s. It would reduce producers' costs, and impact favourably upon output and employment in many sectors of the economy. If undertaken in current conditions of abnormally high unemployment, it would prove much cheaper in the long run to undertake these programmes in the near future than to defer them into periods

Table 16.1 *Suggestions for dual carriageway new roads, broken down into regions*

Region	Road numbers	Route	New mileage (approx.)
Eastern England	A11	Chesterford–Norwich	47
	A15	Lincoln–Scawby	21
	A17	King's Lynn–Newark	58
	A46	Leicester–N. Hykeham (Lincoln)	29
	A47	Norwich S. bypass	14
	A120–M1	Harlington–Stansted	30
	A604–B663	Brampton–Stanwick	17
	B660	Molesworth–Stilton	10
			226
Midlands	A5	Chirk–Wellington	34
	A43	Northampton–Oxford	35
	A46	Coventry SE bypass	5
	A46/439/ 435	M50–Warwick	30
	A453	Kegworth–Measham	18
	B4215/ A436/A40	Ross–Gloucester–Oxford	42
			164
Northern England	A1	Berwick–Newcastle	47
	A57	Hyde–Sheffield	27
	A57/61	Sheffield SW bypass	7
	A58	Leeds–Wetherby	8
	A66	Scotch Corner–Workington	70
	A556	Altrincham (M56)–Lostock Graham	6
	A590	Barrow–M6	20
	A591	Kendal–Windermere	6
	A627	Oldham–Stockport	9
	A637	Huddersfield–West Bretton	11
	A677/646	Halifax–Preston	28
	A689	Bishop Auckland–Billingham	11
			250
Scotland	A1	Berwick–Edinburgh	48
	A9	Dunblane–Inverness	91
	A70/A73	Abington–Edinburgh with spur to Ratho	43
	A74	Gretna–Happendon (widening)	59
	A77	Glasgow–Kilmarnock	10
	A92	Inverkeithing–Kirkcaldy	13
	A94/929	Dundee–Stonehaven	26
	A977/91/ 914	Kincardine Bridge– Tay Bridge	40
			330

Table 16.1 *cont.*

Region	Road numbers	Route	New mileage (approx.)
Southern England	A3	Guildford–Portsmouth	15
	A20	Dover–Folkestone	7
	A21	Hastings–Tonbridge	28
	A23	Bolney–Brighton	12
	A24	Dorking–Worthing	7
	A27	Havant–Worthing	12
	A256/257	Bridge (Canterbury)–Cliffs End	18
	A259/8 2095/ A269/A2100	Mountfield–Pevensey	13
			112
South-West England	A30/303	Andover–Redruth	126
	A34	Beacon Hill–Newbury	7
	A36	Bristol–Ower (Southampton)	68
	A359	Sparkford–Yeovil	7
	A361/373	Barnstaple–Tiverton	33
	A380	Ashcombe–Torquay	8
			249
Wales	A40	Abergavenny–Brecon	18
		Carmarthen–Haverfordwest	21
	A48	Carmarthen–Cross Hands	12
	A55	Bangor–Chester	25
	A465	Abergavenny–Neath	30
	A467	Abertillery–Cross Hands	10
	A468/469/ 472	Nantgarw–Newbridge	12
	A483	Chester–Chirk	20
	A4059	Abercynon–Hirwaun	11
			159

when national labour markets are likely on historical evidence to be considerably tighter. Lastly, it would help to provide jobs for those whose livelihoods would suffer from the effect of the phased withdrawal of some of the fiscal privileges on housing, advocated in section 16.4.2 above.

It was understandable for the public and for governments in the 1970s to recoil in horror from the tragic environmental effects of certain road-building programmes in the 1960s (on medieval cities such as Worcester, for example) and to place great emphasis on the need to regain control over public-sector financial deficit. The government's financial position has now strengthened. It enjoys a large surplus after allowance for inflation and cyclical correction. See Miller (1985) for recent estimates. Planners have become more sensitive to environmental concerns. So the time is ripe for a more balanced attitude.

Other areas in which public investment appears to offer a high social rate of return in Britain can also be identified. A recent report commissioned by the Government drew attention to deficiencies in the stock of publicly owned housing (some 6 million dwellings) and identified the need for repair and renewal expenditure of the order of £20 billion. The sewers of many larger British cities are now about 100 years old, and thought likely to require urgent renovation or reconstruction. What little remains of this or greater antiquity above ground often needs restoration and refurbishment. These may not be new investment prospects on the grand scale. But they are none the less valuable for that. Expenditures under these headings will typically be more labour intensive than new construction projects.

Within the realm of public transport, there is a strong case for exploring the feasibility of improving rail–road and rail–air interchanges. The British railway network has been inherited from an era when it offered a virtually complete transportation system; today the only promising areas for traffic growth are the points of potential complementarity with other transport modes. It is astonishing that the world's busiest international airport, London Heathrow, has no direct railway service, despite being encircled by railway lines. The new underground rail service is a welcome advance, but the stopping trains that operate on it are slow. A modest investment in tunnels would allow non-stop trains to service Heathrow from both Baker Street and Victoria or Waterloo. An investment of perhaps £8 million would link Manchester Airport directly with Manchester and neighbouring population centres. Consideration should also be given to building new 'parkway' stations on main lines from central London close to M25 intersections. This could lead to major savings in traffic congestion costs and commuting times.

Turning to environmental issues, one welcomes the recent British Government's decision to stop giving farmers grants to remove hedgerows, and wonders whether they should not now be bribed to restore them. Relatively low-yielding agricultural land in the green belts surrounding London and other major cities might be better laid out as parkland. Tree-planting programmes, in both urban and rural areas, could be extended and increased. More power lines could be replaced by subterranean cable in areas of outstanding beauty. Particularly ugly buildings clad in concrete, a substance known for thousands of years but until the excrescences of the modernist movement in architecture rightly rejected for the external surfaces of important edifices, might be refaced in a less hideous material.

16.4.11 *Current Public Expenditure Programmes*

It would be foolish to attempt a complete survey of the various headings of central and local government current expenditures. This section will be devoted to discussing two selected areas where a prima facie case exists for greater expenditures: health and education.

In its understandable desire to control public spending, British governments over the past decade have attempted to freeze the costs of the National Health Service. There are several reasons for thinking that this is unwise. Labour productivity in health, as in so many other service industries, is notoriously difficult to increase. If technical progress causes wages to rise elsewhere in the economy, and labour market equilibrium conditions require, as they must, rates of pay to rise in health and other service industries, the central issue will be what should happen to the share of health spending in total national income. Intuition suggests that the demand for health care is elastic to income per head but inelastic to price. If this is so, one must accept that the share of national income devoted to health-care expenditures should display a positive time trend in a growing economy. This certainly accords with evidence in the United States (where health care is, of course, in the main provided privately). This conclusion is reinforced if one takes account of two factors: increases in life expectation (itself partly a reflection of improving public health), which must increase the demand for medical services; and the pattern of advances in medical technology, which tends to increase the range of expensive treatments and surgery available, rather than lower costs. The case for accepting a rising ratio of health expenditure to national income is quite independent of whether such services are provided privately or publicly.

Within the area of education, one is struck by the fact that the proportion of school-leavers who undertake tertiary education in universities or polytechnics (currently 9 per cent) is far below comparable figures in most other Western countries. In the United States, for example, it is nearly 40 per cent. The decision to freeze the absolute numbers entering tertiary education in the early 1980s, when a demographic bulge coincided with an almost unparalleled jump in unemployment rates, is especially depressing. The marginal real resource cost of extending graduate-level education to a higher proportion of the population is modest, particularly if the student–staff ratio is allowed to drift upwards somewhat, and high national unemployment rates are prevailing at the time. The gains from increasing graduate education will be sizeable, especially if it is concentrated in computing, business studies, technological subjects and other disciplines for which substantial future needs can be identified. In the arena of secondary education, one would welcome 'twinning schemes' between schools and local employers, greater emphasis on technical subjects and a major attempt to improve and widen instruction in mathematics and foreign languages. Far too many British school-leavers are monoglot and innumerate. Detailed comparisons with other West European countries should be undertaken on this, and the results publicized. One anticipates that they would make worrying reading.

There is one area, however, in which a pressing case can be made for reduced expenditure. This is the prison service. At the time of writing, the average direct financial cost of incarceration has reached £13,000 per year. Prisons have become grossly overcrowded. The utility of imprisonment is dubious. They too often serve as academies of crime: prisoners educate each other in the techniques of their trade, and develop contacts for future use. Recidivism statistics are alarming; prisons do not seem to perform their reformatory function. For less serious crimes, greater consideration might be given to suspension of certain civil rights (such as passports and driving licences), to weekend custodial sentences that do not impair the convict's ability to maintain his job and to supervised activities of social value (repairing roads, for example). For very serious crimes, international trade in custodial services has some appeal: a period of confinement in an African or Soviet gaol might be a highly cost-effective deterrent. Britain does not seem to have a comparative advantage in prison services.

In general, one fears that the pendulum has swung too far in Britain away from microeconomic considerations of the costs and benefits of public expenditure, to macroeconomic preoccupation with the public authorities' budgetary position. Such benefit–cost calculations as are undertaken impute a real cost of capital far above the yield on indexed government bonds, and typically now fail to shadow-price labour at a rate that reflects the high level of unemployment. It is time to rectify these mistakes. Britain's current rate of unemployment is some 8 per cent above its long-run average over the past 135 years. The total annual financial cost of this may be estimated at about £13 billion. Recognition of the fact that some 90 per cent of the National Debt is unindexed, with interest payments bloated to incorporate allowance for expected inflation, may lead one to subtract a further £6 billion or so. The permanent, real financial surplus of the aggregated public sector is therefore some £9 billion annually at the time of writing, once allowance has been made for cyclical abnormalities in unemployment and for the distortionary effects of expected inflation. The non-recurrent revenue from public-sector asset sales, which should not be included in any permanent surplus or deficit calculations, trims this last figure to a true surplus of about £4 billion. There is certainly ample room, therefore, for a substantial increase in public-sector current and capital expenditure, particularly if microeconomic benefit–cost calculations, properly conducted, reveal a large net social gain. It is noteworthy that this argument cannot be applied to Canada, the United States or Ireland which are all running unsustainable, excessive fiscal deficits on any definition. Britain is extremely fortunate to have a healthy fiscal base which permits higher levels of public expenditure when these are justified by microeconomic considerations.

16.5 Unemployment Policy: A Summing Up

This chapter began with a detailed scrutiny of subsidies on the number of employees, financed by a tax on wages. It was seen that favourable effects upon employment should certainly be expected to ensue. Such a scheme has the powerful advantage of working with the grain of market forces and presenting workers with a higher, but more elastic demand for their services. We then turned to consider some popular remedies for the unemployment problem: import restrictions, lowering unemployment benefits, a long-run relaxation of monetary policy, cutting work hours, and incomes policy. None of these offers a trustworthy or efficient solution to the problem.

Finally section 16.4 was devoted to exploring a package of policies that do offer greater hope of success, at least in the British context. These include income tax and benefit reforms designed to increase the relative attractiveness of employment to those who appear most sensitive to this, while increasing benefits for those most adversely affected by employment; relatively minor policies to combat fraud, stimulate profit-sharing and improve the flow of information within firms to employees; central and important proposals to subsidize employment increases from the proceeds of a wage tax, and to provide job guarantees for the long-term unemployed; measures to alleviate unemployment among black workers; a call for a further small exchange rate depreciation, before full re-entry into the European Monetary System; and a plea for some major increases in public expenditure, particularly in the realms of higher education, health and highway construction. Many of the 11 proposals suggested refer exclusively to the British case, but several – in particular the calls for employment subsidies and job guarantees for the long-term unemployed – could be applied with success in many other countries too. I would not wish to argue that certain measures recently adopted, such as the Youth Training Schemes, have nothing to commend them. They are valuable and should be continued. But they need to be supplemented by a broader range of measures acting directly on the causes, not the symptoms of mass unemployment.

Unemployment is *the* central problem of our age. Unemployment involves a tragic waste of scarce human resources. It is demeaning, debilitating, grossly unfair and massively expensive. Ultimately it threatens the fabric of society. It is all too obvious that it will not cure itself. Active, adventurous policies are urgently required. The greatest chances of success lie with policies built upon sound microeconomic reasoning, rather than crude macroeconomic measures of a traditional Keynesian kind. We must avoid trying to build pyramids, or returning to rapid inflation. The answer lies primarily in improving incentives and helping market forces to work much more effectively. This emphatically does not mean across-the-board cuts in unemployment benefits, or starving the unemployed back into employment. It means, above all, increasing the producers' demand for labour by employment subsidies, while at the same time adopting other measures to make that demand appear more elastic to workers and their representatives. Some relaxation of fiscal policy, particularly when so clearly justifiable on microeconomic criteria, is an essential adjunct to such policies. We can only hope that such policies will be implemented soon. It is worth taking some risks to reduce unemployment. The costs of not cutting it are nothing short of frightening.

Notes

Chapter 1

1 At the Thirteenth International Conference of Labour Statisticians, held at Geneva in October 1982.

2 In 1983, for example, an average of nearly 76,000 people were out of work in New Zealand, nearly 2000 of whom were vacation workers. 17,126 were (on average) employed in the private sector Job Creation Programme, and another 21,579 under the Project Employment Programme in the public sector (*Monthly Abstract of Statistics*, September 1985, New Zealand Department of Statistics, p. 25).

3 Belgium's relatively generous and largely flat-rate unemployment benefit system means that those on low earnings are much better off unemployed (Minford and Peel (1983), pp. 8 et seq.). Maddison notes that the Netherlands 'has a higher ratio of transfer payments than any other country' (1982, p. 67) and includes erosion of certain social benefits in a list of proposals to remedy the problems of the Dutch employment position.

4 As measured by Feinstein's 'compromise' index of GDP at constant factor cost: see Feinstein (1972).

5 Although many would argue that the dependent variable should be the difference between money wage increases and expected inflation.

6 The knock-on effects of a tariff levied on a particular import are likely to include upwards pressure on the exchange rate (if floating) and on nominal wage rates and costs, which should in turn squeeze the demand for labour in other 'tradables' industries. Devaluation could also conceivably exert negative effects upon the demand for labour in non-traded industries. See Neary (1980).

7 For a sophisticated analysis that includes this possibility, see the lively interchange between Nickell (1984) and Minford (1984) on this, and also in section 16.3.2 in chapter 16 of this book.

8 See for example the symposium in the *Journal of Political Economy* (1982): papers by Collins; Cross; Metcalfe et al.; Ormerod and Worswick; and Benjamin and Kochin.

9 For example, Dimsdale (1984) and Worswick (1984) and Beenstock's reply (1985).

10 However, the aggregated Organization for Economic Co-operation and Development (OECD) data still point to a cycle periodicity of about 5 or 6 years. See table 1.9.

11 A weighted average of reported unemployment rates for Australia, Belgium, Canada, Denmark, Germany, Netherlands, Norway, Sweden, the UK and the US, and author's estimates for Japan, shows unemployment rising from 6 per cent to $7\frac{1}{2}$ per cent in 1926–9. Britain's wholly unemployed averaged 8.2 per cent of the labour force in these years.

12 See Eltis and Sinclair (1981) for an analysis of these effects.

13 According to the author's calculations from data presented in the *Statistisches Jahrbuch der Bundesrepublik*, 1985.

14 See *Social Trends*, 1986, chart 4.21, p. 72.

15 Several boroughs in inner London have suffered unemployment in excess of the national average for decades. This phenomenon is the subject of a recent study by Buck et al. (1986).

16 See *Unemployment: An International Problem* (RIIA, 1935).

17 But the authors mention the possibility of underreporting illness during unemployment; there were financial incentives to underreport it.

Chapter 2

1 See Sinclair (1983), chapter 2, for a proof of these propositions.

2 Technical progress is said to be labour-augmenting when it is equivalent to an improvement in the quality of labour employed in production.

3 The derivative $dn/dz = -f_{en}[f_{ee}f_{nn} - f_{en}^2]^{-1}$, which has the sign of $-f_{en}$ given that a third fixed factor implies that there are diminishing returns to energy and labour, taken together.

4 The general effects on employment of a change in the price of energy in a multi-sector open economy are examined in detail in Sinclair (1983b).

5 The reader is referred to Baumol et al. (1982), Baumol (1982) and Baumol and Willig (1986) for an account of this idea. Brock (1983) and Vickers (1985b) present valuable critical summaries.

6 When more than one firm – or in this case all firms – believe that their own expansion will force other firms to contract. A similar situation will arise if firms place a high emphasis on total revenue as an objective, as in Vickers (1985a).

Chapter 3

1 In the simple assumptions of the model with which this chapter began, the income velocity of circulation of money was a preference-determined constant. Under this assumption, the level of money supply needed to restore Walrasian equilibrium is the product of the co-ordinates of point A.

Chapter 6

1 This will happen when equation (6.1) is replaced by $V_i^\theta = c_i^\alpha (1 - h_i)^{1-\alpha}$ where $1 > \theta > \alpha > 0$.

2 By analogy with risk-aversion (Arrow (1970), Pratt (1964)), relative inequality aversion may be defined as $-us_H''/s_H'$.

3 It is logically possible, one imagines, that ε could even be negative, if society positively enjoyed variety in its members' levels of felicity.

4 Absolute inequality aversion will be $-s_N''/s_N'$.

5 Kay (1979) presents an elegant and detailed model designed to determine the optimum average spare capacity the elasticity system should have to cope with the vicissitudes in the weather, and the changes in the demand for fuel these occasion. This is a very similar question to the 'theatre seat problem'.

Chapter 7

1 The reader is referred to two ingenious papers Barro and Gordon (1983a, 1983b) that develop this point in detail. See also Backus and Driffill (1985a, 1985b) who argue that monetary squeezes raise unemployment precisely because the Central Bank and the organized labour are caught in a damaging poker game in which they try to call each others' bluff. The idea that positive (negative) surprise inflation cuts (raises) unemployment goes back to Lucas (1972).

2 Strictly speaking, this is an approximation: (7.2) should really be written $(1 + r) = (1 + r^*)/(1 - \hat{R}^e)$, which tends to (7.2) when the value $\hat{R}^e$ is small.

Chapter 8

1   The exact figure is highly sensitive to assumptions about the level and future course of (real) oil prices, extraction costs, interest rates and other variables. The reader is referred to Eastwood and Venables (1982) for a penetrating analysis of this.

2   This argument is propounded, amongst others by Sargent and Wallace (1981). A summary can be found in Sinclair (1986a). The ideas behind it are criticized by Buiter (1982) and Liviatan (1984).

3   These are considered in Sinclair (1986c). This paper builds upon earlier models of Dasgupta and Heal (1974) and Stiglitz (1974).

Chapter 9

1   These problems have been studied in detail by Stiglitz and his co-authors. See Rothschild and Stiglitz (1976) and Stiglitz and Weiss (1981, 1983); and the penetrating survey by Stiglitz (1985a).

2   Backus and Driffill (1985a, 1985b) explore an interesting model that formalizes these ideas.

Chapter 10

1   See Lippman and McCall (1976) for a proof of this.

2   If people take time to appreciate what is happening, the duration of job-search will drop in booms and rise in slumps. Average unemployment spells do in fact move in this direction over the business cycle. Further, Vroman (1985) provides an ingenious argument to explain this phenomenon that does not rely upon misperceptions about how (10.2) has moved: if firms post signs declaring that they have no vacancies, and such signs are more prevalent in recessions, average unemployment spells will vary countercyclically under many but not all possible shapes for w. The crucial condition for unemployment duration to vary negatively with aggregate demand is for $\Phi(w)$ to be log-concave. This means that a small rightwards shift in $\Phi(w)$ raises the expected value of the truncated distribution $\Phi(w \mid w > z)$. Burdett and Ondrich (1985) also establish this result which, as they show, governs whether the short-run Phillips curve can be downwards or upwards sloping. (It is downwards sloping if $\Phi(w)$ is log-concave.)

Chapter 11

1   Recall that $\partial\sigma/\partial w < 0$.

2   There can be other reasons for this. The elasticity of demand for the monopolist's product may vary along the demand curve, creating regions where marginal revenue may be cut by marginal cost from above rather than below. This will give rise to discontinuous jumps in the demand for labour, since profit-maximizing firms will never settle there.

3   Sinclair (1980) can be consulted to show how this formula may be derived.

4   Diagrams similar to figures 11.13 and 11.14 appear in Greenhalgh et al. (1983) and Minford (1984). They make their first appearance in Neary (1978).

Chapter 13

1   Diamond and Dybvig (1983) present an interesting model of bank runs that reflects these features.

Chapter 16

1   Autonomous expenditure is the value of consumption, investment, government spending and exports, less imports, that would arise if income were zero.

Bibliography

Akerlof, G. A. and Miyazaki, H. (1980) The Implicit Contract Theory of Unemployment Meets the Wage Bill Argument, *Review of Economic Studies*, vol. 47

Altonji, J. G. (1982) The Intertemporal Substitution Model of Labour Market Fluctuations: An Empirical Analysis, *Review of Economic Studies*, vol. 49

Andrews, M. and Nickell, S. J. (1982) Unemployment in the United Kingdom since the War, *Review of Economic Studies*, vol. 49

Andrews, M. and Nickell, S. J. (1986) A Disaggregated Model of the Labour Market, *Oxford Economic Papers*, vol. 38

Argy, V. and Nevile, J. (eds) (1985) *Inflation and Unemployment*, London

Arrow, K. J. (1970) *Essays in the Theory of Risk Bearing*, Amsterdam

Arrow, K. J. and Honkapohja, S. (eds) (1985) *Frontiers of Economics*, Oxford

Ashenfelter, O. and Card, D. (1982) Time Series Representations of Economic Variables and Alternative Models of the Labour Market, *Review of Economic Studies*, vol. 49

Atkinson, A. B. (1970) On the Measurement of Inequality, *Journal of Economic Theory*, vol. 2

Atkinson, A. B., Gomulka, J., Micklewright, J. and Rau, N. (1984) Unemployment Benefit, Duration and Incentives in Britain: How Robust is the Evidence? *Journal of Public Economics*, vol. 23

Azariadis, C. (1975) Implicit Contracts and Underemployment Equilibria, *Journal of Political Economy*, vol. 83

Azariadis, C. and Stiglitz, J. E. (1983) Implicit Contracts and Fixed Price Equilibria, *Quarterly Journal of Economics*, vol. 98

Baba, Y., Hendry, D. F. and Starr, R. (1985) US Money Demand, 1960–1984, mimeo, Nuffield College, Oxford

Backus, D. and Driffill, J. (1985a) Rational Expectations and Policy Credibility Following a Change in Regime, *Review of Economic Studies*, vol. 52

Backus, D. and Driffill, J. (1985b) Inflation and Reputation, *American Economic Review*, vol. 75

Baily, M. N. (1974) Wages and Employment under Uncertain Demand, *Review of Economic Studies*, vol. 41

Banks, M. H. and Jackson, P. R. (1982) Unemployment and Risk of Minor Psychiatric Disorder in Young People: Cross-sectional and Longitudinal Evidence, *Psychological Medicine*, vol. 12

Barro, R. J. and Gordon, D. (1983a) A Positive Theory of Monetary Policy in a Natural Rate Model, *Journal of Political Economy*, vol. 91

Barro, R. J. and Gordon, D. (1983b) Rules, Discretion and Reputation in a Model of Monetary Policy, *Journal of Monetary Economics*, vol. 12

Barro, R. J. and Grossman, H. I. (1971) A General Disequilibrium Model of Income and Employment, *American Economic Review*, vol. 61

Baumol, W. J. (1982) Contestable Markets: An Uprising in the Theory of Industry Structure, *American Economic Review*, vol. 72

Baumol, W. J., Panzar, J. C. and Willig, R. D. (1982) *Contestable Markets and the Theory of Industry Structure*, New York

Baumol, W. J. and Willig, R. D. (1986) Contestability: Developments Since the Book, *Oxford Economic Papers*, vol. 38

Becker, G. S. (1965) A Theory of the Allocation of Time, *Economic Journal*, vol. 75

Beenstock, M. (1985) Unemployment and Real Wages in the 1930s, mimeo, City University Business School, London

Beenstock, M., Capie, F. and Griffiths, B. (1984) Economic Recovery in the 1930s, Bank of England Panel of Academic Consultants' Panel Paper 23

Begg, D. K. H. (1980) Rational Expectations and the Non-neutrality of Systematic Monetary Policy, *Review of Economic Studies*, vol. 47

Begg, D. K. H. (1982) Rational Expectations, Wage Rigidity and Involuntary Unemployment: A Particular Theory, *Oxford Economic Papers*, vol. 34

Benassy, J. P. (1975) Neo-Keynesian Disequilibrium Theory in a Monetary Economy, *Review of Economic Studies*, vol. 42

Benjamin, D. K. and Kochin, L. A. (1979) Searching for an Explanation of Unemployment in Interwar Britain, *Journal of Political Economy*, vol. 87

Blanchard, O., Dornbusch, R. and Layard, R. G. D. (eds) (1986) *Restoring Europe's Prosperity*, Cambridge, Mass.

Blanchflower, D. G. and Oswald, A. J. (1987) Profit Sharing: Can it Work? in Sinclair (1987)

Boltho, A., Butt Philip, A. A. S., Morris, D. J. and Sinclair, P. J. N. (1979) *Employment Subsidies in Western Europe*: A Study for the US Department of Labor, Washington

Brenner, M. H. (1979) Mortality and the National Economy: A Review, and the Experience of England and Wales, *The Lancet*

Brenner, M. H. (1980) Importance of the Economy to the Nation's Health, in: *The Relevance of Social Science for Medicine*, Eisenberg, L., Kleinman, A. (eds)

Broadberry, S. (1983) Unemployment in Interwar Britain: A Disequilibrium Approach, *Oxford Economic Papers*, vol. 35

Brock, W. A. (1983) Contestable Markets and the Theory of Industry Structure: A Review Article, *Journal of Political Economy*, vol. 91

Bruno, M. and Sachs, J. (1982a) Input Price Shocks and the Slowdown in Economic Growth: The Case of UK Manufacturing, *Review of Economic Studies*, vol. 49

Bruno, M. and Sachs, J. (1982b) Energy and Resource Allocation: A Dynamic Model of the 'Dutch Disease', *Review of Economic Studies*, vol. 49

Buck, N., Gordon, I. and Young, K. (1986) *The London Unemployment Problem*, Oxford

Buiter, W. H. (1981) The Superiority of Contingent Rules Over Fixed Rules in Models with Rational Expectations, *Economic Journal*, vol. 91

Buiter, W. H. (1982) Deficits, Crowding Out and Inflation: The Simple Analytics, Centre for Labour Economics Discussion Paper 143, London School of Economics

Buiter, W. H. and Miller, M. (1981a) Monetary Policy and International Competitiveness: The Problems of Adjustment, in: Eltis, W. A. and Sinclair, P. J. N. (eds) (1981)

Buiter, W. H. and Miller, M. (1981b) The Thatcher Experiment: The First Two Years, *Brookings Papers on Economic Activity*

Buiter, W. H. and Miller, M. (1982) Real Exchange Overshooting and the Output Cost of Bringing Down Inflation, *European Economic Review*, vol. 18

Buiter, W. H. and Miller, M. (1983) Changing the Rules: The Economic Consequences of Mrs Thatcher, *Brookings Papers on Economic Activity*

Buiter, W. H. and Miller, M. (1985) The Costs and Benefits of an Anti-inflationary Policy: Questions and Issues, in: Argy, V. and Nevile, J. (eds) (1985)

Buiter, W. H. and Purvis, D. (1982) Oil, Disinflation and Export Competitiveness, in: *Economic Interdependence under Flexible Exchange Rates*, Bhandari, J. (ed)

Burdett, J. and Ondrich, D. (1985) How Changes in Labour Demand Affect Unemployed Workers, *Journal of Labor Economics*, vol. 3

Carruth, A. A. and Oswald, A. J. (1985) Miners' Wages in Post-war Britain: An Application of a Model of Trade Union Behaviour, *Economic Journal*, vol. 95

Chowdhury, G. and Nickell, S. J. (1985) Hourly Earnings in the US: Another Look at Unionization, Schooling, Sickness and Unemployment using PSID Data, *Journal of Labor Economics*, vol. 3

Clark, P. B. (1985) Inflation and Unemployment in the United States: Recent Experience and Policy, in: Argy, V. and Nevile, J. (eds) (1985)

Coe, D. T. and Gagliardi, F. (1985), Nominal Wage Determination in Ten OECD Countries, OECD Economics and Statistics Working Paper 19

Corden, W. M. (1984) Booming Sector and Dutch Disease Economics: Survey and Consolidation, *Oxford Economic Papers*, vol. 36

Corden, W. M. and Neary, J. P. (1982) Booming Sector and Deindustrialization in a Small Economy, *Economic Journal*, vol. 92

Cournot, A. (1838) *Researches into the Mathematical Principles of the Theory of Wealth* (original in French, 1838; English translation, 1929)

Cukierman, A. (1984) *Inflation, Stagflation, Relative Prices and Imperfect Information*, Cambridge, UK.

Darby, M. R. (1984) Some Pleasant Monetarist Arithmetic, *Federal Reserve Board of Minnesota Quarterly Review*, vol. 8

Darby, M. R., Haltiwanger, J. and Plant, M. (1985) Unemployment Rate Dynamics and Persistent Unemployment under Rational Expectations, *American Economic Review*, vol. 25

Dasgupta, P. K. and Heal, G. M. (1974) The Optimal Depletion of Exhaustible Resources, *Review of Economic Studies*, vol. 41

Davidson, J. E. H. and Hendry, D. F. et al. (1978) Econometric Modelling of the Aggregate Time-Series Relationship between Consumers' Expenditure and Income in the UK. *Economic Journal*, vol. 88

Davidson, J. E. H. and Hendry, D. F. (1981) Interpreting Econometric Evidence: The Behaviour of Consumers' Expenditure in the UK, *European Economic Review*, vol. 16

Diamond, D. W. and Dybvig, P. H. (1983) Bank Runs, Deposit Insurance and Liquidity, *Journal of Political Economy*, vol. 91

Dilnot, A. W. and Morris, C. N. (1983) Private Costs and Benefits of Unemployment: Measuring Replacement Rates, *Oxford Economic Papers*, vol. 35

Dilnot, A. W., Kay, J. A. and Morris, C. N. (1984) *The Reform of Social Security*, Oxford

Dimsdale, N. H. (1984) Employment and Real Wages in the Interwar Period, *National Institute Economic Review*, vol. 114

Dixit, A. K. (1978) The Balance of Trade in a Model of Temporary Equilibrium with Rationing, *Review of Economic Studies*, vol. 45

Dornbusch, R. (1976) Expectations and Exchange Rate Dynamics, *Journal of Political Economy*, vol. 84

Douglas, P. H. and Director, A. (1931) *The Problem of Unemployment*, New York

Eastwood, R. K. and Venables, A. J. (1982) The Macroeconomic Implications of a Resource Discovery in an Open Economy, *Economic Journal*, vol. 92

Edwards, J. S. S. and Keen, M. J. (1985) Inflation and Non-neutralities in the Taxation of Corporate Source Income, *Oxford Economic Papers*, vol. 37

Eltis, W. A. and Sinclair, P. J. N. (eds) (1981) *The Money Supply and the Exchange Rate*, Oxford

Farber, H. S. (1978) Individual Preferences and Union Wage Determination: The Case of the United Mineworkers, *Journal of Political Economy*, vol. 86

Farmer, R. E. A. (1985) Implicit Contracts with Asymmetric Information and Bankruptcy: The Effects of Interest Rates on Layoffs, *Review of Economic Studies*, vol. 52

Feinstein, C. H. (1972) *National Income, Expenditure and Output of the United Kingdom 1855–1965*, Cambridge, UK.

Feldstein, M. S. (1978) The Effect of Unemployment Insurance on Temporary Layoff Unemployment, *American Economic Review*, vol. 68

Feldstein, M. S. (1982) Inflation, Tax Rules and Investment: Some Econometric Evidence, *Econometrica*, vol. 50

Fender, J. (1985) Oil in a Dynamic Two Good Model, *Oxford Economic Papers*, vol. 37

Findlay-Jones, R. A. and Eckhardt, B. (1981) Psychiatric Disorder Among the Young Unemployed, *Australian and New Zealand Journal of Psychiatry*, vol. 15

Fischer, S. (1977) Long Term Contracts, Rational Expectations and the Optimum Policy Rule, *Journal of Political Economy*, vol. 85

Fischer, S. (1985) Contracts, Credibility and Disinflation, in: Argy, V. and Nevile, J. (eds) (1985)

Fischer, S. and Modigliani, F. (1978) The Real Effects and Costs of Inflation, *Weltwirtschaftliches Archiv*, vol. 114

Fisher, I. (1926) A Statistical Relation between Unemployment and Price Changes, *International Labour Review*, vol. 13 (reprinted in the *Journal of Political Economy* (1973))

Friedman, M. (1968) The Role of Monetary Policy, *American Economic Review*, vol. 58.

Friedman, M. (1969) The Optimum Quantity of Money, in: M. Friedman, *The Optimum Quantity of Money and Other Essays*, London.

Gordon, R. J. (1976) Recent Developments in the Theory of Inflation and Unemployment, *Journal of Monetary Economics*, vol. 2

Gordon, R. J. (1982) Why Stopping Inflation may be Costly: Evidence for Fourteen Historical Episodes, in: Hall, R. E. (ed) (1982)

Gravelle, H. S. E., Hutchinson, G. and Stern, J. (1981) Mortality and Unemployment: A Critique of Brenner's Time-series Analysis, *Lancet*

Greenhalgh, C., Layard, R. G. D. and Oswald, A. J. (eds) (1983) *The Causes of Unemployment*, Oxford

Grossman, S. J. and Hart, O. D. (1981) Implicit Contracts, Moral Hazard and Unemployment, *American Economic Review*, vol. 91

Grout, P. A. (1985) Employee Share Ownership Schemes, mimeo, University of Bristol

Grubb, D., Jackman, R. and Layard, R. G. D. (1983) Wage Rigidity and Unemployment in OECD Countries, *European Economic Review*, vol. 21

Hall, P. H. and Heffernan, S. A. (1985) More on the Effects Employment Effects of Innovation, *Journal of Development Economics*, vol. 17

Hall, R. E. (ed) (1982) *Inflation: Causes and Effects*, Chicago

Hall, R. E. and Lazear, E. P. (1984) The Excess Sensitivity of Layoffs and Quits to Demand, *Journal of Labor Economics*, vol. 2

Halliday, J. L. (1935) *British Medical Journal*, 9 and 16 March

Hart, O. D. (1983) Optimal Labour Contracts under Asymmetric Information: An Introduction, *Review of Economic Studies*, vol. 50

Hatton, T. J. (1983) Unemployment Benefits and the Macroeconomics of the Interwar Labour Market: A Further Analysis, *Oxford Economic Papers*, vol. 35

Heffernan, S. A. (1980) Technological Unemployment, M. Phil. Dissertation, University of Oxford

Heffernan, S. A. (1981) Technological Unemployment, D. Phil. Dissertation, University of Oxford

Hendry, D. F. (1983) Econometric Modelling: the 'Consumption Function' in Retrospect, *Scottish Journal of Political Economy*, vol. 30

Hicks, J. R. (1928) *The Theory of Wages*, London

Hotelling, H. (1929) Stability in Competition, *Economic Journal*, vol. 39

House of Lords (1982) Select Committee Report on Unemployment, London

Hughes, G. and McCormick, B. (1985) An Empirical Analysis of On-the-job Search and Job Mobility, *Manchester School*, vol. 53

Jackman, R., Layard, R. G. D. and Pissarides, C. (1983) Policies for Reducing the Natural

Rate of Unemployment, Centre for Labour Economics, London School of Economics Working Paper 587

Jackson, P. R. and Warr, P. B. (1984) Unemployment and Psychological Ill-health: The Moderating Role of Duration and Age, *Psychological Medicine*, vol. 14

Jonson, P. and Stevens, S. (1985) The Australian Economy in the 1930s and 1980s: Some Facts, in: Argy, V. and Nevile, J. (eds) (1985)

Journal of Political Economy (1982) Symposium on Benjamin and Kochin (1979): papers by M. Collins; R. Cross; D. Metcalf, S. J. Nickell and N. Floros; P. A. Ormerod and G. D. N. Worswick; D. K. Benjamin and L. A. Kochin

Kaldor, N. (1936) Wage Subsidies as a Remedy for Unemployment, *Journal of Political Economy*, vol. 44

Kay, J. A. (1979) Uncertainty, Congestion and Peak Load Pricing, *Review of Economic Studies*, vol. 46

Kendrick, J. W. (1962) *Productivity Trends in the United States*, Princeton, NJ

Keynes, J. M. (1936) *The General Theory of Interest, Employment and Money*, London.

Killingsworth, M. (1983) *Labor Supply*, Cambridge, UK.

Knight, F. H. (1921) *Risk, Uncertainty and Profit*, New York

Kydland, F. E. and Prescott, E. C. (1977) Rules, Rather Than Discretion: The Inconsistency of Optimal Plans, *Journal of Political Economy*, vol. 85

Laffont, J. J. (1985) Fix-price Models: A Survey of Recent Empirical Work, in: Arrow, K. J. and Honkapohja, S (eds) (1985)

Layard, R. G. D. (1982) *More Jobs, Less Inflation*, Oxford

Layard, R. G. D. and Nickell, S. J. (1980) The Case for Subsidizing Extra Jobs, *Economic Journal*, vol. 90

Layard, R. G. D. and Nickell, S. J. (1985) The Causes of British Unemployment, *National Institute Economic Review*, vol. 111

Leonard, J. S. (1984) The Impact of Affirmative Action on Employment, *Journal of Labor Economics*, vol. 2

Leontief, W. (1946) The Pure Theory of the Guaranteed Annual Wage Contract, *Journal of Political Economy*, vol. 54

Lippman, S. A. and McCall, J. J. (1976) The Economics of Job Search: A Survey, Parts I and II, *Economic Inquiry*, vol. 14

Lipsey, R. G. (1960) The Relation Between Unemployment and the Rate of Change of Money Wage Rates in the UK, 1862–1957: A Further Analysis, *Economica*, vol. 27

Liviatan, N. (1984) Tight Money and Inflation, *Journal of Monetary Economics*, vol. 13

Lucas, R. E. (1972) Expectations and the Neutrality of Money, *Journal of Economic Theory*, vol. 4

Lucas, R. E. (1973) Some International Evidence on Output–Inflation Tradeoffs, *American Economic Review*, vol. 63

Lucas, R. E. (1976) Econometric Policy Evaluation: A Critique, *Journal of Monetary Economics*, supplement 1

Lucas, R. E. and Rapping, L. (1969) Real Wages, Employment and Inflation, *Journal of Political Economy*, vol. 77

Maddison, A. (1982) The Dutch Employment Problem in Comparative Perspective, in: Maddison, A. and Wilpstra, B. S. (eds) *Unemployment: The European Perspective*, Amsterdam

Malcomson, J. (1985) Incomplete Contracts and Involuntary Unemployment, *Oxford Economic Papers*, vol. 37

Malinvaud, E. (1977) *The Theory of Unemployment Reconsidered*, Oxford

Marston, R. C. (1985) The Geographic Distribution of Unemployment, *Quarterly Journal of Economics*, vol. 100

Meade, J. E. (1983) *Wage-Fixing*, London

Meade, J. E. (1984) *Wage Fixing Revisited*, Institute of Economic Affairs Occasional Paper 72

302   *Bibliography*

Miller, M. H. (1984) Government, Unions and Stagflation in the UK, *National Institute Economic Review*, vol. 109

Miller, M. H. (1985) Measuring the Stance of Fiscal Policy, *Oxford Review of Economic Policy*, vol. 1

Minford, P. (1983) Labour Market Equilibrium in an Open Economy, *Oxford Economic Papers*, vol. 35

Minford, P. (1984) A Review of Unemployment: Cause and Cure: A Response, *Economic Journal*, vol. 94

Minford, P. et al. (1984) *Unemployment: Cause and Cure*, Oxford

Minford, P. and Peel, D. (1983) *Rational Expectations and the New Macroeconomics*, Oxford

Mirrlees, J. A. (1971) An Exploration in the Theory of Optimum Income Taxation, *Review of Economic Studies*, vol. 38

Mitchell, B. R. and Deane, P. (1962) *Abstract of British Historical Statistics*, Cambridge, UK

Moffitt, R. and Nicholson, W. (1982) The Effect of Unemployment Insurance on Unemployment: the Case of Federal Supplementary Benefits, *Review of Economics and Statistics*, vol. 64

Moore, J. (1985) Optimal Labour Contracts when Workers Have a Variety of Privately Observed Reservation Wages, *Review of Economic Studies*, vol. 52

Morgan, P. B. (1985) Distribution of the Duration and Value of Job Search with Learning, *Econometrica*, vol. 53

Morgan, P. B. and Manning, R. (1985) Optimal Search, *Econometrica*, vol. 53

Morris, D. J. and Sinclair, P. J. N. (1985) The Unemployment Problem in the 1980s, *Oxford Review of Economic Policy*, vol. 1

Mortenson, D. T. (1978) Specific Capital and Labour Turnover, *Bell Journal of Economics*, vol. 9

Mortenson, D. T. (1982) Property Rights and Efficiency in Mating, Racing and Related Games, *American Economic Review*, vol. 72

Moylan, S., Miller, J. and Davies, R. (1984) *For Richer, For Poorer? DHSS Cohort Study of Unemployed Men*, London

Muellbauer, J. M. J. (1986) Macrotheory versus Macroeconometrics: The Treatment of 'Disequilibrium' in Macromodels, mimeo, Oxford

Muellbauer, J. M. J. and Portes, R. D. (1978) Macroeconomic Models with Quantity Rationing, *Economic Journal*, vol. 88

Narendranathan, A., Nickell, S. J. and Stern, J. (1982) An Investigation into the Incidence and Dynamic Structure of Sickness and Unemployment in Britain 1965–75, Centre for Labour Economics Discussion Paper, London School of Economics

Narendranathan, A., Nickell, S. J. and Stern, J. (1985) Unemployment Benefits Revisited, *Economic Journal*, vol. 95

Nash, J. (1953) Two Person Cooperative Games, *Econometrica*, vol. 21

Neary, J. P. (1978) Short Run Capital Specificity and the Pure Theory of International Trade, *Economic Journal*, vol. 88

Neary, J. P. (1980) Non-traded Goods and the Balance of Trade in a Neo-Keynesian Temporary Equilibrium, *Quarterly Journal of Economics*, vol. 95

Neary, J. P. (1981) On the Short-run Effects of Technological Progress, *Oxford Economic Papers*, vol. 33

Neary, J. P. and Roberts, K. W. S. (1980) The Theory of Household Behaviour under Rationing, *European Economic Review*, vol. 13

Neary, J. P. and Stiglitz, J. E. (1983) Towards a Reconstruction of Keynesian Economics: Expectations and Constrained Equilibria, *Quarterly Journal of Economics*, vol. 98

Newbery, D. (1981) Oil Prices, Cartels and the Problem of Dynamic Consistency, *Economic Journal*, vol. 91

Newbery, D. (1984) The Economics of Oil, in: van der Ploeg, R. (ed) *Mathematical Methods in Economics*, Chichester

Nickell, S. J. (1979) The Effect of Unemployment and Related Benefits on the Duration of Unemployment, *Economic Journal*, vol. 89

Nickell, S. J. (1984) A Review of Unemployment: Cause and Cure, *Economic Journal*, vol. 94

Nickell, S. J. (1985) The Government's Policy for Jobs: An Analysis, *Oxford Review of Economic Policy*, vol. 1

Nickell, S. J. and Andrews, M. (1983) Trade Unions, Real Wages and Employment in Britain 1951–79, *Oxford Economic Papers*, vol. 35

Okun, A. M. (1978) Efficient Disinflationary Policies, *American Economic Review*, vol. 68

Oswald, A. J. (1982) The Microtheory of the Union, *Economic Journal*, vol. 92

Oswald, A. J. (1983) Altruism, Jealousy and the Theory of Optimal Non-linear Income Taxation, *Journal of Public Economics*, vol. 21

Oswald, A. J. (1984) Three Theorems on Marginal Employment Subsidies, *Economic Journal*, vol. 94

Oswald, A. J. (1985) The Economic Theory of Trade Unions – An Introductory Survey, *Scandinavian Journal of Economics*, vol. 87

Oswald, A. J. (1986) Unemployment Insurance and Labour Contracts under Asymmetric Information: Theory and Facts, *American Economic Review*, vol. 76

Overstone, I. M. K. (1973) Unemployment and Suicide in Edinburgh, *British Journal of Preventive Social Medicine*, vol. 27

Pencavel, J. H. (1984) The Tradeoff Between Wages and Employment in Trade Union Objectives, *Quarterly Journal of Economics*, vol. 99

Phelps, E. S. (1967) Phillips Curves, Expectations of Inflation and Optimal Unemployment Over Time, *Economica*, vol. 34

Phelps, E. S. and Taylor, J. B. (1977) Stabilizing Powers of Monetary Policy under Rational Expectations, *Journal of Political Economy*, vol. 85

Phillips, A. W. (1958) The Relation between Unemployment and the Rate of Change in Money Wage Rates in the UK, 1851–1957, *Economica*, vol. 25

Pigou, A. (1937) *The Economics of Unemployment*, London

Pilgrim Trust (1938) *Men Without Work*, London

Pissarides, C. A. (1985a) Dynamics of Unemployment, Vacancies and Real Wages with Trade Unions, *Scandinavian Journal of Economics*, vol. 87

Pissarides, C. A. (1985b) Short Run Equilibrium Dynamics of Unemployment, Vacancies and Real Wages, *American Economic Review*, vol. 75

Pissarides, C. A. (1985c) Taxes, Subsidies and Equilibrium Unemployment, *Review of Economic Studies*, vol. 52

Platt, S. (1983) Unemployment and Parasuicide in Edinburgh 1968–82, *Unemployment Unit Bulletin*, vol. 10

Platt, S. (1984) Unemployment and Suicidal Behaviour: A Review of the Literature, *Social Science and Medicine*, vol. 19

Pratt, J. W. (1964) Risk Aversion in the Small and the Large, *Econometrica*, vol. 32

Rawls, J. (1971) *A Theory of Justice*, Oxford

Reyher, L., Koller, M. and Spitznagel, E. (1979) *Employment Policy Alternatives to Unemployment in the Federal Republic of Germany*, London

Ricardo, D. (1981) *The Principles of Political Economy*, 3rd edition, in: Sraffa, P. (ed) (1951) *The Works and Correspondence of David Ricardo*, vol. 1

Roberts, K. W. S. (1980) Interpersonal Comparability and Social Choice Theory, *Review of Economic Studies*, vol. 47

Roberts, K. W. S. (1984) The Theoretical Limits to Redistribution, *Review of Economic Studies*, vol. 51

Rosen, S. (1985) Implicit Contracts, *Journal of Economic Literature*, vol. 23

Rothschild, M. and Stiglitz, J. E. (1976) Equilibrium in Competitive Insurance Markets: An Essay on the Economics of Imperfect Information, *Quarterly Journal of Economics*, vol. 90

Rowntree, B. S. and Lasker, B. (1911) *Unemployment: A Social Study*, London

Royal Institute for International Affairs (RIIA) (1935) *Unemployment: An International Problem*, London

Salop, S. C. (1973) Systematic Job Search and Unemployment, *Review of Economic Studies*, vol. 40

Samuelson, L. (1985) Implicit Contracts with Heterogeneous Labour, *Journal of Labour Economics*, vol. 3

Sargent, T. A. (1982) The Ends of Four Big Inflations, in: Hall, R. E. (ed) (1982)

Sargent, T. A. and Wallace, N. (1981) Some Unpleasant Monetarist Arithmetic, *Federal Reserve Board of Minnesota Quarterly Review*, vol. 5

Shackle, G. L. S. (1949) *Expectations in Economics*, London

Shackle, G. L. S. (1972) *Epistemics and Economics*, London

Shaked, A. and Sutton, J. (1984) Involuntary Unemployment as a Perfect Equilibrium in a Bargaining Model, *Econometrica*, vol. 52

Shapiro, C. and Stiglitz, J. E. (1984) Equilibrium Unemployment as a Worker Discipline Device, *American Economic Review*, vol. 74

Shoemaker, P. J. H. (1982) The Expected Utility Model: Its Variants, Purposes, Evidence and Limitations, *Journal of Economic Literature*, vol. 20

Sinclair, P. J. N. (1980) Unions, Closed Shops, Technology and Factor Shares, *Greek Economic Review*, vol. 2

Sinclair, P. J. N. (1981) When Will Technical Progress Destroy Jobs? *Oxford Economic Papers*, vol. 31

Sinclair, P. J. N. (1983a) *Foundations of Macroeconomic and Monetary Theory*, Oxford

Sinclair, P. J. N. (1983b) How Does a Change in the Price of Energy Affect Output and Employment? *Greek Economic Review*, vol. 5

Sinclair, P. J. N. (1985) Nota sobre la Trayectoria Optima de Inflacion, *Monetaria*, vol. 8

Sinclair, P. J. N. (1986a) The Theory of Monetary Policy, in: Sinclair, P. J. N., Sumner, M. and Zis, G. (eds) *Monetary Economics*, London (forthcoming)

Sinclair, P. J. N. (1986b) Savings, Output, Population Growth and Wages, *Bulletin of Economic Research*, forthcoming

Sinclair, P. J. N. (1986c) A Comparison of Simple Contracts, mimeo, Brasenose College, Oxford

Sinclair, P. J. N. (ed) (1987) *Prices, Quantities and Expectations*, Oxford, forthcoming

Singer, H. W. (1937) Interim Papers of the Pilgrim Trust Unemployment Inquiry

Smith, J. P. and Welch, F. (1984) Affirmative Action and Labor Markets, *Journal of Labor Economics*, vol. 2

Snower, D. J. (1984) Rational Expectations, Non-linearities and the Effectiveness of Monetary Policy, *Oxford Economic Papers*, vol. 36

Solon, G. R. (1985) Work Incentive Effects of Taxing Unemployment Benefits, *Econometrica*, vol. 53

Solow, R. M. (1980) On Theories of Unemployment, *American Economic Review*, vol. 70

Solow, R. M. and McDonald, I. M. (1981) Wage Bargaining and Unemployment, *American Economic Review*, vol. 71

Stackelberg, H. von (1934) *Marktform und Gleichgewicht*, Berlin

Stiglitz, J. E. (1974) Growth with Exhaustible Natural Resources: Efficient and Optimum Growth Paths, *Review of Economic Studies*, symposium supplement

Stiglitz, J. E. (1982) Utilitarianism and Horizontal Equity: The Case for Random Taxation, *Journal of Public Economics*, vol. 19

Stiglitz, J. E. (1985a) Information and Economic Analysis: A Perspective, *Economic Journal Conference Proceedings*, vol. 95

Stiglitz, J. E. (1985b) Equilibrium Wage Distributions, *Economic Journal*, vol. 95

Stiglitz, J. E. and Weiss, A. (1981) Credit Rationing in Markets with Imperfect Information, *American Economic Review*, vol. 71

Stiglitz, J. E. and Weiss, A. (1983) Incentive Effects of Termination: Applications to the Credit and Labor Markets, *American Economic Review*, vol. 73

Stoneman, P. A. (1983) *The Economic Analysis of Technological Change*, Oxford

Stoneman, P. A. and Ireland, N. (1986) Technological Diffusion, Expectations and Welfare, *Oxford Economic Papers*, vol. 38

Taylor, J. B. (1980) Aggregate Dynamics and Staggered Contracts, *Journal of Political Economy*, vol. 88

Taylor, J. B. (1985) Rational Expectations Models in Macroeconomics, in: Arrow, K. J. and Honkapohja, S. (eds) (1985)

Tobin, J. (1965) Money and Economic Growth, *Econometrica*, vol. 33

Turnovsky, S. J. (1980) The Choice of Monetary Instrument under Alternative Forms of Price Expectations, *Manchester School*, vol. 48

US Department of Commerce (1975) *Historical Statistics of the United States: Colonial Times to 1970*, US Department of Commerce, Washington

van der Ploeg, R. (1985) Trade Unions, Investment and Employment: A Non-cooperative Approach, Centre for Labour Economics Discussion Paper 224, London School of Economics

Venables, A. J. (1985) The Economic Implications of a Discrete Technical Change, *Oxford Economic Papers*, vol. 37

Vickers, J. S. (1985a) Delegation and the Theory of the Firm, *Economic Journal, Conference Proceedings*, vol. 95

Vickers, J. S. (1985b) Strategic Competition Among the Few: Some Recent Developments in the Economics of Industry, *Oxford Review of Economic Policy*, vol. 1

Vroman, S. V. (1985) No Help Wanted Signs and the Duration of Job Search, *Economic Journal*, vol. 95

Walras, L. (1870) *Elements of Pure Economics or The Theory of Social Wealth* (French original edition, 1870; English translation by W. Jaffé, 1954)

Weitzman, M. L. (1974) Prices vs. Quantities, *Review of Economic Studies*, vol. 41

Weitzman, M. L. (1982) Increasing Returns and the Foundations of Unemployment Theory, *Economic Journal*, vol. 92

Weitzman, M. L. (1984) *The Share Economy*, Cambridge, Mass.

Weitzman, M. L. (1985) The Simple Macroeconomics of Profit Sharing, *American Economic Review*, vol. 75

Wijnbergen, S. van (1985) Oil Price Shocks, Unemployment, Investment and the Current Account: An Intertemporal Disequilibrium Analysis, *Review of Economic Studies*, vol. 52

Worswick, G. D. N. (1984) The Sources of Recovery in the UK in the 1930s, *National Institute Economic Review*, vol. 110

Index

Index by
Jacqueline B. McDermott